Williams' Pacific Tourist and Guide Across the Continent.

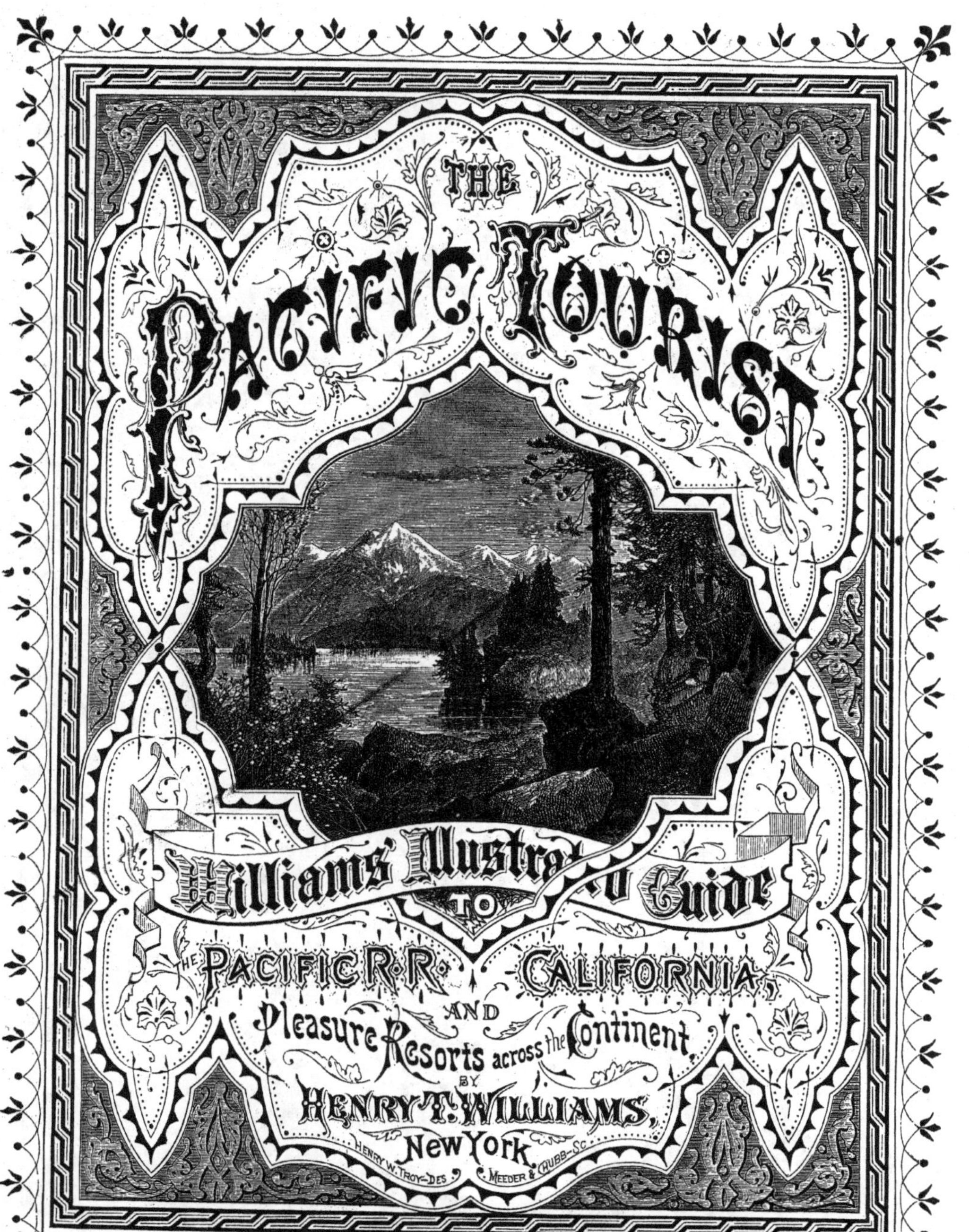
THE
PACIFIC TOURIST
Williams' Illustra d Guide
TO
HE PACIFIC R.R. CALIFORNIA,
AND
Pleasure Resorts across the Continent
BY
HENRY T. WILLIAMS,
New York
HENRY W. TROY—DES.
MEEDER & CHUBB—SC.

PALACE-CAR LIFE ON THE PACIFIC RAILROAD.

The Pacific Tourist.

WILLIAMS'

Illustrated Trans-Continental Guide

OF TRAVEL,

FROM

The Atlantic to the Pacific Ocean.

CONTAINING FULL DESCRIPTIONS OF

RAILROAD ROUTES ACROSS THE CONTINENT, ALL PLEASURE RESORTS AND PLACES OF MOST NOTED SCENERY IN THE FAR WEST, ALSO OF ALL CITIES, TOWNS, VILLAGES, U. S. FORTS, SPRINGS, LAKES, MOUNTAINS,

ROUTES OF SUMMER TRAVEL, BEST LOCALITIES FOR HUNTING, FISHING, SPORTING, AND ENJOYMENT, WITH ALL NEEDFUL INFORMATION FOR THE PLEASURE TRAVELER, MINER, SETTLER, OR BUSINESS MAN.

A COMPLETE TRAVELER'S GUIDE

OF

The Union and Central Pacific Railroads,

AND ALL POINTS OF BUSINESS OR PLEASURE TRAVEL TO

CALIFORNIA, COLORADO, NEBRASKA, WYOMING, UTAH, NEVADA, MONTANA, THE MINES AND MINING OF THE TERRITORIES, THE LANDS OF THE PACIFIC COAST, THE WONDERS OF THE ROCKY MOUNTAINS, THE SCENERY OF THE SIERRA NEVADAS, THE COLORADO MOUNTAINS, THE BIG TREES, THE GEYSERS, THE YOSEMITE, AND THE YELLOWSTONE.

BY

HENRY T. WILLIAMS, EDITOR.

WITH SPECIAL CONTRIBUTIONS BY

PROF. F. V. HAYDEN, CLARENCE KING, CAPT. DUTTON, A. C. PEALE, JOAQUIN MILLER, J. B. DAVIS, F. E. SHEARER.

ILLUSTRATIONS BY

THOMAS MORAN, A. C. WARREN, W. SNYDER, F. SCHELL, H. W. TROY, A. WILL.

ENGRAVINGS BY MEEDER & CHUBB.

Price, $1.50 Railroad Edition, Flexible Covers, 278 pp.

" $2.00 Full Cloth, Stiff Covers, 320 pp.

NEW YORK:

HENRY T. WILLIAMS, PUBLISHER.

1877.

PREFACE.

FEW can form an adequate idea of the immense field required to be covered by a Trans-Continental Guide. The amount of labor, personal travel, and research, all of utmost faithfulness and accuracy, is beyond expression or terms of comparison. Think of the wonderful results accomplished in a few years, by the opening of the Pacific Railroad. In 1850, the Far West was unknown and unexplored. In 1860, its total population was but 619,000, most of whom were residents of the Pacific Coast. In 1870, the population had *doubled.* In 1876, seven years after the opening of the Pacific Railroad, see how wonderful the change. The population of the Far Western States and Territories had again increased 40 per cent. And the Far West now includes this immense field reached only by this Railroad. Population in 1875, 1,524,-703; area of square miles, 1,445,332; area of square acres, 1,332,744,755. The entire capital now invested in Railroad enterprises in this vast region now exceeds $750,000,000. Over 300 towns and stations have arisen on the great Trans-Continental Route and its branches. The annual receipts exceed $30,000,000 a year, and the number of passengers, both through and local, exceed 1,000,000. The tide of pleasure travel has turned westward, and Europe clasps hands with China and Japan across our Continent. Thus have seven short years turned the travel of the world.

This volume represents over nine months' actual time spent in personal travel—over 2,500 *miles—getting with faithfulness all possible facts of interest and the latest information. Over* 40 *artists, engravers and correspondents have been employed, and the whole represents an outlay of nearly* $20,000 : thus making it not only the most elaborate, but the costliest and handsomest Guide Book in the world. No other volume in the world contains so many views of the scenery of the West. The Editor and his Assistants have, in the past seven years, personally traveled over this great Route more than 30 times. More than 100,000 miles of travel on the American Continent have been traversed by the Editor, who during eight years' active service as an associate editor of *The New York Independent,* has conducted four large editorial parties to the wonders of the West, representing over 150 journals and a total circulation of over 3,000,000.

In this volume is combined every possible fact to guide and instruct the pleasure traveler, business man, miner, or settler, who turns his face westward. Herein are found every Railroad Station, and time of the principal Railroads, all Stage Routes, Distances, and Fare to all principal points; all the wonders of Western Scenery, Springs, Mountains, Canons, Lakes, Deserts, Rocks, and Gardens are here described in detail.

The trans-ocean traveler from Europe to the Pacific will find all needful information of Routes on the Pacific Ocean; and the traveler eastward from Australia and Japan will find invaluable help for his route to New York.

Professor F. V. Hayden, the celebrated leader of the United States Geological Exploring Expedition, has contributed specially to these pages an admirably condensed account of the Wonders of the Yellowstone; and with the assistance of A. C. Peale, this Guide is the only publication which gives the most detailed and accurate information of Routes—how to reach it.

The Big Bonanza Mines are also described in glowing language, and add to the interest of these pages.

The Representative Men of the Far West, who have been the energetic projectors and supporters of all its active and successful enterprises, are illustrated in our pages.

I acknowledge, with pleasure, special thanks for the services of Mr. J. B. Davis, late editor of *The Commonwealth,* Topeka, Kansas, and F. E Shearer, of San Francisco, who have done so much by personal travel and effort to make this Guide complete; also to G. W. Savage of Salt Lake City, for photographs.

As the Tourist looks with pleasure upon the sketches of *Thomas Moran,* who more than any other American artist has illustrated the Glories of the West, or upon the scenes illustrated from the paintings of Bierstadt, America's favorite painter, and the sketches by Warren, Will, and others, all from life and accurate in every detail, let him give due credit to Art for these happy embellishments of nature. Wishing every traveler "*bon voyage,*" I am, cordially,

HENRY T. WILLIAMS, *Editor.*

AMERICA'S GREATEST WONDER!

The Pacific Railroad.

HER grandest scenery borders its magnificent pathway; thither is her most popular route of pleasure travel, and most celebrated health resorts; and along these iron lines, the monument of financial intrepidity and daring engineering skill, there is opened a new West, a Continent of itself, richer in wealth than the most sanguine of hopes; and hither, in so short space of time, has poured so immense a volume of trade, as to change the entire commerce of the world.

Industries have arisen by the opening of this great trans-continental line which were never expected or dreamed of by the projectors; the richest of mineral discoveries and the most encouraging of agricultural settlements have alike resulted, where little was thought of, and strangest of all, the tide of travel from the European and the Asiatic countries, and the distant isles of the Pacific Ocean, once the exclusive privilege of English vessels through the Suez Canal, or around the Continent of Africa, actually now crosses the American Continent with far more speed and greater safety. The exclamations of American and European tourists, after a passage over its magnificent route are alike,—"*The greatest wonder of the nineteenth century!*"

Curiosities of History.—To whom the honor belongs of first proposing the plan of a railroad to the Pacific, history can never fully determine. Whitney offered to build it for a grant of thirty miles in width along its track, and it was looked upon as the freaky fancy of a monomaniac. Benton, too, the famous statesman, was once aglow with enthusiasm over the subject, and began to agitate the project, but it was considered the harmless fancy of an old politician. And in 1856, when General Fremont was nominated, the Platform of the National Republican Party contained a clause in its favor—but it was regarded as a piece of cheap electioneering "buncombe," and decidedly absurd. Perhaps the earliest record of a devoted admirer of this project was that of John Plumbe, in 1836. He was a Welshman by birth, an American by education and feeling, a civil engineer by profession, and lived at Dubuque, Ia. He began to agitate the project of a railroad from the great lakes across the Continent to the Territory of Oregon. From that time to his death, in California, several years after the discovery of gold, he never failed to urge his project; earnestly and ardently laboring to bring it before Congress, and attempting to secure a beginning of the great work. To far-seeing statesmen, the idea naturally occurred that in course of time there would arise on the Pacific Coast another empire of trade and commerce and industry, either at San Francisco, or the Puget Sound, which would in time, become the rival of New York and the East, and at once the project was taken up and encouraged by Carver, Wilkes, Benton, Whitney, Burton and others; but all such ideas met with indifference and ridicule.

In 1844, when Fremont made his famous explorations across the plains, which has earned him so world-wide a reputation, so little was known of the geography of that country, that his reports were considered an immense acquisition to the collection of books of physical knowledge of our country. This section was fully 2,300 miles in distance, entirely vacant, no settlement, entirely occupied by roving bands of Indians, and the undisturbed home of the buffalo and antelope. In that year Chicago was but an obscure village, on a prairie without a single inhabitant. And not a single line of railroad was built from the Atlantic westward beyond the Alleghanies, and on the Pacific only one American flag covered a feeble colony. The discovery of gold in California had its effect in directing public attention to the unknown riches of its Western border; and at last Congress woke up to the need of thorough explorations and investigations. In March, 1853, Congress made its first appropriation to explore the Far West, and ascertain if there was really a practicable route to the Pacific. In 1854, Congress appropriated $190,000 additional; and, as a result, nine surveying parties were organized and pursued their work. Ten routes were surveyed between the 32d and 49th parallel of latitude; the eastern ends ranging all the way from Fulton, Ark., to St. Paul, Minn.,—and the western terminal points from San Diego to Puget Sound. The lengths of these routes varied from 1,533 to 2,290 miles.

The continued gold discoveries brought an immense flow of population to the Pacific Coast, and California, more alive to the necessities of such roads than the East, after numerous agitations, at last really made the first initiatory experiment. Early in 1861 there was organized at Sacramento, Cal., the Central Pacific Railroad Company, who by the appointment of T. D. Judah, as chief engineer, began the first and most thorough railroad survey ever made on the Sierras.

Congress then woke up, and in July, 1862, the first national charter was granted. As a curious fact in the act—the utmost limit of time allowed for the completion of the road was fixed at July 1, 1876. In October, 1863, the preliminary organization of the company was completed. A capital of one hundred million dollars authorized, and the first contract for construction begun in 1864, but no practical progress was made till 1865, when on the 5th of November, the first ceremony of breaking ground, at Omaha, was celebrated. Then was begun the great work; the rapid progress of which afterward was a world-wide sensation, astounding engineers, capitalists, and even governments, with the almost reckless daring of construction.

Necessity and Benefits to the Government.

From 1850 to 1860, the population of the far Western States and Territories increased from a mere handful to the large number of 554,301 persons, and in the whole area of 2,000 miles there had been built only 232 miles of telegraph, and 32 miles of railway. The United States Government had established forts and trading stations, and the year 1870 saw the completion of the Pacific Railroad line, Congress and the whole country were astonished to see the rapid rate of development, and the enormous expense of government military service. In that year the population had increased to 1,011,971, there had been built over 13,000 miles of telegraph lines; there were completed over 4,000 miles of railroad; all representing the gigantic capital of $363,750,000. In the reports of distinguished statesmen to the United States Senate, occur these remarks which show the spirit of the times then. Senator Stewart of California, says:

"The cost of the overland service for the whole period, from the acquisition of our Pacific Coast possessions down to the completion of the Pacific Railroad was $8,000,000 per annum, and constantly increasing."

As a curious fact of national economy, these figures will show the result of the Pacific Railroad in saving to the United States Government:

Since the building of the road, the cost of transportation to the government has been as follows:

Amount cash paid to railroad companies for one-half charge of transportation per year about $1,200,000 per annum, say for 7 years—1869 to 1876,	$8,400,000
The cost to the government of military transportation in 1870, was $8,000,000 per annum, and increasing over $1,000,000 per year In 1876, would have been over $14,000,000. Average for 7 years, at $10,000,000 per year,	$70,000,000
Total saving in 7 years to United States Government,	$62,600,000
The actual amount of interest during this time paid by the United States Treasury on bonds issued in behalf of the railroad, average interest, $3,897,129 per year. Total for 7 years,	$27,279,906
Net profit over all expenses to United States,	$42,320,094

These figures do not include vast amounts of incidental items which would have been of incalculable trouble, or immense expense to the United States, such as the indemnities constantly being paid by the United States for destruction of life and private property by Indians; also depredations of Indians on property in government service, increased mail facilities and decreased mail expenses, prevention of Indian wars, the rapid sale of public lands, and the energetic development of the mining interests of all the Territories.

If these can all be correctly estimated, the net gain to the United States by the building of the Pacific Railroad, is over *fifty millions of dollars.*

Hon. Henry Wilson, in a speech before the Senate, Thirty-seventh Congress, boldly said: "I give no grudging vote in giving away either money or land. I would sink $100,000,000 to build the road, and do it most cheerfully, and think I had done a great thing for my country. What are $75,000,000 or $100,000,000 in opening a railroad across the central regions of this Continent, that shall connect the people of the Atlantic and Pacific, and bind us together? Nothing. As to the lands, I do not grudge them."

It is a significant fact, that while the heat and activity of Congressional discussion was most earnest in aid and encouragement of the project, the following sentiments were unanimously entertained by all the members of Congress:

1. That the road was a *necessity* to the government, and if not built by private capital, must be built in time with public funds alone.

2. To encourage the capitalists of the country to come forward and aid the project, the government were willing to give one-half the funds necessary as a loan, and were then merely doing the least part of the whole.

3. That no expectations were entertained that the road would ever, from its own means, be able to refund the advance made by the United States, and no other thought was ever entertained, save of the benefits to accrue to the public from the opening of this grand highway of national interest. No expectations were formed of the ability of the company to pay or repay the interest on the loan, but one thought was considered, that the building of the road was ample compensation and service in its vast aid to industry, and its saving in transportation.

As editor of this Guide, knowing well the resources of the Far West, we positively assert that the government has already, in seven years, realized in both savings and sales, enough money to liquidate one-third the whole principal, and accrued interest of the government loan, and in less than twenty years from the opening of the road, the government gain will be greater than the whole of the financial aid it has ever given. The Pacific Railroad is the right-hand saving power of the United States.

Discouragements. — Notwithstanding all that the government had done to encourage it (by speeches), the work languished. Capitalists doubted it. The great war of the rebellion attracted the attention of every one, and the government, after its first impulses, grew indifferent. A few bold men determined to work incessantly for its completion. And one of the results of the great war was the conviction in the minds of every one—of a closer Union of the States. "*Who knows,*" said one, "*but California and the whole Pacific Coast may secede, and where are we then? We can do nothing to retain them. The Pacific Railroad must be built. It shall be built to keep our country together.*"

The chief engineer of the railroad, Gen. G. M. Dodge, in complimenting the directors on the day of the completion of the last mile of track, says:

"The country is evidently satisfied that you accomplished wonders, and have achieved a work which will be a monument to your energy, your ability, and to your devotion to the enterprise, through all its gloomy, as well as bright periods, for it is notorious that notwithstanding the aid of the government, there was so little faith in the enterprise, that its dark days—when your private fortunes, and your all was staked on the success of the project—far exceeded those of sunshine, faith and confidence."

The lack of confidence in the project, even in the West, was so great that even in localities which were to be specially benefited by its construction, the laborers even demanded their pay *before* they would perform their day's work, so little faith had they in the payment of their wages, or in the ability of the company to succeed in their efforts.

Probably no enterprise in the world has been so maligned, misrepresented and criticised as this, but now it is, by unbiased minds, pronounced, almost without exception, the best new road in the United States.

Rapid Progress. — Though chartered in 1862, yet the first grading was not done until 1864, and the first rail laid in July, 1865. At that time there was no railroad communication from the East; a gap of 140 miles existed between Omaha and Des Moines, and over this it was impossible to get supplies.

For 500 miles westward of the Missouri River, the country was completely destitute of timber, fuel, or any material with which to build or maintain a road, save the bare sand for the road-bed itself, everything had to be transported by teams or steamboats, hundreds and thousands of miles. Labor, and every thing made by labor, was scarce and high.

Railroad ties were cut in Michigan and Pennsylvania, and shipped to Omaha at a cost, often, of $2.50 per tie. Even the splendid engine, of seventy horse-power, used at Omaha for the company's works, was transported in *wagons* across the prairies from Des Moines, the only way to get it. Shops had to be built, forges erected, and machinery put in place, and the supplies, even, for the subsistence of laborers had to be brought by river from the East; yet it was all done.

As the Westerners concisely express it, "*The wind work had all been done, and grading now began.*"

In 1865, 40 miles of track were laid to Fremont. In 1866, 260 miles were laid. In 1867, 240 miles were laid, which included the ascent to Sherman. By January 1, 1868, there had been completed 540 miles. In 1868, to May 10, 1869, 555 miles more were laid, and the road finished—seven years in advance of the time set by Congress, and the time actually spent in construction was just *three years, six months, and ten days.*

To show the enormous amount of materials required in the Union Pacific Railroad alone, there were used in its construction 300,000 tons of iron rails, 1,700,000 fish-plates, 6,800,000 bolts, 6,126,375 cross-ties, 23,505,500 spikes.

Fast Building.—Day after day the average rate of building rose from one to two, three and five miles. Many will remember the daily thrill of excitement as the morning journals in the East made the announcements of so many more miles nearer the end, and as the number of completed miles, printed in the widely circulated advertisements of the company, reached 1000, the excitement became intense, as the rival roads now were fairly aglow with the heat of competition, and so near each other. In previous months there had existed a little engineering rivalry, good natured, but keen, as to the largest number of miles each could lay in one day. The Union Pacific men laid one day *six* miles; soon after the Central followed suit by laying *seven.* The Union Pacific retaliated by laying seven and a half; to this the Central sent the announcement that they could lay ten miles in one day; to this Mr. Durant, the vice-president, sent back a wager of $10,000 that it could not be done. The pride and spirit of the Central Pacific had now been challenged, and they prepared for the enormous contest, one of extraordinary magnitude and rapidity. The 29th day of April, 1869, was selected for the decision of the contest, as there then remained but 14 miles of track to bring a meeting of the roads at Promontory Point.

Work began; the ground had already been graded and ties placed in position, and at the signal the cars loaded with rails moved forward. Four men, two on each side, seize with their nippers the ends of the rails, lift from the car and carry them to their place; the car moves steadily along over the rails as fast as they are laid. Immediately after follows a band of men who attach the plate and put the spikes in position; next a force of Chinamen who drive down the spikes solid to their homes, and last another gang of Chinamen with shovels, picks, etc., who ballast the track. The rapidity of all these motions, which required the most active of exercise and alert movements, was at the rate of 144 feet of track to every minute. By 1.30 P. M., the layers had placed *eight miles of track in just six hours.* Resuming work again, after the noon rest, the track-laying progressed, and at 7 P. M., exactly, the Central men finished their task of 10 miles, with 200 feet over. Mr. James Campbell, the superintendent of the division, then seizing a locomotive ran it over the ten miles of new track in forty minutes, and the Union men were satisfied. This was the greatest feat of railroad building ever known in the world, and when it is known how vast the materials required to supply this little stretch of ten miles, the reader is fairly astonished at the endurance of the laborers. To put this material in place over 4,000 men had been constantly employed. The laborers on that day handled 25,800 cross-ties, 3,520 iron rails, 55,000 spikes, 7,040 fish-plates, and 14,080 bolts, the weight of the whole being 4,362,000 pounds. Upon both roads, for a year previous, there had been remarkable activity.

A total force of 20,000 to 25,000 workmen all along the lines, and 5,000 to 6,000 teams had been engaged in grading and laying the track or getting out stone or timber. From 500 to 600 tons of materials were forwarded daily from either end of the lines.

The Sierra Nevadas suddenly became alive with wood-choppers, and at one place on the Truckee River twenty-five saw-mills went into operation in a single week. Upon one railroad 70 to 100 locomotives were in use at one time, constantly bringing materials and supplies. At one time there were 30 vessels *en route* from New York via Cape Horn, with iron, locomotives, rails and rolling stock, destined for the Central Pacific Railroad; and it is a curious fact, that on several consecutive days, more miles of track were ironed by the railroad companies than it was possible for an ox-team to draw a load over. And when at last the great road was completed, the fact suddenly flashed upon the nation that a road once so distrusted, and considered too gigantic to be possible, was constructed an actual distance of 2,221 miles, in *less than five years,* of which all but 100 miles was done between January 1, 1866 and May 10, 1869—*three years, four months and ten days.*

Pleasure of Overland Travel.—Palace Car Life on the Pacific Railroad.—In no part of the world is travel made so easy and comfortable as on the Pacific Railroad. To travelers from the East it is a constant delight, and to ladies and families it is accompanied with absolutely no fatigue or discomfort. One lives at home in the Palace Car with as much true enjoyment as in the home drawing-room, and with the constant change of scenes afforded from the car window, it is far more enjoyable than the saloon of a fashionable steamer. For an entire week or more, as the train leisurely crosses the Continent, the little section and berth allotted to you, so neat and clean, so nicely furnished and kept, becomes your home. Here you sit and read, play your games, indulge in social conversation and glee, and if fortunate enough to possess good company of friends to join you, the overland tour becomes an intense delight.

The sleeping-cars from New York to Chicago, proceeding at their rushing rate of forty or more miles per hour, give to travelers no idea of the true comfort of Pullman car life. Indeed the first thousand miles of the journey to Chicago or St. Louis has more tedium and wearisomeness, and dust and inconvenience than all the rest of the journey. Do not judge of the whole trip by these first days out. From Chicago westward to Omaha the cars are far finer, and traveling more luxurious, likewise the rate of speed is slower and the motion of the train more easy than on roads farther east.

At Omaha, as you view the long Pacific train just ready to leave the depot for its overland trip, (often over 600 feet in length), giving an appearance of strength, massiveness and majestic power, you can but admit it is exceedingly beautiful and impressive; this feeling is still more intensified when a day or so later, alone out upon the upland plains, with no living object in sight, as you stand at a little distance and look down upon the long train, it seems the handsomest work of science ever made for the comfort of earth's people.

The slow rate of speed, which averages but sixteen to twenty miles per hour, day and night, produces a peculiarly smooth, gentle and easy motion, most soothing and agreeable. The straight track, which for hundreds of miles is without a curve, avoids all swinging motions of the cars; sidelong bumps are unknown. The cars are connected with the Miller buffer and platform, and make a solid train, without the discomforts of jerks and jolts. And the steady, easy jog of the train, as it leisurely moves westward, gives a feeling of genuine comfort, such as no one ever feels or enjoys in any other part of the world.

A Pullman Pacific car train in motion is a grand and beautiful sight too, from within as well as from without. On some lovely, balmy, summer day, when the fresh breezes across the prairies induce us to open our doors and windows, there may often be seen curious and pleasant sights. Standing at the rear of the train, and with all doors open, there is an unobstructed view along the aisles throughout the entire length. On either side of the train, are the prairies, where the eye sees but wildness, and even desolation, then looking back upon this long aisle or avenue, he sees civilization and comfort and luxury. How sharp the contrast. The first day's ride over the Pacific Railroad westward, is a short one to nightfall, but it carries one through the beautiful undulating prairies of eastern Nebraska, the best settled portions of the State, where are its finest homes and richest soil. Opening suddenly into the broad and ever grand Valley of the Platte, the rich luxuriant meadow-grass, in the warmth of the afternoon sun, make even the most desponding or prosaic feel there is beauty in prairie life.

On the second day out, the traveler is fast ascending the high plains and summits of the Rocky Mountains. The little villages of prairie dogs interest and amuse every one. Then come in sight the distant summits of Long's Peak and the Colorado Mountains. Without scarcely asking the cause, the tourist is full of glow and enthusiasm. He is alive with enjoyment, and yet can scarcely tell why. The great plains themselves seem full of interest.

Ah! It is this keen, beautiful, refreshing, oxygenated, invigorating, toning, beautiful, enlivening mountain air which is giving him the glow of nature, and quickening him into greater appreciation of this grand impressive country. The plains themselves are a sight—most forcible; shall we call them *the blankness of desolation?* No, for every inch of the little turf beneath your feet is rich; the soil contains the finest of food in the little tufts of buffalo grass, on which thousands and millions of sheep and cattle may feed the year through. But it is the vastness of wide-extending, uninhabited, lifeless, uplifted solitude. If ever one feels belittled, 'tis on the plains, when each individual seems but a little mite, amid this *majesty of loneliness.* But the traveler finds with the Pullman car life, amid his enjoyments of reading, playing, conversation, making agreeable acquaintances, and with constant glances from the car window, enough to give him full and happy use of his time.

Night time comes, and then as your little berths are made up, and you snugly cover yourself up, under *double blankets* (for the night air is always crisp and cold), perhaps you will often witness the sight of a prairie fire, or the vivid flashes of lightning; some of nature's greatest scenes, hardly less interesting than the plains, and far more fearful and awe-inspiring. Then turning to rest, you will sleep amid the easy roll of the car, as sweetly and refreshingly as ever upon the home-bed. How little has ever been written of "Night on the Pacific Railroad," the delightful, snug, rejuvenating *sleeps* on the Pacific Railroad.

The lulling, quiet life by day, and the sound, refreshing repose by night, are to the system the best of health restorers. Were there but one thing tourists might feel most gratitude for, on their overland trip, 'tis their enjoyment of the exhilarating mountain air by day, and the splendid rest by night. But as our train moves on, it introduces us to new scenes. You soon ascend the Rocky Mountains at Sherman, and view there the vast mountain range, the "Back Bone of the Continent," and again descend and thunder amid the cliffs of Echo and Weber Canons. You carry with you your Pullman house and all its comforts, and from your little window, as from your little boudoir at home, you will see the mighty wonders of the Far West.

It is impossible to tell of the pleasures and joys of the palace ride you will have—five days—it will make you so well accustomed to car life, you feel when you drop upon the wharf of San Francisco, that you had left genuine comfort behind, and even the hotel, with its cosy parlor and cheerful fire, has not its full recompense.

Palace car life has every day its fresh and novel sights. No railroad has greater variety and contrasts of scenery than the Pacific Railroad. The great plains of Nebraska and Wyoming are not less impressive than the great Humboldt Desert. The rock majesties of Echo and Weber are not more wonderful than the curiosities of Great Salt Lake and the City of Deseret. And where more grandly and beautifully could a tourist drop down and finish his tour, than from the grand, towering summits of the Sierras, and amid the golden grain fields of California, its gardens, groves, and cottage blossoms?

When the traveler returns home, nothing will impress him more strongly or beautifully than the loveliness of the Valley of the Platte. Coming eastward, first, he will leave behind the millions of acres of little short buffalo grass, so dry and yellow, and soon comes to a little green. How refreshing it is after days of dry, sere vegetation. Gradually there come other grasses, a little taller and more green; then nearer and nearer to the end of the journey, come the waving of the corn-fields, the vast meadows of tall green grass, and the happy little farms. So complete a transition from the solitude of the uplands to the lovely green verdure of the lowlands of the Platte, is an inexpressible charm to all. No traveler ever returns East but with the most kindly of memories of the grand, and yet simple beauty of the Platte Valley.

Think then, oh reader! of the joys that await thee from the window of thy palace car!

Practical Hints for Comforts by the Way.—To enjoy palace car life properly, one always needs a good companion. This obtained, take a section together, wherever the journey leads you. From Chicago to Omaha, the company in sleeping-cars is usually quiet and refined, but beyond Omaha, there is often an indescribable mixture of races in the same car, and if you are alone, often the chance is that your "*compagnon du voyage*" may not be agreeable. It is impossible to order a section for *one* person *alone*, and the dictum of sleeping-car arrangements at Omaha requires all who come to take what berths are *assigned*. But if you will wait over one day at Omaha, you can make a choice of the whole train, and secure the most desirable berths. When your section is once located, generally you will find the same section reserved for you at Ogden, where you change cars to the Central Pacific Railroad; all through passengers having usually the preference of best berths, and about the same position as on the cars of the Union Pacific.

Fee your porter on the sleeping-car always—if he is attentive and obliging, give him a dollar. His attention to your comfort and care of your baggage and constant watch over the little articles and hand-satchel, against loafers on the train, is worth all you give him. Often larger fees are given. This is just as the traveler feels. The porters of both Pacific Railroads are esteemed specially excellent, obliging and careful.

Meals.—The trains of the Union Pacific Railroad are arranged so as to stop at excellent stations, at convenient hours, for meals. The only disarrangement is at Laramie, which seems to be unfortunate to passengers from either direction. To travelers from the East it furnishes a very early supper, just after dinner at Cheyenne, and to those from the West, it gives a very late breakfast, just before dinner; but there is no other place for an eating-station, except at this point. At Medicine Bow near Laramie, there is a little booth where the Western train coming east, about 7 A. M., often stops ten minutes for hot coffee, sandwiches—an excellent convenience.

Usually all the eating-houses on both the Pacific Railroads are very excellent indeed. The keepers have to maintain their culinary excellence under great disadvantages, especially west of Sidney, as all food but meats must be brought from a great distance.

Travelers need to make no preparations for eating on the cars, as meals at all dining-halls are excellent, and food of great variety is nicely served; buffalo meat, antelope steak, tongue of all kinds, and always the best of beefsteak. Laramie possesses the reputation of the best steak on the Pacific Railroad. Sidney makes a specialty, occasionally, of antelope steak. At Evanston you will see the lively antics of the Chinese waiters, probably your first sight of them. Also they usually have nice mountain fish. At Green River you will always get nice biscuit; at Grand Island they give all you can possibly eat; it has a good name for its bountiful supplies.

At Ogden you will be pleased with the neatness and cleanness of the tables and service. At Cheyenne the dinners are always excellent, and the dining-room is cheerful. To any who either have desire to economize, or inability to eat three railroad meals per day, we recommend to carry a little basket with Albert biscuit and a little cup. This can be easily filled at all stopping-places with hot tea or coffee, and a sociable and comfortable glass of tea indulged in inside the car. The porter will fit you up a nice little table in your section, and spread on a neat white tablecloth.

When the tourist reaches the Central Pacific Railroad he passes beyond the domain of the Pullman Car Company; nevertheless, the new coaches of the Central Pacific Railroad are just as elegant and convenient.

As the comforts of the new cars are far superior to the old ones, which still are used, it would be better to wait over at Ogden one day to make sure of them. The dining-stations of the Central Pacific Railroad are bountiful in their supplies; at all of them fruit is given in summer-time with great freedom. Fish is almost always to be had; no game of value. The food, cooking and service by Chinese waiters is simply excellent. The writer has never eaten nicer meals than those served at Winnemucca, Elko, Battle Mountain and Colfax. The Humboldt Desert is far from being a desert to the traveling public, for its eating-stations always furnish a *dessert* of good things and creature comforts.

A little lunch-basket nicely stowed with sweet and substantial bits of food will often save you the pain of long rides before meals; when the empty stomach craves food and failing to receive it, lays you up with the most dismal of sick headaches; it also serves you splendidly whenever the train is delayed. To be well on the Pacific Railroad *eat at regular hours, and never miss a meal.* Most of the sickness which we have witnessed, has arisen from irregular eating, or injudicious attempts at economy by skipping a meal to save a dollar. We have noticed those who were regular in eating at every meal, passed the journey with greatest ease, most comfort and best health. Those who were irregular, skipping here and there a meal, always suffered inconvenience.

In packing your little lunch-basket, avoid *tongue, by all means*, for it will not keep over a day or two, and its fumes in a sleeping-car are anything but like those from "Araby the blest." Avoid all articles which have odor of any description.

Lunch counters are attached to all eating-stations, so that you may easily procure hot coffee, tea, biscuit, sandwiches and fruit if you do not wish a full meal.

The uniform price of meals at all stations overland, is $1.00 greenbacks. On the Central Pacific, at Colfax pay 75 cents in silver; at Lathrop pay 50 cents silver—the cheapest and best meal for the money, of your whole tour. For clothing on your overland trip, you will need at Omaha the first day, if it is summer, a light spring suit; the next day a winter suit at Sherman. Again, at Salt Lake City and the Humboldt Desert, the thinnest of summer suits, and at the summit of the Sierras, all your underclothing. We can only advise you as you have to pass through so many extremes of temperature, to always wear your underclothing, day and night, through the overland trip, and add an overcoat if the air grows chilly.

Beware of the quick transition from the hot ride over the San Joaquin Valley to the cold sea air on the ferry from Oakland to San Francisco. Invalids have been chilled through with this unexpected sea breeze, and even the most hardy do not love it. Keep warm and keep inside the boat. Thus, reader, we have helped you with kindly hints how to enjoy your trip. Now let us glance, as we go, at each scene of industry where our tour will take us.

HINTS.

1. ***Baggage.***—All baggage of reasonable weight can be checked from any Eastern city direct to Omaha, but is there rechecked.

2. At Omaha all baggage is weighed, and on all excess of over 100 pounds, passengers will pay 15 cts. per pound. This is imperative.

3. ***Railroad Tickets***—are easily procurable for the whole trip across to San Francisco. It is better to buy one through ticket than to buy separately. By returning a different route from Omaha, from the one you went, the tour will be much more interesting, and give you fresh scenery constantly.

4. Buy your tickets only at known railroad offices, and never of agencies. In the West, railroads have offices at the principal hotels. These are usually perfectly reliable.

5. ***To Check Baggage***—be at every depot one-half hour or more before the departure of trains.

6. ***Transfer Coaches.***—In all Western cities there is a line of transfer coaches, which, for the uniform price of fifty cents, will take you and your baggage direct to any hotel, or transfer you at once across the city to any depot. They are trustworthy, cheap, and convenient. The agent will always pass through the train before arrival, selling transfer tickets and checks to hotels.

7. At Salt Lake City, horse-cars run from the depot direct to the hotels; also there is an omnibus transfer. Price, fifty cents.

8. At San Francisco the Pacific Transfer and Baggage Company will take your baggage to any hotel or private residence for 50 cents. Their agent is on every train; you will save time by giving him your check. Hotel coaches charge $1.00. Horse-cars run from the wharf direct to all hotels.

9. Greenbacks are used for all railroad tickets and payment of sleeping-car berths for the entire distance to California; also for all hotels to and including Salt Lake City, but beyond that, everything is payable in silver and gold. For the Central Pacific Railroad, you do not need more than $5 for coin expenses. After reaching San Francisco, you can sell your greenbacks and buy coin as often as necessary. If much coin is needed, buy and use the gold notes which are current everywhere within 300 miles of the city; beyond that the coin only is used. Gold drafts

can be bought in all Eastern cities on San Francisco.

10. The uniform prices of board in the West are $4.50 per day at Chicago, $4.00 per day at Omaha, Denver, and Salt Lake City. In San Francisco, $3.00 gold per day at all hotels. To secure good nice rooms in California, the tourist must submit to extra charges of $1.00 to $1.50 per day.

11. If traveling with ladies, it is good policy, when within 100 miles of each city, where you expect to stop, to telegraph to your hotel in advance, requesting nice rooms reserved, always mentioning that you have ladies.

12. Whenever disposed to take horses and carriage for a ride, look out with sharp eyes for the tricks of the trade; if no price or time is agreed upon, you will have to pay dearly, and the farther west you go, the hire of horse flesh grows dearer (though the value per animal rapidly grows less.) Engage your livery carefully at so much per hour, and then choose your time to suit your wishes. Ten dollar bills melt quicker in carriage rides than any other "vain show."

13. Without much exception, all railroad officers, railroad conductors, Pullman car conductors are gentlemen in manners, courteous and civil. No passenger ever gains a point by loud orders or strong and forcible demands. You are treated respectfully by all, and the same is expected in return. The days of boisterous times, rough railroad men, and bullies in the Far West are gone, and there is as much civility there, often more, than you will find near home.

14. Railroad tickets must always be shown when baggage is checked.

ROUTES.

Route No. 1 from New York.—Take the Pennsylvania Central Railroad which leaves foot of Desbrosses street, by ferry, to Jersey City. To engage a good berth in your sleeping-car, go to a proper railroad office, and secure your berth by telegraph. There are local telegraphs connecting with the principal Pullman office. Do this the previous night, or morning, as then the best berths can be secured. Pullman cars run on the Pennsylvania Railroad to Chicago and St. Louis, direct, without change. Three trains leave per day. To see the richest scenery, take the *morning train* and you will have a good view of nearly the entire State of Pennsylvania by daylight, the valley of the Susquehanna and Juniata, and the famous Horse-Shoe Bend by moonlight. The Pennsylvania Railroad is "*always on time*," the most reliable in its connections.

Route No. 2 from New York.—Leave *via* the Erie Railroad from foot of Chambers or West 23d street. The advantages of this route are numerous. This is the famous Pullman line—where run the only line of dining-cars—between New York and Chicago. The meals are very fine and service excellent. The sleeping-cars on the Erie Railroad belong to the Pullman Company, and are the finest in the world, of extra width and extra comfort. The scenery along the Erie Railroad (by all means take the morning train) is specially fine, and at points is remarkably lovely. The sleeping and dining-cars accompany the train to Chicago. The route passes *via* Salamanca, Atlantic and Great Western and Chicago extension of Baltimore and Ohio Railroad, direct without change, to Chicago. Passengers also can take other sleeping-cars of the train, if they wish, which will convey them direct to Buffalo and Niagara Falls, where there is direct connection *via* the Lake Shore Railroad or Michigan Central to Chicago.

Route No. 3—is *via* the New York Central and Hudson River. Tourists by this route will have the advantage of a daylight ride along the Hudson River, and the Mohawk Valley, which, in early summer, is very fine. The dining-stations on this route, especially at Poughkeepsie, Albany, Utica and Syracuse are the finest in the Eastern States, and meals are super excellent. The sleeping-cars of this line are owned by the Wagner Company, which upon the principal day and night express trains are exceedingly fine, well furnished and luxurious. Wagner cars run by two routes to Chicago, one *via* Buffalo, Cleveland and Toledo, over the Lake Shore and Michigan Southern Railroad, the other *via* Niagara Falls and Detroit over the Michigan Central Railroad. The time made on this route is very rapid, and always exceedingly prompt and reliable.

From Philadelphia.—Tourists uniformly prefer the Pennsylvania Central, though many often wish to visit Baltimore and Washington, and thence see the scenery along the Baltimore and Ohio Railroad, and go westward *via* Cincinnati to St. Louis.

From Baltimore and Washington.—Tourists have choice of either the Northern Central with Pennsylvania Central connections, or the Baltimore and Ohio Railroad. Pullman cars run on either road.

From Boston.—Wagner sleeping-cars run direct over the Boston and Albany Railroad, to Rochester, N. Y., and usually through to Chicago. Though this is an exceedingly convenient route, yet it gives no scenery of consequence. Tourists who desire the best scenery will do well to come direct to New York, the ride by steamer being always pleasant, and from New York make their start, the pleasantest time for departure always being on the fast special express in the morning.

From Cincinnati,—tourists have choice of two routes; 1st, *via* Ohio and Mississippi Railroad, direct to St. Louis, passing over the famous St. Louis Bridge, with omnibus transfer to other railroads; or, 2d, *via* Indianapolis, Bloomington and Western Railroad, which run trains direct to Burlington, Ia., or to Chicago. Pullman sleeping-cars run on either route.

From Chicago,—three roads run across Iowa direct to Council Bluffs.

The Chicago, Burlington and Missouri Railroad—crosses the Mississippi at Burlington, Ia., and passes through Southern Iowa. The Pullman cars are very elegant, and the road popular. This line is now running dining cars attached to its express trains, on both Eastern and Western divisions. It is preferable to get meals on this car than at the eating-stations. The prices are the same; meals splendid.

The Chicago and North-western Railroad—is the shortest line, and crosses the Mississippi at Clinton, Ia. The eating-stations on this route are all very fine. In Iowa, especially, they are the best of the Iowa railroads. The Pullman cars are also very superior. There has recently been added a magnificent Hotel car to express trains, which increases the popularity of the line very greatly.

The Chicago and Rock Island Railroad—crosses the Mississippi at Davenport. The view from the railroad bridge is very beautiful, and the scenery of the railroad in the Des Moines Valley, and westward, is charming. The sleeping-cars on this line are owned by the railroad company, and are very good.

Note.—Upon on railroads west of Chicago, no sleeping-cars run through, except those connected with the morning Pacific express train. These run direct from Chicago to Council Bluffs. At the transfer grounds there, passengers will change cars and take the Union Pacific Railroad train over the bridge to Omaha and the West.

From St. Louis—two routes are open to the tourist. The Missouri Pacific Railroad runs up on the south side of the Missouri River, with Pullman cars, direct for Kansas City, Atchinson, via Lincoln to Omaha.

The St. Louis, Kansas City and Northern Railroad—in direct connection with the *Kansas City, St. Joseph and Council Bluffs Railroad*, run through sleeping-cars from St. Louis direct to Omaha. This line is very popular and reliable in time, and well patronized. Travelers from the Pacific railroad going to St. Louis, will find sleeping-cars of both the St. Louis railroads waiting at the Omaha depot, on arrival of Union Pacific railroad train from the West.

Council Bluffs, Iowa, Railroad Transfer Grounds.—This, as well as Omaha, is a transfer point for all passengers, and the starting point of all trains on the Union Pacific railroad. A recent decision of U. S. Supreme Court, fixes the terminus of the Pacific Railroad on the east side of the Missouri River. The company has complied with the decision, and the necessity for bridge transfer is now entirely removed. At Council Bluffs is also the western terminus of the Iowa Railroads. A Union Depot for all railroads is proposed, and will soon be erected. Henceforth, all passengers, baggage, mails, freight, etc., and trains for the West, will start from this point, as well as Omaha. Passengers, however, usually prefer to take their sleeping-cars at Omaha. The city of Council Bluffs is located about three miles east from the Missouri river, and contains a population of 15,000. Its record dates from as early a period as 1804, when the celebrated explorers, Lewis and Clark, held a council with the Indians, which fact, together with the physical peculiarity of the high bluffs overlooking the town, has given it its name—Council Bluffs.

The city is one of great enterprise, with a large number of public buildings, stores, State institutions, and dwellings, and is the nucleus of a large trade from surrounding Iowa towns, and is supported by a rich agricultural community. It is intimately connected with Omaha—with frequent trains over the bridge, also steam ferry. It will doubtless come more largely hereafter into prominence as a railroad town, though the commercial importance of Omaha, and its trade with the far West, will doubtless be for a long time to come, far superior. The general offices of the Union Pacific Railroad Company will remain, for the present, at Omaha.

At Council Bluffs the Union Pacific Railroad Company have reserved ample grounds, over 1,000 acres, to accommodate its own traffic and that of connecting railroads, and extensive preparations will be made to accommodate the vast traffic of freights, passengers, baggage and stock, which daily arrives and departs.

Here are also located the stock-grounds of the company, which in time will render the locality a large stock-market. The past year over 3,000 cars of stock were transferred over the bridge, and there is ample room for extension.

Sleeping-Car Expenses.—The tariff to travelers is as follows, with all companies, and all in greenbacks:

One berth, New York to Chicago, one and one-half days, by any route,	$5 00
One berth, New York to Cincinnati, one and one-half days, by Pennsylvania railroad,	4 00
One berth, New York to Cincinnati, one and one-half days, by other routes,	5 00
One berth, New York to St. Louis, two days, by any route,	6 00
One berth, Chicago or St. Louis, to Omaha, by any route,	3 00
One berth, Omaha to Ogden, by Pacific Railroad,	8 00
One berth, Ogden to San Francisco, by Central Pacific Railroad,	6 00

MEALS.

All meals at all railroad dining-stations east of Omaha,	$0 75
Except dinners on Erie and New York Central,	1 00
All meals on Union Pacific Railroad,	1 00
All meals on Central Pacific Railroad, first day, currency,	1 00
All meals on Central Pacific Railroad, at Colfax, coin,	75
All meals on Central Pacific Railroad, Lathrop, coin,	50

SCENES IN OMAHA.

1.—General View of Omaha and the Platte Valley. 2.—Post-Office. 3.—High School Building.
4.—Grand Central Hotel. 5.—Missouri River Bridge.

OMAHA.

OMAHA occupies an exceedingly beautiful situation, bold and commanding. Approaching this city from the east, the broad valley of the Missouri river first comes into view. Then, as you near Council Bluffs, the great iron bridge which spans the river is plainly visible. Behind it, looking to the west, is Omaha, covering a part of the low bottom lands, the higher table lands, and the bluffs or hills beyond. On the cover of a book recently written by an English gentleman, on the advantages, etc., of Nebraska, there is a picture, in gilt, of the Union Pacific bridge. On the top of this picture the following expressive legend is inscribed: "To the Plains; To the Mountains; to the Pacific." This legend points the way, and means all it says.

Omaha is the grand gateway through which the western tide of travel and immigration is passing, in search of what may be found, either for amusement, pleasure or profit on these plains, mountains, and the ocean named. It is the half-way house, and resting-place for those who are weary of continual travel, and has sufficient attractions to render a visit profitable and interesting.

Early History.—In June, 1853, as a party of gentlemen were standing in the shade of the bluffs, at whose feet nestled the Mormon town of Kanesville, now Council Bluffs, their eyes rested upon the spot where Omaha now stands. The plateau that ascended gently before them to the finely-rounded hills and covered with a beautiful green carpet, was a most captivating sight. It was a fine location for a city, and the question of embarking in the enterprise of building one was discussed by the party. The project was so favorable in their view, that they shortly after crossed the river and proceeded to make a personal examination of the grounds. They found their anticipations fully realized—the location being even better than it had appeared in the distance. The lines were at once laid down, and the same year surveyed and lithographed. But before the survey, a town company was incorporated under the laws of Iowa, and known as the "Council Bluffs and Nebraska Ferry Company." The date of this organization was July 23, 1853. The honor of naming the town belongs to Jesse Lowe, at whose suggestion it was called Omaha, after a tribe of Indians which is now nearly extinct. The records of Lewis & Clark's expedition up the Missouri river, in 1804, show that they understand the name of this tribe as "Mahas," but we are in the dark as to how or when the letter "O" was prefixed to the name. Having perfected their organization, the next step was to obtain title from the Indians. A preliminary treaty was made with them in the winter of 1853–54, which was ratified by the government, to which the lands reverted; and afterwards the town site was obtained through two patents to two gentlemen who acted for the town company. The first ferry across the river was a cottonwood craft; but it was superseded in 1853 by a steam ferry-boat called the "General Marion." After this event, by means of advertising, the overland travel was rapidly concentrated, and Omaha began to grow. The first house was erected by the ferry company, in 1853, on the corner of Twelfth and Jackson streets. The erection of other buildings quickly followed. In 1854, the first brick kiln was burned; and the *Omaha Arrow*, the first newspaper, made its appearance. The first grave was dug where Turner Hall now stands, for an old squaw of the Omaha tribe, who had been left by her companions to die. How prophetic the words of Whittier in his poem:

> **"Behind the squaw's light birch canoe,**
> **The steamer smokes and raves;**
> **And city lots are staked for sale**
> **Above old Indian graves."**

The first legislature of Nebraska convened in the winter of 1854–5. There was a great strife for the location of the capital, but Omaha triumphed, and in 1856 the capitol building was commenced on the ground now occupied by the High-school building, which was donated by the city.

Busy Times.—In 1856 things were "booming" in Omaha, and corner lots were held and sold for extravagant sums, but the crash of 1857 soon followed, and men who were supposed to be wealthy the year before, found themselves penniless, unable to obtain money enough to get away. These were forced to stay, and by this fact alone many of them are now rich and prosperous. But the discovery of gold in Colorado, in 1859, was a godsend to Omaha. It lifted it from depression and set it marching forward on the road to an enduring prosperity. White-topped wagons from the east came by the thousands. On some of them these words were painted, "Pike's Peak or bust," and "busted" the owners of many of them became as the sequel proved. It was during these flush times that many of the solid merchants and business men of Omaha laid the foundations of their wealth and commercial prosperity. In the winter of 1857 a city charter was granted to Omaha, and Jesse Lowe, one of its original founders, was the first mayor. In 1869, it was chartered as a city of the first class. Up to 1867, the means of public communication with the city were stage-coaches, overland through Iowa, and the steamers on the Missouri river. In the winter the latter ceased to run. Various railroad projects were agitated, but until the year 1862 nothing definite was accomplished. Meanwhile the growth of the city was slow, and attended with varying fortunes and prospects. But in that year an act was passed by Congress, authorizing the construction of a trunk railroad from the 100th meridian—which is about 200 miles west of Omaha—and two branches, from points on the western boundaries of Iowa and Missouri. The first branch that reached the 100th meridian was authorized to build the trunk line. The terminus of the northern branch was fixed by President Lincoln in a proclamation dated November 17, 1863, and from this date the progress of the city has been rapid and substantial. This is manifested by the fact that in 1865 the population had scarcely reached 4,500 souls, while in January, 1875, Omaha had a population of full 20,000,—an increase of 15,500 in ten years. This remarkable increase is due almost wholly to the location of the Union Pacific railroad, and from the fact that this is the initial point and eastern terminus of the road. During those ten years marvelous changes were wrought and wonderful improvements made, until Omaha can now boast of as fine business blocks, hotels, school-buildings and churches as can be found in many older and more pretentious cities in the East; while the manufacturing enterprises now in operation and contemplated, will surely make good its claim as the commercial metropolis of the Missouri valley. Its geographical position is eminently commanding. Its railroad connections are increasing, and as year by year it reaches out its iron arms, more territory will be brought to pay it tribute and establish its supremacy as the seat of influence and power.

The first railroad that reached this city from the East, was the Chicago and North-western—the first train over it arriving on Sunday, January 17, 1867. Then followed the Council Bluffs and St. Joe, the Burlington and Missouri River and the Chicago, Rock Island and Pacific. After these came the Sioux City and Pacific, the Omaha and North-western, and the Omaha and South-western railroads. The last-named road has been leased by the Burlington and Missouri. It extends to Lincoln, the capital of the State; then westward uniting with the Union Pacific at Kearney Junction. It has a branch from its main line at Crete to Beatrice, a thriving town near the southern boundary of the State. The Omaha and North-western is completed about 50 miles, and follows the valley of the Missouri on the west side of that river, north from Omaha. It will probably soon be extended. More railroads are contemplated and will doubtless soon be built.

Omaha is well supplied with churches, and they are generally well supported, though some of them are still without edifices for public worship. All the religious denominations are represented in these establishments, and some of the church edifices are tasteful and elegant,—presenting a fine architectural appearance.

In public schools, however, Omaha is without a peer or a rival in the West. In 1866, the capitol of the State was removed to Lincoln, and the legislature afterwards donated the square and capitol building to Omaha for high school purposes. The old capitol building was torn down, and in its place was erected the present high school building; which for beauty in design and elegance in finish has but few, if any, superiors in the country. It is 176 feet long by 80 feet wide. The spire rises 185 feet from the ground. It fitly crowns a hill, overlooking the city, plains and valley for miles in either direction, and is the first object that meets the eye of the traveler as he approaches the gateway of the Pacific coast. Its cost was about $250,000, and is the pride of the city by whose liberality it was built. Other elegant school buildings have been erected in different parts of the city, the total costs of which, with grounds, including the high school building, amounts to $406,000. There are also several denominational and private schools which are liberally patronized.

Here are the government buildings; such as the head-quarters building used by the commanding officers of the military department of the Platte; the barracks about two miles north of the city, and the elegant post-office, court-house and custom-house combined, finished last year (1875).

There are also numerous elegant private residences, with grounds beautifully ornamented with trees and shrubbery, and magnificent business blocks, which sufficiently attest the solid prosperity of Omaha's business men.

Travelers who take advantage of the opportunity for rest which this city offers, may be always certain of good hotel accommodations. The want of such accommodations was recently felt, not only by citizens, but by the traveling public a few years ago. But, happily, this want has been supplied in the erection of the Grand Central Hotel, by a stock company in 1873. It is a magnificent structure, 132 x 122 feet, and five stories high, with large parlors, dining-rooms and suites of rooms, all elegantly furnished, and is first-class in its management and appointment. Those who enjoy the hospitality of this fine hotel once, are always anxious to do it again. It is, without doubt, the finest structure, and the best managed establishment of the kind between Chicago and San Francisco. Its cost was fully $300,000, not including furniture. Railroad ticket-offices and telegraph-offices may be found on the first floor of this hotel, with furnishing stores, etc., convenient. Its halls and public rooms are heated by steam, and it has water on the lower floors, with gas throughout. The furniture cost over $50,000. It has 150 rooms for the accommodation of its guests.

In manufactures, Omaha begins to loom up. She has an oil-mill, which supplies the extensive demand for linseed oil and oil-cake in the Missouri Valley; several breweries, two distilleries, foundry and machine-shops; carriage and wagon-shops and other manufactories, either in progress or in contemplation. Among these may be found in active operation, the extensive machine-shops, car works and foundry of the Union Pacific Railroad, and the Omaha smelting-works. The shops of the railroad occupy, with the roundhouse, about 30 acres of land on the bottom adjoining the table-land on which most of the city proper is built. Over one million of dollars are paid out annually by the company for office and manual labor alone, in the city of Omaha. This does not include payments for merchandise and supplies. The value of this business, and the location of these shops to the city can therefore be readily seen, and is no small factor in Omaha's prosperity.

One of the principal causes of Omaha's growth and prosperity will be found in the character of its newspapers, the *Herald*, the *Republican* and the *Bee*. The *Omaha Arrow*, the first newspaper, was not strictly an Omaha concern, it being published in the office of the *Kanesville* (Council Bluffs) *Bugle*. The *Nebraskian* was established shortly after the *Arrow* (1854), and lived until 1864. In 1857, the *Weekly Times* was established, which was afterwards absorbed by the *Nebraskian*. In May, 1858, the first number of the *Omaha Republican* was issued. It was consolidated with a rival republican paper, the *Omaha Tribune*, in 1871. The last-named paper was started on the 25th of January in 1870. In 1864, the *Omaha Daily Herald* was first issued. It is democratic in politics, and a lively, vigorous sheet. The *Daily Evening Times* was started in the latter part of 1868, and was moved, the following spring, to Sioux City. In June, 1871, the publication of the *Daily Evening Bee* was commenced. It is republican in politics, and a wide-awake paper. The *Omaha Union* (daily) was also established in 1874, by the Printers' Union, on the co-operative plan. It was a spicy, energetic little sheet, but was short-lived.

Business of Omaha.—Facts Interesting and Curious.—When Omaha was first entitled to the honor of a post-office, the story is told that the first postmaster used his hat for a post-office, which he carried with him wherever he went, delivering to anxious individuals who were waiting eagerly for him, or chased and overtook him. Twenty years after, Omaha possesses a handsome stone post-office worth $350,000, and the finest government building west of the Mississippi River. The total receipts at this post-office for 1875, were $1,089,660.34. The total number of letters and newspapers delivered was 1,313,649; and number of money orders issued and received, 16,070.

In 1861, the first telegraph reached Omaha, and its only office was, for several years, the terminus of the Pacific Telegraph. Now there are 23 telegraph wires radiating in all directions; 15 offices, employing 40 operators. The number of messages per day average 3,500, or about 350,-000 letters, of which about one-third relates to Pacific railroad business.

The total value of school buildings in Omaha is $405,000, and the sum spent for erecting new buildings and stores in 1875, was $360,000.

Omaha is the head-quarters of the army of the Platte, and disburses per annum about $950,000, besides an annual transportation account with the Pacific Railroad Company of $350,000.

In 1865, Omaha did not have a single manufacturing establishment. In 1875, her manufactories employed over 2,000 men. Here are located the largest smelting and refining works in America, the Omaha smelting-works, who employ 135 men, and do an annual business of over $4,000,000. Seven breweries turn out 14,000 barrels of beer. One distillery pays the government a tax of $316,000 per year, and upward of 50 other smaller enterprises, among which is a notable industry, the manufacture of brick; over 500,000,000 brick being turned out of her four brick-yards. The bank capital and surplus exceed $3,000,000.

In overland times, before the building of the Pacific Railroad, or just at its commencement, the wholesale trade of Omaha was wonderful. Single houses handling as much as $3,000,000 per annum. Since that time the courses of trade have been so divided, that the largest sales now of any wholesale establishment do not exceed $1,200,000.

Large quantities of *Utah fruit* are received at Omaha, both dried and fresh, and a large market opened; 40 car-loads were received in 1875, from Salt Lake City. This is one of the greatest curiosities developed by the Pacific Railroad. Corn is shipped west from Omaha to feed the inhabitants of the Salt Lake Valley, while the same cars bring back their surplus fruit. In 1871, the first shipment of fruit was made, 300 pounds. In 1875, the trade amounted to 900,000 pounds.

The business of collecting and drying hides, buffalo robes, pelts and furs alone is $150,000 per year, and to supply the prairie settlements with such modern inventions as the sewing-machine, requires over $250,000 per year; one company alone having sold last year $191,000 worth. One dealer reports a sale of such frivolities as 568 Canary birds, and 331 baby carriages.

Perhaps the best index of the enormous trade of Omaha is gained from the statements of railroad transportation. The total number of cars of freight received at Omaha from the East, in 1875, was 10,045, of which above 3,689 were of coal, and 1,500 additional of grain from the West. The freight paid by Omaha merchants in 1875 upon goods received for consumption was $744,248. From the West there were received 1,277 cars of bullion, 40 of ore, and 4 for soda. These items are of the trade and consumption of Omaha only, and not the main traffic of the railroad.

These are only a few of the many important items which show how vast a business has been built in 20 years, from the smooth, unopened prairie soil, now made rich and active with the hum of industry.

The U. P. R. R. Bridge Across the Missouri River.—The huge bridge, which spans the Missouri, is a fitting entrance to the wonders beyond—a mechanical wonder of itself, it fills every traveler with a sense of awe and majesty, as the first great scene of the overland journey.

The last piece of iron of the last span which completed the bridge was fastened in its place on the 20th of February, 1872. Previous to that time, all passengers and traffic were transferred across the treacherous and shifting shores of the Missouri River in steam-boats with flat keel, and with the ever-shifting currents and sand-bars, safe landings were always uncertain. The bridge comprises 11 spans, each span 250 feet in length, and elevated 50 feet above high water-mark. These spans are supported by one stone masonry abutment, and 11 piers with 22 cast-iron columns; each pier is 8 1-2 feet in diameter, and made of cast-iron in tubes one and three-fourths inches in thickness, 10 feet in length, with a weight of eight tons. As fast as the tubes of the columns are sunk, they are fitted together, seams made air-tight, and process continued till the complete depth and height is attained. During the building of the bridge from February, 1869, when work first commenced, until completion in 1872 (excepting a period of eight months suspension), about 500 men were constantly employed. Ten steam-engines were in use for the purpose of operating the pneumatic works to hoist the cylinders, help put the superstructure into position, to drive piles for temporary platforms and bridges, and to excavate sand within the columns. The columns were sunk into the bed of the river after being placed in correct position by the following method: The top of the column being made perfectly air-tight, all water beneath is extracted by pneumatic exhaustion. Then descending into the interior, a force of workmen excavate the sand and earth, filling buckets which are quickly hoisted upwards by the engines. When the excavation has reached one or more feet, the column sinks gradually inch by inch, more or less rapidly, until a solid bottom is reached.

The least time in which any column was sunk to bed rock from the commencement of the pneumatic process was seven days, and the greatest single depth of sinking at one time was 17 feet. The greatest depth below low water which was reached by any column, at bed rock, was 82 feet. The greatest pressure to which the men working in the columns were subjected, was 54 pounds per square inch in excess of the atmosphere. When solid foundation is once obtained, the interior of the columns are filled with solid stone concrete for about 25 feet, and thence upward with cement masonry, till the bridge is reached.

The total length of the iron structure of the bridge is 2,750 feet. The eastern approach is by an embankment of gradual ascent one and a half miles in length, commencing east of the Transfer grounds, and almost at Council Bluffs, and thence ascending at the rate of 35 feet to the mile to the bridge.

The old depot grounds of the Union Pacific Railroad were on the bank of the river immediately beneath the bridge. When this was constructed, in order to connect the bridge and main line of the railroad, it was necessary to construct, directly through the city, a branch line of road 7,000 feet in length, and construct a new depot on higher ground, of which as a result, witness the handsome, new structure, and spacious roof, and convenient waiting-rooms. From the first abutment to the bank, a trestle-work of 700 feet more, 60 feet in height was constructed; thus the entire length of the bridge, with necessary approaches, is 9,950 feet. Total cost is supposed to be about $2,650,000, and the annual revenue about $400,000. The bridge has figured notably in the discussions of Congress, whether or not it should be considered a part of the Union Pacific Railroad. The recent decision of the United States Supreme Court has at last declared it so to be, and with this is done away entirely the "Omaha Bridge Transfer" of the past.

Preparing for the Westward Trip.—Having rested and visited the principal points of interest in Omaha, you will be ready to take a fresh start. Repairing to the new depot, finished last year (1875), at the crossing of Ninth street, you will find one of the most magnificent trains of cars made up by any railroad in the United States. Everything connected with them is first-class. Pullman sleeping-coaches are attached to all express trains, and all travelers know how finely they are furnished, and how they tend to relieve the wearisome monotony of tedious days in the journey from ocean to ocean. At this depot you will find the waiting-rooms, ticket-offices, baggage-rooms, lunch-stands, news and bookstand, together with one of the best kept eating-houses in the country. You will find gentlemanly attendants at all these places, ready to give you any information, and cheerfully answer your questions. If you have a little time, step into the Union Pacific Land office adjoining the depot, on the east, and see some of the productions of this prolific western soil. If you have come from the far East, it has been a slightly uphill journey all the way, and you are now at an elevation of 966 feet above the sea. If the weather is pleasant, you may already begin to feel the exhilarating effect of western breezes, and comparatively dry atmosphere. With books and papers to while away your leisure hours, you are finally ready for the start. The bell rings, the whistle shrieks, and off you go. The road first winds up a little valley, passing the Bridge Junction 1.5 (one and five-tenths) miles to

Summit Siding,— 3.2 miles from Omaha; elevation 1,142 feet. This place, you will observe by these figures, is reached by a heavy up grade. You are 176 feet higher than when you first started, and but little over three miles away. Here is a deep cut through the hill, and beyond it you strike Mud Creek Valley with a down grade for a few miles. This creek and the road run south on a line nearly parallel with, and about two and a half miles from, the Missouri River until the next station is reached.

Gilmore.—It is 9.5 miles from Omaha, with only 10 feet difference in *elevation*—976 *feet.* The valley is quite thickly settled, and as you look out on the left side of the cars, about four miles from Omaha, you will see a saloon called Half-Way House. At about this point you leave Douglas County and enter Sarpy County. Gilmore was named after an old resident of that locality, now dead. Here you are some nine miles south of Omaha, but only about three west of the Missouri River. Here you will first see what are called the bottom lands of Nebraska. They are as rich as any lands on this Continent, as the remarkable crops raised thereon fully attest. From this station you turn nearly due west, and pass over the lower circle of what is called the ox-bow.

"GOOD-BYE."

Papilion,— 14.5 miles from Omaha; *elevation* 972 *feet,* is the next station, and is a thriving little town (pronounced Pa-pil-yo). It derives its name from the creek on whose banks it is situated. This creek was named by Lewis and Clark in their expedition to Oregon, in 1804, and is derived from a Latin word which means butterfly. The main branch was crossed a little west of Gilmore. It empties into the Missouri River about one mile north of the Platte River. It is reported that the early explorers named, saw an immense number of butterflies in the muddy and wet places near its mouth, and hence the name. These gentlemen explored this stream to its source, near the Elkhorn River. The town was laid out in the fall of 1869 by Dr. Beadle, and is the permanent county-seat of Sarpy County. It has a fine brick court-house, and a brick school-house, hotels, flouring mills and a grain ware-house; is located as are all the towns on the first two hundred miles of this road, in the midst of a rich agricultural country. Sarpy County has two newspapers — one the *Papilion Times,* published at this place, and the other, the *Sarpy County Sentinel,* published at Sarpy Center, some five miles in the country from this station. Sarpy is one of the best settled counties in Nebraska, and has a property valuation of over $3,000,000.

Millard—is named for Hon. Ezra Millard, president of the Omaha National Bank, who has considerable landed property here. The station-house is comparatively new, and there are a few other buildings recently erected. It is pleasantly located, and, like all western towns, has plenty of room to grow. It is 20.9 miles from

Omaha; elevation, 1,047 feet. Evidences of thrift are everywhere visible as you cast your eyes over the rolling prairies, and yet there is ample room for all who desire to locate in this vicinity. You have again crossed the boundary line of Sarpy County, which is a mile or two south-east of Millard, and are again in the County of Douglas.

Elkhorn.—28.9 miles from Omaha, elevation 1,150 feet. This is a growing town, and does a large business in grain; it has an elevator, two stores, a Catholic church, good school-house, and a hotel. A new flouring-mill will be erected this year (1876). It has a sprightly newspaper called the *Independent.* You are now near the famous Elkhorn Valley and River. By a deep cut, the railroad makes its way through the bluff or hill on the east side of this stream, about a mile from the station, and then on a down grade you glide into the valley. The rolling prairies are now behind you and south, beyond the Platte River, which for the first time comes into view. Crossing the Elkhorn River you arrive at

Waterloo,—30.9 miles from Omaha, and only two miles from the last station. A few years since, a train was thrown from the bridge spoken of, by reason of the high water of a freshet. This train had one car of either young fish or fish-eggs in transit; the contents of this car were of course lost in the river, and since that time the Elkhorn abounds in pike, pickerel, bass, sunfish and perch. What the California streams lost by this disaster, the Elkhorn gained, as these fish have increased rapidly in this stream, where they were previously unknown. The elevation of Waterloo is laid down at 1,140 feet. The town has a fine water-power which has been improved by the erection of a large flouring-mill. It also has a steam-mill in process of construction, and a new depot. At this point you enter the Platte Valley, of which so much has been written and which occupies such a prominent place in the history of the country. The Elkhorn and Platte Rivers form a junction a few miles south of this point, and the banks of these streams are more or less studded with timber, mostly cottonwood. In fact, the Elkhorn has considerable timber along its banks.

Valley—is 35.2 miles from Omaha, and is 1,120 feet above the sea. It has a store and hotel, and is the center of a rich farming district. The land seems low, and one would easily gain the impression that the soil here was very wet, but after digging through the black surface soil two or three feet you come to just such sand as is found in the channel of the Platte. In fact, the whole Platte Valley is underdrained by this river, and this is one reason why surface water from hard and extensive rains so quickly disappear, and why the land is able to produce such good crops in a dry season. Water is obtained anywhere in this valley by sinking what are called drive-wells, from six to twenty feet. Wind-mills are also extensively used by large farmers, who have stock which they confine upon their premises, and which otherwise they would have to drive some distance for water. From Valley, the elevations gradually increase as you

NIGHT SCENE. PRAIRIE ON FIRE.

pass to the westward. Next comes a side track called

Riverside,—which is 41.4 miles from Omaha, with an elevation of about 1,140 feet. It will eventually become a station, as many trains already meet and pass here.

Prairie Fires.—During the first night's ride westward from Omaha, the traveler, as he gazes out of his car window (which he can easily do while reclining in his berth) will often find his curious attention rewarded by a sight of one of the most awful, yet grandest scenes of prairie life. The prairies, which in the day-time to some, seemed dry, dull, uninteresting, occasionally give place at night, to the lurid play of the fire-fiend, and the heavens and horizon seem like a furnace. A prairie on fire is a fearfully exciting and fear-stirring sight. Cheeks blanch as the wind sweeps its volume toward the observer, or across his track. Full in the distance is seen the long line of bright flame stretching for miles, with its broad band of dark smoke-clouds above. As the train comes near, the flames leap higher, and the smoke ascends higher, and on their dark bosom is reflected the fires' brilliantly-tinged light. Sweeping away for miles towards the bluffs, the fire jumps with the wind, and the flames leap 20 to 30, or more feet into the air, and for miles brighten the prairies with the awful sight. We have never seen anything of prairie life or scenery possessing such majestic brilliance as the night glows, and rapid advances of a prairie fire. Far out on the prairies, beyond the settlements, the prairie fires, (usually set on fire by the sparks from the locomotives) rage unchecked for miles and miles, but nearer to the little settlements, where the cabins have just been set up, the fire is their deadliest and most dreaded enemy. No words can describe, no pencil paint the look of terror when the settler beholds advancing toward him the fire-fiend, for which he is unprepared and unprotected. When the first sign of the advancing fire is given, all hands turn out; either a counter fire is started, which, eating from the settler's ranch, in the face of the wind, toward the grander coming volume, takes away its force, and leaves it nothing to feed upon, or furrows are broken with the plow around the settler's home. The cool earth thrown up, and all the grass beyond this is fired, while the little home enclosed within, is safe. A curious feature of prairie fires is, that the buffalo grass, the next season, is darker and richer than ever before; and lower down, in sections where the prairie fires are carefully kept off, trees, shrubs, bushes, etc., of many varieties, grow up spontaneously, which never were seen before. So long as prairie fires rage, nothing will grow but the little tufts of prairie grass. Wherever the prairie fire ceases or is kept restrained, vegetation of all description as far west as the Platte, is completely changed. In the fall of the year these fires are most frequent; and creating a strong current or breeze by their own heat, they advance with the rapidity often of a locomotive, 20 or more miles an hour, and their terrible lurid light by night, and blackened path left behind, as seen next day by the traveler, are sights never to be forgotten.

In the lower river counties a prairie fire often originates from the careless dropping of a match, or the ashes shaken from a pipe. The little spark touches the dry grass like tinder—the constant breeze fans the little flame, and five minutes after it has covered yards. The loss to tillers of the soil is often appalling. One of General Sherman's veterans, in describing a prairie fire to a visitor, raising himself to his full six feet height, and with eye flashing as in battle excitement, said: "Mr. C., if I should catch a man firing the prairie at this time, as God helps me, I would shoot him down in his deed." A traveler riding on the prairie said, "only a few miles from me an emigrant, traveling in his close-covered wagon "*with the wind,*" was overtaken by the flames coming down on him unseen. Horses, family, wagon, were all destroyed in a moment, and himself barely lived long enough to tell the tale. Nearly every night in autumn the prairies of the boundless West, show either the near or distant glow of a fire, which in extent has the appearance of another burning Chicago.

"BUSTED."

Pike's Peak or Bust.—This expression has become widely known, and received its origin as

REPRESENTATIVE MEN OF THE UNION PACIFIC RAILROAD.

follows:—At the time of the opening of the Pike's Peak excitement in gold diggings, two pioneers made themselves conspicuous by painting in large letters on the side of their wagon cover:—"*Pike's Peak or Bust.*" In their haste to reach this, the newly discovered Eldorado, they scorned all safety and protection offered by the "train" and traveled alone, and on their "own hook."

For days and weeks they escaped the dangers attending their folly, and passed unharmed until they reached the roving ground of the bloody Sioux. Here they were surrounded and cruelly and wantonly murdered; their bodies were driven through with arrows, and pinned to the earth, and left to the sunshine and storms of the skies.

Fremont—is 46.5 miles from Omaha, and has an elevation of 1,176 feet. It is the county-seat of Dodge County, and has a population of full 3,000. In the year 1875, over $100,000 were expended in buildings in this growing young city. It has never, so far as population is concerned, experienced what may be called a great rush—its growth having been slow and steady. It is located near the south-east corner of the county. Originally the town comprised a whole section of land, but was afterwards reduced to about half a section. The town company was organized on the 26th day of August, 1856, and in that and the following year, thirteen log houses were built. John C. Hormel built the first frame house in 1857. The Union Pacific reached the town on the 24th day of January, 1866, nearly ten years after it was first laid out, and trains ran to it regularly, though the track was laid some 11 miles beyond, when work ceased for that winter. The Sioux City and Pacific road was completed to Fremont late in the fall of 1868. In the expectations of the residents, it was then to become a railroad center, and lots were sold at large prices. This last-named road runs from Blair on the Missouri River, where it crosses said stream and forms a junction with the Chicago and North-western. It then runs north on the east side of said river, to Sioux City. The Elkhorn Valley Railroad completed the first ten miles of its track in 1869, and the balance, some 50 miles, was finished to Wisner in the following year. This road is one of the natural routes to the Black Hills, and it is now stated that it will soon be extended in that direction. It will continue up the Elkhorn Valley to near its source, and then crossing the divide, will strike into the Niobrara Valley, thence westward until the Black Hills are reached. This road is a feeder to Fremont, and very valuable to its trade. The Atchison and Nebraska Railroad, is to be extended from Lincoln to this place, during the present year (1876). The city will then have a direct line to St. Louis and the South, with two direct lines to Chicago and the East. Other railroad projects are contemplated, which will make this place in reality a railroad center.

Fremont has a large, new hotel, the Occidental, and several smaller ones; has the finest opera house in the West, and the largest and finest dry-goods house in the State. It has five or six church edifices, and an elegant public school building, two banks, three or four elevators, a steam flouring-mill, extensive broom factories, and two or three manufacturing establishments where headers are made. It also has a foundry and machine-shop. Occasional changes in railroad time, sometimes discontinue it as an eating station on the road—(passenger trains passing it from the West to Omaha, and not leaving Omaha until after dinner,) but at present trains both ways now stop for dinner.

Fremont is virtually located at the junction of the Elkhorn and Platte Valleys, and from its position naturally controls a large scope of country. Its people are industrious, wide-awake and energetic. It is in the midst of a thickly-settled region, and its future prospects are very flattering.

Fremont has two newspapers—the *Fremont Herald* (daily and weekly), and the *Fremont Tribune* (weekly). The latter was first established, and probably has the largest circulation. The enterprise of newspapers in these western towns, contribute very largely to their growth and prosperity. The town is the fourth in size and population in the State.

The Elkhorn Valley is between two and three hundred miles in length, is well timbered and remarkably fertile, and the railroad which is to do the carrying business of this valley, has its terminus at Fremont.

The Great Platte Valley.—You have now passed over a few miles of the great Platte Valley. At Fremont it spreads out wonderfully, and for the first two hundred miles varies in width from five to fifteen miles. Through nearly all its eastern course, this river hugs the bluffs on its southern side. These bluffs as well as those more distant on the northern side of the valley, are plainly visible from the cars. Before the road was built, this valley was the great highway of overland travel to Colorado, Utah, California, and Oregon. Immense trains of wagons, heavily freighted, have passed over it, in their slow and tedious journeyings towards the setting sun. Leaving the Missouri at different points, the routes nearly all converged in the Platte Valley, and thence westward to their destination. The luxuriant grasses, and the proximity to water, made this the favorite route. It has also been the scene of deadly conflicts with the savages, and the bones of many a wanderer lie bleaching in the air, or are buried beneath some rough and hastily-made mound near the beaten road. But a wonderful change took place with the advent of the road. The "bull-whacker," with his white-covered wagon and raw-boned oxen—his slang phrases, and profane expressions, his rough life, and in many instances violent death—the crack of his long lash that would ring out in the clear morning air like that of a rifle, and his wicked goad or prod—an instrument of torture to his beasts—with all that these things imply, have nearly passed away. Their glory has departed, and in their place is the snorting engine and the thundering train.

The remarkable agricultural advantages of this valley are everywhere visible, and it is rapidly filling up with an industrious and thrifty class of farmers. The land grant of the Union Pacific Company extends for twenty miles on either side of the road, and includes every alternate section of land that was not taken at the time it was withdrawn from the market, for the benefit of the company. If you pass a long distance in the first two hundred miles of this valley without observing many improvements, it is pretty good evidence that the land is held by non-resident speculators, and this fact has a great influence in retarding the growth of the country. Around many of the residences are large groves of cotton-wood trees that have been planted by industrious hands and which give evidence of unusual thrift. In fact, the cotton-wood in most every part of this region is indigenous to the soil, and will thriftily grow where other kinds of timber fail. Trees sixty feet high and from eight to ten inches in diameter, are no uncommon result of six to eight years' growth. The banks of the Platte and the many islands in its channel, were formerly very heavily timbered with cotton-wood, but that on its banks has almost entirely disappeared, together with much that was upon the islands. The favorable State and national legislation in regard to tree planting will cause an increase in the timber land of Nebraska in a very short time, and must of necessity, have an influence upon its climate. Many scientists who are familiar with the circumstances attending the rapid development of the trans-Missouri plains and the elevated plateau joining the base of the Rocky Mountains, assert that this vast region of country is gradually undergoing important climatic changes—and that one of the results of these changes is the annually increasing rainfall. The rolling lands adjoining this valley are all very fertile, and with proper tillage produce large crops of small grain. The bottom lands are better adapted for corn, because it matures later in the season, and these bottom lands are better able to stand drouth than the uplands. The roots of the corn penetrate to a great depth, till they reach the moisture from the under-drainage. One of the finest sights that meets the eye of the traveler, is the Platte Valley in the spring or early summer; to our eastern farmer, it is fairly captivating, and all who are familiar with farms and farming in the Eastern States, will be surprised; no stumps or stones or other obstacles appear to interfere with the progress of the plow, and the black surface-soil is, without doubt, the accumulation of vegetable matter for ages. The Platte Valley must be seen to be appreciated. Only a few years ago it was scarcely tenanted by man, and while the development has been marked, it will not compare with that which is sure to take place in the near future. There is ample room for the millions yet to come, and the lands of the Union Pacific Company are exceedingly cheap, varying in price from $3 to $10 per acre. The alternate sections of government land for the first two hundred miles of this valley are nearly all taken by homesteaders, or under the preemption laws of congress. Much of it, however, can be purchased at a low price from the occupants, who, as a general thing, desire to sell out and go West still. They belong to the uneasy, restless class of frontiers-men, who have decided objections to neighbors and settlements, and who want plenty of room, with no one to molest, in order to grow up with the country. A sod house near a living spring of water is to them a small paradise. They might possibly suffer from thirst, if they had to dig for water, and the labor required to build even a sod house, is obnoxious. But this will not hold good of all of them. There are many occupants of these sod houses in the State of Nebraska, and other parts of the West, who, with scanty means are striving for a home for their wives and children, and they cling to the soil upon which they have obtained a claim with great tenacity, and with sure prospects of success. They are worthy of all praise in their self-sacrificing efforts. A few years only will pass by before they will be surrounded with all the comforts and many of the luxuries of life. These are the experiences of many who "bless their stars" to-day that they have sod houses—homes—in and adjoining the great Platte Valley.

Shooting Prairie Hens.—This is a favorite scene, often witnessed September mornings in the far West. The prairie is covered with its grass, and wild flowers, which last all the season through. Here and there is a stubble field of oats, wheat, or acres on acres of the golden corn, swaying gracefully in the breeze, and perhaps there is a little music from the meadow larks or bird songsters of the fields. The dogs with keenest of scent, hunt out and stir up the game, and as they rise on wing, the ready gun with its aim, and deadly shot, brings them back lifeless. This is probably the most attractive way to look at a prairie hen, for we must confess that after a slice or two of the meat, as usually served at the eating stations of the railroads, from which we escape with danger to our front teeth, and unsatisfied stomachs, we can only exclaim "distance lends enchantment." However tough the meat, if served on the table when first killed, yet if kept till it grows gradually more tender, there is a wild, spicy flavor, which make them very agreeable eating. Buffalo meat and prairie hens are not altogether reliable as viands of the railroad dining stations, still every one must try for himself, with here and there a chance of finding sweet tender morsels.

good an illustration as any, of the rapid growth of some of the western towns and counties. The county was organized in the spring of 1869, two years after the railroad had passed through it,—with Schuyler as the county-seat. In the spring of the present year, 1876, it has an assessed valuation of nearly $1,250,000. Evidences of substantial growth are everywhere visible. The town has about twenty stores, of all kinds, hotel, a substantial brick court-house, several churches, a beautiful school-house, grain elevators, etc. New buildings to accommodate its increasing trade, or its new residents, are constantly going up. There are three flouring-mills in the county, on Shell Creek, a beautiful stream fed by living springs, which runs nearly through the county from west to east, and from one to five miles north of the railroad track. The land in this county is most excellent, especially the rolling up-land north of Shell Creek. Some of the finest crops of spring wheat raised in the West are grown in this vicinity. The people are turning their attention to stock-raising more than formerly, and several flocks of sheep and herds of cattle are now kept in the county, by some of its enterprising stock-men. All of this accomplished in about six years. Schuyler is the second town west of Omaha that has a bridge across the Platte, Fremont being the first. These bridges are very advantageous to the trade of the towns in this valley.

HUNTING PRAIRIE HENS.

Ames—At present simply a side track, 53.5 miles from Omaha, and 1,270 feet above the sea. This was formerly called Ketchum; but bears its present name from Oliver Ames, Esq., one of the builders of this railroad. Observe the size of the trees in the cotton-wood groves and hedges near this place—all planted within the memory of the oldest inhabitant.

North Bend—61.5 miles from the eastern terminus of the road, and 1,259 feet in elevation, a little less than the preceding station. This is a thriving little town, with several stores, hotel, lumber-yard, grain elevator, etc. It is soon to have a bridge across the Platte River, which will materially increase its trade with Saunders County on the south. The opening of many farms in its vicinity have made it quite a grain market. The town is so named from a northward bend in the river, and it is the northernmost point on the Union Pacific in the State of Nebraska. It is the last town west in Dodge County.

Rogers—is a side-track, will eventually become a station; is in the midst of a rich farming country; is 68.5 miles from Omaha, and has an elevation of 1,359 feet.

Schuyler.—The county-seat of Colfax County. It is 75.9 miles from Omaha, with an elevation of 1,335 feet. This town and county, perhaps, is as

Richland.—A small station 83.7 miles from Omaha, with an elevation of 1,440 feet. Up to a late period the land surrounding this station has been mostly held by speculators, but a change having been effected, the town has brighter prospects. Lots are freely given away to parties who will build on them. The location is a very fine one for a town, and it is surrounded by an excellent country. It is the last town west in Colfax County.

Columbus—is 91.7 miles from Omaha. It is 1,432 feet above the sea. A beautiful growing town, with a rich agricultural country to back it. It has several churches, school buildings, brick court-house, two grain elevators doing a large business. Good hotels and other building enterprises contemplated. It is located at the junction of the Loup Fork, with the Platte Rivers, and near where the old overland emigrant road crossed the first-named stream. It now has a population of about 1,500 people, and supports three newspapers—the *Republican*, which, though the youngest, has the most patronage, and the largest circulation; the *Journal*, which was first established, and the *Era*. Columbus has had two lives thus far. The first town-site was jumped by a party of Germans from Columbus, O., from which it takes its name. Afterwards the two interests were consolidated. It was the principal town west of Omaha until the railroad came. The old town, near the ferry crossing, was then moved to its present site near the station. The old town had two or three small stores, a blacksmith's shop and saloons *ad libitum*. It was mostly kept alive by the westward emigration. At that time the Platte Valley was well supplied with ranches and ranchmen, only other names for whisky-shops and bar-tenders. During the week those concerns would pick up what they could from wagon-trains, and Sundays the ranchmen would crowd into Columbus to spend it—the sharpers improving the opportunity to fleece the victims of their seductive wiles. At this time no attention whatever was paid to agricultural pursuits. On the advent of the railroad in 1866, the wood-choppers, the freighters, the ranchmen and others, lured by the charms of a frontier life, jumped the town and country. They could not endure the proximity to, and restraints of civilization. Then the second or new life of the town began. Farmers began to come in, and it was found by actual experiment that the soil was immensely prolific; that it had only to be tickled with the plow in order to laugh with the golden harvests. In the lapse of the few brief years of its second or permanent growth, it has become a great grain market, and probably ships more car-loads each year than any other town on the line of the road. Men draw grain from seventy to eighty miles to this place for a market. It has access to the country south of the Loup and Platte Rivers, by means of good, substantial bridges; while the country north of it is as fine rolling prairie as can be found in any part of the West—well watered and adapted to either grazing or the growing of crops. The men who first came to Columbus were nearly all poor, and it has been built up and improved by the capital they have acquired through their own industrious toil. The town has a good bank, without a dollar of foreign capital. It will soon have other railroads; one from Sioux City, and another to Crete and St. Joe, is projected; while in its immediate vicinity are large quantities of good lands which are held at low prices. These are only a few of the many advantages which Columbus offers to those in search of future homes.

How Buffalo Robes are Made.—George Clother is one of the proprietors of the Clother House at Columbus, Neb. It is one of the best home-like hostelries in the West. Mr. Clother is an old resident, having been in Columbus sixteen years. When he first came, the country was more or less overrun with wandering tribes of Indians, among whom were the Pawnees, the Omahas, the Sioux, and occasionally a stray band from some other tribe. In those days he was accustomed to traffic in furs and robes, and the business has grown with his increasing acquaintance, until it is now both large and profitable, though with the disappearance of both Indians and buffaloes, it is liable to decrease in the future. General Sheridan, we think it was, said that the vexed Indian question would be settled with the fate of the buffaloes—that both would disappear together. During the past few years, the slaughter of these proud monarchs of the plains, has been immense, and will continue, unless Congress interposes a friendly and saving hand. It is safe to say, that millions of them have been killed for their hides alone, or "just for fun," which in this case amounts to the same thing, as their hides have been repeatedly sold for less than a dollar, and regularly not more than $1.50. This slaughtering has taken place principally in the Platte, Republican, Solomon, and Arkansas Valleys, and where a few years since, travelers could see countless thousands of them from the car windows and platforms, on either the Union Pacific, Kansas Pacific or Atchison, Topeka & Santa Fe Railroads, they now, probably will see but few, if any. Their hides have been shipped East, where they make a poor quality of leather. Those only which are taken late in the fall and during the winter months of January and February, are fit for robes. The hair, at this season of the year, is thick and firmly set.

About the time this killing process began in 1870, Mr. Clother entered upon the work of tanning robes, employing for this purpose the squaws of the Pawnee and Omaha tribes. The Pawnee reservation was only a short distance from Columbus, and the "Bucks" were glad of the opportunity of employment for their squaws. Labor is beneath their dignity, and they depise it. Besides this, tanning robes is hard and slow work, and, in their opinion, just fit for squaws. For a

INDIAN TENT SCENE.

few years the squaws of both of the tribes named, have been engaged by Mr. Clother, but the departure of the Pawnees to their reservation in the Indian Territory, precluded the possibility of their employment, and hence in the winter of 1876, the Omahas seem to have a monopoly of the work, though there is not as much to do as formerly. We visited their camp to inspect the process of making robes. It was located in a body of heavy timber, with a thick growth of underbrush, on the narrow point of land where the Loup Fork and Platte Rivers form their junction. The low bushes made a perfect wind-break, and in the midst of the tall trees their Sibley tents were pitched. The barking of numerous dogs greeted our approach, and after making a few inquiries of one or two who could talk broken English, we crawled into the tent occupied by the "Bucks," whom we found intensely interested in gambling—playing a game with cards called "21." In this tent were nine "Bucks" and one squaw; three sat stolidly by—disinterested witnesses of the game; the squaw was engaged at some very plain needle-work, and occasionally poked the partly burned brands into the fire, which was in the center of the tent, and over which hung a kettle of boiling meat; the remaining six, sitting upon a blanket *a la Turk*, were shuffling and dealing the cards. Of course they play for money, and before them were several quarters in currency, and several silver quarters, with some small sticks, which were used as money, and which enabled them to keep an account with each other, of the gains and losses. During this game they passed around, several times, a hollow-handled tomahawk, which was used as a pipe. One would take three or four whiffs, then pass it to the next, and so on, until it had been passed around several times. One of these "Bucks" was called "Spafford." He could talk English quite well. After a while we asked "Spafford" to show us some robes, but he pointed in the direction of his tent, and indicated where they could be found. He said he could not leave the game just then. We went to his tent where we found his mother, who showed us two robes, one of which was hers—a smaller one which she held at six dollars. Spafford had previously told us that $12.00 was the price of his robe. We then began to look for other robes, and saw them in various stages of completion. The process of tanning is simple, and yet, Indian tanned robes far excel those tanned by white men, in finish and value. When the hides are first taken from the animals, they must be stretched and dried, flesh side up; if they are not in this condition when the squaws receive them, they must do it. After they are thoroughly dried, the squaws then take all the flesh off, and reduce them to an even thickness, with an instrument, which, for want of a better name, may be termed an adze; it is a little thin piece of iron, about two inches long on the edge, and two and a half inches deep. This is firmly tied to a piece of the thigh bone of an elk, and is used the same as a small garden hoe, by eastern farmers in cutting up weeds. When the requisite thickness is obtained, the flesh side is covered with a preparation of lard, soap and salt, and the robe is then rolled up and laid by for two or three days. It is then unrolled and again stretched on a frame, like a quilt, with flesh side to the sun; in this shape it is scraped with a thin, oval-shaped piece of iron or steel, resembling a kitchen chopping-knife without the handle; this process usually lasts about two days. The robe is then taken from the frame, and drawn across a rope stretched between two trees, with the flesh side to the rope, until it becomes thoroughly dry and soft. This last process makes it very pliable, requires a good deal of time and strength, and renders the robe ready for market. Before the Indians came in contact with civilization, they used sharpened pieces of bone, instead of the pieces of iron we have named, and in place of the preparation of lard, soap and salt, they used buffalo brains, which are considered altogether preferable to this mixture; the brains of cattle are also used when they can be obtained; but the robes are taken out on the plains, or in the Platte and Republican Valleys, and brought here by wagon or rail, and of course the brains cannot very well be brought with them. The squaws laughed when we pulled out our note-book and began to write, being evidently as much astonished and interested as we; they looked with wonder at the book, pencil, and the words we wrote. While the lazy "Bucks," sit in their tents and gamble, the squaws are laboring hard to secure means for their support. An Indian is constitutionally opposed to labor. He is evidently tired all the time.

Jackson—So called from a former roadmaster of the Union Pacific—is 99.3 miles from Omaha, with an elevation of 1,470 feet. The Loup Valley is just over the hills to your right, and the magnificent Platte bottom lands are still stretching out before you. It has one or two stores and bears a thrifty appearance; at one time it was supposed that this place or Columbus would be made the end of a division, but nothing has been developed on this subject within the past few years.

Silver Creek—109.4 miles from Omaha, and 1,534 feet above the sea. It is the first station in Merrick County, as Jackson was the last in Platte County. North of this station is the Pawnee reservation, one of the finest bodies of land yet unoccupied in the State. This once powerful tribe, between whom and the Sioux a deadly hostility exists, has dwindled down to small numbers, and during 1875, they abandoned their reservation entirely and went to the Indian Territory. An attempt was made a short time since to sell a part of this reservation at an appraised valuation, but it was not successful, and efforts are now being made to bring it into market under the preemption laws of the government at a fixed price, ($2.50 per acre) the proceeds of which are to go to the tribe on their new reservation. When this takes place Silver Creek will have a great impetus to its growth and trade, as it is the nearest railroad station to this reservation.

Clark.—Named after S. H. H. Clark, general superintendent of the Union Pacific; it is sometimes called Clark's, Clarksville and Clark's Station. It is 120.7 miles from the eastern terminus of the road, with an elevation of 1,610 feet. It has three stores, school-house, church, shops and dwellings, and is doing a fine trade; with a rich country around it, and the Pawnee reservation soon to be opened on the north, it is destined to become a thrifty town.

Lone Tree.—The county-seat of Merrick County; has two or three churches, several stores, a brick court-house, a two-story frame school-house, hotel and numerous other buildings. The name of the post-office is Central City. The Nebraska Central Railroad is expected to form a junction with the Union Pacific, here. Local dissensions have injured the town in the past, and must operate to retard its growth in the future. About three miles west of this place a new side track has been put in. It is yet unnamed, though it will probably be called Lone Tree, and it is expected that a post-office with the same name, will be established. Merrick County has two flouring-mills, both of which are run by water, taken from the Platte River. The identical "lone tree," from which the place was named, has long since disappeared, but numerous groves of cotton-wood are everywhere visible. Elevation 1,686 feet; 132 miles from Omaha.

Chapman.—142.3 miles from Omaha, and 1,760 feet above the sea. It is named after a former road-master of the Union Pacific. The town has two stores, school-house, and other buildings, and is in the midst of a fine, thickly settled country.

Lockwood—is 147.8 miles from Omaha, with an elevation of 1,800 feet. It is a side track where trains meet and pass. A store has recently been opened where a lively trade is done.

Grand Island.—The end of the first division of the Union Pacific Railroad, 153.8 miles from Omaha, and 1,850 feet above the sea. The town is named after an island in the Platte River, which is some forty miles long, and from one to three miles in width. It was first settled by a colony of Germans from Davenport, Ia., in 1857. The island is thickly settled, nearly every quarter section being occupied by a thrifty farmer. The soil is wonderfully prolific, being composed of a black vegetable mold, and is especially adapted to corn raising. The old town site of Grand Island was south of the present site, on the old emigrant road. The first three years of this town were very severe on the settlers. They had to haul all their supplies from Omaha, and part of this time they were obliged to live on short rations. They immediately began the cultivation of the soil, but at first had no market for their crops. This was soon remedied, however, by the opening of a market at Fort Kearny, some forty miles west, where they obtained good prices for everything they could raise. In a short time, the rush to Pike's Peak began, and as this was the last place on the route where emigrants could obtain grain and other supplies, the town grew, and many who are now in good circumstances, then laid the foundations of their prosperity. In this vicinity stray buffaloes first appeared to the early settlers of the valley. They never came in large herds, but when hunted by the Indians further west and south in the Republican Valley they would be seen wandering near this place. While the war was in progress, the settlers frequently saw war parties of the Sioux pass to and from the Pawnee camp on the high bluffs south of the Platte River, and opposite Fremont. When they returned from their attacks, they would exhibit the scalps they had taken, and manifest great glee as they swung them through the air, dangling from their spears. In the early spring of 1859, the stages from Omaha began to run. At first they came once a week, then twice, and later, daily. Then the telegraph line was put up. Meanwhile the trans-continental railroad was agitated, and as it became more and more talked about, the settlers here fondly hoped that they were on the exact spot where the three converging lines, as first proposed, would meet. But they were doomed to disappointment. The Union Pacific, Eastern Division, now the Kansas Pacific, grew into an independent line, while the Sioux City & Pacific had its course changed, finally uniting with the Union Pacific at Fremont. But the railroad came at last in 1866. The heavy bodies of timber on the islands in the river and between the Platte and Wood Rivers were nearly all taken for cross-ties. It was only cotton-wood, but it would hold the spikes and rails for a few years until others could be obtained. Then the buildings on the old town site were moved up to the railroad and the town began to grow. The roundhouse for the steam-horses was built, and the town was made the end of a division of the road. An eating-house was erected, and stores, shops, and dwellings followed in quick succession. It is the county-seat of Hall County, and the first station in the county from the east. It has a fine large brick court-house, three church edifices, school-house, hotels, bank, and one of the largest steam flouring-mills in the State. This is one of the regular dining-stations on the road. Last year, 1875, the company put up an elegant hotel for the accommodation of the traveling public, at which all passenger trains stop for meals. It is exceedingly well kept, and under its present management will command the patronage of the public. Like all other towns of any importance in this valley, Grand Island hopes and expects more railroads. A road to connect with the St. Joe & Denver, and the Burlington & Missouri at Hastings, twenty-four miles south, is nearly all graded, and will probably soon be finished. A line is also projected to the north-west, and one to the north-east to reach Sioux City. Its present population is about 1,200, and its prospects for the future are flattering.

The country in this immediate vicinity is well settled by a thrifty class of German farmers, who have dug wealth from the soil, and when rations were scarce and border scares frequent, still hung on to their claims. The road came in 1866, and gave them communication with the outer world. The location of the roundhouse and necessary repair shops, for the division, is a great help to the town, as they give employment to quite a number of skilled mechanics. It is also the location of the government land office for the Grand Island land district. It has two weekly newspapers, the *Times* and *Independent*, both of which are well conducted. The new eating-house, elsewhere spoken of, is the finest on the road, though less expensive than many. It cost about $15,000. This is a breakfast and supper station, and the company has furnished ample accommodations for the patrons of this house.

After leaving Grand Island, a magnificent stretch of prairie country opens to view. The same may be said of the entire valley, but the view in other places is more limited by bluffs and hills than here. After passing Silver Creek, there is a section of the road, more than forty miles, in a straight line, but the extent of prairie brought into vision there is not as large as here. Up to this point, you have doubtless witnessed

EMINENT AMERICAN EXPLORERS AND ARTISTS.

1.—Gen. Custer. 2.—Gen. Fremont. 3.—Lieut. Wheeler. 4.—Prof. F. V. Hayden. 5.—Albert Bierstadt. 6.—Maj. J. W. Powell. 7.—Thomas Moran.

many groves of cotton-wood around the numerous dwellings you have passed, but they begin to diminish now—nearly the last of them being seen at

Alda,—the next station, some eight miles west of Grand Island, 161.5 miles from Omaha, at an elevation of 1,907 feet. There are one or two stores, a school-house, and several dwellings. It is two miles east of Wood River, which is spanned by the first iron bridge on the line. All regular passenger trains stop at this station and receive and deliver mails. In other parts of the country, Wood River would be called a rivulet or small brook, but such streams are frequently dignified with the name of rivers in the West. It forms a junction with the North Channel of the Platte River, just south of Grand Island. Its rise is in the bluffs across the divide, north of Plum Creek, and its general course is due east. The road runs along its southern bank for several miles, and in several places it is fringed with timber. When the road was first built through here, it was well timbered, but it was nearly all taken for construction purposes and fuel. In early days, say in 1859–60, this valley was the frontier settlement of the West, and a few of the old pioneer log houses are still standing, though very much dilapidated. The settlers had a few "Indian scares," and lost some stock, but beyond this, no great depredation was done. Fort Kearny was their first market-place to which they hauled their surplus grain and provisions. Though Wood River is so small, it nevertheless supplies three flouring-mills with power for grinding, and there are several mill sites unoccupied. The first mill is near the iron bridge already spoken of, and the others will be noticed further on.

Wood River—is the name of the next station. It has two or three stores, several dwellings, and a new depot building. It is 169.6 miles from Omaha, and 1,974 feet above the sea. The old station was two miles further west, and the Catholic church still remains to mark the place where it stood. The country around here was first settled by some Irish families; they are industrious and worthy citizens, and have developed some fine farms. Prairie, or blue joint-grass has been principally seen thus far, but now you will observe patches of buffalo grass which increase as you go west, and of which we shall speak hereafter. This is the last station in Hall County.

Shelton—comes next—a side track, depot, a few dwellings, and another of those flouring-mills spoken of. In January, 1876, the water in Wood River was sufficient to keep three run of burrs going in this mill for about twenty out of every twenty-four hours. The flour made at nearly all the mills on the Union Pacific finds a ready market in the mountain towns west, to which it is usually shipped. Shelton was named after the present cashier of the Union Pacific road at Omaha. It has an elevation of 2,010 feet, and is 177.4 miles from the eastern terminus of the road.

Successful Farming.—The little farms which now fill up the Platte Valley as far as North Platte are occupied by people who came from the older States, with very little cash capital, and by homesteading or warrant or purchase from the railroad on time, they have made many a snug home. To show what has been done by real industry, we quote from actual records the figures of the success of a farmer in Platte County. Beginning with the year 1867, and up to the year 1874, seven years, he cultivated in wheat and corn, an average of sixty to eighty acres wheat, and fifty acres corn; total 130 acres. His receipts from these two crops only, in seven years, was $13,314.05; expenses, $4,959.92; profits, $8,354.13, besides increase of value of land, which is fully $2,000 more. This is what was done with a capital of less than $2,000.

Tree Planting in Nebraska.—The Nebraskans celebrate a special day in the spring months as a holiday, in which the entire population join hands in a hearty exercise at tree planting; this is called *Arbor Day*. Travelers will notice from the car windows on their first day's ride westward from Omaha, quite a number of pretty groves of trees, planted both as wind-breaks for their farms, and also for timber plantations. The tree most popular is the cotton-wood, which grows very easily, sure to start, and is quite luxuriant in foliage; however it is valuable for shelter and stove-wood only, not for manufactures. As an instance of rapidity of growth, there are trees in the Platte Valley, which planted as cuttings, have in thirteen years measured 22 inches in diameter. Little boys are tempted by large premiums from their parents to test their capacity at tree planting on Arbor Day, and astonishing rapidity has occasionally been known, one farmer in one day having planted from sunrise to sundown, 14,000 trees, and in the course of one spring season, over 200,000. Settlers, as fast as they arrive, aim to accomplish two things. First, to break the sod for a corn field; next, to plant timber shelter. The winds which blow from the west are very constant, often fierce, and a shelter is of immense value to stock and fruit trees. Hedges of white willow, several miles in length, have been laid, which at five years from cuttings, have made a perfect fence 15 feet high; one farm alone has four miles of such continuous fence, which at four years of age was a complete protection. The rapidity of growth in the rich alluvial soil of the Platte Valley reminds one of tropical luxuriance. A grove of white ash, in twelve years, has grown to an average of 26 inches in circumference, and 30 feet high. Walnut trees, in eight years, have measured 22 inches in circumference, and 25 feet high. Maple trees, of twelve years, measure 43 inches around four feet from the ground. Elms of fourteen years, show 36 inches in girth, and a foot in diameter. Honey Locusts, eleven years of age, are 30 feet high, and 30 inches around. Cottonwood trees, of thirteen years, have reached 66 inches in circumference, and 22 inches in diameter. White willow, same age, 45 inches in circumference.

Gibbon,—the last station on Wood River, is 182.9 miles from the Missouri by rail, and has an elevation of 2,046 feet. It was formerly the county-seat of Buffalo County, and had a fine brick court-house erected. But the county-seat was voted to Kearny Junction in 1874, and the building is now used for school purposes. It has a hotel, several stores, and another of those flouring-mills, in plain sight from the track. The Platte River is some three miles distant, to the south, and glistens in the sunlight like a streak of silver; the level prairie between is studded with farm-houses, and in the late summer or early autumn numerous stacks of grain and hay are everywhere visible around the farmers' homes. The bluffs, south of the Platte, rear their low heads in the distance, and your vision is lost on prairie, prairie, prairie, as you look to the north. Beautiful as these prairies are in the spring and early summer, their blackened surface in the fall, if burned, or their dull drab color, if unburned, is monotonous and wearying.

Shelby—has an elevation of 2,106 feet, is 191.3 miles from Omaha. The town is named Kearny, and takes its name from General Kearny, who was an officer in the regular army during the Mexican war. Old Fort Kearny was located near this station, south of the Platte River, and the military reservation of government land still remains, though it will probably soon be brought into market. The rights, if they have any, of "squatter sovereigns" will here be tested, as nearly every quarter section in the whole reserve is occupied by them, some of whom have made valuable improvements in the shape of buildings, etc. It was formerly a great shipping point for cattle, but the advancing tide of settlements has driven stock-men, like the Indians, still further west. Occasionally, however, Texas herds are grazed near here, and the herders sometimes visit Kearny Junction, a few miles west, and attempt to run the town; they murdered a man there in 1875, in cold blood—shot him dead on the threshold of his own door—and this so incensed the inhabitants in the vicinity that they will not, probably, allow them to visit the town in future. The murderer was arrested, has been convicted, and time will tell whether he will be hung or not. Texas herders, as a class, are rough fellows, with long hair and beard, wide-rimmed hats, best fitting boots they can get, large spurs jingling at their heels, a small arsenal, in the shape of Colt's revolvers, strapped to their waists with a careless *negligee* appearance. Their chief pleasure is in a row; their chief drink is "whisky straight," and they usually seem to feel better when they have killed somebody. Houses of prostitution and tippling saloons follow close in their wake. They are generous to their friends, dividing even the last dollar with a comrade who is "broke;" cowardly, treacherous and revengeful to their enemies. Human life is of but little account with them. Their life is one of constant exposure, and very laborious. They are perfect horsemen—usually in the saddle sixteen out of every twenty-four hours—and their great ambition seems to be to become "a devil of a fellow," generally. Nor does it require much care or effort on their part, to fill the bill. Thousands of them on the plains in their native State, in Kansas, Colorado, Wyoming, and Nebraska "have died with their boots on," and we suppose thousands more will perish the same way. Living violent lives, of course they meet with violent deaths. They are a peculiar race, answering, perhaps, a peculiar purpose. The community in which they live, and the country generally, will be better off when they have passed away, for almost ninety-nine out of every hundred goes

> "Down to the vile dust from whence he sprung,
> Unwept, unhonored and unsung."

Kearny has now nothing but a side track, depot and water-tank, with a section-house and the remains of an old corral from which cattle used to be shipped. The reservation included not only land on both sides of the river, but a large island which extends east and west quite a number of miles. The fort was south of the river, and scarcely a vestige now remains to mark the spot where the buildings formerly stood. This fort was built in 1858, by Colonel Charles May, of Mexican war fame. Three miles west of the old fort was Kearny City, which was a considerable town in the old overland times, but it disappeared with the advent of the railroad. The southern part of the reservation is covered with sand-hills, and useless, except for grazing. Notice how the buffalo grass appears and how its extent is increased as you go further west. The new houses around the station, especially those of the squatters on the reservation, are increasing, which indicates that the country is fast settling up.

Kearny Junction.—A lively, enterprising town, 195.3 miles from Omaha, with an elevation of 2,150 feet. It is the junction of the Burlington and Missouri Railroad only, and owes its rapid development to this fact more than to anything else. Formerly the St. Joe and Denver Railroad ran trains to this place, using the track of the Burlington and Missouri from Hastings, a smart little town twenty-four miles south of Grand Island. But this has been abandoned and it is supposed the road will build an independent line to some point on the Union Pacific during the year 1876. Grand Island and Kearny Junction both hope to get it. Kearny Junction was laid out by the town company in September, 1872, about the same time the Burlington and Missouri Railroad arrived; the first house was built in August, 1872, and the town has grown very rapidly ever since; it now has a population of 1,000 souls, four church edifices, two daily newspapers, the *Times* and the *Press*, two brick bank buildings and other brick blocks, with hotels, numerous stores, school-house, court-house, etc. It has a daily stage line to Bloomington, a thriving town some sixty miles south in the Republican Valley, and quite an extensive trade from it and the South Loup Valley on the north; some of the stores here do quite a wholesale trade. The town is finely located on a gradual slope, and from the hills or bluffs on its north side the land in seven counties can be distinctly seen; it has the vim and energy which usually characterizes Western towns; it is an aspirant for the capital if it is ever moved from Lincoln, and has ground on the hill reserved for the location of the State buildings; it also expects a railroad from Sioux City, and one from the Republican Valley; altogether its future prospects are bright. Splendid crops of wheat, corn, oats, barley, broom-corn, potatoes, cabbages, and onions are raised in this vicinity during favorable seasons, but we regard the stock business as the best paying and surest investment for settlers; the buffalo grass, to our mind, is a sure indication of it. Kearny Junction is very healthy, and invalids would here find an agreeable resting-place.

Stevenson—has an elevation of 2,170 feet, and is 201.2 miles from the Missouri River. It is simply a side track with a section-house near by. The way settlers have pushed up this valley during the last five years, is marvelous.

Elm Creek—is 211.5 miles from Omaha, with an elevation of 2,241 feet. In the first 200 miles of your journey, you have attained an altitude more than a thousand feet above Omaha, where you started, and yet the ascent has been so gradual that you have scarcely noticed it. Elm Creek was so named after the creek which you cross just after leaving the station going west. It was formerly heavily timbered with elm, ash, hackberry and a few walnuts and cotton-woods; but the necessities of the road when it was built required it all and more too. The town has one or two saloons, stores, school-house and a few dwellings. The creek rises in the bluffs north-west, and sluggishly worries through them and the sand, till it is finally swallowed up by the Platte. But little timber remains in this vicinity. The next station, some nine miles west of Elm Creek, called

Overton—has the usual side track, school-house, a store and some few dwellings. This valley, to this point and beyond, would have been thickly settled long before this but for climatic reasons which we need not name. The Platte Valley extends on either side here nearly as far as the eye can reach. The town is 220.5 miles from Omaha, at an elevation of 2,305 feet.

Josselyn,—A side track; will eventually become a station; named after the pay-master of the Union Pacific Road. It is 225.1 miles from Omaha, with an elevation of about 2,330 feet above the sea.

Plum Creek.—So named from a creek on the south side of the river, which flows into the Platte nearly opposite the town. The stage-station, on the old overland road was located on this creek and in those days it was considered quite an important point It was the scene of a number of conflicts with the savages—in fact one of their favorite points of attack; eleven white persons were killed and several wounded during one of these attacks. Four miles west of the present town-site they captured and burned a train of cars in 1867; one of the train men was scalped and recently was still living in or near Omaha; one was killed, and the others, we believe, made their escape. The nature of the bluffs here is such that they had a good opportunity to attack and escape before the settlers and emigrants could rally and give them battle. The creek rises in a very bluffy region, and runs north-east into the Platte. Plum Creek is the county-seat of Dawson County; has about 500 inhabitants; a fine brick court-house with jail underneath, one church edifice, school-house, two or three hotels, stores, warehouses, etc. It is a point where considerable broom-corn is purchased and shipped; has a semi-weekly stage line across the Republican Valley to Norton, in the State of Kansas, and a weekly newspaper. There is a substantial wagon bridge across the Platte River, nearly three-quarters of a mile in length. It is located in the midst of a very fine grazing country, though in favorable seasons crops have done well. With irrigation, perhaps they might be made a certainty. This town also enjoys quite a trade with the upper Republican Valley. It was formerly a favorite range for buffaloes, and large quantities of their bleaching bones have been gathered and shipped by rail to St. Louis and places east. It is 231.4 miles from Omaha, with an elevation of 2,370 feet.

Battle with the Indians at Plum Creek.—While the railroad was being built, the engineers, graders and track-layers were frequently driven from their work by the Indians. Not only then, but after the track was laid and trains running, it was some times torn up and trains ditched, causing loss of lives and destruction of property. One of these attacks took place near Plum Creek, as we will now relate. In July, 1867, a train was ditched about four miles west of the above-named station. It was by a band of southern Cheyennes, under a chief called Turkey Leg, who now draws his rations regularly from Uncle Sam, at the Red Cloud agency. He is a vicious looking fellow, his appearance naturally suggesting him as a fit subject for a hanging bee. At a small bridge, or culvert, over a dry ravine, they had lifted the iron rails from their chairs on the ties—raising only one end of each rail—about three feet, piling up ties under them for support, and firmly lashing the rails and ties together by wire cut from the adjoining telegraph line. They were pretty cunning in this arrangement of the rails, and evidently placed them where they thought they would penetrate the cylinder on each side of the engine. But not having a mechanical turn of mind exactly, and disregarding the slight curve in the road at this point, they missed their calculations, as the sequel shows, as one of the rails did no execution whatever, and the other went straight into and through the boiler. After they had fixed the rails in the manner described, they retired to where the bench or second bottom slopes down to the first, and there concealed themselves in the tall grass, waiting for the train. Before it left Plum Creek, a hand-car with three section men was sent ahead as a pilot. This car encountered the obstacle, and ran into the ravine, bruising and stunning the men and frightening them so that they were unable to signal to the approaching train. As soon as the car landed at the bottom of the ravine, the Indians rushed up, when two of the men, least hurt, ran away in the darkness of the night—it was little past midnight—and hid in the tall grass near by. The other, more stunned by the fall of the car, was scalped by the savages, and as the knife of the savage passed under his scalp, he seemed to realize his condition partly, and in his delirium wildly threw his arms out and snatched the scalp from the Indian, who had just lifted it from his skull. With this he, too, got away in the darkness, and is now an employe of the company at Omaha.

But the fated train came on without any knowledge of what had transpired in front. As the engine approached the ravine, the head-light gleaming out in the darkness in the dim distance, fast growing less and less, the engineer, Brooks Bowers by name, but familiarly called "Bully Brooks" by the railroad men, saw that the rails were displaced, whistled "down brakes," and reversed his engine, but all too late to stop the train. The door of the fire-box was open, and the fireman was in the act of adding fuel to the flames within, when the crash came. That fireman was named Hendershot, and the boys used to speak of him as "the drummer boy of the Rappahannock," as he bore the same name, and might have been the same person whose heroic deeds, in connection with Burnside's attack on Fredericksburg, are now matters of history. He was thrown against the fire-box when the ravine was reached, and literally roasted alive, nothing but a few of his bones being afterwards found. The engineer was thrown over the lever he was holding in his hands, through the window of his cab, some twenty feet or more. In his flight the lever caught and ripped open his abdomen, and when found he was sitting on the ground holding his protruding bowels in his hands. Next to the engine were two flat cars loaded with brick. These were landed, brick and all, some thirty or forty feet in front of the engine, while the box cars, loaded with freight, were thrown upon the engine and around the wreck in great disorder. After a time these took fire, and added horror to the scene. The savages now swarmed around the train and whooped and yelled in great glee. When the shock first came, however, the conductor ran ahead on the north side of the track to the engine, and there saw Bowers and Hendershot in the position we have described them. He told them he must leave them and flag the second section of the train following after, or it, too, would be wrecked. He then ran back, signaled this train, and with it returned to Plum Creek. Arriving there in the middle of the night, in vain did he try to get a force of men to proceed at once to the scene of the disaster. No one would go. In the morning, however, they rallied, armed themselves and went out to the wreck. By this time it was near ten o'clock. The burning box cars had fallen around the brave engineer, and while the fiery brands had undoubtedly added to his agony, they had also ended his earthly existence. His blackened and charred remains only told of his suffering. The rescuing party found the train still burning—the Indians had obtained all the plunder they could carry, and left in the early morning. In the first gray dawn of the morning they manifested their delight over the burning train in every possible way, and their savage glee knew no bounds. From the cars not then burned they rolled out boxes and bales of merchandise, from which they took bright-colored flannels, calicos, and other fancy goods. Bolts of these goods they would loosen, and with one end tied to their ponies' tails or the horn of their saddles, they would mount and start at full gallop up and down the prairie just to see the bright colors streaming in the wind behind them. But the end of this affair was not yet. The avenging hand of justice was on the track of these blood-thirsty villains, who, for some inscrutable reason, are permitted to wear the human form. In the spring of that year, by order of General Augur, then in command of the military department of the Platte, Major Frank North, of Columbus, Neb., who had had no little experience in the business, was authorized to raise a battalion of two hundred Pawnee Indians, who were peaceable and friendly towards the whites, and whose reservation is near Columbus, for scouting duty. It was the old experiment of fighting the devil with fire to be tried over again. These scouts were to fight the various hostile bands of the Sioux, Arrapahoes, and Cheyennes, and assist in guarding the railroad, and the railroad builders. At the time this train was attacked, these scouts were scattered in small detachments along the line of the road between Sidney and the Laramie Plains. General Augur was immediately notified of it, and he telegraphed Major North to take the nearest company of his scouts and repair as soon as possible to the scene of the disaster. At that time, Major North was about fourteen miles west of Sidney, at the end of the track, and his nearest company was some twelve miles further on. Mounting his horse, he rode to their camp in about fifty minutes, got his men together, and leaving orders for the wagons to follow, returned, arriving at the end of the track at about four o'clock in the afternoon. By the time these men and horses were loaded on the cars, the wagons had arrived, and by five o'clock the train pulled out. Arriving at Julesburg, they were attached to a passenger train, and by midnight, or within twenty-four hours after the disaster took place, he arrived at the scene. Meanwhile other white troops, stationed near by, had arrived. In the morning he was ordered by General Augur to follow the trail and ascertain whether the attack had been made by northern or southern Indians. With ten men he started on the scout. The sharp-sighted Pawnees soon struck the trail. They found where the hostile band had crossed the river, and where they had abandoned some of their plunder. They followed the trail all that day, and found that it bore south to the Republican Valley. From this fact, and other indications that only Indians would notice, he ascertained that the attacking band were southern Cheyennes. Returning from this scout, after about thirty-five miles' travel, he reported to the commanding officer at Omaha, and received orders to remain in the vicinity, and thoroughly scout the country, the belief being generally entertained among the officers that, if not followed, the Indians would soon return on another raid. Subsequent events proved this belief to be true, and they had not long to wait. In about ten days, their camp being at Plum Creek, one of the scouts came running into camp from the bluffs south of Plum Creek, and reported that the Indians were coming. He had discovered them in the distance, making their way in the direction of the old overland stage station, which they soon after reached. Arriving here, they unsaddled their horses and turned them loose in an old sod corral to feed and rest. They then began preparations to remain all night. The scouts, however, proposed to find out who and what they were before the evening approached. Major North first determined to go with the company himself, but at the urgent solicitation of Capt. James Murie, finally gave him charge of the expedition. There were in the command, two white commissioned officers—Lieut. Isaac Davis, besides the Captain — two white sergeants, and forty-eight Pawnees. The company marched from their camp straight south to the Platte River, which they crossed; then turning to the left followed down its bank under the bushes to within about a mile and a half of the creek. Here they were discovered by the Cheyennes. Then there was mounting in hot haste—the Cheyennes at once preparing for the fray. There were one hundred and fifty warriors to be pitted against this small band of fifty-two, all told. But the Cheyennes, up to this time, supposed they were to fight white soldiers, and were very confident of victory. Forming in regular line, on they rushed to the conflict. Captain Murie's command, as soon as they found they were discovered, left the bushes on the river bank and went up into the road, where they formed in line of battle and were ordered to charge. As the order was given, the Pawnees set up their war-whoop, slapped their breasts with their hands and shouted "Pawnees." The opposing lines met on the banks of the creek, through which the scouts charged with all their speed. The Cheyennes immediately broke and fled in great confusion, every man for himself. Then followed the chase, the killing and the scalping. The Indians took their old trail for the Republican Valley, and put their horses to their utmost speed to escape the deadly fire of the Pawnees. Night finally ended the chase, and when the spoils were gathered, it was found that fifteen Cheyenne warriors had been made to bite the dust, and their scalps had been taken as trophies of victory. Two prisoners were also taken, one a boy of about sixteen years and the other a squaw. The boy was a nephew of Turkey Leg, the chief. Thirty-five horses and mules were also taken, while not a man of the scouts was hurt. After the chase had ceased, a rain-storm set in, and tired with their day's work, with the trophies of their victory, they returned to camp. It was about midnight when they arrived. Major North and a company of infantry, under command of Capt. John A. Miller, had remained in camp guarding government and company property, and knowing that a battle had been fought, were intensely anxious to learn the result. When the Pawnees came near, it was with shouts and whoops and songs of victory. They exhibited their scalps and paraded their prisoners with great joy, and spent the whole night in scalp-dances and wild revelry. This victory put an end to attacks on railroad trains by the Cheyennes. The boy and squaw were kept in the camp of the Pawnees until late in the season, when a big council was held with the

Brule Sioux, Spotted Tail's band, at North Platte, to make a new treaty. Hearing of this council, Turkey Leg, chief of the Cheyennes, sent in a runner and offered to deliver up six white captives held in his band for the return of the boy and the squaw. After the necessary preliminaries had been effected, the runner was told to bring the white captives, that the exchange might be made. The boy held by the scouts was understood to be of royal lineage, and was expected to succeed Turkey Leg in the chieftaincy of the tribe. After the exchange had taken place, the old chief would scarcely allow the boy to leave his sight—such was his attachment to him, and manifested his delight in every possible way over his recovery. The white captives were two sisters by the name of Thompson, who lived south of the Platte River, nearly opposite Grand Island, and their twin brothers; a Norwegian girl taken on the Little Blue River, and a white child born to one of these women while in captivity. They were restored to their friends as soon as possible.

The Next Attack.—The Indians were not willing to have the iron rails that should bind the shores of the continent together laid in peace, and made strenuous and persistent efforts to prevent it. On the 16th of April, 1868, a "cut off" band of Sioux, under a scalawag chief, named Two Strikes, attacked and killed five section-men near Elm Creek Station, taking their scalps, and ran off a few head of stock. They were never pursued. On the same day, and evidently according to a pre-arranged plan, a part of the same band attacked the post at Sidney. They came up on the bluffs north of the town and fired into it. But no one was injured from their shooting at that time. Two conductors, however, named Tom Cahoon and William Edmunson, had gone down the Lodge Pole Creek, a little way to fish. They were unobserved by the Indians when the firing took place. Hearing the reports they climbed up the bank to see what was going on, and being seen by the Indians, they at once made an effort to cut them off, though they were only a mile or so from the post. The savages charged down upon them, and shot Cahoon, who fell forward on the ground. The Indians immediately scalped him and left him for dead. Mr. Edmunson ran towards the post as fast as he could, and drawing a small Derringer pistol, fired at his pursuers. Thinking he had a revolver and would be likely to shoot again if they came too close, they did not venture up as they had done, but allowed him to escape. He got away with some eight or nine arrow and bullet wounds together and carrying four arrows sticking in his body. He was taken to the hospital, and rapidly recovered from his wounds. After the Indians had gone, the citizens went after the body of Mr. Cahoon, whom they supposed dead, but to their surprise he was still alive. They brought him into the post, where he recovered, and is now running on the road.

Attack at Ogalalla.—In September of the same year, the same band of Sioux attempted to destroy a train between Alkali and Ogalalla. They fixed the rails the same as at Plum Creek. As the train came up the rails penetrated the cylinders on each side of the engine, as it was a straight track there; the engine going over into the ditch, with the cars piling up on top of it. The engineer and one of the brakemen who was on the engine at the time, were thrown through the window of the cab, and were but little hurt. The fireman was fastened by the tender against the end of the boiler, and after the train had stopped, there being no draft, the flames of the fire came out of the door to the fire-box upon him, and the poor fellow was literally roasted alive. He was released after six hours in this terrible position, during which he begged the attendants to kill him, but lived only a few moments after his release. All the trains at this time carried arms, and the conductor, with two or three passengers, among whom was Father Ryan, a Catholic priest of Columbus, Nebraska, seized the arms and defended the train—the Indians meanwhile skulking among the bluffs near the track, and occasionally firing a shot. Word was sent to North Platte, and an engine and men came up, who cleared the wreck. Meanwhile word was sent to Major North, then at Willow Island, to take one company of his scouts and follow the Indians. He came to Alkali and reported to Colonel Mizner, who was marching from North Platte with two companies of cavalry, all of whom started in pursuit. They went over to the North Platte River, crossed that stream and entered the sand-hills, where the scouts overtook and killed two of the Indians; the whole party going about thirty-five miles to a little lake, where the main body of Indians had just left and camped, finding the smouldering embers of the Indian fires still alive. That night some of the white soldiers let their camp fires get away into the prairie, and an immense prairie fire was the result. This, of course, alarmed the Indians, and further pursuit was abandoned, much to the disgust of the scouts. Colonel Mizner also claimed that his rations were running short, but from all the facts we can learn, he lacked the disposition to pursue and capture those Indians. At least, this is a charitable construction to put upon his acts.

In October of the same year (1868), the same band of Indians attacked the section-men near Potter Station, drove them in and run off about twenty head of horses and mules. Major North and his scouts were immediately sent in pursuit. Leaving camp at Willow Island, the command was soon on the ground. It was evidently a small raiding party, and Major North sent a

Lieutenant and fifteen of his men after them. They struck their trail, followed them to the North Platte River, which they crossed, followed and overhauled them in the sand-hills, killing two, recapturing a part of the stolen horses, and returned without loss. The Indians have made some efforts to ditch a few trains since that year, but have effected no serious damage. Their efforts of late have mostly been confined to stock stealing, and they never seem so happy as when they have succeeded in running off a large number of horses and mules. When the road was first built it was their habit to cross it, going south and north, several times in each year. They roamed with the buffaloes over the plains of Nebraska, Colorado, Wyoming and Kansas. The effort of the government of late has been to confine them on their reservations, and the rapid disappearance of the buffaloes from the regions named have given them no excuse for hunting in the country now crossed by railroads and filling up with settlers.

Coyote—is the next station, simply a side track with a section-house near by. But little timber is visible at this place, though the bottom lands begin to widen, giving an extended view. This is not a timber country, and wherever it is found, the traveler will please bear in mind that it is the exception and not the rule. The islands in the river doubtless had some timber, but the most of it has long since disappeared. Occasionally you may see a few scattering trees which have been left by the prairie fires, and which stand in inaccessible places. This side track is 239.1 miles from Omaha, and 2,440 feet above the sea. The next station is

Cozad—so named after a gentleman from Cincinnati, Ohio, who purchased about 40,000 acres of land here from the railroad company; laid out the town; built quite a number of houses; induced people to settle here; has resold a good deal of his land, but still has about 20,000 acres in the immediate vicinity. Along the railroad track, west of Plum Creek, the traveler will notice that the buffalo grass has been rooted out by what is called prairie or blue-joint grass. This last is an annual grass and is killed by frost, after which it resembles dark colored brick—a reddish brown appearance. It has but little nutriment after the frost comes, but if cut and cured in July or August, makes an excellent quality of hay. The buffalo grass is just over the divide a little way, but is giving way to that just named. Some men of capital near Cozad, are interesting themselves in sheep raising, and frequently from this place west you will see large herds of cattle. Cozad is 245.1 miles from Omaha, with an elevation of 2,480 feet. It has two or three stores, school-house, hotel, several large dwellings, and with favorable seasons for growing crops in the future, will become quite a town. The Platte Valley at this point is about twenty miles wide.

Willow Island—is the next station; so named from the large number of willow bushes on the island in the river near by. It is 250.1 miles from the Missouri, and has an elevation of 2,511 feet. The prairie or blue-joint grass still continues along the side of the track, and the bluffs on the south side of the river seem more abrupt. They are full of ravines or "draws," and these sometimes have timber in them. At this station a large quantity of cedar piles and telegraph poles are delivered. They are hauled some forty miles from the canons in the South Loup Valley. There is a store at this station and a corral near by where stock is kept; with a few old log and mud buildings, rapidly going to decay in the vicinity. The glory of this place, if it ever had any, has long since departed, but it may, nevertheless, yet become the pride of stock-men, who shall count their lowing herds by the thousand.

Grand Duke Alexis' First Buffalo Hunt.

During the visit of the Grand Duke Alexis of Russia, to the United States, the imperial party were escorted to the plains, and enjoyed the excitement of a buffalo hunt, over the western prairies. Connected with the chase were some incidents of rare curiosity and pleasure. As the only representative of the great Russian nation, he has seen the novelty of military life on the frontier; shaken hands with partially tamed Indian warriors, and smoked the pipe of peace in ancient style. Among the company were Buffalo Bill, a noble son of the wild West, and Generals Sheridan and Custer. The red men appeared in a grand pow-wow and war-dance, and indulged in arrow practice for his particular benefit.

The party started from camp Alexis, Willow Creek, Nebraska, in January, 1872. For the hunt the Duke's dress consisted of jacket and trowsers of heavy gray cloth, trimmed with green, the buttons bearing the Imperial Russian coat-of-arms; he wore his boots outside his trowsers, his cap was an Australian turban, with cloth top; he carried a Russian hunting knife, and an American revolver recently presented to him, and bearing the coat-of-arms of the United States and of Russia on the handle.

General Custer appeared in his well-known frontier buckskin hunting costume, and if, instead of the comical sealskin cap he wore, he had only had feathers fastened in his flowing hair, he would have passed at a distance for a great Indian chief.

Buffalo Bill, the famous scout, was dressed in a buckskin suit trimmed with fur, and wore a black slouch hat, his long hair hanging in ringlets down his shoulders.

Game was sighted in a long canon with broken sides and high hills on either side, forming a magnificent arena.

The Grand Duke and Custer started off, and as they went Custer pulled out his revolver, and said, "Are you ready, Duke?" Alexis drew off his glove, grasped his pistol, and with a wave of his hand replied, "All ready now, General." Buffalo Bill had been selected to show the Grand Duke how the buffaloes would stand at bay when suddenly attacked. A cow was singled out to show him how fleet of foot the females are, and the speed and skill essential to overtake and kill them. As soon as she espied them she started off at full speed, the Duke and Custer after her. Finding herself hard pressed, she ran up a steep declivity on the right side of the canon, and gaining a footing on the slope, kept along the narrow ledge, while the Duke and Custer followed in a line along the bottom of the canon. The chase was most exciting, and the Grand Duke, exhibiting an enthusiasm and daring which the most experienced western hunter could not have surpassed, pressed his game until she turned upon him. Describing a semi-circle with his horse, he dashed to the other side of her, and taking deliberate aim, discharged the contents of his revolver into her fore shoulder, as quick as a flash of lightning. The buffalo fell dead upon the instant. Thus, as he telegraphed to his father, the Czar of Russia, he killed the first wild horned monster that had met his eye in America. The sport continued for two days, and ended with a series of Indian festivities.

GRAND DUKE ALEXIS KILLING HIS FIRST BUFFALO.

Warren—is a side track 260.4 miles from Omaha, and 2,570 feet above the sea. A section-house stands near by. The valley here narrows, and the bluffs on both sides come near the river.

Brady Island—is the next station, with an elevation of 2,637 feet, and 268.4 miles from the eastern terminus of the road. The island in the river, from which the station is named, is quite large, and formerly had considerable timber for this country. An occasional tree may yet be seen.

McPherson—is 277.5 miles from Omaha, and 2,695 feet above the sea. It is the station named after the fort which is located south of the Platte River, on a military reservation, and nearly opposite the station. There is a wagon bridge across the river connecting the two places. The fort is about seven miles from the station, and is located near some springs formerly called "Cotton-wood Springs." It bears the name of the gallant general who fell before Atlanta, in 1864, in the war for the preservation of the Union. But few soldiers are now kept at this fort, though at the time the war was in progress, and afterwards during the building of the road, and in the years of Indian conflict that raged on the frontier, it was a post of considerable importance. Immense quantities of hay are annually cut near this place, with which government and private contracts are filled. A part of the Seventh Iowa Cavalry, under Major O'Brien, camped on the site of the fort in 1866, and afterwards troops from the regular army were stationed here.

Gannett—named after J. W. Gannett, Esq., of Boston, and present auditor of the Union Pacific Railroad—is a side track with adjacent section-house; is 285.2 miles from Omaha, and 2,752 feet above the sea. All the stations for from fifty to a hundred miles east of this, are located in an excellent grazing country, and cattle and sheep are coming in to occupy it.

Five miles from Gannett, the railroad crosses the North Platte River on a pile bridge. There is a side track and two section-houses just east of the river, the side track for hay cars, and one of the section-houses near the bridge for the watchman, who walks its entire length after the passage of every train. The bridge is planked by the railroad company, and rented by Lincoln County, so that wagons, teams and stock have free passage. After leaving Cozad, the number of settlers' cabins and houses diminishes till you come to the North Platte Valley. South of the river between Fort McPherson and North Platte, there are quite a number of homesteaders, who have farmed it for a few years, with indifferent success, having to contend with drought and grasshoppers. The soil has been proven to be prolific, but some plan of irrigation will have to be adopted, before agriculture can be made a paying investment. In choice locations, however, such as pieces of low bottom land near the river, crops of potatoes and "garden truck" have been successfully raised for several years.

We have now entered upon the great stock-growing region of the continent, where cattle and horses can be grown and kept the year round without hay, and where the buffalo grass, excepting along the streams, affords the rich nutriment that produces fat, and renders cattle ready for market without grain.

The North Platte River will be crossed again at Fort Steele. It has its source in northern Colorado, west of the Medicine Bow Mountains. The Laramie River, which you cross just beyond Laramie City, and the Sweetwater, which rises in the Wind River Mountains north of Point of Rocks, and runs through the great South Pass, are two of its principal tributaries. It drains an immense region of country, and is fed by innumerable streams and springs from the Black Hills of Wyoming, the Wind River Mountains, the Medicine Bow Mountains, the Sweetwater Mountains, the Big Horn Mountains, Rattlesnake Hills and other elevations. The traveler must not be confused by the term "Black Hills." The Black Hills of Wyoming are those which you cross between Cheyenne and Laramie City, the summit of which you reach at Sherman. These are not the Black Hills of which so much has been said of late, in connection with the discovery of gold and the Sioux Indians. They are called the Black Hills of Dakota, and the nearest point to them on the railroad is Sidney. From the immense amount of water which runs into the North Platte River, it is a mystery what becomes of it all, as the river is shallow and sluggish where it is crossed near its mouth. Its treacherous bottom of ever varying and shifting quicksands, like that of the South Platte, does not make it a good fording stream for wagons, though the water, except in certain seasons of of the year, is the smallest obstacle. Up to the spring of 1875, this river was the southern boundary of what the Sioux Indians claimed as their reservation, and it was only by the payment of a special appropriation of $25,000, that they relinquished the right to hunt as far south as this river. The principal military posts on the stream, are Forts Fetterman, usually occupied by but few troops, and Laramie. The latter is at present the principal military depot for both troops and supplies off the line of the railroad, in this part of the West. It is 90 miles from Cheyenne, its nearest railroad station, and the point from whence nearly all the frontier expeditions into northern Wyoming, western Dakota, and the Big Horn and Powder River countries, start. The Laramie River and the North Platte form a junction near the fort.

The South Platte, which the railroad still follows for about eighty-five miles, is similar to the North Platte, so far as external observations go. It rises in the mountains south and west of Denver, receives a large number of tributaries; the chief of which is the Cache La Poudre, which forms a junction with it at Greeley, and then pursues a due east course to the Missouri River. The junction with the North Platte is formed a few miles below the bridge just spoken of. On neither of these streams, nor on any of their tributaries can agricultural pursuits be carried on without irrigation, and not always with success with irrigation. The hand of the Almighty has placed its ineffaceable mark upon all this vast region of country—that it is His pasture ground and adapted, so far as is known, to no other purpose. Millions of buffaloes have ranged over these bleak and desolate-looking plains for ages past, and from the short grass which grows in abundance thereon, have derived a rich sustenance. They have gone or are fast going, and the necessities of the civilization which follows, calls for beef and mutton. These plains must become the great beef-producing region of the continent. They are the Almighty's pasture grounds, and if there are not a thousand cattle upon a hill, there will surely be "cattle upon a thousand hills." The numerous tributaries to these two rivers are from ten to fifteen miles apart, with high rolling prairies between—affording abundance of water with adjacent pasture, and this pasture is the home of the richest natural grasses.

Before you reach the North Platte River, you will see conclusive evidence of the adaptability of these plains to stock-raising, and from this time on to where the river is again crossed, you will see numerous herds of cattle and flocks of sheep. The snows of winter in these elevated regions are dry, and not frequent. Driven by fierce winds, they will fill the hollows and small ravines, while the hills are always left bare, so that cattle and sheep can always obtain access to

CROSSING THE PLATTE, BY EMIGRANT TRAIN, IN OLD OVERLAND DAYS.

the ground, and the buffalo and bunch grasses with which it is covered. While hay must be cut for the sustenance of sheep during the few days storms may last, and for the horses and cattle that may be kept up; the vast herds, whether of cattle or horses, will go through the most severe winter that has ever been known in this region without hay or shelter, except that afforded by the ravines. The experiment has been repeatedly tried, and the vast herds that are now kept in this region, attest the success of that experiment. In Lincoln County, of which the town of North Platte is the county-seat, there are probably 60,000 head of cattle alone. Eastern farmers and stock-raisers will see that the attempt to provide hay for this vast number would be useless, and if required would render the keeping of so many in a single county unprofitable. The expense of providing hay would in the first place be great, and the expense of confining the cattle and feeding it out would be still greater. And if the buffaloes have lived in this country year after year, during the flight of the centuries without hay, why may not cattle and horses do likewise? The stock-grazing region to which allusion is here made, comprises in fact all the country west of the 100th meridian of longitude, to the base of the Rocky Mountains, and the elevated plateaus or great parks lying between the eastern and western ranges of the same mountains; while the extent north and south reaches from the Gulf of Mexico to the northern boundary line of the United States. Three great railroad lines already penetrate this vast stock range, and a decade will hardly pass away before other lines will follow. A ready outlet to the best stock markets in the country is therefore always accessible and always open.

But with all the natural advantages of this region, not every one who may be captivated with the idea of a stock ranche and lowing herds, can make it a success. The business requires capital and care—just the same attention that is given to any other successful business. Nor can it be safely entered upon under the impression that a fortune can be made in a day or in a year. It is a business liable to losses, to severe winters, unfavorable seasons and a glutted market. It does not run itself. By reason of a single hard winter, one man in the stock business has been known to lose a hundred thousand dollars, and the losses that same winter were proportionally severe upon those who were not as able to suffer them. It is a business which, if closely attended to, promises large returns upon the capital invested, and which, at the same time, is liable to heavy losses. It is more sure than mining and more profitable than agricultural or dairy-farming. But we shall have more to say of this hereafter, with specific illustrations as to what can be done in both sheep husbandry and cattle raising. Returning to the two rivers, one of which we crossed near their junction—the vast area of bottom lands continue to widen, and for a long distance each has its broad valley. Leaving the North Platte here we shall ascend the South Platte to Julesburg. About one mile west of the bridge, we arrive at

North Platte,—the end of another division of the Union Pacific Railroad. It is 291 miles from Omaha, and 2,789 feet above the sea. It is a thriving city, and outside of Omaha has the most extensive machine and repair shops on the line of the road. The roundhouse has twenty stalls, and it, together with the machine and repair shops, are substantially built of brick. In these shops engines and cars are either repaired or entirely built over,—a process which cannot hardly be called repairing, but which nevertheless renders them as good as new. The engine-room for the machine-shops, is a model of neatness; everything in and around it being kept in perfect order.

The town has about 2,000 inhabitants, two wide-awake newspapers; the *Republican* being a weekly, and the *Western Nebraskian* being a semi-weekly, together with several wholesale and retail stores and shops of various kinds. The Railroad House is the largest and leading hotel. About 150 men are given constant employment in the shops. There are also one or two companies of troops stationed here, not to protect the railroad from the savages, for that necessity has passed, but for economy in keeping and convenience for frontier duty. The town also has two or three church edifices, a brick court-house and brick school-house, both new, and both presenting a fine appearance. There are also several elegant private residences. It is beautifully located, and has excellent drainage. The bluffs or hills are in near view, both north and south, and give quite a picturesque appearance to the country in the immediate vicinity. The Black Hills excitement, in regard to the discovery of gold, has had some effect upon the town, and a railroad off to the north-west is talked. It is the home of some of the leading stock-men of this section of country. Near this city, in 1875, Col. E. D. Webster and Mrs. A. W. Randall, wife of the late ex-postmaster-general Randall, formed a copartnership to engage in the dairying business, and erected a cheese factory. During the year they manufactured about 30 tons of cheese, which brought them a fair return. Colonel Webster claims that the experiment has demonstrated that the business can be carried on with profit, and he believes it will eventually become the leading feature of this part of the country. He further says that the only drawback at present is the scarcity and unreliability of help, it being difficult to obtain a sufficient number of "milkers" at a reasonable price to milk a large number of cows. In 1876 the firm proposes to make cheese from the milk of from one to two hundred cows, and the balance of their herd—some five hundred—will be devoted to stock-raising. This dairy establishment is one of the new enterprises of North Platte, and, if successful in the future, will make it the prominent cheese-market of the West.

The town has abundant attractions for invalids needing rest—there being antelope and deer in the hills, fish in the streams, and an abundance of pure air to invigorate the body. It has a bright future and is destined to become one of the leading towns on the line of the railroad. Formerly it was an eating-station, but as now run, trains pass it in the night. The road was finished to this town in the fall of 1866, from which time until the following June it was the point where all overland freight was shipped. It was a rough town then, but this state of affairs did not last long, and the character of the place rapidly improved with the arrival of permanent settlers. There were a few Indian scares, but no serious attack was made by the savages upon the town. Two or three trains were ditched and wrecked, both east and west, but this was the extent of the damage done by them. Of this, however, we shall have more to say in another place.

CHIMNEY ROCK, NEAR NORTH PLATTE.

Chimney Rock.—Near North Platte is the far-famed Chimney Rock, two and a half miles from the south bank of the Platte River. It is composed of a friable yellowish marl, which can be cut readily with the knife. It rises in the form of a thin, perpendicular shaft above a conical mound, whose base slopes gradually out toward the plains. It appears to be the renewal of the old chain of hills and rocks which bounded the valley, but which, from their softness of material, have been disintegrated by wind and weather. This possessing harder material has withstood these effects, although it is steadily yielding. In the days of Fremont's expedition, it was estimated that it was over 200 feet in height, but other travelers and explorers who had seen it years before, stated that its height had been as great as 500 feet. In those days it was a landmark visible for forty or fifty miles; now it is hardly 35 feet in height. Around the waist of the base runs a white band which sets off its height, and relieves the uniform yellow tint. It has often been struck by lightning.

The Overland Pony Express.

The Pony Express (of which few now remember those days of excitement and interest) was started in 1860, and the 3d of April, that year, is the memorable date of the starting of that first trip. In those days, the achievements of the Pony Express were attended with an eager excitement hardly less interesting than the building of the Pacific Railroad itself. "*Overland to California in thirteen days,*" was repeated everywhere as a remarkable achievement. The first company organized was formed in California in 1858 or 1859, under the name of the Central Overland California and Pike's Peak Express. At that time, with no telegraph or even stage line across the continent, this attempt was considered extraordinarily audacious. The services planned and executed by the company were a pony express, with stations sixty miles apart, the entire distance from St. Joseph, Mo., to Sacramento. The time occupied between ocean and ocean was fourteen days, and from St. Joseph to San Francisco, ten days. And the schedule of the company required the pony express to make trips in the following time:

From St. Joseph to Marysville,	12 hours.
From St. Joseph to Fort Kearny,	34 hours.
From St. Joseph to Laramie,	80 hours.
From St. Joseph to Fort Bridger,	108 hours.
From St. Joseph to Salt Lake,	124 hours.
From St. Joseph to Camp Floyd,	128 hours.
From St. Joseph to Carson City,	118 hours.
From St. Joseph to Placerville,	226 hours.
From St. Joseph to Sacramento,	232 hours.
From St. Joseph to San Francisco,	240 hours.

An express messenger left once a week from each side with not more than ten pounds of matter. The best of riders were chosen from among trappers, scouts and plains men, familiar with all the life of the route, fearless, and capable of great physical power, endurance and bravery. The ponies were very swift and strong, a cross between the American horse and Indian pony, and after each run of sixty miles, waited till the arrival of the messenger from the opposite direc-

OVERLAND PONY EXPRESS PURSUED BY HIGHWAYMEN.

tion, when each returned. The riders were constantly exposed to dangers from Indian attacks and pursued by highwaymen; and to compensate them for this risk they received the large salary of $1,200 a month each; and the modest price charged for the conveyance of business letters was $5.00, gold, per quarter ounce. At the time of the departure of the first messenger from St. Joseph, a special train was run over the Hannibal and St. Joseph Railroad to bring the through messenger from New York, and a "*Pony Express Extra*" was issued of two pages, by the St. Joseph *Daily Gazette*, containing telegraphic news from all parts of the world, with a heavily leaded account of the new enterprise, and sending greetings to the press of California.

The route from St. Joseph, after reaching the Platte Valley, followed just north of the present track of the Pacific Railroad to Laramie, then up the Sweet Water to Salt Lake, and down the Humboldt to Sacramento. Night and day the messengers spurred their ponies with the greatest speed each could endure. Often on arriving at an express station the messenger, without waiting to dismount, tossed his bag to another already waiting, and each were off at once, back again, and thus for eight days the little express bag traveled, arriving at the rail terminus, rarely a minute behind the prescribed time, a total distance of 2,000 miles.

For two years this system was kept up, until the telegraph line was finished in 1862, when the company dissolved with a loss of $200,000. As an instance of rapid speed, once, very important dispatches—election news—were carried from St. Joseph, Mo., to Denver City, Col., 625 miles, in sixty-nine hours, the last ten miles being made in thirty-one minutes. On this and next page, we give two illustrations characteristic of these times. One engraving is taken from a painting of G. G. M. Ottinger, of Salt Lake City, which represents the express rider dashing along and cheering the telegraph

OLD PONY EXPRESS STATION AT CHEESE CREEK, NEBRASKA.

men who were erecting the poles. This is an actual scene, as, in the summer of 1862, while the telegraph was under construction, the flitting by of the Pony Express was an almost daily occurrence. An illustration is also given of one of these express stations at Cheese Creek, Neb., which was soon afterwards abandoned as a thing of the past. The government mails were carried by special contract of the Overland Mail Company with the United States government, which was started in 1858, who contracted with them to run a monthly mail from San Francisco to the Missouri River for a consideration of $650,000 annual compensation. Of this company, John Butterfield who drove the first coach, was president. The route chosen was the Ox Bow, via. Santa Fe, but in 1860 the Indians became so troublesome that the route was changed to that of the Pony Express, and soon afterwards a daily mail was established at an expense of $1,000,000 annually. The incidents of overland stage life have been repeated over and over again in books of Western adventure. Here and there were lonely post-offices away out on the distant prairies or plains. No passengers to set down or take up, the driver throws out his mail-bag, catches the one thrown to him, and whirls on without stopping, or scarcely checking the speed of his team. Morning, noon or night comes the inevitable "*refreshment station*," such as it is, where the weary passengers, well shaken up, were glad to regale themselves on pork and beans, corn bread, and "slumgullion"—the Far Western name for tea. Toward the middle of the night, perhaps, the driver may be heard shouting loudly, or with terrific whoop—a mile or so before his station is reached the keepers have heard it—and as his stage rattles up, the new relay of horses is ready, and in two or three minutes the stage is on its way again. After a few days' journey, the travelers become used to the swinging motion of the stage, and sleep as naturally as if made for such a life.

PONY EXPRESS SALUTING THE TELEGRAPH.

A Word with Invalids.

Thousands of invalids, especially consumptives, visit the mountains and California coast, every year, in search of health, and to try the effect of a change of climate in restoring them to activity and vigor. There can be no question but that many have been benefited by the change, and it is a fact equally patent that many have left good homes, kind friends, and plenty of care—to die alone and among strangers. With this last class the main trouble is, they wait too long in the East before starting. The disease, more or less rapid in its strides, gets too firm a hold upon the system—becomes too deeply rooted to be easily thrown off; then they start for health and rest that cannot be found, and most always go too far in search of it. There are a few words of advice to these people, which are the result of years of observation and experience on the plains and among the mountains.

First, the discovery of *a tendency* to lung and throat diseases should be a sufficient incentive to prompt one to *an immediate* change of climate. Do not wait until a change becomes hopeless because of the advanced stages of the disease.

Second, *do not at first go too far.* This is another mistake frequently committed by those who finally get started.

Third, *do not go too fast.* Remember the railroad from Omaha, in less than two days, will take you to an altitude of more than 8,000 feet, and this is a severe test on a pair of healthy lungs, to say nothing of its effect upon weak ones. First go as far as Grand Island, and stop. This place is 1,850 feet above the sea, and you are in the midst of a fine prairie country, with a generally clear atmosphere and balmy breezes. Here are good hotel accommodations, in a thickly settled region, where you can obtain plenty of fresh milk, cream and eggs, and such other articles of diet as are necessary and conducive to your welfare. Ride or walk out from town; go around among the farmers, and if, after a month or so, you improve and wish to go farther, buy a team and wagon, and from this place go along leisurely overland, camping out if the weather is favorable. There are opportunities for hunting and fishing, along the road, which will afford amusement and recreation. When you get to Kearny Junction, stop a few weeks. Notice the effect of your new mode of life and the climate upon your health, and if you simply hold your own, it is safe for you to take another step up the Platte Valley in your westward journey. Leisurely pursue your way, either along the stream or on the adjoining highlands, still camping out, until you reach North Platte. Then take another rest, look around the country, mount your horse and ride out to the cattle ranches and live with the herders for a time. Do not be in a hurry to get away, and after you have been here a month or six weeks, if you still improve, or even hold your own with the character of the life herein prescribed, it will be safe for you to go still farther, and in the same manner. But if you are not benefited by the trip thus far, it will be better for you to return to your homes and friends, where loving hands can smooth your pillow and administer comfort during your declining days.

SHOOTING DUCKS ON THE PRAIRIES.

If the journey has benefited you, pursue it overland and camping out, to Sidney or Cheyenne, up the Lodge Pole Valley and along side of the railroad, or at Julesburg go up the South Platte Valley to Greeley. You are now, if at Cheyenne, over 6,000 feet above the sea, and between 5,000 and 6,000 feet at either Greeley or Denver, in the midst of a rarified and dry atmosphere. If your health is regained, do not think of returning, for this is almost sure to bring on a relapse, which is usually sudden, and from which there is no escape; your safety depends upon your remaining in these high altitudes, and on the high and dry plains of the West. A trip down in New Mexico, and across the plains to

Arizona, will also prove beneficial. In the old overland times, thousands of consumptives regained their health in driving teams, and by slowly crossing the plains, who would have died if the same journey had been taken on the cars. By the latter mode, the change from a damp and heavy atmosphere in the East, to the rarified and dry air of the plains and mountains, is too sudden; and after all, if the disease has become thoroughly seated, it is doubtful if any change will be effectual. It is an experiment which should only be tried with all possible safeguards thrown around it.

Buffalo Grass.—After you have passed the stations of North Platte and Sidney, you will observe the entire country carpeted with a short, dried up grass growing in little bunches. This is the famous buffalo grass which covers thousands of miles of the plains northward and southward and westward. Though it gives to the country a dried look, as if the very appearance of desolation and sterility, yet it is the richest grass ever known in the world. The entire State of Nebraska is famous for its remarkable variety of grasses. The Platte Valley is the home of no less than 149 varieties, all native to the soil, and were it not for the extraordinary beauty and luxuriance of the green carpet the grasses make, the Valley of the Platte would be almost wholly devoid of interest. The buffalo grass is rarely over two to three inches in height, and its seed is produced on flowers almost covered by leaves close to the ground. It grows in little tufts, broad and dense, and is exceedingly rich and sweet, having no less than 3 6-10 per cent. of saccharine matter. When making its first growth in the spring, it is green, then dries on its stem and remains the rest of the year like cured hay on the open ground, retaining all its sweetness. Without a single exception, horses, mules and stock of all descriptions, will forsake all other kinds of grass until all the buffalo grass within reach has been consumed. While the buffaloes roamed over this country it was their natural food, but with their disappearance and the coming of the white man, it is disappearing to give place to others. Leaving North Platte, the next station is

Nichols,—299.4 miles from Omaha, and 2,882 feet above the sea. It is simply a side track with section-house near, in the midst of the level bottom lands between the two rivers, both of which are in sight. Before reaching North Platte it will be observed that the bottom narrows, and that the bluffs or sand-hills in some instances approach the river's bank. But after leaving the town, for nearly twenty miles west, the level prairie between the rivers spreads out in view, with bluffs on either side beyond. Between North Platte and this station there are a few settlers, but the territory is mostly occupied as the winter range of Keith & Barton's herd of cattle, as they are easily confined between the rivers with little help.

O'Fallon's—is the next station. It is 307.9 miles from Omaha, with an elevation of 2,976 feet. It is a telegraph station. O'Fallon's Bluffs are plainly visible south of the South Platte River, which they closely approach; at this point we lose sight of the Valley of the North Platte—a ridge of low hills jutting down from the west, while the railroad follows the south river. The railroad reached this place late in the fall of 1866, but North Platte was the terminal station until Julesburg was reached in 1867. If there was any timber on the streams in this vicinity, it has long since disappeared. On an island in the South Platte the Indians used to camp, and from their hiding places in the sand-hills and bluffs, frequently attacked emigrants and trains, but as before remarked, with the buffaloes, the Indians disappear.

Dexter—is simply a side track where trains occasionally meet and pass. It is 315.2 miles from Omaha, and has an elevation of 3,000 feet. The bluffs here come very near the river, and they are utilized in the building of a corral—the rocky ledge answering all the purposes of a fence. The monotony of the scenery up to this point now passes away, and the traveler will always find something in the ever-varying views of rocks, bluffs, streams and plains that will interest him in the journey.

Alkali.—A telegraph station, 322.4 miles from the Missouri River, and 3,038 feet above the sea. The alkali spots which have been witnessed in the soil since we left Omaha, are now more frequent, and the station naturally takes its name from these characteristics. This station has a small depot, side track and section-house; is in the midst of a fine grazing country, and opposite an old stage station south of the river.

Roscoe.—Simply a side track, 332.0 miles from Omaha, with an elevation of 3,105 feet. Just before reaching this place, and in this vicinity, the railroad passes through more sandy bluffs that approach the river.

Ogalalla—is the next station, 341.6 miles from Omaha. Elevation 3,190 feet. It is the county-seat of Keith County, Nebraska, and is destined to be the Texas town on the line of the Union Pacific. The regular trail for driving cattle from Texas may be said to terminate here. It has a depot, water tank, side tracks, cattle chutes, store, one or two boarding-houses, saloon, etc. It is the head-quarters and outfitting place of a large number of ranchmen, who have herds of cattle in this vicinity. It is some twelve miles from the North Platte River, where a number of herds find ample range. In 1875, it is claimed that nearly 60,000 head of Texas cattle were driven to this point, and afterwards distributed to various parties to whom they were sold. A large number of them were taken to the

Indian agencies at Red Cloud and Spotted Tail. There will be numerous buildings erected soon to accommodate the growing necessities of the town. Leaving Ogalalla we next come to

Brule,—so called from the Brule Sioux, a band of which Spotted Tail is the chief. Red Cloud is chief of the Ogalalla Sioux. This is probably the most powerful tribe of Indians now existing in the country, and when all united they are said to be able to raise at least 10,000 warriors. Those of them who have been taken east to Washington and other eastern cities, seem to have lost their belligerent feelings toward the whites, and will not probably go to war with them unless misled by tricksters or influenced by some other powerful motive. The young "bucks" who have remained on their reservations, however, think they can whip the whole country in a very short time if they should once get at it. This station was a favorite crossing place with this band of Sioux during the years when they used to hunt on the rivers south, or go on their scalping and horse-stealing expeditions. Brule is 351.2 miles from Omaha, and has an elevation of 3,266 feet. North of this place, on the North Platte, is Ash Hollow, a celebrated camping ground for Indians and the scene of a great victory over them by General Harney, in 1859. The whole tribe of Sioux probably have a greater admiration for General Harney, to-day, than for any other living American. Physical force is the only power which they can be made to respect and fear. Next comes

Big Spring,—which is 360.9 miles from the eastern end of the road, with an elevation of 3,325 feet. It is so named from large springs which break to the surface of the ground at the foot of the bluffs, on the right-hand side of the road going west, and in plain sight of the cars. The water tank, at this station, is supplied from these springs. The water is excellent, and the station is quite a camping place for those who continue to journey overland. This is a telegraph station.

Barton,—called after Hon. Guy C. Barton of North Platte. It is 368.7 miles from Omaha, and 3,421 feet above the sea—simply a side track where trains meet and pass. Beyond this station, a short distance, the old town of Julesburg can be seen across the river. Late in 1875, a stray herd of about six hundred buffaloes quietly passed over the old town site to and from the river, where they went for water. It will probably be their last visitation to this part of the country.

Julesburg,—377.4 miles from Omaha, and 3,500 feet above the sea. It was named after Jules Burg—a frontier character who was killed by one Jack Slade, another rough, in the old overland stage times. The old town was across the river, some four miles below the present station, and was a pretty rough place. The station is opposite old Fort Sedgwick, now abandoned, and was the proposed junction of a branch railroad up the South Platte River by way of Greeley to Longmont, from which a railroad is completed to Denver. This branch is graded nearly the entire distance, and bridged part of the way. By an agreement made in 1875, the Union Pacific, or men in the company, relinquished the proposed and completed roads in Colorado to the Kansas Pacific, and the latter road relinquished its through business to the Pacific coast, and its efforts to compel the Union Pacific to pro rate with it from Cheyenne west. This arrangement effected the entire suspension of all efforts to complete this branch, and Julesburg is now, as formerly, a way-station on the Union Pacific. It is, however, quite a place for shipping stock, has one or two stores, some adobe houses and stables, with cattle-yards and chutes. The completion of this branch road would have been of great benefit to the Union Pacific, and to the entire State of Nebraska, by reason of the coal which is found in large quantities near Boulder, and which, if obtained there, would save some three or four hundred miles in hauling over very heavy grades, as is now done. It is doubtful if it is ever completed. At this point the Union Pacific passes through the north-eastern corner of Colorado, and here it leaves the South Platte River and ascends Lodge Pole Creek to within a few miles of Cheyenne.

The early pioneers who went to Utah, California and Oregon overland, usually crossed the South Platte River at this place, and followed up the Lodge Pole to Cheyenne Pass. In fact, there were many routes. One up the North Platte, one up the South Platte, one up the Lodge Pole, and others. The northern route passed through what is known as the Great South Pass, about 65 miles north of the Point of Rocks. The Lodge Pole route crossed the Black Hills at Cheyenne Pass, and the South Platte route followed up the Cache La Poudre and Dale Creek, until it struck the great Laramie Plains south-west of Sherman.

Fort Sedgwick, of which we have spoken, was established in May, 1864, and was named after the gallant commander of the Sixth Corps, army of the Potomac, who was killed at the battle of Spottsylvania Court-House while sighting a gun, and whose loss was greatly lamented by the entire army, and especially the corps he commanded. Among "the boys" he was familiarly spoken of as "Farmer John."

Incidents in the History of Julesburg.

The overland stage company had quite an important station at Julesburg, south side of the river, and about a mile east of the location of Fort Sedgwick. It was in 1865, before any rails had been laid on the Union Pacific. The stage company had accumulated a large quantity of supplies at this station, and the Indians knowing this, and ever hostile to the travel of the whites through this region, had their cupidity aroused. Troops were scattered all along the route, and frequently had to escort the stages from one station to another. At Julesburg, the road crossed the South Platte, followed the Lodge Pole up to Sidney, and then crossed over to the North Platte, which it ascended to Fort Laramie and beyond. Capt. N. J. O'Brien was in command at the fort, with one company of the Seventh Iowa Cavalry, and two pieces of artillery. On the 7th of January, 1875, the Sioux and Cheyennes, one thousand strong, discovering the small force to defend it, attacked the fort with great bravery. They had previously run the stage into the station, killing one man and one horse. When their presence was discovered, Captain O'Brien made the best disposition possible with his small force. He left a sergeant with some twelve men in the fort, to handle the artillery, and mounting the rest, thirty-seven men and one officer, besides himself, went out to meet the savages. The charge was sounded, and in they went. About a mile from the fort there is a projecting hill in the bluffs, back of and around which the main body of the Indians were concealed. As the men neared the top of this hill, they saw the large force opposed to them, but never flinched. The Indians charged upon them with great fury, and for quite a time the unequal contest was continued. But his ranks having become depleted by the loss of fourteen of the thirty-seven enlisted men, the captain ordered them to fall back, which they did in good order, but leaving their dead comrades to fall into the hands of the blood-thirsty foe. The Indians perceiving their disposition to fall back, redoubled their efforts, and endeavored to cut them off from the fort. They attacked with greater fury and boldness than ever, and came very near effecting their purpose. The men, however, fell back in good order, and were successful in gaining the fort. The Indians now surrounded this, but the artillery was brought out and served with good effect, so that they were kept at bay, and eventually night put an end to the conflict. In the night the Indians withdrew, and when the morning broke, not one was in sight. But now comes the most horrible part of this incident. The men went out to find, if possible, the bodies of their dead comrades. They found them, but nearly all were beyond recognition; stripped of every vestige of clothing, mutilated beyond account, cold and stark they lay, in the places they had fallen; their fingers, toes and ears cut off, their mouths filled with powder and ignited, and every conceivable indignity committed upon their persons. Sorrowfully they gathered up these remains, and conveyed them to the fort, where they were decently buried; but the recollections of that awful night, did not fade from the memories of the survivors of that company. In subsequent battles with the savages, their courage was quickened and their arms nerved to deeds of daring, which cost many a warrior his life, and gave him a sudden exit to his happy hunting grounds. The loss of the savages in this battle, could not, at the time, be accurately ascertained,

INDIAN ATTACK ON AN OVERLAND STAGE.

but from the best information since obtained, admitted by the Indians themselves, they had sixty-three warriors killed in this engagement. None were found on the field, as they always carry their dead away with them.

On the second day of February, less than a month from the above attack, they appeared in the vicinity of the fort again, and attacked and burned the station house of the stage company, other out-buildings and stores, and one or two houses adjoining. Five miles below the station was a ravine called the Devil's Dive, through which the stages passed. Captain O'Brien and four or five men were escorting the coach with three or four passengers, one of whom was a lady. As he ascended the bank of the ravine going toward the fort, he saw a smoke, and riding up to the top of a hill, he saw Indians. Returning to the coach, he had every man, passengers and all, carefully examine his arms, and caused the coach to proceed slowly along. Soon the road neared the bank of the river, and here he met some teamsters with wagons, who, beyond a pistol or two, were unarmed, and who had left the station for some object, less than a half hour before. They now became aware of the situation, and were greatly alarmed. These men the captain ordered to return and keep near the stage, which they did, all moving slowly toward the station and fort. Meanwhile the heads of Indians were popping up quite frequently, over the bluffs in the distance. Arriving near one of these, the captain boldly rode to the top, and taking his blanket swung it three times over his head. The Indians saw this, and supposed he had a large force in the rear, which he was signaling to come up, and they began to fly. The river was frozen, and sand had been scattered over two roadways on the ice. They took everything they could from the burning station and houses, and beat a retreat across the river. At the first sign of their leaving, the stage-driver and teamsters put their animals to their utmost speed, and ran into the fort, the captain arriving there in time to give the Indians a few parting shots from his artillery as the last of them ran across the river. The shots ricocheted along the ice, and caused the Indians to drop some of their plunder, though doing no further damage, as we could learn.

These are only two of the many incidents in our frontier history, that will soon be beyond the reach and knowledge of either the present or future generations.

The Great Indian Battle at Summit Springs.

On the divide south of the South Platte River, and about midway between old Fort Morgan and old Fort Sedgwick, opposite to which Julesburg now stands, there are some fine springs—the only good water in quite a region of territory. They are now called Summit Springs; and are near the summit of a divide from which the water, when there is any, runs north and south.

In the winter of 1869, Major Frank North, before alluded to, received orders to recruit his scouts for the summer campaign. He organized one company in February, and two the following April, the total number in the three companies being one hundred and fifty men, exclusive of their white officers. In April of that year, General Carr, taking two of these companies and eight of the Fifth Cavalry, then stationed at Fort McPherson, was ordered to scout the country in the Republican, Solomon and Saline Valleys and their tributaries, and strike any marauding bands of Indians he might find. At that time, the Indians were raiding the advanced settlements in the lower Republican and Solomon Valleys, burning houses, killing and scalping men, women and children, and stealing all the horses they could find. The third company of the scouts had not then been organized. As soon as this was done, Major North was ordered to take them across the country from Fort Kearny, and join General Carr's command, at the mouth of Prairie Dog Creek, in the Republican Valley. This he did, effecting a junction about the 5th of May. After scouting the country between the Republican and Solomon for about a month, the command returned to the Republican, where it met a supply train, which had been sent out from Fort McPherson, and then proceeded up the valley. On arriving at the mouth of Medicine Creek, they struck the trail of a large village. This was on the first day of July, and they continued to follow it up the river for about one hundred and twenty-five miles. The trail then left the valley, and bore off to the North, until it struck Frenchman Creek, then up that creek to its source, and then over a divide to Summit Springs, about thirty-five miles from the headwaters of the Frenchman. The Indians of this village kept pickets out as a sort of a rear-guard, but did not think of an attack from another quarter. The Pawnee scouts were constantly in the advance, and kept the command well informed of the condition and disposition of the Indians. They had discovered the rear-guard of the Indians, without being themselves seen, reporting their situation, and telling just how the attack should be conducted, in order to be successful. A wide detour would have to be made, and the Indian village, encamped in a ravine near the springs, would have to be approached and attacked from the west. Every precaution was taken to conceal the movements of the troops. The attack was made on the 11th day of July. The heavy wagon train was left in the rear, and the best horses with their riders, were selected for the march, which was supposed to be, with the detour mentioned, at least fifty miles. The command arrived within about a mile and a half of the Indians undiscovered, at about three o'clock, P. M., but before the dispositions and arrangements for making the final charge had been fully completed, one company of cavalry unnecessarily exposed itself, and this precipitated the attack. The Indians were Sioux, forty lodges, Cheyennes, forty-five lodges—eighty-five in all. They had been in the raids together, and were to separate the next day. They had evidently concluded to take one day at these splendid Springs, for the enjoyment of their farewell pow-wow, but it proved to be a "bad medicine day" for them. When they saw the company of cavalry that had unfortunately been exposed to their view, they ran out to gather in their horses, which were quietly feeding in the vicinity of their camp, a mile or more away. There was no time for delay. The troops and scouts charged down upon them with all their speed. The scouts, as usual, set up their infernal war-whoop, and went in with a rush. The Indians were wholly unprepared for the attack, and some of them were quietly lounging in their tents. In fact it was nearly a complete surprise. They were all under the lead of Tall Bull, a noted Cheyenne chief and warrior, and numbered about five hundred men, women and children—nearly or quite two hundred being warriors. Seventeen squaws and children were taken prisoners, and as near as could be estimated, one hundred and sixty warriors were slain, among them Tall Bull, the chief. He was seen, as the troops approached, mounted upon his horse, with his wife and child behind him, trying to escape, but when he found his retreat cut off, he ran into a "pocket" or "draw," in the side of a ravine, with almost perpendicular sides, where some fifteen other warriors had taken refuge. He had a very fine horse, which he led to the mouth of this "pocket" and shot dead. He then took his wife and child and pushed them up on the bank of the "pocket," telling her, as he did this, to go and give themselves up, perhaps their lives would be spared. The squaw and her child, a beautiful girl, went straight to Major North, and raising her hands in token of submission, drew them gently over his face and down his form to the ground, where she sank upon her knees, her child standing beside her. While Major North can talk Pawnee like a native, he could not understand what she said, but as all Indians use sign language to a great extent, he readily interpreted her motions to mean that she surrendered, and wanted him to spare their lives. He motioned her to rise, which she did, and told her by signs to go a little way, sit down and stay there, and she would not be harmed. She then, by signs, indicated that there were seven living braves still in the "pocket," and asked him to go in after them, doubtless thinking that her husband might be saved with herself. He declined this request,

INDIAN COSTUMES.

especially as the Indians were shooting every one they could see from their concealed position, it being simply a question of life for life, and further told her that the braves in the ravine would all be killed. The troops and scouts staid around this "pocket," until satisfied that there were no living Indians there, and, on entering, found sixteen dead warriors and one dead squaw, lying close together, among whom was Tall Bull. In their raids in the Solomon Valley, they had captured two white women, whose lives they had spared for purposes worse than death, and at the time this attack was made, they were still alive. One of them had been taken by the principal Sioux chief, and the other was appropriated by Tall Bull, whose wife, doubtless from motives of ignorant jealousy, was accustomed to give her severe whippings, at least six days out of every seven, and her body showed the marks where she had been repeatedly bruised and lacerated by Tall Bull's squaw. The white woman who was appropriated by the Sioux chief, when he found she was likely to be rescued, was shot dead by him, and only gasped for breath a few times after being found by some of the officers, unable to utter a word. As near as could be learned, her name was Susanna. It was afterwards ascertained that she was a Norwegian woman, and General Carr, in his report of the battle, calls the Springs, Susanna Springs, after this woman, and near which she was decently buried, and which name they ought to bear now.

PAWNEE CHIEF IN FULL DRESS.

When the charge was first begun, Captain Cushing of the scouts, passing by the lodge of Tall Bull, entered it. The chief, as before stated, had fled with his wife and child at the first approach of danger, but in his lodge there remained the other captive woman, whom he had shot and evidently left for dead. She was a German woman, unable to speak English, and up to this time, had supposed, from the presence of the scouts, that the fight was between Indians, and that whatever the result, there would be no change for the better so far as she was concerned. As the captain entered the lodge, he saw this woman in a sitting posture, nearly denuded, with the blood running down her waist. When the chief left the tent, he had shot her in the side, aiming at her heart, but the bullet struck a rib, glanced, passed part way around her body, and came out near the spine. As the fight had just commenced, Captain Cushing told her by motions and as best he could, to stay there and she would be taken care of, but not comprehending his meaning, and now, for the first time, realizing that white men were engaged in the battle, she thought, as he started to go, that she was to be left, and with the most pitiful moan ever uttered by human lips, she lifted her arms, clasped him around his limbs, and in every possible way, begged him not to leave her with the savages. Others passing by, he called them in, and the woman was partially made to understand that she would be cared for. He disengaged himself from her embrace, and after the fight had ended, returned and took her to the surgeon, who saw that her wounds were not fatal, that they were properly dressed, and provided for her as best he could on the return march to Fort Sedgwick, opposite where Julesburg now stands, where she was placed in the hospital and soon recovered. A few months later, having no home or friends where she was taken captive, she was married to a soldier, who was discharged by reason of expiration of service. The troops and scouts captured in this fight, nearly six hundred head of horses and mules, all the tents of the two tribes, an immense quantity of buffalo meat and robes, fifty guns of various kinds, with pistols, fancy Indian head-dresses, trinkets, etc., and $1,900 in twenty-dollar gold pieces, which the Indians had taken from this German woman's father at the time she was captured. About $900 of this gold was restored to the woman, and if the white soldiers had been as honest and generous as the brave Pawnee scouts, when the appeal for its restoration was made, every lost dollar would have been returned. Of the $900, the scouts gave up over $600. The seventeen prisoners taken, included Tall Bull's wife and child. They were first carried to Fort Sedgwick, then sent to Omaha, where they were kept under guard for about six weeks, and then sent to the Whetstone Agency, on the Missouri River above Yankton. The widowed squaw married a Sioux Indian at the Red Cloud Agency, where she is now living.

Prairie Dogs.—The little villages of prairie dogs which are seen frequently by passengers from the car windows, soon after leaving Sidney, and line the track for many miles, are full of curious features of animal life. Ladies clap their hands, and children shout with glee at sight of these cunning little creatures. It is a pretty little animal, curious in shape, always fat, grayish red color, about sixteen inches in length, and always lives with a multitude of its companions in villages. It has a short, yelping sound, which it is very fond of uttering, and has some resemblance to the bark of a young puppy. The curious mounds or burrows are of considerable dimensions, dug in a sloping direction at an angle of forty-five degrees with the surface of the ground. After descending two or three yards they make a sudden turn upward, and terminate in a spacious chamber.

In the same hole with the prairie dog is found frequently the *burrowing owl*, and often upon the summits of their little burrows may be seen the solemn owl on one side of the hole in stately silence; while on the other side is the lively little prairie dog, squatted on the fattest part with head bobbed up, and fore paws hanging down, ready at the slightest noise to dart headfirst into his hole. In some of these holes rattlesnakes have been found. What harmony or congruity there can be in the lives of these three diverse species of creatures to help form a happy family, no one can give the reason, but all accounts seem to agree that the stately owl and the treacherous snake make their home with the little dogs, to abuse the hospitality of their four-footed friends by devouring their young.

The scene presented by one of these dog villages is very curious. The prairie dog is no less inquisitive than timid. On the approach of an intruder, the little creature gives a sharp yelp of alarm, and dives into its burrow, its example being at once followed by all its neighbors. For an instant the village appears to be deserted; but soon their curiosity gets the better of their prudence, and their inquisitive little noses are seen protruding from their burrows, to ascertain the cause of the alarm, a curiosity which often costs them dear. The prairie dog is remarkably tenacious of life, and unless shot in the head is sure to escape into its hole. The writer has often seen attempts to shoot them from the train as it passes. Away scampers the little dog, stomach so full that it touches the ground, while little feet pulled for dear life for its own hole, and by its side or under it traveled the livelier bullet, each tearing up a stream of dust quicker than the eye can follow. Attempts have been made to tame them as pets, but they rarely ever live long, and have too apt a way of biting off fingers. They live only on the roots of grasses, not being flesh eaters.

Burton, an early traveler across the continent in 1861, was immensely interested in his examination of a prairie dog village. The Indians call them "*Wish-ton-wish*," from some slight resemblance to this cry.

"Wish-ton-wish" was at home, sitting posted like a sentinel upon the roof, and sunning himself in the mid-day glow. It is not easy to shoot him; he is out of doors all day, but timid and alert; at the least suspicion of danger he plunges with a jerking of the tail, and a somersault quicker than a shy young rabbit, into the nearest hole, peeping from the ground, and keeping up a feeble little cry, (wish-ton-wish!) more like the notes of a bird than a bark. If not killed outright, he will manage to wiggle into his home. The villages are generally on the brow of a hill, near a creek or pond, thus securing water without danger of drowning. The holes, which descend in a spiral form, must be deep, and are connected by long galleries, with sharp angles, ascents and descents, to puzzle the pursuer. Lieutenant Pike had 140 kettles of water poured into one without dislodging the occupant. The precincts of each village are always cleared of grass, upon which the animals live, as they rarely venture half a mile from home. In the winter time they stop the mouth of their burrows, and construct a deeper cell, where they live till spring appears.

The Indians and trappers eat the flesh, declaring it to be fatter and better than that of the squirrel. If the meat is exposed for a night or two to the frost, all rankness will be corrected. In the same hole are found rattlesnakes, the white burrowing owl, tortoises and horned frogs, the owl often gratifying his appetite by breaking open the skull of a young dog, with a smart stroke of his beak."

Iliff, the Cattle King of the Plains,

Has a range 150 miles long, a herd of 26,000 head, and is called the Great Cattle King of the plains, and has the "boss ranche" of this western country. This ranche is in northern Colorado. It begins at Julesburg, on the Union Pacific Railroad, and extends to Greeley, 156 miles west. Its southern boundary is the South Platte River; its northern, the divide, rocky and bluffy, just south of the Lodge Pole Creek. It has nearly the shape of a right-angled triangle, the right angle being at Greeley, the base line being the South Platte River. The streams flowing through it are, first,

PRAIRIE DOG CITY.

the river just named, Crow Creek, and other small creeks and streams which take their rise in living springs, in and near the bluffs of the divide mentioned, and flow in a southerly direction into the South Platte River. It includes bottom and upland ranges, and has several camps or ranches. The chief ranche is nearly south of Sidney, and about forty miles from Julesburg. At this ranche there are houses, sheds, stables, and corrals, and more than two sections of land fenced in. All the cattle bought by Mr. Iliff are rebranded and turned over to him at this place. Here are his private stock yards, with corrals, chutes, pens and all necessary conveniences for handling cattle. It is near the river, and of course has fine watering facilities, while from the adjoining bottom lands plenty of hay may be cut for the use of the horses employed in herding. He cuts no hay for his cattle; they live the entire year on the rich native grasses on his range, and with the exception of a severe winter, now and then, the percentage of loss is not very great.

Mr. Iliff is a thorough cattle man, and from his long experience has a perfect knowledge of the business. He began in 1860, and during the war had government contracts to fill, in New Mexico and other frontier territories. He supplied most of the beef to the contractors who built the Union Pacific Railroad, and brought immense herds of cattle from Texas and the Indian Territory which were driven along the line of the road to supply the army of laborers with beef. He has been engaged in the stock business in Kansas, New Mexico, and now in Colorado, and thinks his present location is admirably adapted to it, if the sheep men will only keep out. Cattle and sheep will not do well on the same range together. Success in either requires separation. Mr. Iliff has purchased and now owns more than twenty thousand acres of the range he occupies, which, of course, includes the choice springs and watering places within its limits, and will, undoubtedly, purchase more land as soon as it comes into market.

He now has more than 26,000 head of cattle, of all ages, sizes and conditions. The number of calves branded on his ranche, last year, reached nearly 5,000 head, and his sales of three and four-year-old steers and fat cows, last season, reached nearly the same number. He realized about $32 per head, net, on these sales. At this rate, 4,000 head would bring him the snug little sum of $128,000. To take care of this immense herd, he employs from twelve to thirty-five men—very few, usually, in the winter months, and the largest number during the "round ups" in the spring. During the shipping season of 1875, he had twenty-four men who were employed in cutting out of his herd the four-year-old steers that were ready for market, some fat three-year-olds, and such fat cows as were no longer fit for breeding purposes. While engaged in this work, the same men gather the cows with unbranded calves, which they put into the corrals near by, and after the calves are branded they are turned loose with the herd again. By the introduction of thoroughbred Durham bulls, his herd is rapidly being graded up. In addition to the cattle raised on his ranche, he deals largely in Texas and Indian cattle, and last season advertised for 20,000 head of Texas cattle to be delivered on his ranche during the driving months of 1876. These cattle must be yearlings, two and three-year-old steers, and for them he expects to pay $7, $11 and $15 per head, respectively. This is, at least, 10 per cent. advance on the prices paid for the same kind of cattle in 1875, and indicates their growing scarcity in Texas. If he does not obtain this number from Texas, he will supply the deficiency with Oregon and Montana cattle, which are now beginning to come East.

Mr. Iliff estimates the increase of cattle from his home herd—outside of purchases and sales—to be about 70 per cent. per year, and about equally divided as to gender. He does not separate his bulls from the herd, but allows them to remain with it the entire year. In this part of his management, we believe he makes a mistake, as the percentage of increase would be much larger if no calves were born during the severe winter and spring months of each year. The loss in calves at these times must be very great. The shipping points for his ranche are at Pine Bluffs and Julesburg, on the Union Pacific, and at Deers' Trail on the Kansas Pacific. The most of his cattle, however, are shipped over the first-mentioned road.

Lest any one should come to the conclusion that this business is all profit, and that the expenses and losses do not amount to much, let us further state that Mr. Iliff's policy is to keep his expenses as low as possible, having the keeping and safety of his cattle constantly in view. In 1875, the expenses of herding, cutting hay for horses, etc., amounted to less than $15,000. But the losses from thefts and death, some years, are frightful. The winter of 1871–2 was very severe. There were deep snows over his range that remained on the ground a long time, and the storms were incessant. In the midst of these storms, Mr. Iliff visited the ranche, and found his cattle literally dying by thousands. On the islands in South Platte River, he found and drove off into the sand-hills and bluffs, on the south side, after great exertion, some 2,700 head, and of this number less than half were recovered. Their bleaching bones now whiten the plains in the vicinity where they were frozen and starved to death, and those finally recovered were found in two different States and four different Territories in the Union. More than $20,000 were expended in efforts to find them; nor was this all. It was impossible to tell, for a number of years, how great the loss had been. His books showed more than 5,000 head unaccounted for. No trace of them, beyond skeletons, could be found. At last, in the spring of 1874, this number was charged to profit and loss account, and the books balanced for a new start. Could they have been sold the fall previous, they would have averaged at least $18 per head, and at this rate would have amounted to $90,000.

It will thus be seen that the cattle business is not all profit; that it is liable to losses the same as any other business. Taking the years together, with ordinary care and judgment, the business will pay large profits and prove a desirable investment. We would not, however, advise every man to undertake it. It is a business that must be learned, and to succeed in it men must have experience, capital, and a good range. Mr. Iliff has all of these, and hence is meeting with corresponding success. The 26,000 head he now has, he thinks, on an average, are worth $18 per head. This rate would place the capital he has invested in cattle at the sum of $468,000. In addition to this he has 160 head of horses and mules, worth at least $10,000, which are used, principally, in herding, together with wagons, horses, fences, corrals, sheds, stables, mowing-machines, tools and implements, and the large track of land before mentioned. Half a million dollars is a low estimate to name as the sum he has invested in this business, and yet from its very nature he is liable to lose half of it in the next year. Like other business ventures, if a man goes into it, of course he takes the chances, but with care and good management we see no reason why he should not, in nine cases out of ten, win every time. Let the facts speak for themselves. Ordinary men can't raise a half million dollars, every day, for such an investment, and if they could command that amount, very few would desire a stock ranche and the cattle business.

THE BULLWHACKER OF THE PLAINS.

Bullwhackers.—A curious character of overland life, when the plains were covered with teams, and long trains of freight-wagons, was the bullwhacker. He is in size and shape usually of very large proportions; very strong, long, unkempt hair, and face covered with the stiffest of beards. Eight or ten yoke of oxen were usually attached to each wagon, and often two wagons were doubled up; i. e., the tongue of the second wagon passed under the body of the wagon just before it, and then securely fastened. By the side of his wagon hang his trusty axe and ready rifle, and on the tops of the wagons were spread the red blankets used for their cover at night. Of the bullwhacker, it is said that his *oath* and his *whip* are both the longest ever known. The handle of the ordinary whip is not more than three feet in length, but the lash, which is of braided rawhide, is seldom less than twenty feet long. From the wooden handle, the lash swells gradually out for about six feet, where it is nearly ten inches in circumference (the point called the "belly"); from here it tapers to within a foot of the end, which terminates in the form of a ribbon-shaped thong. This is called by some facetiously a "persuader," and under its influence it will make the ox-team progress at the magic rate of twenty miles per day. The effect on a refractory ox is quite forcible. The lazy ox occasionally receives a reminder in the shape of a whack in the flank, that causes him to double up as if seared with a red-hot iron.

The bullwhacker is universally regarded as the champion swearer of America. He is more profane than the mate of a Mississippi River packet, and his own word is good to the effect that he "*kin drink more whisky.*" The writer who heard this, says that "accompanying this statement were *some of the most astounding oaths that ever fell on the ear.*"

General Sherman humorously tells a story in defence of the extremely profane mule-driver who kept his trains so well closed up during the long marches of the army under his command. It is to this effect: "One of the members of a freighting firm in St. Louis desired to discourage the continual blasphemy of the bullwhackers in their employ. Orders were accordingly issued to their train-masters to discharge any man that should curse the cattle. The wagon-masters were selected more for their piety than for any extensive knowledge of their duties in the handling of trains. The outfit had not proceeded more than a hundred and fifty miles, before it was stuck fast. A messenger was dispatched to the firm with the information that the cattle would not pull a pound unless they were *cursed as usual.* Permission to do this was requested and granted, after which the train proceeded to Salt Lake, to which place good time was made."

The bullwhacker is astonishingly accurate with his lash. One of his favorite pastimes is to cut a coin from the top of a stick stuck loosely into the earth. If the coin is knocked off without disturbing the stake, it is his; if the stake is disturbed, the thrower loses the value of the coin. A curious incident is told of a bullwhacker, noted for the accuracy with which he throws his lash. He bet a comrade a pint of whisky that he could cut the cloth on the back of his pantaloons without touching the skin beneath. The bet was accepted. The individual put himself in position, stooping over to give fair chance. The blow was delivered carefully but in earnest, and thereon ensued the tallest jump ever put on record. The owner being minus a portion of his skin, as well as a large fragment of his breeches, and the bullwhacker's sorrowful cry, "*Thunder, I've lost the whisky.*"

Chappell,—387.4 miles from Omaha. Elevation 3,702 feet. It is a side track with section-house near by. Trains meet and pass here, but passenger trains do not stop unless signaled.

Lodge Pole—has an elevation of 3,800 feet, and is 396.5 miles west of Omaha. The creek from which this station is named, rises in the Black Hills of Wyoming, west of Cheyenne, and is fed by springs and numerous small streams near its source. It generally has water in its channel the entire year. In occasional places it sinks into the sand, runs a distance under-ground, and then reappears on the surface again. The valley of the Lodge Pole is quite narrow—the bluffs on either side at times approaching near the track. The whole region of country upon which we have now entered, is covered with buffalo grass, and affords both winter and summer grazing for immense herds of cattle and flocks of sheep. Stockmen claim that both cattle and sheep will do better in this region than farther east, for the reason that the native grasses are more nutritious, and that there is less snow in the winter.

Colton,—406.5 miles from Omaha, and 4,022 feet above the sea. It is simply a side track, named in honor of Francis Colton of Galesburg, Ill., and formerly general ticket agent of the road.

Sidney—is 414.2 miles from the Missouri River, and 4,073 feet above the sea. It is the end of a sub-division of the road, and has a roundhouse and machinery adequate for making minor repairs. The railroad reached and passed here in August, 1867. The rocky bluffs which jut up close to the town, were quarried by the railroad men, and stone obtained for various construction purposes. It is now a regular eating-station, where all passenger trains stop for breakfast and supper. The railroad hotel is kept by J. B. Rumsey, and passengers may be assured of good meals, with plenty of time to eat, as the trains stop thirty minutes. Sidney is the county-seat of Cheyenne County, Neb. The military post here known as Sidney Barracks, was laid out in 1867, and built in January, 1868, by Colonel Porter. The town has several stores, hotels, saloons and general outfitting establishments. It is the nearest railroad point to the Black Hills, it being only 185 miles by actual measurement to Harney's Peak, and the adjacent gold fields, over an excellent wagon road, with wood and water convenient of access. Several parties have already outfitted here for these mines, and the town expects to obtain quite a share of the travel to that region. It has a weekly stage line already established to Spotted Tail's Agency, which could easily be made a daily line. It is the point where large quantities of military and Indian supplies are shipped to the agencies and military posts adjoining. It also has a weekly newspaper, *The Sidney Telegraph*, which is quite an enterprising sheet. The town still has the characteristics of a frontier place, and not a small number of roughs have died here "with their boots on." In December, 1875, a man was found hanging to a telegraph pole one morning, who had shot another in cold blood, and without provocation. He was taken from the jail and jailer by masked men and strung up as aforesaid. The town was begun about the time the railroad passed through. D. Carrigan, now probate judge of the county, and James and

Charles Moore being the first settlers. James Moore was the post trader here for a long time. He is now dead. In the time of the Pony Express he made the remarkable trip of 280 miles in fourteen hours and three-quarters. The town has had trouble with Indians, and was once attacked by them, as related in another place. Even after the trains were running regularly, the Indians would seek for revenge in ditching them and in killing all the employes they could. Section-men always went armed, ready to defend themselves in case of attack. In April of 1869, the Indians attacked two section-men who had gone to the creek for water, and one of them, Daniel Davidson, was killed—his body being literally filled with arrows. Right north of the town, where the traveler can see a small column of stones, was an old fort or breastwork, the remains of which are still visible, which was used as a place of defense in case of Indian raids. A bridge across the North Platte River, on the road to Spotted Tail's Agency, would largely increase the trade and importance of the town. In 1875, the assessed valuation of Cheyenne County was about $1,250,000. There are a large number of stockmen in the county.

Beautiful Cloud Effects.—Artists and all travelers, as they get nearer and nearer to the summit of the Rocky Mountains, will often have fine opportunities to see some magnificent cloud effects. The most glorious sunset ever witnessed by the writer, was one beautiful evening in passing down the line of the Denver Pacific Railroad from Cheyenne. Long's Peak, grand in its sublimity of snow, was surrounded with a collection of clouds, so poised that the rays of the setting sun showed us each side of them. On the hither side the fleecy clouds were lighted up with the grandest of crimson and golden colors; in their midst opened little circular or oval windows, which, letting light upon their upper portions, seemed to be of molten silver; while in their depth of deep azure blue—more beautiful than we can describe—there seemed to glow the intense colors and reflections from the bosom of a mountain lake. Every few minutes the clouds, at our distance from them, changed their position, and new colors, forms, and rays came and went, and when at last the sun itself dropped slowly behind the very point of the peak, and it shone out in startling clearness with the grand display of rainbow-colored clouds above; the sight seemed like a heavenly vision. The editors of the New York and Eastern Editorial Excursion Party of 1875, who witnessed the scene, expressed but one sentiment of admiration, that it was far the most superb cloud and sunset scene ever witnessed. Such scenes are very frequent, and exceedingly captivating to those who have a true artist's eye and appreciation of colors and effects.

An English traveler (to whom beautiful sunsets are unknown) when once traveling from Ogalalla toward Laramie, over the plains, says, "As we journeyed, the sun approached the horizon, and the sky and numerous clouds assumed columns of strange and wonderful beauty. The 'azure vault' itself was of all possible shades of light green, and also of clear light blue; some of the clouds were of solid masses of the deepest indigo, while a few were black, some were purple, and others faintly tinged with crimson and gold. Two days before, I had witnessed cloud effects almost equally fine. There is no monotony in the glorious dawns or beautiful sunsets, which are the rule on these elevated plains, and which go far to relieve the tameness of the landscape.

"As evening approached, on my journey to Laramie, and I neared my destination on the great mountain plains, I saw hovering over one of the snow-capped peaks, a richly colored cloud, so curious in form, and withal so perfect that it might well have been considered a miraculous omen, in the superstitious days of old. It was a most accurate representation of a long waving ostrich plume, in varying tints of crimson and purple and gold; I gazed on it with pleasure and wonder till it faded away."

Sunset in a Storm.—The Earl of Dunraven, in an account of his travels, mentions with wonder these extraordinary sunset scenes: "Just before sundown, the gorgeous flaunting streamers of bright yellow and red that were suddenly shot out across a lurid sky were most wonderful to behold. If the vivid colors were transferred to canvas with a quarter of their real brilliancy, the eye would be distressed by the representation, and the artist accused of gross exaggeration and of straining after outrageous effects.

"These stormy American sunsets are startling, barbaric, even savage in their brilliancy of tone, in their profusion of color, in their great streaks of red and broad flashes of yellow fire; startling, but never repulsive to the senses, or painful to the eye. For a time the light shone most brilliantly all over the western hemisphere, breaking through a confused mass of dazzling purple-edged clouds, massed against a glowing, burnished copper sky, darting out bright arrows through the rifts and rents, and striking full upon the mountain top.

"But not long did this glorious effulgence last. The soul of the evening soon passed away; as the sun sank, the colors fled. The mountains became of a ghastly, livid greenish color, and as the faint rose light paled, faded slowly upward and vanished, it really looked as though the life were ebbing away, and the dull gray death-hue spreading over the face of a dying man."

Sunset Scene on Mount Washburne.—The Earl of Dunraven ascending, in the summer of 1874, the summit of Mt. Washburne was rewarded at sunset with a scene of extraordinary magnificence, which he relates as follows: "The sun was getting very low, and the valleys were already steeped in shade. To the east all was dark, but in the western heavens long flaming streaks of yellow were flashing across a lowering sky. The masses of black clouds were glowing red with an angry flush. The clear white light of a watery sun had changed into broad streaks of flaunting saffron. Across all the hemisphere, opposed to it, the setting orb was shaking out the red and yellow folds of its banners, challenging the forces of the storm, which was marshaling on the horizon its cloud warriors resplendent in burnished gold.

"The sun sank behind a cloud, and I turned away to descend; but as we went, the sun, though invisible to us, broke through some hidden rift in the clouds, and shone out bright and strong, splashing its horizontal rays full against the opposite slope, and deluging the lower portions of the valley with a flood of intense cherry-colored lurid light. The hills reddened as if beat upon by the full glare of a great furnace. It was a sight most glorious to see. The beauty of it held us and forced us to stop. The glow did not gradually ripen into fullness, but suddenly, and in all its intensity, struck upon a prominent ridge, lighting up the crags and cliffs, and even the rocks and stones, in all their details, and then by degrees it extended and spread on either side over the foot-hills, bringing out the projecting slopes and shoulders from deep gloom into clear light, and throwing back the valley into blackest shade. Every rock and precipice seemed close at hand, and shone and glowed with such radiance that you could trace the very rents and crevices in the cliff faces, and mark the pine trees clinging to the sides, while in comparison the deep recesses of the chasms and canons seemed to extend for miles back into dark shadow. As the sun sank, so rose the light, rushing upward, surging over the hills in a wave of crimson mist, really beautiful to behold, and illuminating the great bulk of the range, while the peaks were still darkly rearing their sullen heads above the tide, and the valleys were all filled with gray vapors. At last the glare caught the mist, and in an instant transformed it from gray cloud into a gauzy, half-transparent veil, light, airy, delicate exceedingly, in color like the inner petals of the rose. Then, as the sun dropped suddenly, the light flashed upon the summit, the peaks leaped into startling life, and the darkness fell."

Brownson.—Simply a side track. Elevation 4,200 feet above the sea. Distance from Omaha, 423.2 miles. The station was named after a former general freight agent of the Union Pacific. From Sidney, and in this vicinity, the bluffs are rugged, and look like fortifications or the old castles that we read about. They are simply indications of the grand scenery which is to follow.

Potter.—433.1 miles from Omaha. Elevation 4,370 feet. It is a telegraph station. West of Potter you cross the bed of a dry creek, which leads into the Lodge Pole.

Bennett.—Another side track, at which passenger trains do not stop. There is a fine stock ranche near by, and the grazing in this vicinity is excellent. The station is named after Colonel Bennett, the efficient superintendent of the Pullman Palace Car Company at Omaha. It is 442.3 miles from the eastern terminus of the road, with an elevation of 4,580 feet.

Antelope.—451.3 miles from Omaha. Elevation, 4,712 feet. A telegraph and coal station, with side tracks and section-house. In November, 1875, the Indians, who have a liking for good and fast horses, equal to that of Bonner, the *New York Ledger* man, went to the ranche of Mr. Jones, a Kentuckian, about twenty miles south of this station, and stole some forty head of blooded horses and mares which he had there for breeding purposes. They are supposed—believed—to have gone north, and if Uncle Sam's Indian agents would withhold rations from the tribe until they were brought back, or make a thorough search for them, they could undoubtedly be found. Many of the animals were thoroughbreds, and very valuable. Here is another violation of the Sioux treaty. Mr. Jones will have to pocket his loss, while Uncle Sam will, of course, pocket the insult. Antelope is the home of some old hunters, and if the traveler desires to hear their experiences, let him stop a day and interview Jack Evans, who has a ranche here, and Mr. Goff, who has been engaged in the business some fourteen years.

Landscape of the Colorado Plains.—There is a charm in life on the great plains. To one who visits it for the first time, it seems lonely indeed, and yet it is never wearisome.

Now come great rolling uplands of enormous sweep, then boundless grassy plains, and all the grandeur of vast monotony and desolation. Sometimes the grand distances are broken by rugged buttes and bluffs. As they rise in sight, the traveler is as eager in his curiosity as the sea voyager just catching his first view of the distant shore. Over all these plains there is a sparkling, enthusiasm-giving atmosphere, crisp, strong, magnetic, and a never-failing breeze; even in the hottest days, or portions of the day, the air is bracing, and rarely ever is the sky long cloudless.

That vastness of solitude, boundless plains, and boundless sky, that stretch of blue, that waste of brown, never a tree, river, bird, or animal, home or life of any nature, who can describe the sensations, which are so overpowering.

As you approach the mountains, the Colorado plains assume more verdure, as they are better watered by the little streams from the foot-hills, or bedewed by the mountain showers. In summer time the landscape is green, and the plains covered with flowers, while in autumn, with the yellow of the prairie grass, the flowers ever stay, new ones coming as old ones disappear. The sunflower is the most profuse of all the species of vegetation that spring up wherever the soil is opened. For thousands of miles, wherever the railroad or a wagon route has made its way across the country, there spring up parallel rows of the ever-living sunflower. In the eastern portions of the plains of Nebraska and Kansas, near the Missouri River, may be seen square miles of sunflowers, 7 to 9 feet high; as we travel farther west, they gradually dwindle until they are, in Colorado, only 3 to 9 *inches* in height, the oddest little plant in nature, yet perfect in shape and growth.

years yet to come, to be only the grazing-field of thousands of buffalo or herds of cattle. Water is scarce, irrigation is impossible, rains uncertain, and in many parts the soil is full of soda and alkali. The western march of settlement practically ends at the one hundredth meridian of longitude—North Platte.

Coyotes.—Pioneers, Indians and drivers, unite in the most thrilling exclamations of their detestations of this, the meanest of the animal tribe that infest the plains. Just after twilight, if you happen to be encamped on the plains, you will hear not far off the quick bark of a single coyote. This is the first call, the bugle cry. Then come answers, and the pack of wolves assemble rapidly; and just as darkness closes down, you have but one enjoyment left, to listen to the most

COYOTES.

Into this vast area of plains, which reaches from east to west 500 miles, and north to south 1,000 miles, there can be poured nearly all the population of Europe and Asia. Swallowing up by the thousands, the plains, with open mouth, wait with insatiate appetite for more. Into this area can be put the whole of India. It is twice as large as Hindostan, and as large as the whole of the United States east of Chicago.

Agriculture is certain as far west as the three hundredth mile from the Missouri River; from thence westward, to the immediate vicinity of the mountains, no crops can at present be raised. This reach of 200 miles or more is, for many

dismal of howling matches. As each new comer arrives he is welcomed with a howl. Each howl is short, and by the band there seems to be a chosen few who execute them in proper manner, with all the variations. After these few have performed some of their most "striking airs," a silence of a few moments' duration follows, and then the whole band breaks out with the most unearthly noises, which are second to no other noises of plains and mountains. Kit Carson once said of these howls, "that it was only a little dispute as to which coyote had, as the winner of the match, the right to take the stakes (steaks)." A traveler says of them: "It is quite impossible to do full justice to this wolf music. There is no racket known to the inhabitants of the more civilized sections of our country which will compare with it. All the felines in the neighborhood would not make a noise which would begin to equal wolf music." Strange as it may seem, the rough pioneer esteems this music his sweetest lullaby, for as one of the old "rough and readies" says: "If any redskin should take it under his scalp to look about camp, every cuss of them coyotes would shut up his trap and wake the fellows up with the *quiet*." So long as the coyote cries there is no danger from Indians—the moment he ceases, danger is near—so the pioneer esteems their music his best lullaby, and their bark his safety. Occasionally the pack, toward early morning, will make a raid into the traveler's camp, and grab any edibles or pieces left within reach; even sometimes seizing the very haversack upon which the sleeper's head is pillowed, but seldom ever touching the persons of the campers. As morning approaches, they retire to a safe distance from camp, and squatted on their haunches like dogs, wait till the party leaves.

The *plains men* have an old saying, "That the coyotes can smell a *States feller*, and then you will not see a coyote anywhere within sight of camp." The explanation for which is supposed to be as follows, given also by the old plains men: "States fellers shoots at any live thing as jumps in their sight, whether it is any 'count to them or no."

Adams.—A side track 457.3 miles from Omaha; elevation 4,784 feet. The country here is considerably broken, and between the bluffs on either side huge boulders crop out.

Bushnell,—463.2 miles from Omaha, and 4,860 feet above the sea. It is simply a side track with water tank. In coming up this valley the railroad crosses the Lodge Pole Creek, or its little branches, several times. Near Bushnell is a trestle bridge across the creek.

Hailstorms.—This region of country is frequently, in summer, visited with hailstorms and cloud-bursts. In the summer of 1875, a train was overtaken by one of these hailstorms, and not a whole pane of glass was left in the side of the cars toward the storm. The glass in skylights on the top of the cars was broken, and many of the hailstones, as large as a man's fist, bounded through the cars on the opposite side. The wooden sides of the cars were dented, and the sheet-iron casing of the engine-boiler looked as though it had passed through a violent case of the small-pox. When these cloud-bursts occur, the drops of rain seem as large as walnuts, and come so fast that the entire surface of the ground is covered—the surplus water not having time to run off. In such storms the road is liable to washouts, and great care is necessary in the running of trains to avoid accidents.

Bushnell is the last station in Nebraska. Just across the line, between it and Wyoming, comes

Pine Bluffs,—473.2 miles from Omaha; elevation 5,026 feet. The little station takes its name from the stunted pines along the bluffs. Pine timber once was plenty here, but it disappeared when the road was built. It is the great trail and crossing point for Indians passing from the buffalo grounds on the Republican to Horse Creek and North Platte River. Was several times attacked by Indians during construction of road, several were killed and large amounts of stock stolen. It is now the head-quarters of Judge Tracy's cattle ranche, and several carloads of cattle are shipped each year. Muddy Creek is just west of station, has water most of the time, yet Lodge Pole Creek, beyond Egbert, sinks in the sand. Water can be found in the bed of the stream by digging 3 to 9 feet. This is a telegraph station, with side track, cattle-yards and chutes.

Tracy,—478.8 miles from Omaha; elevation 5,149 feet. It is a side track named in honor of Judge Tracy of Cheyenne.

Egbert,—484.4 miles from Omaha; elevation 5,272 feet. It is a side track with water tank. Three miles south of this side track runs the Muddy, which has quite a settlement of ranchemen. The Lodge Pole at this point is still dry, and the company dug thirty-two feet for the water which supplies their tank. The road here leaves the main valley of the Lodge Pole, to the right, and runs up a branch, in which the bed of a creek is visible, but which never has water in it except after the cloud-bursts spoken of.

Burns,—490.7 miles from the Missouri River, with an elevation of 5,428 feet. The grade is now quite heavy as we are going up on to the divide between the Lodge Pole and Crow Creek. Burns is simply a side track where trains occasionally meet and pass.

Hillsdale,—a telegraph station with side track and section-house. The place takes its name from a Mr. Hill, who was killed here by the Indians at the time the road was located. He belonged to the engineer corps of the road. The company's well here, which supplies the water tank, is 72 feet deep. North and south of this station numerous sheep ranches have been opened. By looking straight west, up the track, you can here obtain the first glimpse of the Black Hills of Wyoming—and they will come into plain view as you ascend the heavy grade toward the divide. Hillsdale is 5,591 feet above the sea, and 496.4 miles from Omaha. Notice the grade indicated by the elevations as you pass these stations.

Atkins,—502.6 miles from Omaha, and 5,800 feet above the sea. It is a side track, simply, with water tank and section-house near by. The well which supplies this station with water is over 200 feet deep. Here the traveler obtains a good view of the Black Hills stretching off to the right. Still up the grade you go, reaching the summit of the divide in the first snow shed on the line of the road just beyond

Archer,—which is 508 miles from the starting place, with an elevation of 6,000 feet above tide-water. This station is a side track with section-house near by. A short distance farther, you enter the shed; it seems like passing through a tunnel. In the distance there are mountains "to the right of you," and mountains "to the left of you," but we shall see more of them hereafter. Leaving the snow shed we are now on a down grade into Crow Creek Valley, which makes its way through the bluffs off to the left. Soon we come to a deep cut through the spur of a bluff, passing which, we cross a bridge over a dry ravine, and then continue up the hill to the "Magic City" of the plains, called Cheyenne.

Long's Peak.—Travelers will notice, a few hours before reaching Cheyenne, the snow-clad summit of this bold peak, rising above the distant horizon. It is about sixty miles south-west of the Union Pacific Railroad, and the highest mountain in northern Colorado. The view we here give is taken from Estes Park; a beautiful

LONG'S PEAK FROM ESTES PARK.

little park on its north-western slope, and about twelve miles distant from the summit. This park is about four miles wide, and six miles long, is well sheltered, easy of access, and beautifully covered with pine and spruce trees, scattered easily about over the grassy surface, which gives to it a true park-like loveliness. It is partially occupied by a few families who have taken up permanent homesteads, and has been for a long time an excellent pasture for large herds of cattle which live here the entire year. It is also becoming quite a pleasure resort, and has many attractive features to interest the health seeker and tourist. Excellent fishing, in lovely little trout streams, can be found all over the vicinity. From this valley is the only practicable route for ascending the peak. Long's Peak is 14,271 feet in elevation, and about 6,300 feet above the park. Its construction is of the boldest and most decided character, with great walls, deep canons; and on its sides there are gorges and caverns among the grandest on the continent. Its summit is divided into two sharp crests, the western one being the highest and most difficult of ascent. It is a famous landmark for a stretch of country of more than a hundred miles from north to south.

Buffaloes. — Buffalo hunting is a pastime tourists can now have little hope to indulge in. Few or no buffaloes ever appear within sight of the car windows of the overland trains, and the vast herds which once roamed for thousands of miles and continually up and down the great plain, are passing away, or disappearing from their old haunts to find some nook or corner more quiet and secure. Thousands of them have been killed during the past two or three winters for commercial purposes. The hides are stripped off and sold for as low prices as $1.50, while the bones are gathered in heaps near the railroad station and freighted eastward to be used for commercial fertilizers. In one winter it is estimated that on the lines of the Union and Kansas Pacific Railroad there were killed over 100,000 head.

A Smart Indian Trade. — The Indians which in olden times used to visit the military posts, were noticeable for their great anxieties to trade, and for their great shrewdness, which had often the spice of humor.

At one of the posts a Kiowa chief endeavored to consummate a bargain for an officer's wife, by offering as an equivalent a large number of *fat dogs;* the number was so large that the Indians present thinking it was impossible for the officer to withstand so tempting an offer, made haste to express their willingness to *help eat the dogs*, if there were more than the white man could manage for himself.

But it is among the Indians themselves that the sharpest species of trading is seen. In the great passion of the Indian for "fire-water"— whisky—there comes out, in their trade for it, all the possible shrewdness and cunning of the races.

At one time, as a military officer relates the story, there was a Kiowa village, beautifully located for the winter near a grove of old cotton-wood trees. The fact that the village was rich in buffalo robes and other skins became known to a band of the Cheyenne tribe. Stealing would not answer, as there were too many Kiowas and too few Cheyennes. But the shrewdness of the Cheyennes appeared soon in the shape of a bottle of whisky; how they obtained it was a mystery not explained.

With their whisky, the Cheyennes proceeded to the Kiowa village, exhibited their bottles, and distributed around a few judicious smells of the refreshing corn juice; every now and then giving the bottle a shake, so that the aroma should be thoroughly appreciated by *their friends the Kiowas.*

The smells were freely accepted, and there was an uncommon desire manifested to know more (i. e., get better acquainted) of the Cheyennes. Pipes were produced and duly smoked; after which the visitors announced their willingness to trade, as they said.

"They had not brought much whisky, as they did not know that their brothers, the Kiowas would like to see it. The little that they had with them was good and very strong," (with water) "when the Kiowas had tasted of it they would see." The Cheyenne was liberal, "he would give so much," (holding up the bottle and marking with the thumb something like half an inch of the whisky). "But seeing that the Kiowas were not in haste to trade, the Cheyennes would smoke with them." Meanwhile a kindly disposed bottle-holder was dispensing smells of the whisky to a few Kiowas, who were loud in their announcements of the number of fine robes which they possessed. This second smoke was quickly finished, and the Cheyenne again exhibited the *fire-water*, marking it as before by the location of the thumb on the bottle.

A general exclamation followed, for to the Kiowa's eye the position of the thumb on the bottle was so very much higher (i. e., so much less whisky than before). To this Cheyenne had no consideration; the trouble he said, was with the eyes of the Kiowas, which could not be expected to see big like those of a Cheyenne. Another smelling time ensued, which was followed by an instantaneous exhibition by the Kiowas of tin cups and robes, and the Cheyennes began to pour out the whisky.

While pouring out the promised grog, the position of the thumb on the bottle was regarded by each Kiowa with the most exact scrutiny, which effectually prevented all attempts to shove up the gauge. And it was noticeable by the care of the bottle-holders, that when the bottle was held up after each pass, no Indian could detect the

THE DOME OF THE CONTINENT, GRAY'S PEAK, COLORADO.

slightest variation between the whisky mark and the position of the finger on the bottle.

The Kiowas did not get drunk, and the Cheyennes left the village with all their ponies loaded with robes, having as they freely remarked, made a "*heap smart trade.*"

Astonishment of Indians at the Locomotive and Telegraphs.—When the first locomotive was seen passing over the plains, an Indian guide in the employ of the United States, exclaimed with inexpressible surprise, "Good Medicine, *good medicine.* Look look," at the tu-te (toot). As he passed under the telegraph wires which then were stretching along the Platte, through which the wind as it swept, made the whirr and singing sound of a *prairie harp*, this guide heard the sound, and directly declared that they were talking "*medicines.*" This was supposed to be the creations of the *great spirit*, and everything of supernatural nature was "*medicine.*"

The Indians have rarely ever molested the telegraph wires which spanned the continent. Perhaps the following incident may have much to do with their respectful and distant attitude:—Shortly after the wires were erected, the attaches of the Telegraph Company invited a number of Indian chiefs to meet them at a given point, and from thence to travel, one party East and the other West.

When they had reached a distance of 100 miles apart, each party was invited to dictate a message to the other, which was sent over the wires. Then turning backward, they rode rapidly toward each other, and two days later met and compared notes. They were greatly astonished, and expressed themselves convinced that the "*Great Spirit*" had talked to them with the wires. They decided from that time it would be well to avoid meddling with the wires.

Soon after a little incident happened, which, in the minds of the Indians, seemed to settle forever the opinion that the telegraph belonged to the Great Spirit. A young Sioux Indian was determined to show that he had no faith in the Great Spirit's connection with the wires, so he set to work with his hatchet to cut down one of the telegraph poles. A severe thunder-storm was going on at a distance; a charge of electricity being taken up by the wires, was passed to the pole which the Indian was cutting, and resulted in his instant death. After that the tribe never molested the telegraph again.

An Indian Prayer.—The following actual translation of an Indian prayer will give an idea of their feelings and longings, and the extent of their moral sentiments. It is a prayer to the Great Spirit by a Crow Indian:

"I am poor; that is bad."

"Make me a Chief; give me plenty of horses; give me fine clothing. I ask for good spotted horses."

"Give me a large tent; give me a great many horses; let me steal fine horses; grant it to me."

"Give me guns by cheating; give me a beautiful woman; bring the buffalo close by."

"No deep snow; a little snow is good."

"Give me Black Feet to kill or to die; close by, all together."

"Stop the people from dying, it is good."

"Give instruments for amusements, blankets too, and fine meats to eat."

"Give the people altogether plenty of fine buffalo, and plenty to eat."

CHEYENNE.

"Magic City of the Plains,"—516 miles from Omaha; elevation, 6,041 feet. Thus truly is it named, for it is at present the most active and stirring city on the entire line. Travelers will here take a dinner in comfortable style at one of the best kept hotels between the two oceans. It is a good place to rest after a tiresome journey, and it will pay to stop a few days and enjoy the pure air and genial sun in this high altitude. The hotel is owned by the railroad company, and is 150 feet long by 36 wide, with a wing 25 feet square. It has an elegant dining-hall, around which hang the heads of antelope, deer, elk, mountain-sheep, black-tailed deer, buffalo, etc., all nicely preserved and looking very natural. It is two stories high, the upper floor being well furnished with sleeping-rooms for guests. Cheyenne is the capital of Wyoming and the county-seat of Laramie County. Cheyenne has had its ups and downs. Once very lively when the road was building, then it fell dead and motionless. Now it has arisen again, and is the largest town on the railroad between Omaha and Salt Lake City, having a population of fully 4,000, and rapidly growing. There are two causes for this growth. First, the stock interests which center here, and second, the recent gold discoveries in the Black Hills. Up to the year 1875, it was the terminus of the Denver Pacific Railroad, and had the advantages of a competing line of railroad; but since the virtual consolidation of the Kansas Pacific and Union Pacific interests, it no longer enjoys these advantages. During the last two years there has been a large increase in the permanent buildings of the city. In 1875, the Inter-Ocean hotel was completed—a fine brick structure three stories high, and other large and elegant brick blocks with iron and glass fronts. In proportion to its population, Cheyenne has more elegant and substantial business houses than most any other western city. Its inflation period has long since passed away, and its future growth, like its present, will be substantial and permanent. The town has a fine court-house and jail, which cost $40,000, a large public school building, a good city hall, and a brick opera-house. This is a wonderful change for a place known the world over by its fearful sobriquet of "Hell on Wheels." Churches have come where gamblers once reigned; and in five years as many edifices for religious purposes have been erected. The Episcopalians, Methodists, Presbyterians, Congregationalists and Catholics have all comfortable church buildings. The school accommodations, owing to the rapid growth of the city, will soon have to be enlarged. At first sight the traveler would naturally inquire, what there was to build and sustain a town here? The soil is not prolific, nor is the country around it. Crow Creek bottom is quite narrow, and in the most favorable seasons, by irrigation, "garden truck" may be raised, but beyond this everything looks barren and desolate. The soil has a reddish appearance, and appears to consist of decomposed granite underlaid in the valleys with sand and on the uplands with rock. In fact, a man who attempts to farm it for a living in this region of country is simply fooling away his time.

Stock Interests.—The rich nutritious grasses with which the great plains are covered are here found in all their excellence, and the large territory east of the base of the Black Hills, north as far as the North Platte River and south to the Gulf of Mexico, is now sustaining millions of sheep and cattle. Cheyenne is located in the midst of one of the best sections of this territory, and all around it are the ranches of stockmen—men engaged in growing cattle, sheep, horses and mules for market. With the exception of sheep, no hay is cut for these animals except for those kept up for use. Winter and summer they thrive and fatten upon nothing but the native grasses. Cheyenne is the central and natural trading-point for these ranchmen and stock growers. Another large and valuable element of its prosperity is the railroad trade—the company having here quite extensive machine and repair shops, with a commodious roundhouse. Hunting and exploring parties also supply themselves with outfits at this place, and immense quantities of military and Indian supplies also pass through here for the posts and Indian agencies north.

To give an idea of the stock business which centers here, and its rapid increase, let us state that 375 cars of cattle were shipped in 1874. which represent 7,500 head. In 1875, the shipments increased to 525 cars, or 10,500 head, with prospects for a large increase in 1876 and future years. It may be well to state here, the shipments from other points in this grazing belt of the country:

North Platte	in 1875	shipped	96	cars, or	1,920	head.
Ogalalla,	"	"	207	"	4,140	"
Julesburg,	"	"	216	"	4,320	"
Sidney,	"	"	93	"	1,860	"
Pine Bluffs,	"	"	208	"	4,160	"

This statement does not include the cattle marketed at home or supplied to the Indian agencies in the north. Sixty thousand head of cattle, seventy thousand sheep and four thousand horses and mules are the estimated number owned and held in Laramie County alone. The development of the cattle and stock interests of this vast upland region is something never thought of nor entered the heads of the projectors of the railroad. In 1867, when the railroad first arrived, there was not probably a hundred head of all kinds owned in the whole territory, outside of those belonging to contractors and stage lines. Now it is a leading interest, and represents millions of dollars. Like all other frontier towns, Cheyenne has a history, and it is similar to that of others. It was once a very fast town, and it is not very slow now. On the 1st day of July, 1867, it had one house built and owned by Judge J. R. Whitehead, on Eddy street, between Sixteenth and Seventeenth. That house stands to-day, and is known as the Whitehead block. It was built of logs and smoothly plastered, outside and in.

Rough Times.—When it was known that this was to be the winter terminus of the road, there was a grand hegira of roughs, gamblers and prostitutes from Julesburg and other places down the road to this point, and in the fall of that year and winter of '68, Cheyenne contained 6,000 inhabitants. Habitations sprang up like mushrooms. They were of every conceivable character, and some were simply holes in the ground, otherwise termed "dug-outs." Town-lots were sold at fabulous prices. Every nation on the globe, nearly, was represented here. The principal pastimes were gambling, drinking villainous rot-gut whisky, and shooting. Shooting scrapes were an every-day occurrence. Stealing anything from anybody was the natural habit of the thieving roughs. Knock downs and robberies were daily and nightly amusements. But these things had to come to an end, and their perpetrators, some of them, to a rope's end. The more respectable portion of the citizens became weary of the depredations on property and life. Vigilance committees were organized, and "Judge Lynch" held court, from which there were neither appeals nor stay of executions. Juries never disagreed, nor were there vexatious delays and motions for a new trial. Witnesses were unnecessary and demurrers of no account. Nor would "the insanity dodge" avail. The victims were known and "spotted" beforehand, the judgments of the courts were unerring and generally righteous. No gallows were erected, because telegraph poles and the railroad bridge across Crow Creek were convenient of access. When Cheyenne was only six months old, so frequent were the murders and robberies, and the city authorities so powerless, that a vigilance committee was organized. The first knowledge of its existence happened thus: Three men were arrested on the 10th day of January, 1868, charged with having stolen $900. They were put under bonds to appear before the court on the 14th of the same month. On the morning of the day after they were arrested, they were found on Eddy street, tied together, walking abreast with a large piece of canvas attached to them, on which the following words were conspicuous: "$900 *stole; $500 returned; thieves—F. St. Clair, W. Grier, E. D. Brownville. City authorities please not interfere until 10 o'clock a. m. Next case goes up a tree. Beware of Vigilance Committee.*" Within one year after its organization, the "vigilantes" had hung and shot twelve desperadoes and sent five to the penitentiary. Since that time Cheyenne has been ruled by the law-and-order party, though even these may seem rather lax to eastern people not accustomed to the manners and customs of the frontier. Yet the people enjoy "peace."

On the 13th day of November, 1867, the track layers reached the city limits, and on the 14th the first passenger train arrived. The arrival of the track layers was greeted with music, a display of bunting, while the inhabitants turned out *en masse* to meet them. On the 14th an enthusiastic meeting of citizens was held to extend a public greeting to the railroad officials who had arrived on the first train, among whom were Sidney Dillon, Esq., now president of the company, and General Casement of Ohio, the champion track layer of the continent.

The first city government was organized, by the election of officers, on the 10th of August, 1867. The first newspaper was issued on the 19th of September, called the *Cheyenne Leader*, and has maintained its existence ever since—publishing daily and weekly editions. Other papers have since been started, but they were short-lived, until the publication of the *Cheyenne Daily News*, which is a spicy little daily. As the town is now able to support two papers, the *News* (just merged into the *Daily Sun*,) will continue to flourish.

Cheyenne is well laid out, with broad streets at right angles to the railroad, and has an abundant supply of pure water. Irrigating ditches run through the streets. A ditch was dug from Crow Creek to some natural "hollows" or reservoirs north of the town, which form beautiful little lakes. From these the water for the streets is taken by ditches. As a result, trees and shrubbery will soon ornament the streets and yards of the city, which will greatly add to its attractiveness and beauty. There are a few local manufactories already in existence and more will follow, and on a larger scale. With the wool which is soon to be annually shipped from this place, we should think a woolen factory would be a great desideratum.

Precious Stones.—In the adjacent mountains, on the hills and bluffs near by, and in the valleys of the streams in this vicinity, a large number of curious and precious stones, gems rich and rare, have been found. They are very plenty in their natural state, their chief value being in the cost of cutting by a lapidary and mounting by a jeweler. In the immediate neighborhood of Cheyenne the following are found: Moss-agates, in great profusion; topaz, in colors; garnet or mountain ruby; they are usually found in the little heaps of sand thrown up by ants; opals variegated, rare as yet, and valuable; petrifactions of wood and shells, which when cut, polished and mounted, are splendid; amethysts, onyx, black and white, for cameos and jasper. All of these have been found in this vicinity, though some are rare. The most beautiful moss-agates are found about halfway to Fort Laramie, on Chugwater Creek. Messrs. Joslyn & Park, an old and reliable firm of manufacturing jewelers, in both Cheyenne and Salt Lake City, have made this business a specialty, and possess the largest and finest collection of stones in the country. Some of them are exceedingly beautiful. Fine specimens of petrified palm-wood may be seen at their store. They are both beautiful and rare. The fact that petrified palm-wood and petrified bones of the rhinoceros have been found in this territory, shows that some six million years ago—comparatively recent—there was a tropical climate in this region of country, when the palm flourished in luxuriance, and the rhinoceros sported in the warm streams or cavorted around on their sunny banks. Travelers who are willing to omit their dinner can improve the half hour allowed by the railroad, by a hurried run over to this store, which is but a block away.

Prospects.—At present, the greatest cause of the growth and prosperity of Cheyenne is the discovery of gold in the Black Hills of Dakota. This cause will last until, if that country will warrant it, a railroad is built there. The discoveries of gold seem to be extensive and inexhaustive, and the building of a railroad from some point here or on the Union Pacific or Missouri River, will rapidly follow. Such a road might for a time at least injure the trade of the town. But at present its prospects are flattering, and its business men are reaping a rich harvest from their investments. The opening of northern Wyoming to settlement, the development of the vast mineral resources of the territory, and the continued prosperity of her stock interests, will give to the "Magic City of the Plains" the trade, growth and influence which her location demands.

Health.—As a resort for health-seekers, Cheyenne has superior advantages. It is about a thousand feet higher than Denver, with an atmosphere not only rarefied but dry. It has good hotels and livery accommodations. Ponies are cheap, and invalids can purchase them and ride over the hills and dales at pleasure. There is also an abundance of game in the vicinity—antelope, rabbits, deer, etc. A bear weighing over 1,500 pounds, was killed near here in 1875. It is the largest one we ever saw. Its skin has been preserved, and the bear has been mounted in good shape. Frequent excursions can also be taken in the warm summer weather to Fort Laramie, Cheyenne Pass, and other places which will expand the lungs

SCENES IN THE BLACK HILLS.

1.—Golden Park. 2.—Genevieve Park. 3.—Custer Park. 4.—Limestone Peak. 5.—Harney's Park.

and invigorate the body. The results of several years' observations at the United States Signal Station here, show that the temperature is more even, taking the years together, than in many places East or on the Pacific coast. The hottest days do not equal those which frequently occur in the East, and in the summer months the nights are deliciously cool, assuring the invalid good sleep under plenty of blankets. We predict a great rush of invalids and health-seekers to this place and vicinity, in the near future. Although Cheyenne is a good place to sleep, yet the people are wide-awake and "owly" nights.

Rapidity of Business at Cheyenne.— On the 22d of July, 1867, the first lots were offered for sale by the Union Pacific Railroad Company at Cheyenne—66 by 132 feet for $150. Thirty days after, these lots sold for $1,000 each, and in two to three months thereafter, the same lots were again resold at $2,000 to $2,500. On the 15th of July, 1867, there was but one house at Cheyenne. Six months thereafter, there were no less than *three thousand.* The government freight which was transported over the plains to Cheyenne, from November, 1867, to February, 1868, four months, amounted to 6,000 tons, and filled twelve large warehouses, and for a long time subsequently averaged 15,000,000 to 20,000,000 pounds annually.

During the fall and winter, there were three forwarding companies whose business in transporting goods, exclusive of government supplies, averaged 5,000,000 pounds per month. Stores were erected with marvelous rapidity. One firm constructed an entire store, 25 by 55 feet, quite substantial, in just forty-eight hours; three hundred firms were in operation that winter, doing mostly a wholesale business; of this number, over seventy made sales of over $10,000 per month each, and with some firms sales reached over $30,000 per month.

The first post-office was established October 30, 1867; salary $1.00 per month. In two months the United States mails had increased so enormously as to average 2,600 letters per day, and in two months more this was doubled, and salary increased to $2,000 per year. Though business declined as soon as the terminus of the road was moved, yet it now has a solid business. The population in 1875 was about 4,000, and there was invested in new buildings, in the single year of 1875, no less than $430,000.

The Black Hills Gold Discoveries.

For several years the impression has obtained that there was gold in the Black Hills of Dakota, and every exploration under the auspices of the government has tended to encourage and strengthen this impression. In 1860, Colonel Bullock, now a resident of Cheyenne, was an Indian agent and trader where Fort Laramie now stands. He saw a squaw in his store, one day, with something in her mouth. He said, "Let me see that." She gave it to him, and it proved to be a nugget of gold, worth about three dollars. He said, "Give that to me." She told him she would, for some raisins and candy. These he gave her, and afterwards gave her coffee and sugar to its full value. He showed the gold to his interpreter, and requested him, if possible, to find out where it came from. The interpreter did his best, but the squaw would only say that it was picked up in the bed of a creek, and that the Indians would kill her if she told where it was. During his long experience as a trader with the Indians, Colonel Bullock frequently saw small nuggets of gold, but could never find out where the Indians obtained them, and the inferences he drew from all the information he could obtain were to the effect that the Bear Lodge country, nearly north of the Inyan Kara mountain, was the region where this gold came from. According to the most recent information on the subject, the eastern boundary line of Wyoming strikes the Black Hills nearly in the center,—that about one-half are in Dakota and the other half in Wyoming. Harney's Peak and Dodge's Peak are in the former, while the Inyan Kara and Bear Lodge Mountains are in the latter territory. The question of the existence of gold there and other precious metals, can no longer be doubted. The official report of Professor Jenny sufficiently establishes this fact. It also establishes the fact that in a small portion of the country which he examined, it is found in paying quantities. It remains, therefore, for the hardy miners and sturdy pioneers to demonstrate still further whether it is there in large quantities. Thus far every thing has been against them, and they even now are upon forbidden ground, liable at any moment to be driven out of the Hills by United States troops. But there is an implied understanding and belief now becoming quite prevalent that they will be allowed to remain,—that the government will not molest them again. If only this result can be obtained, it will be satisfactory to the miners. They do not fear the Indians; they only ask, if the government will not protect them, that it will not interfere with their mining operations nor destroy their property. Nor will they attack the Indians,—they are safe if they keep away and do not disturb them. If, however, they are attacked, self-defence will require vigorous measures for protection. The law of the case, as we understand it, is simply this: that the reservations agreed upon by the treaty of 1868 are in Dakota territory; that a part of the Black Hills only are in that territory, nor is there any evidence or indications that they ever occupied this part beyond the cutting of a few lodge-poles. The facts are that the Indians are in Nebraska instead of Dakota, and that they are really afraid of the Black Hills because of the terrific storms that visit them, when, "from peak to peak, the rattling crags among, leaps the live thunder," and the pranks of livid lightning are fearful to behold. They have a superstitious reverence for these Hills, and believe them to be the home of the Great Spirit. The treaty only gives them the right to hunt in Wyoming, as far west as the crests of the Big Horn Mountains, whenever there is sufficient game to warrant the chase. With the exception of this proviso, therefore, the whole territory of Wyoming is open to exploration, settlement and development. The next question is,—Will the government protect the pioneers in their explorations? or must they protect themselves in going where they have an undoubted right to go?

The Black Hills are mainly confined to a region of territory lying between the forks of the Cheyenne river. In addition to the gulch and placer diggings, already discovered, there have been a few discoveries of what appears to be rich quartz lodes of gold and veins of silver. This region is about one hundred miles long and eighty miles wide. French Creek, Spring Creek, Rapid Creek, Box-elder Creek, Elk Creek and others head in these Hills, and flow mainly in an eastern direction, emptying into the south fork of the Cheyenne. The north fork seems to hug the hills pretty closely with small creeks and streams, yet unexplored, heading in the mountains and flowing into it. The north fork heads in Pumpkin Butte, a mountain a little north-west of Fort Fetterman, on the North Platte river. West of the northern portion of the Black Hills, there are several ranges of mountains and several streams which flow north into the Yellowstone River. All accounts of this region of country, as far west as the Big Horn Mountains, unite in the report of its rich mineral character, and we believe the richest mineral discoveries ever known on this continent will be made here in the next few years.

AGNES PARK.—BLACK HILLS.

How to get to the Black Hills.—Within the past year of 1876 and 1877, there have been opened three distinct routes to the Black Hills, and it is now easy of access. The principal routes are via the Union Pacific Railroad, and stage line from either Sidney or Cheyenne. A longer route is occasionally used by steamers up the Missouri River to Sioux City, Yankton and Port Pierre, and thence by wagon across the plains and "bad lands" of Dakota. This route is long and circuitous, with not as good wood, water or grazing, as the Southern route. From Cheyenne there is a good natural road, which runs to Fort Laramie, a distance of 90 miles, over which the U. S. mails have been carried for many years. It passes through a country with good ranches, at convenient distances apart. From Fort Laramie to Custer and Deadwood City, there is a good wagon road, which has recently been shortened 60 miles, so that the entire distances are as follows:

Cheyenne to Fort Laramie 93 miles; to Custer City, 260 miles; Hill City, 275 miles; Golden City, 295 miles; Rapid City, 315 miles; Elizabeth City, 347 miles; Deadwood, 348 miles; Crook City, 360 miles.

The Cheyenne and Black Hills Stage line now runs regularly, daily trips over the road with a superior outfit for transportation of all classes of passengers. Hitherto the Cheyenne route has been the principal one since it has been the depot of supplies. It is the only route used by the Government Supply trains, is in the proximity of four government military forts and stations, and along the entire route there is an ample supply of wood, water and grain. It is also the line of the telegraph to the Black Hills, which connects Deadwood and Cheyenne. The time occupied in stage travel to the principal places of the Black Hills is from 48 to 60 hours.

Sidney has also become a large outfitting point, and there is now invested nearly $100,000 capital in transportation, equipments for passengers and freight to the Black Hills mines.

Stages leave Sidney every morning at 8 o'clock, and make the distance in following time:

Red Cloud Agency in 20 hours; Buffalo Gap (the point of intersection with stage for Custer, 30 miles West) in 30 hours, and reaches the entire distance to Deadwood in 48 hours.

By the Sidney route distances are as follows:

To Red Cloud Agency, 109 miles; Buffalo Gap, 171 miles; French Creek, 184 miles; Battle Creek, 196 miles; Rapid River, 214 miles; Spring Valley, 228 miles; Crook City, 246 miles; Deadwood, 256 miles. The advantage of distance in favor of the Sidney route is nearly one-fourth less than by any other route.

Result of the Opening of the Black Hills.—During the past season of 1876, the yield of the gold mines was nearly $2,000,000. Cheyenne bankers are said to have bought above $900,000 worth of gold dust, and various amounts have been forwarded in other ways, besides what has been kept in the Hills. This result has been entirely from *placer mining*. One mining party known as the Wheeler party, has realized nearly $500,000 in one season. Extraordinary success attended their work; $2,600 were cleared in only 42 hours' work, and in general, on Deadwood Creek, the average to the miners on each claim was $300 to $700 per day. Nearly all the yield of the Black Hills in 1876 was gleaned in the vicinity of Deadwood and Whitewood gulches.

Quartz mining has been attempted. First assays were but $38 per ton, and the average of the ores thus far experimented upon, vary from $30 to $50 per ton. There is enough ore available to fill fifty 100 stamp mills for 20 years.

Miners with mortar and pestle have taken ore from some of these quartz lodes, and realized as high as $15 per day. Since the settlement of Deadwood, prices of living have gradually declined, until good day board now averages only from $7 to $10. Freight from Cheyenne and Sidney now costs but $3 to $4 per 100 lbs. The width of the mineral belt is now definitely ascertained to be but 10 to 15 miles, but it stretches 100 miles long. The agricultural value of the Hills is beyond all words of expression. The valleys have been found to be surpassingly fertile, the rain-fall regular and constant, and were any one dissatisfied with mining, still there is room for thousands of farms and peaceful homes.

A statement is made, apparently of unquestioned accuracy, of an explorer on Spring Creek, who, with three others, and one day's sluicing, took out $38 coarse gold, the pieces varying from three cents to three dollars in value. One man prospecting on Iron Creek, sixty miles farther off, took out $23.67 from one pan of dirt. Mr. Allen, the recorder of mining claims, took from his claim four pounds of coarse gold in one month, and all reports agree in an average of seven to twenty-five cents per pan, which will turn out per day $7 to $50 to each man.

As a proof of the existence of gold, it is but necessary to quote from the authority of Professor Jenny's report of a visit in July, 1875, whereof writing to the Department of the Interior at Washington, he announces the discovery of gold in paying quantities near Harney's Peak; deposits very rich, with plenty of water in the streams: "The gold is found in quartz ledges of enormous dimensions. Whether the mines be valuable or not, there is a vastness of future wealth in the grass lands, farms and timber. The soil is deep and fertile; the rain-fall more abundant than any other point west of the Alleghanies." In the summer of 1875, an expedition headed by General Custer visited this region, wherein he describes finding an abundance of wild fruits, strawberries, raspberries, gooseberries in wonderful profusion; and frequently the wild berry was larger and more delicious flavor than the domestic species in the Eastern states.

A miner writing from personal view thus speaks of the richness of the section thus far discovered: "I found several miners working their claims, as yet in a crude and primitive manner. Some of them working with a Chinese rocker cleaned up from five to seven pennyweights of gold, the result of but three hours' work. Twenty-five miles north-west of Spring Creek, I found the largest vein of gold quartz I have ever seen, being from 300 to 600 feet in width, and traceable for over 40 miles in length. I also found a vein of white crystallized quartz about four feet in width, in which gold was plainly visible. I obtained some specimens, fabulously rich; one piece was sent to the Omaha smelting works which averaged $42,000 to the ton. At Rapid Creek the prospects are still better than in Spring Gulch. Castle Creek is the richest found in the Black Hills. One claim has been worked to the bed-rock, in the channel, which paid $6.00 of gold to one cubic foot of gravel."

The best mines have proved by the latest discoveries to be on the west side of the Hills, and aside from the value of the precious metal, the superb salubrity of the climate, and the natural richness of the soil, make it extraordinarily attractive. An explorer describes the country as "the richest ever seen or heard of between the Missouri River and Central Oregon. Excellent timber in the greatest abundance; as fine pasturage as I ever saw; rich black loam soil; splendid water; showers every few days; no disagreeable winds; a delicious, bracing atmosphere to either work or rest in; a splendid diver-

LIGHTNING SCENE ON THE PRAIRIES.

sity of hill and valley; prairie and timber forest; a landscape of which the eye never tires."

During one week, 800 miners passed through Hill City, *en route* for the mines of Whitewood and Deadwood. In most of the creeks the bed-rock lies 15 to 20 and 40 feet below the surface. On the 1st of March there were estimated to be over 10,000 people in the Black Hills, and rapidly accumulating at the rate of 1,000 per week, which would be still greatly augmented when the summer weather opens.

A Terrible Thunder-Storm.—The Black Hills of Dakota are the fear of Indians, because of the frequent thunder-storms. Col. R. I. Dodge, United States Commander of Black Hills Expedition, 1874, states that in this region "thunder-storms are quite frequent, terrific in force and power, and fearful in the vividness, the nearness of the lightning. Scarcely a day in summer that there is not a thunder-storm in some part of the hills.

"One afternoon, from the top of one of the high mountains, near Harney's Peak, I saw five separate and distinct storms, occurring at the same instant in different parts of the hills. One of these struck our party with fatal results.

"A heavy rain-storm coming on, two soldiers and the boy took refuge under a tall pine. All three were seated on a rock about six feet from the trunk of the tree, and each held in his hand the reins of his horse's bridle. At the flash, the three persons and horses were thrown to the ground, one of the soldiers being pitched quite a distance, alighting on his head. The surgeon was promptly on hand. Each person had been struck on the cheek bone, just under the eye. The fluid passed down the person of each, going out at the ball of the foot, boring a hole in the shoe sole as clean and round as if made by a bullet, and raising a large blood blister on the bottom of the foot. Neither had any other mark whatever. Skipping from the men to the horses, the flash prostrated all, striking each just over the eye. Two soon recovered their feet, and the third was killed.

"During this storm, which lasted scarce half an hour, more than twenty trees were struck by lightning within a radius of a few hundred yards.

"At another time, I witnessed another curious and unaccountable phenomenon. I was on a high mountain of the Harney Group. Within four miles of me, in different directions, were three thunder-storms, their clouds being probably 500 or 1,000 feet below me. Though I could see the vivid and incessant flashes of lightning, *not a sound of the thunder could be heard.* Throughout the Hills the number of the trees which bear the mark of the thunder-bolt is very remarkable, and the strongest proof of the violence and frequent recurrence of these storms. The electric current acts in the most eccentric way. In some cases it will have struck the very top of a lofty pine, and passed down, cutting a straight and narrow groove in the bark, without any apparent ill effect on the tree, which remains green and flourishing; at other times the tree will be riven into a thousand pieces, as if with the blows of a giant axe, and the fragments scattered a hundred feet around."

Rainbows.—"The rainbow of the Black Hills is a marvel of perfection and beauty. Two or three times wider than the rainbow of the States, it forms a complete and perfect arch, both ends being, sometimes, visible to the beholder, and one so near and distinct that there would be little difficulty in locating the traditional 'pot of gold.' Very frequently the rainbow is doubled, and several times I saw three distinct arches, the third and higher being, however, a comparatively faint reflex of the brilliant colors of the lower."

DEVIL'S TOWER—BLACK HILLS.

Mountains. — Harney's Peak is 7,440 feet above tide-water, the other peaks are

Crook's Monument,	7,600 feet elevation.
Dodge's Peak,	7,300 feet elevation.
Terry's Peak,	7,200 feet elevation.
Warren's Peak,	6,900 feet elevation.
Custer's Peak,	6,750 feet elevation.
Crow Peak,	6,200 feet elevation.
Bare Peak,	5,200 feet elevation.
Devil's Tower,	5,100 feet elevation.

The *Devil's Tower* is one of the most remarkable peaks of the world. General Dodge describes it thus: "An immense obelisk of granite, 867 feet at base, 297 feet at top. It rises 1,127 feet above its base, and 5,100 feet above tide-water. Its summit is inaccessible to anything without wings. The sides are fluted and scored by the action of the elements, and immense blocks of granite, split off from the column by frost, are piled in huge, irregular mounds about its base. The Indians call this shaft "*The Bad God's Tower.*"

Game.—The Hills are full of deer, elk, bears, wolves, cougars, grouse, and ducks. The streams have an abundance of fish, although of but few sorts.

After careful investigation General Dodge closes with this expression of careful judgment:

Opinion of General Dodge.—"I but express my fair and candid opinion when I pronounce the Black Hills, in many respects, the finest country I have ever seen. The beauty and variety of the scenery, the excellence of the soil, the magnificence of the climate, the abundance of timber and building stone make it a most desirable residence for men who want good homes.

"As a grazing country it can not be surpassed, and small stock farms of fine cattle and sheep can not fail of success.

"Gold there is every-where in the granite—gold enough to make many fortunes, and tempt to the loss of many more.

"Here is a country destined, in a few years, to be an important and wealthy portion of the great American Republic."

There is little doubt that in a few years this section, from the Black Hills of Dakota to and across the Big Horn region, and all northern Wyoming, will be a rich field of industry, as have been Colorado and Utah. The illustrations we give are from photographs taken by General Custer in his famous Black Hills Exploring Expedition of 1875, and represent this country to be of great scenic beauty.

COLORADO.

Pleasure Resorts.—Colorado is an empire of itself in enterprise, scenic beauty and abundance of pleasure resorts. In 1870, few or none of these were known, and towns were small in number and population. Since that time, it has become a center of great railroad activity, has grown in wonderful favor as an attractive region for summer travel; and as a country for health-giving and life-giving strength, it has drawn thither thousands who have made it their permanent home.

The Denver Pacific Railroad runs direct from Cheyenne, southward, to Denver, and trains connect with the mid-day trains of the Union Pacific Railroad from each direction, east and west, leaving usually about three P. M., arriving at Denver about eight P. M. The distance, 106 miles, is mainly over a vast level plain, covered only with the short gray buffalo grass, but parallel with the main range of the Rocky Mountains, and not more than 15 to 20 miles from their eastern base. The scenery from the western side of the car, as the train, in summer afternoons, gradually moves southward, with the brilliant rays of the afternoon sun illuminating the long range of snow-capped peaks, and the window is opened to admit the pure mountain invigorating air, is charming in the highest degree. Travelers will do well to arrange their Western trip, if for pleasure, so that a good two weeks or a month may be spent in this lovely section. It is a region of capital living, excellent hotels, every modern convenience to make life abound with good home comforts, and excellent society for those who choose to make it their temporary home. The citizens are mostly from the East, engaged in farming, stock raising, and active business, with but a small proportion devoted to mining, and are more orderly and peaceful than in most of the mining localities of the mountains. Colorado shares the enviable reputation of possessing the best class of citizens, the most active business developments, the loveliest scenery, and most rapid increase of population of all the Western Territories. Life everywhere is safe; travel is easy; the mountains are full of neat little homes, all filled with the quieter class of settlers from the far East, and the reputation of the community for law and order, and peace, is eminently proverbial.

This Territory was first opened practically to the rest of the country by the completion of the Denver Pacific Railroad, an enterprise started originally by the capitalists of Denver to afford quicker connection with the Union Pacific than by stage The enterprise was begun in the fall of 1867, when, by subscription and county bonds, nearly $1,000,000 were raised, and completed June 24, 1870. It was operated for a series of years independently of either the Union or Kansas Pacific Railroad, but at last, in 1872, was sold to the latter, by whom it is now controlled. The road has never paid any dividends on stock, and barely pays expenses and in terest on the bonds. The distances and principal stations on the railroad are as follows:

Cheyenne to Summit,	10 miles.
Cheyenne to Cass,	21 miles.
Cheyenne to Pierce,	41 miles.
Cheyenne to Greeley,	55 miles.
Cheyenne to Evans.	59 miles.
Cheyenne to Johnson,	75 miles.
Cheyenne to Hughes,	89 miles.
Cheyenne to Denver,	106 miles.

Soon after leaving Cheyenne, the railroad descends some very heavy grades, at one place nearly 100 feet to the mile, and passes over the ridges which form the northern bluff limits of the South Platte Valley. From these rough bluffs and plains can easily be seen the snow-clad summit of Long's Peak, the great landmark of northern Colorado. The railroad soon reaches a more open country, the wash from the mountains with smooth, clear surface, and at last descends into the valley of the South Platte, up which it passes to Denver. On its course it passes through two flourishing colonies, one of which is

Greeley,—Named in honor of Horace Greeley. It was settled in May, 1870, by a small colony from the East, who obtained by homesteading and purchase about 100,000 acres of fine alluvial soil in the Valley of the *Cache La Poudre* River. This is the largest stream that flows eastward from the mountains of north Colorado, its water being pure and flow constant. Irrigating ditches were constructed, and the entire colony has had an abundance of water for all agricultural purposes. The town for several years has increased with steady rapidity, and the population is slightly over 2,000. It has had many drawbacks incident to new settlements — grasshoppers, frost, want of knowledge of climate, and methods of raising crops. Still these are mostly overcome, and the community feel greatly encouraged. The crops of the last year are said to have reached a value of over $200,000. At this place are located some of the finest grist-mills of the entire West. The place has achieved considerable reputation as a temperance town. No intoxicating liquors being permitted on sale. This restriction is of but little consequence to those who *will have*

WILLIAMS' CANON, COLORADO SPRINGS.

BY THOMAS MORAN.

it, as it can easily be obtained at the next station, six miles away, but it has kept a class of loafers and idlers off, who otherwise would have been a curse to any community.

Evans—is a small settlement of about 1,000, which is the number of two colonies, one from St. Louis and one from Boston, Mass. There are about 60,000 acres of land occupied in the vicinity.

Denver—is the capital of the Territory (which will soon become a State). This has become a large railroad point. From it diverge the Kansas Pacific, 636 miles eastward to Kansas City, the Denver and Rio Grande Railroad, Narrow Gauge, southward, 156 miles to Canon City, Pueblo and Trinidad, the Boulder Valley Railroad to Boulder, and the Colorado Central Railroad to Idaho Springs and Central City in the mountains.

Its population exceeds 16,000, and its location is most advantageous for easy trade and communication with all the principal points of the Territory. Located on an open plain, about thirteen miles from the Rocky Mountains; there is a grand view of the entire range from Long's Peak on the north to Pike's Peak on the south. While eastward, northward and southward stretches the vast upland plains which is so impressive with its boundless extent. The city is full of thrift, of life; and trade is always splendid. The buildings which grace the principal streets are made principally of brick, and in general appearance, are superior to those of any city west of the Missouri River. Daily, weekly and monthly newspapers thrive. Here is a branch of the United States Mint, gas-works, water-works, horse-railroads, and a multitude of hotels. The best of which are the Grand Central, Inter-Ocean, American, Sargent, Broadwell and Villa Park. From this point the traveler can radiate in all directions in search of pleasure resorts.

Notes to Tourists.—The uniform railroad fare in the Territory averages ten cents per mile. Stage routes run all through the mountains, fare from ten to twenty cents per mile. The uniform rate of board is four dollars per day, and almost every-where can be found excellent living; the nicest of beef steak, bread and biscuit. In many of the mountain resorts plenty of good fishing can be found, and delicate trout are common viands of the hotel tables. The best season of the year for a visit to Colorado is in July and August. As then the snow has nearly disappeared from the mountains, and all the beautiful parks and valleys are easily approachable. Those who wish to include both Colorado and California in a pleasure trip will do well to visit California first, during April May and June, and then on return spend July and August leisurely in the cozy little home resorts of Colorado. Although it must be confessed that the scenery of the Colorado mountains is far the most impressive and most beautiful when *first seen*, before reaching the greater magnificence of the Yosemite and Sierras. Living in Colorado is more nearly like New England customs than in California, and to those who seek Western travel, for health, the climate of Colorado is much more favorable than that of California.

The Denver and Rio Grande Railroad—will carry the traveler southward from Denver, along the base of the Rocky Mountains, to some of the most noted pleasure resorts of the territory. This little narrow gauge is a wonder of itself, representing nearly $1,000,000 of capital, and operating over 200 miles of road, it has developed a traffic exceeding $500,000 per year, where six years ago the stage route did not realize $1,000 per month, and the prospects for the future for its trade with the miners of the San Juan Country, Trinidad, Sante Fe, are most encouraging, as the new gold discoveries become better developed. Seventy-six miles south of Denver, on this line, are clustered three little places of resort, practically one in interest, Colorado Springs, Colorado City, and

Manitou Springs.—The former is the railroad station, a lively town, which in five years has risen from the prairie to a population of 3,000. Six miles distant from the Springs at Manitou, are collected several elegant hotels, and in the vicinity are numerous soda springs—iron springs and medicinal baths—of great virtue. The location of this resort, with its wonderful collection of objects of natural interest and scenery, have earned for it the title of "Saratoga of the Far West." Travelers find here beautiful scenery in the Ute Pass—Garden of the Gods—Glen Eyrie, numerous beautiful canons, Queen Canon —Cheyenne Canon, grand and impressive, and towering over all is the lofty summit of Pike's Peak, 14,300 feet high, up which ascends a trail to the government signal station, the highest in the United States. Travelers, who frequently ascend this peak are rewarded, when on a clear day, with a glimpse of grand and glorious views of the peaks and mountains, southward and westward.

In this vicinity is located a pretty little canon about 15 miles in length, with walls of rock rising to uniform height of 600 and 800 feet above a very narrow foot pass below. This canon was discovered and named, in 1870, by a party of editors, *Williams' Canon*, in honor of H. T. Williams, their commander. This was the first visit of an Eastern party, of any notoriety, at the Springs. No railroad was then built, and not a house was to be seen, nor even a rancheman's cabin. The scenery of this canon, (*see illustration*), is at various points wild in the extreme, and the colossal walls of rocks are of such shape and formation that they give to the observer an excellent general idea of the characteristic canon scenery of the mountains. The canon has never been fully explored, and at present is the scene of fifty or more claims of gold discoveries.

GATE-WAY TO THE GARDEN OF THE GODS

Pleasure travelers are uniformly glad that they have made a visit to these points, as they excel in interest any other points in the Western trip. Southward from Colorado Springs, the next most noted resort is Canon City and the

Grand Canon of the Arkansas.—This is a scene of remarkable beauty and magnificence; at one point can be seen the river winding its way for ten miles, at the base of huge perpendicular rocks which rise fully 1000 and 2000 feet above the current. This is the grandest canon view in Colorado. Westward from Colorado Springs is the South Park, a noted route for travelers who enjoy camping out, and a fine drive through the mountains.

Garden of the Gods. — The Beautiful Gate.—This is also a famous pleasure resort at Manitou, near Colorado Springs. Midway between the Station and Springs is located one of the most beautiful and curious little parks, and upheaval of rocks that Western scenery can display. Descending from parallel ridges into a little park, the traveler sees in front of him a beautiful gate of two enormous rocks, rising in massive proportion to the height of 350 feet, with a natural gateway between of 200 feet in width, with a small rock in the center. Standing a little eastward, the observer gets the view illustrated in our engraving. At the right is another parallel ridge of rocks, pure white, which contrasts finely with the dark red of the rocks of the gate. Through the gate, in the long distance is seen the summit of Pike's Peak, eighteen miles away. Around these rocks is a little grassy park of fifty or more acres, in which according to the mythological stories of the people, the "gods" found such lovely times in play that they christened it a garden. These two parallel ridges of white and red rocks extend for many miles at the foot of the mountains, and form other curious formations at Glen Eyrie, Monument Park and Pleasant Park, although much less in size and impressiveness. The locality is the most famous in all Transcontinental travel.

The Dome of the Continent—Gray's Peak.—Westward from Denver, 65 miles, and 14 from Georgetown, Colorado, rises the grandest and most beautiful of the mountains of Colorado. The way thither is one of easy approach, through valley and mountain roads of gradual ascent, past Idaho Springs, one of the most charming of summer resorts, and past all the mines of Golden, Empire, Georgetown, and the silver mines of the Palisades. Near to the summit are two very successful mines, Baker and Stevens, which are dug out of the perpendicular face of a rock fully 200 feet in height. Rising above all the ranges of the Colorado Mountains of north Colorado, Gray's Peaks are the grand Lookout Points, from which to view to advantage all the vast mountain range. In a clear day the observer can embrace in his range of vision a distance of 100 miles, in each direction, northward, southward and westward, and even eastward to over the plains east of Denver. From this point are plainly discernible Pike's Peak, 80 miles away, Mount Lincoln, 50 miles; Mount of the Holy Cross, 60 miles; Long's Peak, 50 miles; the City of Denver, 65 miles, and even the summit of the Spanish Peaks, 150 miles southward, and the higher ranges of the Uintah Mountains, 150 miles westward. The total range of the vision being not less than 200 to 250 miles. Beneath them at the foot, lie the beautiful rivers and lakes of Middle Park; southward the vast extended plains of South Park, and everywhere near at hand multitudes of little grassy parks, like valleys dotted with the groves of spruce and pine, as if planted for a grand pleasure ground. The height of the Peak is 14,351 feet, and is the easiest of access of all the mountains of Colorado. Travelers and pleasure tourists who desire one grand sight, never to be regretted, must not fail to include this in their Western visit for the sublimity and grand exaltation as from so lofty a height one views a sea of huge mountains, is a thing always to live in one's memory. There is a fine road to within three miles of the summit, through charming verdure-clad canons and valleys and the rest of the way can be made over a fine trail by horseback, even to the summit.

Westward from Denver are Idaho Springs, Georgetown, Gray's Peak, Middle Park, Clear Creek, and Boulder Canons, with the mining attractions of Central City, Georgetown, Empire, Caribou, and Black Hawk, where the observer can witness sights of extraordinary beauty. We can not possibly describe the attractions of these resorts. They are at once terrible, overpowering, lonely, and full of indescribable majesty. Amid them all the tourist travels daily, imbibing the life-giving, beautiful, fresh air full of its oxygen to quicken and stimulate the system; the eye drinks in the wealth of scenery, and loves to note the beauties of the wonderful glowing sunlight, and the occasional cloud-storms, and wild display of power and glory.

We know of no country better worth the title of the "*Switzerland of America*" than Colorado, with its beautiful mountain parks, valleys, and springs. Go and see them all. The tour will be worthy of remembrance for a life-time.

The editor of this Guide expects soon to issue *The Colorado Tourist*, devoted more especially to the attractions of Colorado, as the limits of this Guide can not begin to possibly describe a hundredth part of the objects of interest within that little region—a *world of pleasure travel by itself.*

Of Life in Colorado,—a prominent writer has said: "At Denver I found, as I thought, the grade of civilization actually higher than in most Western cities. In elegance of building, in finish, in furniture, in dress and equipages, that city is not behind any this side of the Atlantic border. The total absence of squalidity and vis-

MOUNTAIN OF THE HOLY CROSS, COLORADO.

ible poverty, and I may also say of coarseness and rowdyism, impressed me on my visit very strongly, as did the earnestness, activity and intensity of life which is everywhere so apparent."

P. T. Barnum once said of Colorado, in a lecture: "Why, Coloradoans are the most disappointed people I ever saw. Two-thirds of them came here to die, and they *can't do it.* This wonderful air brings them back from the verge of the tomb, and they are naturally exceedingly disappointed."

The average temperature is about 60° the year round—the air is bracing, winter mild, and days almost always full of clear skies and bright warm sunshine. The purity and dryness of the atmosphere are proverbial.

Mountain of the Holy Cross.—The name of this remarkable mountain is renowned to the ends of the earth, and is the only one with this name in the world. It is the principal mountain of the Sawatch Range, just west of the Middle Park of Colorado, and exceedingly difficult of access. The Hayden party were several days in merely finding an accessible way of travel to reach its base. The characteristic features which give it its name is the vertical face, nearly 3,000 feet in depth, with a cross at the upper portion, the entire fissures being filled with snow. The cross is of such remarkable size and distinct contrast with the dark granite rock, that it can be seen nearly eighty miles away, and easily distinguished from all other mountain peaks. The snow seems to have been caught in the fissure, which is formed of a succession of steps, and here, becoming well lodged, it remains all the year. Late in the summer the cross is very much diminished in size by the melting of the snow. A beautiful green lake lies at the base of the peak, almost up to the timber line, which forms a reservoir for the waters from the melting snows of the high peaks. From this flows a stream with many charming cascades. The height of the mountain is 14,176 feet above tide-water. The perpendicular arm of the cross is 1,500 feet in length, and fully 50 feet in breadth, the snow lying in the crevice from 50 to 100 feet in depth. The horizontal arm varies in length with the seasons, but averages 700 feet. The mountain was ascended by the Hayden party only with the greatest difficulty, after 5,000 feet of climbing—fifty pounds of instruments on each back, and obliged to pass thirty hours on the summit, with no shelter, protection, fuel or provisions, except one pocket lunch.

Military Posts.

At Cheyenne is Camp Carlin, which is principally a depot for quartermasters' supplies. Three miles north on Crow Creek is Fort D. A. Russell, named in honor of the gallant commander of the first division of the sixth army corps, who fell at the battle of Winchester while leading his men to victory. It is a fifteen-company post; its grounds are well laid out, with fair buildings for officers and men. The creek runs on two sides of the enclosure and "a spur" from the railroad leads to it. This fort was established by General Augur, about the first of August, 1867. The reservation on which it is located contains 4,512 acres. It is a distributing point for both troops and supplies. In the winter quite a large number of troops, principally cavalry, are kept here; but in summer they are at out-stations on the frontier.

Fort Laramie.—This fort is on the North Platte River, ninety-two miles from Cheyenne. It was established in August, 1869, by Major W. F. Sanderson. It was formerly a trading-post and a great resort for the northern Indians. The trappers and hunters among them and among the whites used to visit this place to trade their furs for supplies. The fort derives its name from Laramie River, which unites with the North Platte near this point. The government has a reservation here of fifty-four square miles. The old overland road to Oregon passes this place, and it is also on the direct road to Montana, the Big Horn and Powder River regions. It is probably the most important post on our frontier at present. A semi-weekly stage line connects it with Cheyenne, which will soon be made daily. In 1875, thieving bands of Sioux found their way in west and also south of this fort and killed one or two herders and stole a few horses. If trouble with the Sioux should come in consequence of the occupation of the Black Hills by miners, the location of this fort is very convenient for the distribution of forces for either offensive or defensive operations.

Fort Fetterman—Is located on the south side of the North Platte River, about eighty miles from Fort Laramie. It is named in honor of Lieutenant-Colonel W. J. Fetterman, who was killed by the Indians at the Fort Phil Kearny massacre, in December, 1866. It was established in July, 1867, by Major Dey, of the United States Army, and has a reservation of sixty sections of land adjoining. It is at present a base of supplies for troops in that vicinity, and is an important link in the chain of forts that should be re-established in the Powder and Tongue River countries. Two or three military posts between this fort and Atlantic City, in the great south pass at the base of the Wind River Mountains, would prevent the annual horse-stealing raids of the Indians on the Laramie plains.

Old Fort Casper—Is one of the forts that should be re-established. It is about sixty miles west of Fort Fetterman, on the North Platte River, at the old overland stage crossing, and was abandoned in 1867. At that time there was a bridge across the river there, which cost $65,000, and which was soon after burned by the Indians.

THE UINTAH MOUNTAINS.—SCENE NEAR GILBERT'S PEAK.

Fort Reno.—Established by General P. Edward Connor, on Powder River, about ninety miles north-west of Fort Fetterman, during the war, and Fort Phil Kearney; established by Colonel Carrington, at the forks of the Big and Little Piney Creeks, in 1866, have both been abandoned, and should both be re-established. Fort C. F. Smith was on the old Montana road, near the base of the Big Horn Mountains in Montana, some ninety miles from Fort Phil Kearney; established in 1866 and abandoned at the same time the other posts were given up. The region of country in which these forts were established is very fine for grazing, buffaloes living there the entire year, with an abundance of other game. It is a famous hunting region for the Indians; but since the government has inaugurated the policy of feeding them, they have become too lazy to hunt. Nothing but a horse-stealing raid can rouse the ambition of an ordinary Indian.

Powder River Country.—The Powder River, so named from the dark powder-colored sand in its bed, rises in the Big Horn Mountains, north and north-west of Old Fort Casper, and runs in a general north-easterly direction till it empties into the Yellowstone River. It drains an immense area of country, flows through a large region of fine grazing lands, and has in the mountains and hills on either side, untold treasures of rich metals and precious gems. It has hitherto been forbidden ground to white men, but those who have passed through it give glowing descriptions of its luxuriant fertility, its grand scenery and its mineral wealth. The demand for gold must soon cause it to be opened, and if it should not prove as rich in minerals as has been predicted, it will nevertheless be one of the finest grazing-regions in the country, producing vast herds of cattle, sheep and horses, which will add to the material wealth of the country. There are also heavy bodies of timber on the hills and mountains which border this river, and which will soon be needed to build the homes of the people who are to inhabit this mountain region of the Continent. Its wonders are just beginning to be told. They have yet to become known. When fully realized, the overcrowded population of the East will be drawn to it as the magnet draws the iron; the wilderness will bud and blossom as the rose, and a State will rise from the ground now roamed over by wild beasts and tenanted by savages.

The Tongue River Country.—This is similar in some of its general features to that bordering the Powder River, with this exception,—the soil is said to be more fertile and better adapted to agricultural pursuits. The Tongue River rises in the Big Horn Mountains, in the central portion of northern Wyoming, and runs north into the Yellowstone River. It abounds in the usual varieties of fish, and game is abundant along its banks. It is a very crooked stream,—its ways being more devious than those of a modern whisky-maker. It only awaits the advent of white men and women to become an empire of itself. A ready outlet to the best stock-markets in the country is needed to render it accessible and always open.

Hazard—is 522.4 miles from Omaha, with an elevation of 6,325 feet. It is a side track and telegraph station, and there is a sheep ranche near by. As you leave Cheyenne, looking off to the right, you will see the Black Hills of Wyoming stretching to the north, and you will wonder how you are to get by them. To the left, Long's Peak rears its snow-capped summit high into the air. It is one of the famous mountains of Colorado, and you have a better view of it on the Denver Pacific Road than from the Union Pacific. It is always crowned with snow and frequently obscured by clouds. How grand it looks, and how huge it appears in the distance. After leaving Hazard, the road enters a "draw," or ravine, and the monotony of the scenery over the plains is past. From this place on, the mountains will be constantly in sight. The next station is

Otto,—530.6 miles from Omaha, and 6,724 feet above the sea. Here, looking to the right, you will see an old road-bed, partly graded. It was abandoned and the track was laid on the present grade. Every opportunity for obtaining the rugged views, both to the right and left, should be observed and taken advantage of. The station itself is simply a side track with telegraph office.

Granite Canon—is the next station, 535.6 miles from Omaha, and 7,298 feet in altitude. You approach this station high upon the side of a ravine, and through deep cuts in granite spurs. Stunted pines, like lone sentinels, are seen on the bleak hills, where they have for ages withstood the frosts of time. The station has a few houses, a lime kiln, telegraph office, and the accompanying side track where trains meet and pass. The cuts, through a reddish granite, are short but very heavy. Snow sheds are now quite frequent.

Buford,—542.5 miles from Omaha; elevation, 7,780 feet. It is a telegraph station. As you leave it on your left, the "Twin Mountains,' two peaks in the Black Hills, lift their rocky heads above the barren waste around them. Near these mountains the noted desperado, Jack Slade, once had his retreat. The country here is covered with short buffalo grass, cut with ravines and draws, abounding in fine springs, and in places, covered with pine trees. The dark hues of the pine give the hills their name, "black," and in places the timber is quite heavy. A short distance to your right, Crow Creek rises and winds its way among the hills to the plains below. Four and a half miles north from Buford, near the valley of Crow Creek, mines of copper and silver have been discovered. The ore assays over $50 per ton, but is very refractory. It will eventually become a silver mine, as the copper in nearly all such cases runs out.

Sherman—is 549.2 miles from Omaha, at an elevation of 8,242 feet. At the time the road was completed here, it was the highest railroad point in the world, but there are higher places now reached by rail in South America. It has been reached by an ascent so gradual that you have hardly noticed it. In the past few years there have been many changes in grade of the Union Pacific, and wherever possible, the track has been raised above the cuts, so the snow, unless in immense quantities, now causes but little impediment to travel. At Sherman, the snow never falls very deep, but there is a constant breeze, that most Eastern people would pronounce a gale, and the snow is constantly drifting and packs so hard wherever it finds lodgment, that it is exceedingly difficult to displace, requiring an immense power of snow-plows, engines and shovelers. As you approach Sherman, you will see the balanced rocks, and to the right of the station, about one-quarter of a mile, is a rugged peak, near which are graves of some who are quietly sleeping so near heaven, and a solitary pine tree, like a sentinel keeping guard over them. Sherman is a telegraph station, has a hotel, one or two saloons, several houses, and a roundhouse where an engine is kept for use in cases of emergency. The difference in elevation between this place and Cheyenne is 2,201 feet, and distance nearly 33 miles. The average grade from Cheyenne is 67 feet per mile, and the maximum grade of any one mile is 90 feet. From Sherman to Laramie, the distance is 23.4 miles; the average grade is 50 feet to the mile, while the maximum grade of any one mile is the same as on the eastern slope—90 feet to the mile. These grades indicate why this route across the Black Hills was selected in preference to others where the altitude was not as great—the approach on either side being more gradual, though the elevation is greater. Nearly all trains between Cheyenne and Laramie have two engines attached so that they may be easily controlled. It is a steady pull to the summit, from each side, and the heavy down grades from it require a great deal of power to properly control trains. About ½ mile west of Sherman on the left side of the road, is "Reed's Rock," so called from one of the civil engineers who laid out the road. The man who deprives newspapers of their proper advertising patronage, has been along and defaced the upper layers of this rock with sentences more suggestive than elegant. You will obtain a fine view of it as you pass west.

SKULL ROCKS, NEAR SHERMAN.

Dale Creek Bridge—is about two miles west of Sherman. This bridge is built of iron, and seems to be a light airy structure, but is really very substantial. The creek, like a thread of silver, winds its devious way in the depths below, and is soon lost to sight as you pass rapidly down the grade and through the granite cuts and snow sheds beyond. This bridge is 650 feet long, and nearly 130 feet high, and is one of the wonders on the great trans-continental route. A water tank, just beyond it, is supplied with water

DALE CREEK BRIDGE.

from the creek by means of a steam pump. The buildings in the valley below seem small in the distance, though they are not a great way off. The old wagon road crossed the creek down a ravine, on the right side of the track, and the remains of the bridge may still be seen. This stream rises about six miles north of the bridge, and is fed by numerous springs and tributaries, running in a general southerly direction, until it empties into the Cache La Poudre River. The old overland road from Denver to California ascended this river and creek until it struck the head-waters of the Laramie. Leaving Dale Creek bridge, the road soon turns to the right, and before you, on the left, is spread out, like a magnificent panorama,

The Great Laramie Plains.—These plains have an average width of 40 miles, and are 100 miles in length. They begin at the western base of the Black Hills and extend to the slope of the Medicine Bow Mountains, and north beyond where the Laramie River cuts its way through these hills to join its waters with the North Platte. They comprise an area of over two and a half millions of acres, and are regarded as one of the richest grazing portions of country. Across these plains, and a little to the left, as you begin to glide over them, rises in full view the Diamond Peaks of the Medicine Bow Range. They are trim and clear-cut cones, with sharp pointed summits—a fact which has given them their name, while their sides, and the rugged hills around them, are covered with timber. Still farther in the shadowy distance, in a south-westerly direction, if the atmosphere is clear, you will see the white summits of the Snowy Range—white with their robes of perpetual snow. Even in the hottest weather experienced on these plains, it makes one feel chilly to look at them, they are so cold, cheerless and forbidding.

In the hills we have just passed, there is an abundance of game, such as mountain sheep, bear, antelope, and an occasional mountain lion, while Dale Creek and all the little brooks which flow into the South Platte River are filled with trout. The speckled beauties are not found however, in the streams which flow into the North Platte. This is a well-established fact, and we have yet failed to discover any satisfactory reason for it, though some of these brooks, flowing in opposite directions, head not more than fifty yards apart.

Skull Rocks.—These rocks, found near Dale Creek, are excellent samples of the granite rocks which are so abundant in this section, and show how they bear the effects of the severe weather. All the massive rocks, which, like the ruins of old castles, are scattered all over the Black Hills, were once angular in form, and square masses, which in time have been worn to their present forms by the disintegrating effects of the atmosphere.

Tie-Siding,—555.2 miles from Omaha; elevation, 7,985 feet. This is a telegraph station, with side tracks for the accommodation of the numerous cars which are loaded with ties, fence-poles and wood. Vast quantities are hauled from the mountains in the vicinity of the Diamond Peaks to this siding. There are a few houses, and the inevitable saloon—houses occupied mostly by woodchoppers and teamsters—while the saloons generally take the most of their money. A short distance from this station two soldiers of an Iowa cavalry regiment were killed by Indians at the overland stage station, in 1865. The pine board and mound which marks their resting-place will soon disappear, and there will be nothing left to mark the spot where they fell. Near Tie-Siding are extensive ranches occupied by sheep during the summer. The general direction of the traveler is now north. In fact, after leaving Dale Creek bridge, you turn towards the north, and continue in that direction, sometimes even making a little east, until you pass Rock Creek Station, a distance of about seventy miles by rail. We have now fairly entered upon the great Laramie Plains. The next station is

Harney,—simply a side track, 559.3 miles from the eastern terminus, with an elevation of 7,857 feet. We are going down grade now pretty fast. The old stage road can be seen to the left, and the higher mountains of the Medicine Bow Range shut in the western view.

Red Buttes,—near the base of the western slope of the Black Hills—is 563.8 miles from Omaha; elevation, 7,336 feet. So-called from the reddish color of the Buttes between Harney and this place, on the right side of the track. This red appearance of the soil on both hill and plain, indicates the presence of iron. It would seem that at some remote period the whole valley was on a level with the top of these Buttes, and they, composed of harder and more cohesive substance than the soil around, have withstood the drain and wash of ages, while it has settled away. They are of all sorts of shapes. The nearest about half a mile from the track, and excite no little interest from their peculiar forms, in the mind of the traveler who is at all curious on such subjects; some of them are isolated, and then again you will see them in groups. There are quite a number in sight from the car windows, and their close inspection would warrant the tourist in stopping at Laramie and making them and other objects in the vicinity a visit. Red Buttes is a telegraph station, with a few settlers in the neighborhood. These plains have been called the paradise for sheep; but of this subject we will speak in another place.

Fort Sanders,—570.3 miles from Omaha; elevation 7,163 feet. This is a station for the military post which was established here in June, 1866, by Col. H. M. Mizner of the 18th United States Infantry. Its buildings for both officers and men are mainly of logs, and many of them are both substantial and comfortable. The post can be seen from a long distance in every direction; is close to the track and on the old military road leading across the Black Hills by way of Cheyenne Pass to Fort Walbach at the eastern base of the hills, now abandoned, and to the military posts near Cheyenne. It will probably be abandoned in a short time.

Laramie—is 572.8 miles from Omaha, and 7,123 feet above the sea. It is the end of a division of the Union Pacific Railroad, is a regular eating-station on the road, has large machine and repair shops, and is destined to become from its mining and manufacturing capacities yet undeveloped, the largest city on the road in Wyoming. It is located on the Laramie River, in the midst of the Laramie Plains, has fully 3,000 people, is the county-seat of Albany County, has numerous churches and schools, several public buildings, brick and stone blocks, with streets regularly laid out at right angles to the railroad; is well watered from one of the mountain streams in the vicinity, and altogether is one of the most promising towns on the line of the road. It is called the "Gem city of the Mountains," and its altitude and close proximity to the hills behind it give it a fair show for the name. The rolling mills of the company, giving employment to from 150 to 300 men, are located and in operation here, in the northern limits of the city. It is expected and understood that a foundry and smelting works for reducing iron ore will soon be established in connection with the rolling mills. At present these mills have all they can do in rerolling the worn out rails of the track, which are brought here for that purpose. The water-power in the Laramie River will also soon be utilized in the erection of woolen mills and factories for refining soda and other minerals with which this country abounds. The mineral resources of Wyoming have not been developed. The slight explorations which have thus far been made only demonstrate the fact of their existence in untold quantities. Laramie, for instance, has within a radius of thirty miles the following named minerals: Antimony, cinnabar, gold, silver, copper, lead, plumbago, iron, red hematite iron, brown hematite, specular iron, sulphate of soda, gypsum, kaolin or porcelain clay, fire clay, brick clay, coal, sand, limestone, fine quality, sandstone for building purposes within two miles of the city, and good wagon roads to all the places where these materials are found. Laramie, from its location and surroundings, must become a manufacturing city, and upon this fact we base the prophecy of its future greatness and prosperity. There are lakes of soda within the distance named that must soon be utilized. A simple chemical process only is required to render this article into the soda of commerce—immense quantities of which are used in this country annually, and most of it comes from foreign countries. It is expected that a soda factory will be started at Laramie within the next year.

Sheep-Raising.—We have before remarked that the Laramie Plains were a paradise for sheep. The success which has attended sheep husbandry on these plains sufficiently attests this fact. It is true, first efforts were not as successful as they should have been, but this is reasonably accounted for in the lack of experience of those who engaged in it, and a want of knowledge of the peculiarities of the climate. It has generally been claimed that sheep will live and do well where antelope thrive. While this theory holds good in the main, it has nevertheless been ascertained that sheep on these plains require hay and shelter in order to be successfully carried through the storms of winter. It is also true that this hay may not be needed, or but a little of it used, but every preparation for safety requires that it should be on hand to be used if necessary. The winter is rare indeed, in this locality, that makes twenty successive days' feeding a necessity. Usually the storms last two or three days, perhaps not as long, when hay and shelter are required. Another fact about this business is that the climate is healthy, and seems especially adapted to sheep. If brought here in a sound and healthy condition, they will remain so with ordinary care, and the climate alone has been effectual in curing some of the diseases to which they are subject. Within the last few years a great number of men have invested capital in sheep husbandry in the vicinity of Laramie, and without an exception they have done well where their flocks have received the requisite attention and care. Among the shepherd kings of the plains may be mentioned the firms of Willard & Kennedy, King & Lane, Rumsey & Co., T. J. Fisher & Co., and others. The firm first named have about 6,000 in their flock, and have accommodations at their different ranches for 10,000 sheep. They place this number as the limit of their flock. Their home ranche is on the Laramie River, about twenty miles due west from the city, and is worthy of a visit from any traveler who desires information on the subject. They are Boston men, and are meeting with success because they give their personal care and attention to the business. Their sheep are divided into flocks of about 2,500 each; this number is all that can be well cared for in a flock. One man, a pony and one or two good shepherd dogs are all that are necessary to care for a flock, though some flocks are cared for without the pony or dogs. Mexican herders or shepherds are considered the best, and usually cost about $25 per month and board. They have long been accustomed to the business in New Mexico, and the most of them don't know enough to do anything else. The wool of graded sheep will usually more than pay all the expenses of the flock, leaving the increase as clear profit, and the increase depends to a large extent on how well the flock is managed; it is ordinarily 80 per cent. Some have had an increase of their flocks as large as 90 per cent., others as low as 60 per cent. Some of the successful sheep men have begun their flocks with Spanish Merinos, others with French Merinos, others with Cotswolds, and others still with Mexican sheep. These last are very hardy; have small bodies and coarse wool. The ewes are usually good mothers, and all of them will hunt and dig through the snow for grass, while other breeds would not. Mexican sheep will live and thrive where tenderly raised eastern sheep will die. They are cheap and easily graded up. On the other hand, when once acclimated, graded sheep cost no more care than others, and their wool will bring double the price in the market. Each class of sheep has its advocates on these plains, and each class has been successful. As an illustration of what care and attention will do in the sheep business, we call attention to the facts and figures in the case of T. J. Fisher & Co., quoting from memory. In August, 1873, Mr. Fisher bought some 690 ewes. At the end of the first year he had a few over 1,300 sheep and lambs, together with the wool clip from the original number purchased, in the spring of 1874. At the end of the second year, in August, 1875, he had over 1,900 sheep and lambs, together with the wool clip in the spring of that year. His sheep being graded, the wool more than paid all expenses of herding, cutting hay, corrals, etc. His ranche is on the Little Laramie River, some fourteen miles from the city. While nearly all who have entered upon this business have been remarkably successful, so far as we are able to learn, Mr. Fisher has been the most successful, in proportion to the capital invested. Tourists desiring further information on this subject will do well to visit his ranche and inspect his method of conducting the business. Messrs. King & Lane, and Rumsey & Co., have some very fine Cotswold and Merino sheep, and a visit to their flocks will abundantly reward any one who desires further information on the subject.

Stock Statistics.—The total number of stock grazing on the plains of Laramie County, January 1, 1876, was as follows:

Sheep,	78,322 head,	worth	$3,	value,	$234,966
Horned cattle,	87,000 "	"	20,	"	1,740,000
Horses and mules,	2,600 "	"	50,	"	130,000
	Total,				$2,104,966

The average weight of fleece of sheep sheared last spring, was 9 lbs. per sheep. The average increase in flocks is 60 to 90 per cent. per annum, and the average increase of capital, is 50 to 60 per cent. per year.

Sheep husbandry is destined to become the feature of the Laramie Plains, and the wool which will soon be raised in this vicinity will keep thousands of spindles in motion near the very place where it is produced, thus saving to both producer and consumer vast sums which are now lost in transportation.

Early Times.—In April, 1868, the first town lots in Laramie were sold by the railroad company. There was a great rush for town lots—excitement ran very high, and the history of Cheyenne in this respect, where men made fortunes in a day, was repeated here. In fact, a month or two prior to the beginning of the sale, the town site was covered with tents, wagons, dugouts, etc., of parties waiting for the day of sale. With that sale, the settlement of the town began. The first week, over 400 lots sold and building began rapidly. In less than two weeks something over 500 buildings and structures of some kind had been erected. This was an example of western growth that would astonish the slow-going denizens of the Atlantic States. It is true these structures were of a peculiar character, and such as were usually found in the towns for the time being made the business terminus of the road. Some were of logs, some of cross-ties, others were simply four posts set in the ground with canvas sides and roofs. Others still were made of boards, in sections, and easy to be moved when the next terminus should be made known.

The iron rails that were soon to bear the iron horse were laid past the town on the 9th day of May, 1868, and on the day following, the first train arrived and discharged its freight. Laramie maintained the character of all these western towns in the early days of their settlement. The same class of human beings that had populated and depopulated North Platte, Julesburg, Cheyenne, and other places, lived and flourished here until the next move was made. They were gamblers, thieves, prostitutes, murderers — bad men and women of every calling and description under the heavens, and from almost every nationality on the globe—and when they could prey upon no one else, would, as a matter of course, prey upon each other. The worst that has ever been written of these characters does not depict the whole truth; they were, in many cases, outlaws from the East—fled to escape the consequences of crimes committed there, and each man was a law unto himself. Armed to the very teeth, it was simply a word and a shot, and many times the shot came first. Of course those who were respectable, and who desired to do a legitimate business could not endure for a long time, the presence and rascalities of these border characters. There being no law in force, the next best thing was a resort to "lynch law." This was the experience of Laramie.

Laramie is now an orderly, well-governed city, where the rights of person and property are respected, and forcibly reminds one of the quiet towns in the East. All saloons and other places of like character, are closed on the Sabbath, the churches are well attended, and the schools are liberally patronized. It is one of the most attractive towns on the line of the Union Pacific road, and offers many advantages to those who desire, for any reason, a change of location.

In addition to other public institutions elsewhere mentioned, Laramie has the location of the territorial penitentiary, a small wing of which is already constructed, and which is plainly visible only a short distance west of the railroad track. Laramie is also one of the regular eating-stations on the route. The company has a large hotel which is well kept by Major H. B. Rumsey. It is a breakfast and supper station, and travelers may be assured of good meals at the usual price. In connection with the dining-hall, there is a lunch stand supplied with the usual variety of refreshments. A manufactory for soda is talked of, and if the mines of this article are properly developed, Laramie will soon supply the world with soda enough to raise, not only biscuits and bread, but no small sum of money as a return for the investment. The rolling mills and machine and repair shops of

EARLY MORNING SCENE ON THE LARAMIE PLAINS.

the company are sources of perpetual trade and income, and must of necessity increase with the annually increasing business of the company. A visit to the soda lakes, gold mines, Iron Mountain, Red Buttes and other places of interest in the vicinity, together with good hotel accommodations, will surely lure the traveler to spend a few days in this "Gem city of the Mountains."

Laramie Peak.—This is the highest peak of the Black Hills Range in Wyoming and Colorado, north of Long's Peak, and is about 10,000 feet high. The Hayden exploring party, who were encamped at its base, describe witnessing a sunset scene of rare beauty. The sun passed down directly behind the summit of Laramie Peak. The whole range of mountains was gilded with a golden light, and the haziness of the atmosphere gave to the whole scene a deeper beauty. The valleys at the base of the Cotton-wood and Laramie Rivers are full of pleasant little streams and grassy plains. Sometimes these valleys expand out into beautiful oval park-like areas, which are favorite resorts of wild game, and would be exceedingly desirable for settlements. Emigrants would find here beautiful scenery, pure air and water, and a mild and extremely healthy climate. Cereals and roots could be easily raised, and stock-raising could be made a source of wealth to them and the whole community.

The Windmills of the Union Pacific Railroad.—The traveler notices with interest the ever frequent windmills which appear at every station, and are such prominent objects over the broad prairies. They are used for supplying the locomotives and station houses with water. Probably no finer specimens exist in the United States than are found on the lines of this road. We give an illustration of the one at Laramie:—

Its height is about 75 feet. The base is 15 feet by 25 feet. The tank for holding the water is about half the height of the tower. The arms or wings of this machine are 25 feet in length, and the fan or weather-director at the opposite end of the shaft is nearly 25 feet in length, the whole being balanced on this beam. In the tank is a large hollow globe floating in the water. This globe is so connected with levers that when the water has reached a certain height, the slats or fans are thrown in line with the wind, and the machine stops. As the water is drawn off for supplying the locomotives, the ball falls, and the machine is again put in motion. It is thus self-regulating and self-acting. The water is thrown up by a forcing pump. A curious fact may be here mentioned. These tanks, when closely covered, have thus far proved that there is enough caloric in the water to prevent it from freezing. The cost is upward of $10,000.

WINDMILL AT LARAMIE.

Wind River Mountains.—These mountains, seen on the map and just north of the railroad, are destined soon to celebrity, for their mining value, although as yet but partially explored. Two well-known peaks rise among them, Fremont's Peak and Snow's Peak, the latter being the highest, its elevation is given by Fremont as 13,570 feet. The mountains are filled with a dense growth of a species of the nut pine, which furnishes food for innumerable birds and squirrels, and supplies the Indians with their favorite food.

Indian Burial Tree.—Among the Indian tribes there are quite a number whose custom is to honor their dead with burial places in the tops of favored trees. The Comanches, Apaches, Cheyennes, Arrapahoes and Kiowas all do this. After an Indian is dead, his corpse is securely wrapped like a mummy; with it are put food, arms, tobacco, etc.,—which its spirit is supposed to want in his trip to the happy hunting-ground,—and the whole covered with an outer covering made of willows. All the Indians of the tribe celebrate mourning both before and after this is done; then the body is placed upon a platform, constructed in some old tree, usually a large cotton-wood. The feet of the departed Indian are turned with care to the southward, for thither resides the Great Spirit,—so the Indians say—and thither he is going. In some of their favorite groves, as many as eight or ten bodies have been found in a single tree. Another mode of burial is to erect a scaffold on some prominent knoll or bluff. These customs are prevalent among those Indian tribes which are most roving, and live in the saddle. "Foot Indians," those which inhabit the plains, and are peaceable, most invariably bury their dead in the ground—always, however, accompanied with such good things as he will need in his trips thereafter in the new hunting-grounds.

INDIAN BURIAL TREE, NEAR FORT LARAMIE.

The Black Hills of Wyoming, and the Medicine Bow Range.—In going west, the first range of real mountains the traveler meets with are what are called the Black Hills of Wyoming. They are really the first range of the Rockies. They begin at the valley of the North Platte River, directly south of Fort Fetterman, and unite with the Medicine Bow Range in northern Colorado, south-west from Sherman. Laramie Peak and Reed's Peak, north of the Laramie Canon, are the highest peaks in this range. The waters which flow from them east of the Black Hills, and those which flow west from the Medicine Bow Range, all unite in the North Platte River, which describes a half circle around their northern extremity, and then flows eastward to the Missouri River. This range of mountains, as before stated, is crossed at Sherman. They have not been prospected to any great extent for the precious metals, but gold, silver, copper, iron and other minerals are known to exist. Iron is found in large quantities. About 18 miles north-east from Laramie is Iron Mountain, on the head of Chugwater Creek. It is said to be nearly pure, and will some day be developed. There has been talk of a railroad from Cheyenne with a branch to this mountain, but nothing has been done yet. In searching for a route for the Union Pacific Railroad, a survey of the Laramie Canon was made, but it was found to be impracticable for a railroad. It, however, has grand scenery, and will become a place of resort, by tourists, as soon as the Indian question is settled. The Black Hills virtually connect with the Medicine Bow Range at both extremities, bearing to the left around the circle of the North Platte, and to the right south

MEDICINE BOW MOUNTAINS, FROM MEDICINE BOW RIVER.

of Sherman. The canons of both the Laramie and Platte Rivers are rugged and grand. Laramie Peak has an elevation of 10,000 feet, and lies in plain view off to the right from Lookout to Medicine Bow Stations.

Crossing the Black Hills, the road strikes the Laramie Plains, and then the Medicine Bow Range rises grandly before you. At Laramie City—the road running north—you look west and behold Sheep Mountain in front, whose summit is 10,000 feet above the sea; to the left of this is Mt. Agassiz, so named in honor of the distinguished scientist who gave his life to the cause he loved so well. To the right of Sheep Mountain, which is in the Medicine Bow Range, you discover what seems to be a large depression in the mountains. This is where the Little Laramie River heads, and across it, to the right, still other peaks of this range lift their snowy heads. The range is now on your left until you pass around its northern bend and into the North Platte Valley again at Fort Steele. On the northern extremity, Elk Mountain looms up, the best view of which can be obtained as you pass from Medicine Bow Station to Fort Steele, provided, of course, you look when the foot hills do not obscure your vision. The Medicine Bow Range is also full of the precious metals, mostly gold, but has not been developed. The Centennial Mine, located by a party of gentlemen from Laramie, on the first day of January, 1875, is on the mountain just north of one of the branches of the Little Laramie River, and in a clear day, with a good glass, can plainly be seen from Laramie City. Nearly all the streams which head in the Medicine Bow Mountains will show "color" to the prospector, but the lodes are mostly "blind," and can only be found by persistent search. This range is also heavily timbered, and abounds in game, and except the highest peaks, is free from snow in the summer. The timber is mostly pine, and immense quantities are annually cut for railroad ties, telegraph and fence poles and wood. Nearly every ranche on the Laramie Plains is supplied with poles for corrals, sheds and fences from the Black Hills or Medicine Bow Range. The Laramie Plains is the great basin between these two ranges, and the road has to pass northward a long distance in order to find its way out. Leaving the grand views of these mountains, the traveler enters upon a vast, dreary and unproductive waste—fitly called a desert. Still its rough and broken appearance with rocks, hills, and mountains on either side afford a strange and pleasant relief from the dull monotony of the eastern plains.

Leaving Laramie City, the track passes close to the company's rolling mills, from the tall chimneys of which there are huge volumes of black smoke and occasional flames, constantly belching forth. We soon cross the Laramie River on a wooden truss bridge, and run along near its banks to

Howell,—which is a side track, eight miles from Laramie, and 580.8 miles from Omaha; elevation, 7,090 feet. Passing over the plains, walled in by mountains on either side, we reach the next station,

Wyoming,—over fifteen miles from Laramie, and 588.4 miles from Omaha; elevation, 7,068 feet. Having reached the highest altitude on the line of the road between the two oceans, at Sherman, you see we are now going down hill a little, and from this time until we cross the Sierras, there will be a constant succession of "ups and downs" in our journey. Wyoming is on the Little Laramie River, which empties into the Laramie River near the station. It is a telegraph station with a few houses in the vicinity—in the midst of a fine grazing country, with sheep and cattle ranches in sight. Leaving Wyoming, the aspect of the country soon changes. A bluff on the right lies near the track, the country becomes more undulating as we pass on, and the grass seems to grow thinner except on the bottom near the stream. Sage brush and greasewood, well known to all frontier men, begin to appear. We have seen a little of sage brush before in the vicinity of Julesburg, and Sidney, and now strike it again.

Cooper's Lake,—598.9 miles from Omaha, with an elevation of 7,044 feet It is a telegraph station with the usual side track and section-houses. The station is named from the little lake near by, which can best be seen from the cars at the water tank, beyond the station. It isn't much of a lake, nor can much of it be seen from the car windows. The water is said to look very green in the summer, and to differ but little in appearance from the green grass which surrounds it. The lake itself is about half a mile wide, and a mile and a half long, and about two miles from the track, though it does not seem half that distance. It is fed by Cooper and Dutton Creeks, but has no visible outlet.

Lookout,—607.6 miles from Omaha, and about thirty-five miles from Laramie; elevation, 7,169 feet. The road left what may be called the Laramie bottom at the last station, and now winds through a rolling country, which soon becomes rough and broken, with the sage brush constantly increasing. Notice the changes in the elevation as you pass along.

Miser,—615.9 miles from Omaha; elevation, 6,810 feet. There are quite a number of snow-sheds on this part of the road, with numerous cuts and fills. Near here coal has been found. It is in the vicinity of Rock Creek, which is said to be the eastern rim of the coal fields discovered on this elevated plateau, in the middle of the Continent. From the last station to this, and beyond, you have fine and constantly changing views from the moving train, of Laramie Peak, away off to the right, and of Elk Mountain to the left. Sage brush is the only natural production of the soil in this region, and is said to be eaten by antelope and elk in the absence of grass or anything better. It is also said that sheep will feed upon it, and that wherever antelope live and flourish, sheep will do likewise. Miser is a telegraph station with the usual side track and section-house.

Rock Creek,—so-called from a creek of the same name, which the road here crosses. It is 624.6 miles from the eastern terminus of the road, with an elevation of 6,690 feet above the sea. Rock Creek rises in the north-eastern peaks of the Medicine Bow Range, and runs in that direction to this station, near which it turns toward the west and unites with Medicine Bow River, near Medicine Bow Station. Parties who are anxious to fish, may find plenty of what are called "suckers" in this creek, and also in the Laramie Rivers. The road now follows in its general course Rock Creek, until it empties into the Medicine Bow River. There is the usual telegraph office, side track and section-house at the station, with a broken country around.

Wilcox.—A side track for the passing of trains, 632.3 miles from Omaha, and 7,033 feet above the sea. The next station is

Como,—named after Lake Como, which the

road here passes. One peculiarity of this lake is that it is near Rock Creek—separated from it by a ridge of hills estimated at 200 feet high,—with no visible outlet. The station is 640.2 miles from Omaha, and 6,680 feet above the sea. The lake has been estimated to be 200 feet above the surface of Rock Creek, from which it is separated as above stated. It is fed by warm springs, which also supply the water tank of the company at the station. In a cold day the steam from these springs can be seen at some distance. It is also a great resort for ducks, and sportsmen can obtain fine shooting here in the proper season. If lizards are fish with legs, then we have fish with legs abounding in this lake and vicinity. These animals are from 6 to 18 inches in length, with a head a good deal like that of a frog, and tufts or tassels where the gills would be on a fish. They have four legs and crawl around to a certain extent on the land. There are two kinds of these lizards, one differing from the other in size and color more than in shape, and either kind are devoured by the ducks when they can be caught. The lake is about one mile wide in the widest place, and two and a half miles long.

Valley of the Chugwater. — The Chugwater Valley is about 100 miles long. It has been for many years a favorite locality for wintering stock, not only on account of the excellence of the grass and water, but also from the fact that the climate is mild throughout the winter. Cattle and horses thrive well all winter without hay or shelter. The broad valley is protected from strong cold winds by high walls or bluffs. The soil everywhere is fertile, and wherever the surface can be irrigated, good crops of all kinds of cereals and hardy vegetables can be raised without difficulty.

In this valley and near the source of the Chugwater, are thousands of tons of iron ore, indicating deposits of vast extent and richness, which can be made easily accessible whenever desirable to construct a railroad to Montana.

Medicine Bow—is 647.3 miles from Omaha; elevation, 6,550 feet. The river, from which the station is named, was crossed a short distance before we reached the station. It rises directly south, in the Medicine Bow Mountains, and runs nearly north to the place where it is crossed by the railroad, after which it turns toward the west and unites with the North Platte, below Fort Steele.

There is a roundhouse of five stalls, in which one or more engines are kept, to assist trains up and down the steep grades between here and Carbon. It is also a point from which a large quantity of military supplies for Fort Fetterman and other posts are distributed. The government has a freight depot here. There are one or two stores, with the inevitable saloon and several dwellings, in the vicinity. There is a good wagon road from this place to Fort Fetterman, distance ninety miles, and it is by far the nearest route to the gold fields in the Black Hills of Dakota, for passengers and miners from the West. The Indians were disinclined to leave this region and even now hardly know how to give it up. In the summer of 1875, they came here and stole a herd of between three and four hundred horses that were grazing on Rock Creek. Some of these horses have been seen and recognized at the agencies of Red Cloud and Spotted Tail; and when demand was made for them, the owners were quietly told by the Indian agents to make out their claims and present them to the proper authorities to be paid. But the cases of their payment are like angels' visits, few and far between. Some of the horses stolen belonged to Judge Kelly, member of Congress, from Pennsylvania. Medicine Bow is in the midst of a rough, broken country, over which millions of antelope and jack rabbits roam at pleasure. When the road was built here immense quantities of ties and wood were cut in the mountains south, and delivered at this place.

Curiosities of Indian Life and Character.—The entire country, from North Platte over as far as the western border of Laramie Plains, has been for years the roving ground of the Indians, of whom we could tell many interesting facts respecting their life and the curious interviews the overland scouts, trappers, etc., have had with them. To a man, every scout will unite in denunciation of their treachery. Jim Baker,—an old Rocky Mountain trapper,—once told, in his characteristic manner the following, to General Marcy:

"They are the most onsartainest varmints in all creation, and I reckon thar not mor'n half human; for you never seed a human, arter you'd fed and treated him to the best fixins in your lodge, just turn round and steal all your horses, or anything he could lay his hand on.

"No, not adzackly! he would feel kinder grateful, and ask you to spread a blanket in his lodge if ever you passed that way. But the Indian, he don't care shucks for you, and is ready to do you a heap of mischief as soon as he quits your feed. No, Cap'," he continued, "it's not the right way to give 'um presents to buy peace; but ef I was governor of these yeer United States, I'll tell you what I'd do. I'd invite 'um all to a big feast, and make believe I wanted to have a big talk, and as soon as I got 'um all together, I'd pitch in and scalp half of 'um, and then t'other half would be mighty glad to make a peace that would stick. That's the way I'd make a treaty with the dog-ond, red-bellied varmints; and, as sure as you're born, Cap., that's the only way.

"It ain' no use to talk about honor with them, Cap.; they hain't got no such thing in 'um; and they won't show fair fight, any way you can fix it. Don't they kill and scalp a white man, when'ar they get the better on him? The mean varmints, they'll never behave themselves until you give 'um a clean out and out licking. They can't onderstand white folks' ways, and they won't learn 'um, and ef you treat 'um decently, they think you're afeard. You may depend on't, Cap., the only way to treat Indians, is to thrash them well at first, then the balance will sorter take to you and behave themselves."

Indian observations on the character of the American and English people, are often pretty good. An Indian once describing to an Englishman the characteristics of the different people he knew, said as follows, most naively:

"King George man, (English) very good; Boston man, (American) good; John Chinaman, not good; but the black man, *he no better than a dog*."

They are particularly curious about negroes, as they do not feel certain whether the black goes all through. Some years ago, a party of negroes escaping from Texas, were captured by some of the Comanches, who *scraped their skin to settle this question.*

At the time of the presidency of Lincoln, an Indian, while conversing with an English missionary, asked him who was the chief of the English. He was told. "Ah! Queen Victoly," for they can't pronounce it. "Is she a woman?" "Yes." "Who is the chief of the Boston men, (American)?" "Mr. Lincoln." "Ah! I thought so; but another Indian once told me that it was Mr. Washington. Are Mr. Lincoln and the English woman-chief good friends?" "Yes, excellent friends." He thought for a moment, and, finally, said eagerly: "Then if they are so good friends, *why does not Mr. Lincoln take Queen Victoly for his squaw?*"

The Indians are very fond of card-playing, and, perhaps in no other way can their natural treachery be so well illustrated, and desire to take advantage of others by cheating.

An Indian once, while at a wayside village, near the mines, and withal a natural born swindler, explained to his white hearers how he could manage to cheat while dealing the cards.

While playing in the open air, in some valley, near some rocks, with a young Indian, while dealing the cards, he would shout out as if he saw some lovely forest maid passing near or ascending the rock or sides of the hill: "Aah, nanich skok tenans klatchmann (Hallo! look at that young woman!)" While the Indian looked around, "old Buffalo" immediately took the opportunity of dealing double to himself, or of selecting an ace or two before his opponent turned around.

A semi-civilized Indian, named Black Beaver, once visited General Marcy at St. Louis, and on his return back to his native camp, he prided himself not a little on his knowledge of cities and men, white and civilized. Camping one night with a Comanche guide, the General overheard the two in an apparently earnest and amicable talk. The General inquired of him afterward what he had been saying.

"I've been telling the Comanche what I've seen among the white folks. I tell him 'bout the steamboats, and the railroads, and the heep o' houses I see in St. Louis, but he say Ize—— fool. I tell him the world is round, but he keep all o' time say, 'Hush, you fool, do you spose I'ze child? Haven't I got eyes? Can't I see the prairie? You call him round? Maybe so; I tell you something you not know before. One time my grandfather he made long journey that way (West), when he got on big mountain, he see heep water on t'other side, just so flat as he can be, and he see the sun go straight down on t'other side. S'pose the world flat he stand still?'"

General Marcy attempted to explain to him the telegraph, but there he was nonplussed. "What you call the magnetic telegraph?" He was told. "You have heard of New York and New Orleans?" "Oh, yes." "Very well; we have a wire connecting these two cities, which are 1,000 miles apart, and it would take a man thirty days, on a good horse, to ride it. Now, a man stands at one end of this wire in New York, and by touching it a few times, he inquires of his friend in New Orleans, what he had for breakfast. His friend in New Orleans touches the other end of the wire, and in ten minutes the answer comes back, *ham and eggs*."

Beaver was requested to tell this to the Comanche, but he remained silent, his countenance all the time covered with a most comical, puzzled expression. Again he was asked to tell him, when he observed, "No, Captain, I not tell him that, for I don't b'lieve that myself."

He was assured that it was a fact, but no amount of assurances could induce him to pin his faith on such a seemingly incredible statement. All he would reply was simply,

"Injun not very smart; sometimes he's big fool, but he holler pretty loud; you hear him, maybe, half a mile; you say 'Merican man he talk thousand miles;' I 'spect you try to fool me now, Cap'n. *May be you lie*."

Polygamy is quite frequent among many of the Indians of the plains, and some amusing stories are told of the way they get their wives. One such is told of an Indian boy of only eighteen, whose father, considering that he had arrived at the years of discretion, presented him with a lodge, several horses, and goods enough to establish him in life. The first thing the precocious youth did was to go and secretly bargain with a chief for his daughter, enjoining secrecy, and then to a second, third and fourth, the result of which was, that on a fixed day, he claimed all four ladies, to the astonishment of the tribe and the indignation of the fathers. But he obtained his wives and marched them off to his wigwam. Not only this, but the chiefs determined that a youth who could do so bold an act, must be a person of discretion, and deserved and gave him a seat in the council among the warriors and the medicine men.

Of the want of books and writing among the Indians, they give the following explanations:

"It is impossible. The Great Spirit at first made a red and a white boy; to the red boy he gave a book, and to the white boy a bow and arrow, but the white boy came round the red boy, stole his book, and went off, leaving him the bow and arrow, and, therefore, an Indian could not make a book."

Carbon,—656.5 miles from Omaha, with an elevation of 6,750 feet. A telegraph station with usual side tracks for passing trains, and for the coal business which is done here. This is the first station on the line of the road, where the company obtains a supply of coal. A shaft about 120 feet deep has been sunk, and veins of coal opened about six feet thick. The coal is hoisted to the surface by means of a stationary engine, and dumped into cars by means of chutes, or into large bins from which it is taken to supply passing engines. From 50 to 150 men are employed in these mines, and a good many of them live in board shanties, adobe houses, and dug-outs along the side of the track. The coal is mostly used by the company—but little being sold as it is not as good for domestic purposes as the coal found at Rock Springs. Leaving Carbon we pass through a rugged country, with scenery sufficiently attractive to keep the traveler on the constant lookout, to

Simpson,—a side track, with section-house, 663.5 miles from Omaha, and an elevation of 6,898 feet. Passenger trains do not stop and on we go to

Percy,—668.1 miles from Omaha, and 6,950 feet above the sea. From Simpson to this station, you can obtain the finest view of Elk Mountain on the left. We have not been able to ascertain its elevation, but its comparative short distance from the road causes it to look high and grand. It can be seen from a long distance, either east or west, and is the noted peak of the Medicine Bow Range. It seems to jut out from the main ridge, and looking from the west, stands in bold relief against the sky. The station is named in honor of Colonel Percy, who was killed here by the Sioux Indians, when the road was being surveyed. At this station passengers who desire to visit Elk Mountain, and the region in its immediate vicinity will leave the cars. During the construction of the road large quantities of wood and ties with timber for bridges, were cut in the mountains and foot hills, and hauled to this station. At the foot of Elk Mountain stood Fort Halleck now abandoned, and a station of the Overland Stage Company. There were many skirmishes with the Indians in this vicinity in those days, and now and then you will be able to find an old settler who will entertain you for hours, in the recital of wild adventures and hair-breadth escapes. A visit to the site of the old fort and the region of country around, together with a close view of the grand scenery of the mountains, will amply repay the traveler for his time and money. About four miles south of Percy, fine veins of coal were discovered in 1875, but they have not been opened or tested. One is nine and the other over twenty feet in thickness. Notice a suggestive sign as you pass the station. It is "Bowles's Hotel," and of course, indicates that everything is perfectly "straight" within.

South of this station there is some very fine grazing land, mostly in the valleys of the little streams that head in the Medicine Bow Range, and flow westward into the North Platte River, and a considerable quantity of hay is cut during favorable seasons.

A Curious and Exciting Race.—Engineers have told of a curious scene on the Pacific Railroad not far from the Laramie Plains, of a race between the locomotive and a herd of deer. At daybreak, the locomotive, with its long train of carriages and freight cars, entered a narrow valley or gorge, where runs quite a rivulet of clear and cold mountain water. On the banks of this stream a large herd of red deer were standing, occasionally lapping the refreshing element. The timid creatures, startled by the presence in their midst of the "iron horse," knew not what course to pursue in order to get away from it. The engineer, to add to their evident perplexity, caused the whistle to send forth its loudest and most discordant shriek. This was enough for the deer. To get beyond reach of this new enemy, they started up the road, taking the course the locomotive was pursuing. The race became exciting. It was a superb trial of steam and iron against muscle and lung. The engineer "put on steam," and sent his locomotive with its burdensome train, whirling along the track; but for many miles—six or seven it was estimated—the frightened animals kept ahead, fairly beating their antagonist. At last the pursued and pursuer got into a more open country. This the deer perceiving, they sprang on one side, and, with unabated speed, ran to a safe distance, where beyond reach of locomotive or rifle, they stood and gazed with dilated eyes—their limbs trembling from unusual exertion, and gasping for breath—at their fast receding enemy.

Dana—is the next station—simply a side track. It is 674.2 miles from Omaha; elevation, 6,875 feet. The rugged, broken character of the country with cuts for the track, and fills in the

DEER RACE WITH TRAIN ON THE U. P. R. R.

valleys, will interest the observing tourist if he passes by in daylight.

St. Marys,—681.7 miles from Omaha, with an elevation of 6,751 feet. It is a telegraph station with accompanying side tack, section-house, etc. From this station to the next, the bluffs are rugged and wild, the road passing through a short tunnel and several deep cuts. There is nothing but the changing scenery as you move along with the train, to relieve this country from its desolate appearance. Sage brush and greasewood continue to be the only products of the soil.

Walcott,—a side track 689.5 miles from the Missouri River, and 6,800 feet above the sea. After leaving this station, the road winds around the bluffs, passing through some very deep cuts, near one of which there is a stone quarry from which stone is taken by the company for road purposes at Green River. A side track to the quarry has been laid and stone easily loaded on the flat cars used for their transportation. Suddenly bursting through one of these cuts we enter the valley of the Platte, through what is called Rattle Snake Pass, by the railroad men, and arrive at

Fort Steele,—which is 695.3 miles from Omaha, 122.5 miles from Laramie, and has an elevation of 6,840 feet. It is a telegraph station, and the site of the government post of the same name. We cross North Platte River just before arriving at the station, and are 4,051 feet higher than when we crossed the same stream at North Platte City, near the junction of the two Plattes in the State of Nebraska. Fort Steele was established on the last day of June, 1868, by Col. R. I. Dodge, then of the Thirtieth United States Infantry. It is considered a good strategic point, as well as a convenient base of supplies, in case of a campaign against the Indians. The buildings are mostly of logs, and none of them very comfortable. In 1875, the government finished a fine stone hospital building here. The station also does considerable government business, and there is a government depot for receiving and storing supplies near the track. The valley of the North Platte at this upper crossing is quite narrow, without the broad and fertile bottom-lands we were accustomed to see below as we whirled along its banks. From the head of this river in the North Park of Colorado, to a point as far down as Fort Laramie, its route describes the form of a horseshoe. Its tributaries from the east mostly rise in the Medicine Bow Range, and flow westward. They are principally Douglas Creek, Fresh Creek, Brush Creek, Cedar Creek, Spring Creek, and Pass Creek. They are beautiful streams with fine grass valleys and partially wooded banks. Its tributaries from the west are Beaver Creek, Grand Encampment Creek, Cow Creek, Hot Spring Creek, Jack Creek, and Sage Creek. Hot Spring Creek is so named from the hot sulphur springs which are found near its mouth. All the streams which rise in the Medicine Bow Range, and flow into the North Platte, show the "color" of gold where they have been prospected, and some rich diggings are said to have been discovered at the head of Douglas Creek. We believe it will not be long before the Medicine Bow Mountains will develop into a rich mining country. The waters of the Hot Springs referred to are claimed to possess remarkable medicinal virtues, and are from 40 to 45 miles from Fort Steele, up the right bank of the river. The wonders of even these desolate plains do not begin to be known, and when they are fully realized, the world will be astonished at the results. About three miles west of Fort Steele is the site of Benton—the town that was—now wholly abandoned. For a short time it was the business terminus of the road, while its construction was going on, and possessed all the characteristics of the railroad towns in those days. At one time it had a population estimated as high as five thousand souls. Old iron barrel hoops, rusty tin cans, a few holes in the ground, a few posts and stumps, and nearly or quite a hundred nameless graves in close proximity, are all that now remain to mark the place where Benton was. It grew in a day, and faded out of sight as quickly. But it was a red-hot town while it lasted. A death, sometimes two or three of them, with corresponding burials, was the morning custom. Whisky was preferred to water because it was much easier to obtain, and unrestrained by civilized society or wholesome laws, the devil in men and women had full sway, and made free exhibitions of his nature. The town was three miles from the North Platte River, where all the water was obtained and hauled in, price ten cents per bucket, or one dollar per barrel. In that town, a drink of regular old "tangle-foot" whisky, at "two bits" (twenty-five cents) would last a good deal longer than a bucket of water, to say nothing of the superior satisfaction it would give. The railroad reached and passed Benton in July, 1868. The valley of the N. Platte River begins to be occupied by cattle men, as stock can be carried through the severest winters, thus far experienced, without hay. It has superior advantages, not only for grazing, but its numerous "draws" or ravines afford friendly shelter in case of storms.

View on the North Platte, near Fort Fred Steele.—The Platte River here is over 700 miles from its mouth near Omaha, and has an elevation of 6,845 feet. Upon the plains it was a wide, shallow stream, with sand-bars and shifting currents. Here it is a deep, clear, cold stream, and but little distant from its source among the perpetual snow banks of the Rocky Mountains.

Grennville—is the next station, 703.7 miles from Omaha with an elevation of 6,560 feet above the sea. It is simply a side track for the meeting and passing of trains. Passenger trains seldom stop. The next station and the end of a subdivision of the road is

Rawlins,—named in honor of Gen. John A. Rawlins, General Grant's chief of staff and his first secretary of war. The springs near here bear the same name, but it has been incorrectly spelled, heretofore. This station is 137.9 miles from Laramie, and 710.7 miles from Omaha. It has an elevation of 6,732 feet. We are going up hill again. The town has a population of about 600 souls, a large majority of whom are railroad employes. The company has erected a hotel for the use of its employes and the traveling public, and has a roundhouse and machine-shops which are kept pretty busy in the repair of engines.

VIEW ON THE PLATTE, NEAR FORT FRED STEELE.

The water used by engines on this division is strongly impregnated with alkali and other substances, which form scales on the inside of the boiler and adhere to the flues. The engines are, therefore, carefully watched and every precaution taken to guard against accidents. North of the town, is what might be called in some countries, a mountain. Near the east end of this mountain valuable beds of red hematite—iron ore—have been found. This ore is very pure, and, when ground, makes a very hard and durable paint. It is said to be water and fire-proof when used in sufficient quantities. The dark red freight and flat cars which you see on the line of the road belonging to the company, have been painted with this material, and it is rapidly growing into public favor as its merits become known. There are two mills here for the manufacture of this paint, and a large quantity is always on hand. Forty miles due north from Rawlins are the Ferris and Seminole mining districts. These mines were visited, in 1875, by Professor Hayden and Professor Thompson. The lodes operated by the Vulcan Mining Company, indicated gold, silver and copper, mixed with iron. This company is composed mostly of mechanics and employes of the Union Pacific. They first sunk a shaft on the vein and obtained ore at about 60 feet from the surface that assayed well and gave indications of a rich mine. They then commenced a tunnel, and from their monthly wages, during nearly two years or more, contributed and expended about $24,000. At a distance of about 365 feet, they struck the vein, and have a large body of rich ore in sight and on the dump. A mill will soon be put in, when the company will begin to realize something for their outlay. The Elgin Mining Company have also put in a tunnel, and are reported to have struck a rich vein. The developments, thus far made, indicate that the copper and silver will soon run out, and that the mines will be essentially gold-bearing. South of Rawlins about 60 miles, in the Snake River Region, are fine grazing fields, already occupied, to a certain extent, by cattle men, and mining country yet undeveloped. Placer diggings have been found and worked to some extent, and indications of rich quartz lodes are prevalent, some having already been discovered. A colony of farmers and miners from the vicinity of Denver, Col., have settled in that region, and more are constantly going in. About a mile and a half from Rawlins, east, is a large sulphur spring. It is untaken, as yet. We could not ascertain whether the waters had been analyzed or not, though they are claimed to possess the usual medicinal qualities of water from similar springs. The springs frequently alluded to as Rawlins Springs, are on the left of the track, and a little west of the town. The small creek which passes through the place, is known as Separation Creek, and empties into the North Platte River north of Fort Steele. There are, also, immense beds or lakes of soda, tributary to this station, some of which is nearly pure. When they are utilized, as they doubtless soon will be, and the industry is developed, employment will be given to many laborers now idle, together with fortunes to those who have the nerve and capacity to successfully carry it on. We are informed that from twelve to fourteen millions of dollars are annually paid in customs duties on the article of imported soda, alone. Rawlins is in the midst of a broken, desolate country, and depends upon railroad importations for nearly everything upon which its people live, though there is a fine country reported both north and south. In addition to the other buildings named, it has the usual quantity of saloons, together with several stores, at which a thriving trade is done. The future of the town will depend largely upon the developments in the mining districts spoken of.

Summit.—A side track, nearly seven miles from Rawlins, and 717.4 miles from Omaha; elevation, 6,821 feet. Heavy grades now for quite a distance.

Separation.—One would naturally suppose from the name, that the waters flowing east and west, divided or separated here, but such is not the fact. It is reported that a party of engineers who were surveying and locating the road, separated here to run different lines—hence the name. It is a telegraph station, 724.1 miles from Omaha, and 6,900 feet above the level of the sea. The artesian well at this station, which supplies the water tank is 860 feet deep. The water from these wells is not always pure—frequently having a brackish or alkali taste.

Fillmore,—named in honor of a former division superintendent of the road, now in the stock business, with ranche at Wyoming. It is 731.6 miles from Omaha; elevation, 6,885 feet. Simply a side track in the midst of a barren, broken country.

Creston,—738.6 miles from the eastern terminus of the road, and 7,030 feet above the sea. It is a telegraph station, with the usual side tracks and section-house. Three miles farther west, and we reach the summit of the divide which separates the waters of the two oceans. This is the crowning ridge in the backbone of the Continent, and a desolate place it is. It is the summit of the Rocky Mountains. "What was this country made for?"—We asked a fellow-traveler. "To hold the rest of it together"—was the ready reply. That is good; the best reason for its existence we've had. It is of some use after all. Allowing 60 feet grade for the three miles west of Creston, to the actual summit of the divide, and we are then 1,122 feet lower than at Sherman. It is true there are no lofty peaks here, with snowy crests the year round, but an immense roll, over which we glide and never think that we are crossing the summit of the rock-ribbed Rockies. At this divide a short distance north of the track, a pole was once erected with a flag to mark the spot, but it has fallen before the fierce gales which sweep over this elevated ridge, and which seem to have withered everything they touched. Standing on the rear platform of the train, looking east you notice the undulations of the road as it passes beneath you; Elk Mountain of the Medicine Bow Range, and the far distant Black Hills rise grandly in view as you approach the crest, but suddenly you have passed to the other side, and a stretch of country two hundred miles long drops from your view in an instant. On this part of the road the most difficulty with snow is usually experienced in the winter. There is a constant breeze here, and frequent storms, though a few miles farther it may be clear and pleasant. In the great snow blockade of the winter of 1871–2, the telegraph poles were frequently buried in the drifts. The Western Union Company had their wires elevated on poles planted in the snow in several places, to keep them above the drifts. In that blockade, the worst ever known since the road was built, there were seventeen days without trains. Since then the track has been raised, snow fences planted, sheds erected and every possible appliance used to insure the safe and speedy passage of trains. Looking again to the north you can see the snowy heads of the Wind River Mountains, with the peak named after Fremont, the gallant Path-finder of the West, towering against the sky. Notice the dark shades of the timber lines as they press against the eternal snows with which they are covered. Looking forward to the west, if you have a chance, Pilot Butte, north of Rock Springs, one of the great landmarks of the plains, is clearly visible. To the south you behold the mountains where the tributaries of the Snake River rise, and whence they flow into the Pacific Ocean. Passing rapidly down the grade we arrive at

Latham,—746.1 miles from Omaha, and 6,900 feet above the sea. Passenger trains do not stop as it is only a side track. On we go to

Washakie,—so called after a Shoshone chief, reputed to be friendly to the whites, whose tribe fights the Sioux when there is opportunity. It is 753.7 miles from Omaha; elevation, 6,697 feet; and nearly 200 feet lower than at the last station.

Red Desert.—The country near is reddish in appearance, but the place is named after the *Red Desert*, near which is an immense basin of its own, similar to the Salt Lake basin. It lies 500 feet below the level of the country, has no outlet, and extends from the South Pass on the north, to Bridger's Pass on the south, and east from summit of the divide to Tipton on the west, a very singular depression right on the divide of the Continent. The little stream just seen before reaching this place, flows south and is lost in this basin. The country near is alkali, and subject to high water and heavy rains, giving great difficulty to preserve the security of road-bed and track. Station is 763 miles from Omaha; elevation 6,710 feet.

Tipton,—a side track for meeting and passing trains. It is 769.6 miles from the "Big Muddy," with an elevation of 6,800 feet. We have been going up hill again—leaving the valley of the Snake River. The snows of winter leave heavy drifts along here, but the railroad men have learned by experience how to manage them quite successfully. When the drifts have reached the top of the fences in height, they go along and raise the fences to the top of the drifts, fastening them as best they can in the snow. This they repeat as often as necessary, and thus, the snow, in many instances, is kept away from the track, but the drifts become pretty high.

Table Rock,—named from a rock resembling a table south of, and about six miles from the station. It is 776.3 miles from Omaha, and 6.890 feet above the sea—is a telegraph station. There is a long, evenly cut bluff south of the track, estimated to be 600 feet in height. On what appears to be the north-west corner of this bluff a square, table-like, projection rises—the table—and presents a very odd appearance. It can be seen for quite a distance, as you look to the left from the cars. The table projects about 60 feet above the bluffs adjoining, though it does not seem half that distance. Next we come to

Agate,—781.3 miles from Omaha, and 6,785 feet above the sea. South of this station and to a certain extent, in its immediate vicinity, moss agates are found. The stones, however, are not clear and well-defined. They are smoky and dark, rendering them nearly valueless. Agate is only a side track where trains seldom stop. Down the grade we pass to

Bitter Creek,—a telegraph station, 786.3 miles from Omaha, with an elevation of 6,685 feet. At this station, we first strike the well-known Bitter Creek Valley, through which we shall pass to Green River. About four miles below this station, on the south side of the track, the old overland stage and emigrant road struck the valley, as it came in from Bridger's Pass, and across the Snake River Valley. The railroad reaches Bitter Creek through a "draw" or dry ravine which unites with the valley proper, at the station. The old stage-road struck the creek farther south, and before it reaches the railroad. This was formerly quite a station, and the end of a passenger division. It has a small round-house, with five stalls and turn-table, upon which the engines and snow-plows are turned. Between this station and Rawlins, as has been observed, are very heavy grades, requiring two engines to pull a train. These extra engines come with trains as far as this station, and then assist eastward bound trains back again. A large quan-

SCENES ON GREEN RIVER.

tity of bridge timber is also kept here, ready for any emergency. In the great washout at the foot of this valley, in the spring of 1875, large quantities were used. Bitter Creek is rightly named. Its waters are so strongly impregnated with alkali that they are almost useless. Nevertheless, at the head of this creek, where it is fed by cold, clear springs, for more than ten miles from the station, trout have been caught, though they are small. The rugged scenery along this valley will interest the traveler, as the views are constantly changing. There are no machine-shops for repairs here, only the five-stall roundhouse. The creek has been dammed for the purpose of supplying the water tank, though the water is not the best for boilers. The whole region of country, from a point east, as far as Rock Creek to Green River, is underlaid with coal. It frequently crops out in this valley. The coal is lignite and will not "coke" like the bituminous coal. There are also indications of iron and other minerals, in the immediate vicinity of the valley. Occasionally, you will see little shrub pines on the bluffs—but no timber. These pines have tried to grow, but the sterility of the soil is against them. They find it almost impossible to "take root." Sometimes it seems, as you pass down the valley and look ahead, as though the train was going square against the rocks, and would be dashed in pieces; but a sudden curve, and you have rounded the projecting bluffs, and are safely pursuing your journey. Again, it seems as though the bluffs were trying to shake hands across the chasm, or making an effort to become dovetailed together. They assume all sorts of shapes, washed out in places by the storms of ages—smoothly carved as if by the hand of the sculptor—and again, ragged and grotesque. The geology of the Bitter Creek and Green River Valleys, will afford a chapter of curious interest, and will amply reward him who searches thoroughly after the knowledge. Professor Hayden and Major Powell have the best reports on the formation and geology of this region.

Black Buttes—is the next station, 795.4 miles from Omaha, and 6,600 feet above the sea. It is a telegraph station with accompanying side tracks. Formerly there was a coal mine worked here, said to belong to Jack Morrow, now of Omaha, and quite a noted frontier character in his day. It furnishes excellent coal, easily accessible, the vein being from six to eight feet thick. As you approach the station, notice the balanced rock north of the road and within 50 feet of the side track. The buttes from which the station is named are south of the creek, and plainly visible.

Hallville,—named after a noted contractor who graded the road through this part of the valley. A few posts and adobe walls are all that remain of the camp. It is simply a side track, 800.9 miles from Omaha, with an elevation of 6,590 feet.

Point of Rocks—is a station with a history. It was formerly quite a town, but its glory has departed with the causes which brought it into existence. It was formerly the point of departure and the outfitting place for the Sweetwater Gold District, South Pass City, Atlantic City, Camp Stambaugh, and other places in the region of the Great South Pass at the foot of Wind River Mountains, and is the nearest railroad point to those places, to-day, with a good wagon road not much traveled. Distance to South Pass City, 65 miles. The rocks from which this place is named are on a high point south of the track, and a little east of the station. They seem in the distance like faint outlines of huge perpendicular columns, not very high, but really 365 feet perpendicular above their base surroundings. Their summit is about 1,100 feet above the track. At the base of the rocks proper, and about 735 feet above the track, seven sulphur springs break out, three of which are large ones, the balance being small.

North of the track, and three-fourths of a mile west of the station, is an iron spring, reputed to possess remarkable medicinal qualities, several invalids, especially females, having been highly benefited by drinking and bathing in its waters. Four miles north of the station is a huge sulphur spring, with water pouring forth from the ground. The artesian well, which supplies the water tank here, is 700 feet deep. Water is pumped out by steam power. Wells & Fargo's Overland Express Company had a station here, and their old adobe buildings, rapidly going into decay, may still be seen across the creek, at the base of the bluffs. In the "piping" times of the town several buildings were commenced, but the collapse was so sudden that they were never completed. This station is 806.7 miles from Omaha, and 6,490 feet above the sea. If the springs in the vicinity are improved, it will become a great resort for invalids, and those who desire to realize the beneficial effects of their healing waters.

Thayer,—simply a side track, 812 miles from Omaha, with an elevation of 6,425 feet. The moving trains will give the tourist an ever-varying view of the grand and beautiful scenery of this valley.

Salt Wells,—818.2 miles from the eastern

terminus of the road, and 6,360 feet above the sea. It is a telegraph station, and in the construction period of the road, was a place where considerable timber, wood, etc., was delivered. The water from the well here has a saltish, alkaline taste, hence the name. Three and one-half miles north, there is a salt or alkali basin, which has no visible outlet in which the brackish waters stand the most of the year.

Baxter,—826.2 miles from Omaha; elevation, 6,300 feet—A side track where passenger trains do not stop. The valley narrows in this vicinity, and the rugged rocks with their ragged edges, if possible become more interesting to the observer.

CASTLE ROCK.

Rock Springs,—831.6 miles from Omaha, and 6,280 feet above the sea. This is the great coal station on the line of the Union Pacific Road. The company not only furnishes the finest lignite coal to be found, for its own use, but supplies the market at every point along its entire line. Rock Springs coal for domestic purposes is only surpassed by anthracite. It has but little of the sulphurous smell of other soft coal, burns into ashes without clinkers, and without the black soot which characterizes other coal. These mines, with others, were formerly operated by the Wyoming Coal Company. Their product is annually increasing; wherever the superior merits of the coal have become known it speedily supplants other kinds in use. In 1875 the company mined 104,427 tons, or 10,442 cars allowing the usual ten tons per car. They did not, however, ship this number of cars as considerable coal is furnished to all the engines that pass, and consumed by the people living in the town. They are now working two veins, one six and the other about nine feet in thickness.

Lawrence,—840.6 miles from Omaha, with an elevation of 6,200 feet. A side track for passing trains between Rock Springs and

Green River,—which is the end of the Laramie division of the road, 273.8 miles from that place, and 846.6 miles from Omaha, with an elevation of 6,140 feet. This is a regular eating-station, breakfast and supper, and *is now* one of the best kept hostelries on the road. This place will eventually be a popular resort for those who are seeking for fossiliferous remains, and those who delight in fishing. Here is the outfitting point for hunting and fishing parties who desire to go either north or south, and here is the head center for Rocky Mountain specimens, fossils, petrifactions, etc., and travelers would like to know beforehand just what accommodations they can obtain. Mr. Kitchen is able to provide for all, in elegant style, at reasonable prices. Here, also, he has on exhibition and for sale the specimens alluded to—such as beautiful moss agates, fossil fish, petrified shells and wood, with others which we are not able to name. Parties of men are employed to search the hills, mountains and valleys in this vicinity, for these specimens, and when found, to bring them in. The stock is, therefore, continually replenished with rich and rare gems and fossils, and they may here be obtained at any time.

THE TWIN SISTERS, GREEN RIVER.

Being the end of a division, Green River has a large roundhouse with fifteen stalls, and the usual machine and repair shops. The railroad bursts into the valley through a narrow gorge between two hills, then turns to the right and enters the town, crossing the river beyond on a wooden truss bridge. The old adobe town, remains of which are still visible, was on the bottom-land directly in front of the gorge.

Green River is now the county-seat of Sweetwater County, Wyoming, and has a population of about 500 souls. Efforts have been made by Mr. Fields and a few others to reclaim the soil, but thus far with indifferent success, though Mr. Fields was quite successful, in 1875, with a crop of potatoes, cabbages, turnips, radishes, and other "garden truck." His wheat, oats and barley did not ripen, though he says they were planted too late in the season, and that the experiment was not a fair test. The valley of Salt Lake has been reclaimed by the Mormons, and crops may yet be raised here upon similar soil (alkali), though the elevation is some 2,000 feet greater than at Salt Lake.

The high projecting tower north of the track, crowning a bluff, is 625 feet higher than the river level below, and about 615 feet higher than the track. Other rocks, as "The Sisters" and "The Twin Sisters" will be readily recognized by the passing traveler.

"Wake up, wake up," said an old lady to her husband, as the train approached the station one morning last year; "here is Solomon's temple petrified," said she, as she gave him another shake. The old gentleman rubbed his eyes, gave another yawn, and finally looked out, to see what excites the curiosity of every traveler, as he arrives at this place. Sure enough: it seems as though some great temple once stood here, or several of them, and in the wrecks of time, left their gigantic pillars standing, as a reminder of their former greatness.

The Green River.—The peculiar color of this river is not owing to the fact of any discoloration of the water; that, when the banks of the stream are not filled by freshets of itself or some of its tributaries, is very pure and sweet, and of the usual color of clear water, but is owing to the green shale through which it runs, and which can readily be seen in the bluffs in the vicinity and for quite a distance up Black's Fork, and

PETRIFIED FISH CUT, GREEN RIVER.

WEST BANK GREEN RIVER, LOOKING EASTWARD.

which is supposed to contain arsenic or chloride of copper, which becomes detached by drainage and fastens itself to the pebble stones and bottom of the stream, causing the water, as you look into it, to bear the same color. This river rises in the Wyoming and Wind River Mountains, is fed by numerous tributaries, and flows in a general southerly direction, until it unites with the Colorado River. The scenery along its banks, most always rugged, in some places is sublime. Where it is crossed by the railroad, its valley is narrow, enclosed on either side by high bluffs, which have been washed into numerous fanciful shapes by the storms of time, and which are crowned, in many instances, by columns, or towers, forcibly reminding one of the towers, battlements and castles, spoken of in the old feudal times. Its tributaries, nearly all have narrow fertile valleys, which are being occupied by stockmen, and which afford both hay and shelter for stock. South of the railroad, it winds through the famous Colorado Canon, so well and grandly described by Major Powell, the explorer. The river and its surroundings must from their very nature, always be a source of interest to the scientist, and will soon become a popular resort for fossil hunters, gem searchers and sportsmen.

Brown's Hole.—This is a beautiful scene just below Red Canon, the water is calm, quiet, and peaceful, like a mirror, with wonderfully distinct reflections. Here is the last quiet stretch of the river ere it enters into the turbulent passage of the deeper, gloomier, and larger canon below. The sandy beach, at the left, shows the foot-prints of numerous deer, bears, and elk that frequent the bank.

Brown's Hole is an expansion of the valley of Green River, and is about five miles wide and thirty miles long. This is a name given by the old trappers,—40 years ago, or more—and has been a favorite wintering place for stock. Little or no snow falls in the valleys, and they are so well surrounded by high mountains, that the bleak winds of winter cannot reach them. The valley is covered with wild sage and bunch grass—and at the time of the visit of the Hayden Exploring Party, there were 2,200 head of Texas cattle, just driven in, to fatten for the California market. In the north sides of the valley, the beds of rock have, by the action of the weather, become shaped into innumerably beautiful, architectural forms, like the ruins of pyramids.

Giant's Club.—This is fairly a giant in dimensions,—as its proportions are really colossal. It rises with almost perpendicular sides, and is impossible to scale by ascent. The rock is valuable for its curious composition, as it bears evidences of having once existed at the bottom of a lake. The rock lies in regular strata, all horizontal, and most of these contain fossils of plants and fishes. The plants are all extinct species, and closely allied to our fruit and forest trees; among them, however, are some palms, which indicated this to be, in original times, when the deposit was formed, a very warm climate. Professor Hayden, in examining this rock, and others near, found the plants in the upper part of the rock, and about a hundred feet lower down, discovered the remains of fishes, all of them belonging to fresh water, and all extinct species. They were imbedded in oily shales, and insects were found with them, in a remarkable state of preservation. With the fishes were also found feathers of birds, and a few reeds.

Peculiarities of the Green River Rocks. —To the curious formation of rocks which give all this region its characteristic features, is given the name of the Green River Shales; the sediments are arranged in regular layers, mostly quite thin, but varying from the thickness of a knife-blade to several feet. These peculiar layers, or bands, are quite varied in shades of color. In some of the thin slabs of shale, are thousands of beautiful impressions of fish, sometimes a dozen or so within the compass of a square foot. Impressions of insects and water plants are also sometimes found. At Burning Rock Cut, the road is cut through thin layers of a sort of cream-colored, chalky limestone, interspersed with strata of a dark brown color, saturated with petroleum as to burn freely. The Cut derives its name Burning Rocks, from the fact that during the building of the road the rocks became ignited and burned for some days, illuminating the labor of the workmen by night—and filling the valley with dense clouds of smoke by day.

GIANT'S CLUB, GREEN RIVER.

GIANT'S TEA-POT, GREEN RIVER.

Curious Scenes along the Green River. —At the mouth of Henry's Fork there is a view on Green River of great beauty, which derives its principal charm from its vivid colors. The waters of the river are of the purest emerald, with banks and sand-bars of glistening white. The perpendicular bluff to the left is nearly 1,500 feet above the level of the river, and of a bright red and yellow. When illuminated by full sunlight, it is grand, and deserves its full title "The Flaming Gorge." It is the entrance to a gateway to the still greater wonders and grandeurs of the famous Red Canon that cuts its way to a depth of 3,000 feet, between this point and its entrance into Brown's Hole.

Leaving Green River the railroad crosses the bridge, turns to the right, and runs along under the bluffs — the highest being about 350 feet high, and almost over the river in one place—for about three miles, when it again turns to the left, passing the divide where there is an unnamed side track, and along a hilly, broken country.

The Sweetwater.—This stream rises in the Wind River Mountains, directly north of Point of Rocks and Salt Wells, in the great South Pass, discovered by General Fremont, and runs in a general easterly direction uniting with the North Platte River about 80 miles north of Fort Steele. South of it is the Sweetwater Mountain Range. North of it lay the Rattlesnake Hills, which are said to be one continuous chain of broken ragged rocks heaped upon each other in confused masses. They are utterly barren and desolate, and beyond the snakes which give them their name, are avoided by almost every living thing. Near the mouth of this river, Independence

Rock, a noted landmark of the plains, rises. It is on the line of the Indian trail, to the upper North Platte Region, and near it has been found immense deposits of soda in lakes which are said to be nearly pure, and which are soon to be worked. The valley of this stream is rarely covered with snow in winter, and affords excellent grazing for stock the entire year. Were it not so exposed to Indian raids in summer, it would soon be occupied. The care of stock requires horses and beyond the killing of a few head for beef occasionally, the Indians do not trouble it; the horses are what they want, and what they come after and scalps will be taken, if necessary to obtain them. Placer, gulch and quartz gold has been discovered in the Wind River Mountains, near the Great South Pass, and fortunes have been made and lost in that mining district in a very short time. They have been made by the mining sharks, who sold their mines to the inexperienced and uninitiated from the East, and lost by the parties who were "taken in." There are however valuable mines in this vicinity (nearly all gold), which will some day be developed. To the east of the Wind River Mountains the Shoshone or Snake River Indian reservation has been laid off. The principal towns are Atlantic City, South Pass City and Miner's Delight, a mining town. Near Atlantic City is Camp Stambough and still farther north on the east side of the same mountain, is Camp Brown, the latter being near the boundary line of the Indian reservation referred to. Very fine hot mineral springs have been found on or near this reservation, which will eventually be extensively patronized. The main road by which these places are reached, leads out from Bryan and Green River. From the latter place four-horse coaches are run tri-weekly, while from the former a great quantity of government freight is annually shipped. The road crosses the river near the mouth of Big Sandy Creek, and follows up this stream, and its south branch to Pacific Spring, after which it crosses a low divide to a tributary of the Sweetwater. While the road from Point of Rocks is much shorter yet this route is said to be the best as it follows the valley of a stream all the way, and avoids sand-hills which are very trying to stock. From Green River the road at present traveled, passes up the valley until it strikes the Big Sandy, where it intersects the road from Bryan. The nearest peaks seen on the north side of the track, as you pass the divide just west of Creston, are those of the real Rocky Mountain Range, and extend in a north-westerly direction to the head of the Wind River Mountains, from which they are only divided by the Sweetwater Valley. Before the Lodge Pole Valley Route was discovered *via* the Cheyenne Pass, the North Platte and Sweetwater Route *via* the South Pass and Big Sandy was the main, in fact the great overland route, traveled by the Mormons and California emigrants. At the time the railroad was built, however, the Lodge Pole Route was the one mainly traveled. The vast region north of the railroad between the Black Hills and Green River Valley, contains within itself the germs of a mighty empire, only waiting for the united efforts of capital and labor for development.

Bryan,—over 13 miles from Green River, and 860 miles from Omaha, with an elevation of 6,340 feet or just 200 feet higher than at Green River. This station was formerly a division terminus at which time it was a place of considerable importance. The government has a depot here, where its freight for Camp Stambaugh, Camp Brown and other places is received. The majority of the freight for the Sweetwater Mining District and the settlements at the base of the Wind River Mountains, South Pass City, Atlantic City, etc., is also shipped from this place, the distance to the latter city being 90 miles. Bryan is the first station where the railroad strikes Black's Fork of the Green River. This fork rises in the Uintah Mountains, directly south of Piedmont, and runs in a north-easterly direction till it reaches Bryan, then turns toward the south-west and unites with Green River some twenty miles below the town of Green River. The valley at Bryan is quite broad in places, and thickly covered with sage brush and greasewood. The soil is said to be fertile and capable of producing large crops with irrigation.

Fort Bridger, eleven miles south of Carter Station, is on this stream, and at that place over 300 bushels of potatoes have been raised from a single half acre of ground. This shows what this virgin soil can do if irrigated. The tableland on the elevated benches that the traveler will observe on either side of the road, is said to be equally rich, and would be equally as prolific if it could be irrigated. As you approach Bryan, look away to the south and south-east, and you will behold the towering peaks of the Uintah Mountains, 70 or 80 miles off. They do not look so distant, but then distance is very deceptive in this country. Bryan is a telegraph station with a store, saloon, and a few houses—all that's left to tell the story of its better and departed days. Its early history is the same as all the railroad towns we have mentioned, with roughs, cut-throats, gamblers, villains, etc., and their cleaning out by vigilance committees, under law administered by "Judge Lynch."

We now pursue our way up the valley of Black's Fork. Four miles west of Bryan, the road first crosses this stream which it follows to Church Buttes.

Marston—is the next station—a side track 21 miles from Green River, and 867.6 miles from Omaha; elevation, 6,245 feet. From the apparently level plains which the road crosses, abrupt buttes or bluffs rise as if built by human hands as mounds to conceal some treasure, or to perpetuate some remarkable incident in history. They form a curious study, and awaken no little interest in the mind of an observing traveler. To the left of the track there are a number of low buttes as you approach

Granger,—the next station, 877.2 miles from Omaha, and 6,270 feet above the sea. It is a telegraph station, named in honor of an old settler here, and is the principal shipping point on the line of the Union Pacific, for Montana and Idaho cattle. These cattle are driven to this point from the territories named, and the shipments are increasing every year. Yards and chutes have been erected for their accommodation and use. Near the station are one or two stone houses. The road here crosses Ham's Fork, a tributary of Black's Fork, which rises some 70 miles north-west, and which, the old settlers say, is really the main stream of the two. The banks of this stream, as far as you can see, are lined with bushes, and farther up, its valley produces luxuriant grass, from which hay is cut, and upon which numerous herds of cattle feed. An oval peak rises on the north side of the track, beyond which, in the distance, may be seen a range of bluffs, or mountains, which rise up between Ham's Fork and Green River. From Granger to the next station, are buttes on both sides of the track, while, to the left, the high peaks of the Uintah Range tower up in the distance, affording one of the grandest views on the line of the road. This is the region of moss agates, gems of various kinds, and precious stones. Agates are found all along the line of the road from Green River to Evanston, in great profusion. The most of them, however, are valueless, but occasionally specimens of rare beauty are picked up. On what are called "the bad lands," about 7 miles south of the road, however, the finest agates, with other beautiful gems, are obtained with little difficulty. In Ham's Fork water agates, creamy white, and amber colored, may be occasionally picked up. They are quite rare, and when cut by the lapidary, are held to be of considerable value.

View of Uintah Mountains.—The view we give an illustration of, on page 80, is one of the finest in the Far West. The scene is taken from Photograph Ridge, at an elevation of 10,829 feet. In the foreground is a picturesque group of the mountain pines. In the middle distance flows Black's Fork. The peaks or cones in the distance have their summits far above the limits of perpetual snow, and from 1,500 to 2,000 feet above the springs that are the sources of the streams below. These cones are distinctly stratified, mostly horizontal, and there are frequently vast piles of purplish, compact quartzite, which resemble Egyptian pyramids on a gigantic scale, without a trace of grit, vegetation, or water. One of these remarkable structures stands out isolated from the rest, in the middle of the Valley of Smith's Fork, and is so much like a Gothic church, that the United States Surveying Party gave it the name of Hayden's Cathedral, after the leader of the exploration.

CHURCH BUTTES ON BLACK'S FORK.

Church Buttes,—887.7 miles from Omaha; elevation, 6,317 feet. The particular buttes, from which the station derives its name, are about 10 miles south of the station, on the old overland stage road, but buttes rise up from the level plains in this vicinity in every direction. They are, however, fast washing away. The annual increase in rain-fall on this desert, since the completion of the railroad and the stretching of five telegraph wires, is remarkable, and is especially noticed by the old settlers. These rains, with the frosts of winter, are having a noticeable effect on the buttes. Isolated peaks have disappeared entirely—and prominent projections have been materially lessened. There are still a large number, however, chiseled by the action of frosts and rains into fantastic shapes which will excite the attention and rivet the gaze of the traveler, as he passes by; but, if their annual diminution continues, in less than half a century, they will have lost their interest. Near this station is the last crossing of Black's Fork, which now bears away to the left, while the road ascends another of its branches, called the Big Muddy. What has been said in reference to agates, etc., of the other stations, will apply to Church Buttes with equal force.

Curious Scientific Explorations.—Church Buttes is a curious formation, located on the line of the old overland stage route, about one hundred and fifty miles east from Salt Lake, and at this point having an elevation of 6,731 feet. The formation is part of the *Mauvaises Terres*, or Bad Lands, and consists of a vast deposit of sedimentary sandstones, and marly clay, in perfectly horizontal strata, and contain within their beds, some very remarkable paleontological remains. The peculiar effects of stormy weather and flood, in the past, has carved the bluff-lines into the most curious and fantastic forms—lofty domes and pinnacles, and fluted columns, these rocks resembling some cathedral of the olden time, standing in the midst of desolation.

Professor Hayden, in speaking of them says, "Distance lends a most delicious enchantment to the scene, and the imagination can build many castles from out of this mass of most singular formation. A nearer approach dispels some of the illusions, but the mind is no less impressed with the infinite variety of detail and the scattered remains of the extinct life of some far distant age."

In this section are found "moss agates," in the greatest abundance, being scattered all over the surface of the country. Standing upon one of the summits of the highest point of the "Bad Lands," Hayden says, "as far as the eye can reach, upon every side, is a vast extent of most infinite detail. It looks like some ruined city of the gods, blasted, bare, desolate, but grave, beyond a mortal's telling." In 1870, a geological expedition, headed by Prof. O. C. Marsh, of Yale College, and known as the "Yale College Expedition of 1870"—visited the "Bad Lands" and made a geological examination. They were accompanied by Buffalo Bill, a military troupe, and ten Pawnee Indians, as guides. On the way, Professor Marsh endeavored to explain the mighty changes of geology and the grand discoveries they would make—and as Buffalo Bill intimated, some of them were "*pretty tough yarns.*" The desolation of the country can only be imagined, not described—hour after hour the party marched over burning sand-hills, without rocks or trees, or signs of water, while the thermometer stood at 110° in the shade of the wagons. After fourteen hours in the saddle, one of the soldiers, exhausted with heat and thirst, finally exclaimed: "*What did God Almighty make such as this for?*" "*Why,*" replied another more devout trooper, "*God Almighty made the country good enough, but it's this deuced geology the professor talks about, that spoiled it all.*"

For fresh water the party had to thank the favor of a thunder-shower, during which they drank from the rims of each other's hats. Their researches resulted in the discovery of the remains of various species of the camel, horse, mammals, and others new to science. A branch of this expedition exploring the canons and plains of Northern Colorado, discovered a large deposit which contained great quantities of fossil turtles, and rhinoceros, birds, and the remains of the *areodon*,—a remarkable animal combining the characteristics of the modern sheep, pig and deer. The remains of another monster, the *Titanotherium*, were found of such vast proportions, that a lower jaw measured over *four feet* in length. At Antelope Station, in one of these areodon beds, remains were found of several species of horse;—one a three-toed animal, and another which, although full grown, had attained the height of but two feet. In an exploration near Green River—the expedition found petrified fishes in abundance, and a small bed, containing fossil insects, *a rare discovery*. Here were beetles and dragons, flies and grasshoppers; a gigantic fossil mosquito, and an extinct flea of great dimensions were also discovered. At Fort Wallace, Ks., the party found a trophy in the form of a skeleton of a sea serpent nearly complete, which alone required four days to dig out and bring to the camp. This monster when alive could not have been less than 60 feet. It had a slender eel-like body and tail, with mouth like a boa-constrictor.

Among the curious incidents which happened, was the discovery of a genuine Sioux Indian burial ground. The dead were reposing on platforms of boughs elevated above the ground, and supported at the four corners by poles about eight feet in height. On one of these tombs lay two bodies,—a woman, decked in beads and bracelets, and a scalpless brave, with war paint still on the cheeks, and holding in his crumbling hand, a rusty shot-gun, and a pack of cards. Several incidents occurred from the abundance of rattlesnakes. Several animals were bitten by them, and the country at some places fairly swarmed with them. Numbers were killed every day by the horses' feet, and while members of the party would occasionally bathe in the river, these reptiles would bask upon the bank of the stream near their clothes, as one of them says, "Their humming soon became an old tune, and the charm of shooting the wretches wore away for all but one, who was collecting their rattles as a necklace for his lady love."

Hampton,—a little over 50 miles from Green River, 897.1 miles from Omaha, and 6,500 feet above the sea. It is simply a side track where, occasionally, trains meet and pass. Approaching this station, two large buttes lift themselves above their fellows on the left side of the track, while beyond, a low, dark ridge may be seen covered with cedars. In this ridge is an abundance of game and good hunting at almost any season of the year. The game consists of elk, coyotes, wolves, deer, bears, etc. About three miles before you reach the next station, you will notice off to the right of the track, a long, low, dark ridge. It is also covered with cedars, and it strikes the road near Bridger Station. There are also plenty of cedars in the bluffs to the left before you reach

Carter,—the next station, which is 904.6 miles from Omaha, and 6,550 feet above the sea. The station is named in honor of Col. Dick Carter, whose home is here, and who has lived here since the completion of the railroad. It is the nearest railroad station to Fort Bridger, which is located on Black's Fork, 11 miles due south, and reached by daily stages from this point. Colonel Carter is about to try the experiment of raising crops at this station. He has built a dam across the creek and dug a ditch nearly 2,000 feet long, which will irrigate the ground he proposes to till. Near Carter, also, one can hardly go amiss of moss agates and other curious specimens. About 20 miles a little north-west of this station, is a mountain of coal on a tributary of Little Muddy. In this mountain are found three splendid veins of coal, of total thickness of 87 feet, which can be traced over ten miles, also layers of slate 25 to 30 feet in depth. The coal resembles cannel coal, and makes excellent coke for smelting purposes. Seven miles north of Carter, a white sulphur spring was discovered in the summer of 1875, whose waters will equal, if not surpass those of the celebrated springs of Virginia. Within about a hundred yards of these sulphur springs, and at the same time, a chalybeate spring was also discovered, but its waters have not yet been analyzed, though their medicinal qualities are said to be excellent. There is also, a fine fresh water spring near by. A branch railroad from Carter would pass these springs, and reach the mountain of coal in a distance of 24 miles.

Smith's Fork, a branch of Black's, is about five miles south of Fort Bridger, and Henry's Fork, of Green River, is some 25 miles still farther south, and is noted for its rich grazing. It is mostly occupied by stockmen as a winter range, and large numbers of cattle are annually wintered without hay in its valley. Smith's and Henry's Forks are filled with trout, and afford fine fishing, while there is an abundance of game, such as elk, deer, antelope and bear to attract the hunter and sportsman. A plenty of sage hens give fine shooting in the summer months. Carter is a telegraph station, and has a store from which ranchemen, hunters, and others obtain supplies. It was formerly an eating-station on the road and was renowned for the splendid trout which were served up by Colonel Carter, who was its proprietor. A government road to Fort Ellis, Montana, and the Yellowstone Park, has been surveyed from this station by way of Bear River Valley and the Soda Springs in Idaho. It is some 80 miles nearer than by Ogden or Corinne, over a fine route, and will probably be opened in a year or two.

Bridger,—914.1 miles from Omaha, with an elevation of 6,780 feet. It is a telegraph station named in honor of Jim Bridger, who was a noted hunter and guide, for government and other expeditions. Since leaving Bryan, we have been going up hill all the time, and our ascent will now be rapid until we pass the divide between Piedmont and Aspen. The country is exceedingly broken and rough on each side of the track, while the valley of the Big Muddy narrows up, as we approach the summit.

Leroy,—is the next station. It is 919.1 miles from Omaha, and 7,123 feet above the level of the sea. In passing over only five miles of road, we have ascended nearly 350 feet. Leaving this place, you will observe old telegraph poles still standing on the left of the track. They mark the line of the old overland road. About two miles west of Leroy, at the base of a hill or bluff, south of the track, are some excellent Soda Springs. They are near the road, and trains sometimes stop to enable passengers to drink the water. In 1875, an emigrant train stopped at these springs a few minutes, when one of the passengers, on the way to the springs, picked up a most beautiful moss agate, in which there were six clearly defined, conical shaped trees, each one perfect in shape and form. The hills and valleys in this vicinity continue to abound in agates and other curious specimens, while soda, iron and fresh water springs, are numerous, sometimes in close proximity to each other.

Piedmont.—Here the road, after crossing it, leaves the Muddy, which comes in from the south. This station is ten miles from Leroy, 929.1 miles from Omaha, and has an elevation of

7,540 feet. In summer, the scenery along this part of the road is delightful, while in winter the storms are severe, the wind blowing almost a constant gale, while the snow drifts mountains high. There are several snow sheds along this part of the road, the longest being on the summit, 2,700 feet in length. The road having to wind around the spurs and into the depressions of the hills, is very crooked, in one place doubling back on itself. We are now crossing a high ridge in the Uintah Mountains, and the second highest elevation on the Union Pacific. Off to the left these mountains in higher, grander forms, lift their summits toward the clouds, and are most always covered with snow, while their sides are lined with dark green—the color of the pine forests, which partially envelop them. While the road was being built, large quantities of ties, telegraph poles and bridge timber, were cut on the Foot Hills, near these mountains, and delivered to the company. About two miles northwest of Piedmont, is a wonderful Soda Spring. The sediment or deposits of this spring have built up a conical-shaped body with a basin on the top. In this basin the water appears, to a small extent, and has evidently sometime had a greater flow than at present; but, as similar springs have broken out around the base of this cone, the pressure on the main spring has, doubtless, been relieved, and its flow, consequently, lessened. The cone is about 15 feet high and is well worthy of a visit from the tourist. At Piedmont, the traveler will first observe the permanent coal pits, built of stone and brick, which are used in this country for the manufacture of charcoal for the smelting works of Utah. There are more of them at Hilliard and Evanston, and they will be more fully described then.

INTERIOR OF SNOW SHEDS, U. P. R. R.

Leaving Piedmont, the road makes a long curve, like a horse-shoe doubling on itself, and, finally, reaches the summit of the divide in a long snow shed, one of the longest on the road.

Aspen,—the next station. It is 938.5 miles from Omaha, and has a reported elevation of 7,835 feet. It is not a great distance — only about two miles —from the summit. Evidences of change in the formation of the country are everywhere visible, and the change affords a marked relief to the weary monotony of the desolate plains over which we have passed. Down the grade we now pass rapidly, with high hills on either side of the track—through a lovely valley, with an occasional fill, and through a deep cut, to the next station.

Hilliard,—a new station, opened for business in 1873, is 943.5 miles from Omaha, with an elevation of 7,310 feet. The town owes its importance to the Hilliard Flume & Lumber Company, which has extensive property interests here, and in the vicinity. In approaching the town from Aspen, the road passes down a "draw" or ravine, through a cut on a curve, and near this place enters the Bear River Valley, one of the most beautiful, and so far as has been demonstrated, fertile valleys of the Rocky Mountains. Two things excite the curiosity of the traveler if he has never seen them before; one is the coal pits, and the other is the elevated flume under which trains of cars pass. This flume, built of timber and boards, is 24 miles long, and is 2,000 feet higher where it first takes the water from Bear River, than where it empties the same at Hilliard. The greatest fall in any one mile is 320 feet. The timber which is brought to the station by this flume, is obtained in large amounts in the foot hills of the Uintah Mountains, or on the mountains themselves and is mostly pine. The saw-mill of the company, erected at the head of this flume, has a capacity of 40,000 feet in 24 hours, with an engine of 40 horse-power. Over 2,000,000 feet of lumber were consumed in the construction of this flume, and its branches in the mountains. Through it cord-wood, lumber, ties and saw-logs are floated down to the railroad. The cord-wood is used for charcoal. You will observe the conical shaped pits in which it is made, near the railway track, on the right, as you pass westward. There are 29 pits or kilns at Hilliard, nineteen small ones, and ten large ones. The small kilns require twenty-six cords of wood at a filling, and the large ones forty cords. The small ones cost about $750, each; the large ones $900. These kilns consume 2,000 cords of wood per month, and produce 100,000 bushels of charcoal as a result, in the same time. There are other kilns about nine miles south of the town, in active operation. There are fine iron and sulphur springs within three-fourths of a mile of the station. The reddish appearance of the mountain we have just passed indicates the presence of iron in this vicinity in large quantities, and coal also begins to crop out in different places as we go down the valley. Bear River is renowned for its trout. They are caught south of the road in the mountain tributaries, and north of Evanston, in Bear River Lake. Though the country has somewhat changed in appearance, and a different formation has been entered upon, we have not passed the region of agates and gems, precious and otherwise. They are found in the vicinity of Hilliard, in large quantities, together with numerous petrifactions of bones, etc., with fossilized fish, shells, ferns and other materials.

Twenty-five miles a little south-west of Hilliard are found two sulphur mountains. The sulphur is nearly 90 per cent. pure, in inexhaustible quantities.

ROCK CUT, NEAR ASPEN.

The scenery of the Upper Bear River is rugged and grand. About 20 miles south of Hilliard is a natural fort which was taken possession of by a gang of horse thieves and cut-throats, under the lead of one Jack Watkins, a genuine frontier ruffian, who, with his companions, for a long time resisted all attempts at capture.

The hills and mountains in this vicinity abound in game, and offer rare inducements to sportsmen. The country around both Hilliard and Evanston is the natural home for bears, elk, deer, catamounts, lynx, wolves, coyotes, wolverines, beaver, mink, foxes, badgers, mountain lions, wild cats, jack rabbits, etc., grouse sage hens, quails and ducks in the spring and fall. Not far north of Evanston, on Bear River, is *Bear Lake*, ten miles in length, and from five to eight in breadth. The boundary line between Idaho and Utah passes directly across the lake from east to west.

Soda Springs.—Farther north, at the Big Bend of Bear River, the most interesting group of soda springs known on the Continent, occupy some six square miles. To those graced with steam vents, Fremont gave the name of Steamboat

Springs, from the noise they make like a low-pressure engine. Near by is a spring with an orifice brightly stained with a brilliant yellow coating of oxide of iron, from which the water is thrown up two feet.

Independence Rock.—This has long been a noted landmark, for travelers on the old overland wagon route. Its base which borders the road is literally covered with names and dates, some of them even before Fremont's expedition crossed the Continent—many more well known. The Sweetwater River flows immediately along the southern end of it, and on the opposite side of the stream is another ridge similar to it, continuing from the south-west, which was once connected with it. It is a huge example of disintegration; its rounded form resembles an oblong hay-stack, with layers of rocks lapping over the top and sides of the mass. Thin layers have been broken off in part, and huge masses are scattered all around it. On some portions of the sides they lap down to the ground, with so gentle a descent that one can walk up to the top without difficulty. The rock has a circumference of 1,550 yards. The north end is 193 feet in height, and the opposite end, 167 feet, with a depression in the center of 75 feet.

INDEPENDENCE ROCK.

Devil's Gate on the Sweetwater.—Following up the valley from Independence Rock, and five miles north, is another celebrated natural curiosity. *The Devil's Gate*, a canon which the Sweetwater River has worn through the Granite Ridge cutting it at right-angles. The walls are vertical, being about 350 feet high, and the distance through is about 300 yards. The current of the strêam through the gate is slow, finding its way among the fallen masses of rock, with gentle, easy motion, and pleasant murmur.

Fifteen miles farther above the Devil's Gate, is another conspicuous landmark,—the *Twin Peaks*, which really are but one high peak in the ridge, cleft down the centre, dividing it in two, nearly to the base.

View in the Uintah Mountains.—The view we give on page 80, is taken from Photograph Ridge, elevation, 10,829 feet,—by the Hayden Exploring Expedition, and is one of the grandest and most perfect mountain views in the West. The traveler, as he passes rapidly through Echo and Weber Canons, and casually notices the chain of mountains at the south, can form no idea of their beauty and grandeur. Professor Hayden says of this view "In the foreground of our view is a picturesque group of the mountain pines. In the middle distance, glimmering in the sunlight like a silver thread, is Black's Fork, meandering through grassy, lawn-like parks, the eye following it up to its sources, among the everlasting snows of the summit ridge. The peaks or cones in the distance, are most distinctly stratified and apparently horizontal or nearly so, with their summits far above the limits of perpetual snow, and from 1,500 to 2,000 feet above the springs that rise from the streams below."

Gilbert's Peak,—is one of the highest peaks of the Uintah Mountain Range, named after General Gilbert of the U. S. A. It has near its summit a beautiful lake of 11,000 feet, and above this rises the peak abruptly 2,250 more. Total, 13.250 feet.

Throughout these mountains are very many lakes,—which gather among the rocks bordered with dense growth of spruce trees, and form a characteristic feature of the scenery.

Bear River City.—After leaving Hilliard, the road, as it continues down the valley of Sulphur Creek, passes the site of Bear River City, a once famous town, but which now has not a single building to mark where it once stood; a mile and a half west of Hilliard will be seen the headboards of the graves of early-day rioters. The city was laid out in 1868, and for a time there was high speculation in lots, and once the population reached as high as 2,000 persons. Frequent garrotings, deaths and robberies, led to the organization of a vigilance committee, who hung three of the desperadoes. An active fight afterwards ensued between the citizens and the mob, who had organized to revenge the death of one of their number. The citizens were well protected by the wall of a store, and by active firing killed 16 of the rioters, with other losses, never known. From that day the place was dropped by the railroad, and it faded entirely away.

THE DEVIL'S GATE ON THE SWEETWATER.

Millis — is the next station, 947.5 miles from Omaha, with an elevation of 6,790 feet. It is an unimportant side track, where trains occasionally pass. Its location is about a mile and a half below or west of the site of Bear River City. Leaving Millis the road soon crosses Bear River over a low trestle-work—an opening being left in the embankment for the passage of surplus water in time of freshets. The entire valley here has been known to be covered with water in the spring.

Evanston,—957 miles from Omaha; elevation, 6,770 feet. It is the county-seat of Uintah County, Wyoming Territory, and the last town going west, in Wyoming. It contains about 1,500 people, and is a thriving business place, owing to proximity of the coal mines, its lumber interests and the location of the division roundhouse of twenty stalls, with car and machine-shops—giving constant employment to a large number of men. The town is located on the western bank of Bear River, and has abundant water power that might be utilized in various manufactories. A large saw-mill, run by a lumber company, gets its logs from the mountains toward the head of the stream. They are rolled into the river, and floated down to the mill. This place, also, has a few charcoal kilns—lumber, coal and charcoal, being the principal products of the town. Evanston is a regular dinner station—trains from the east and west stopping thirty minutes for dinner. You will dine at the "Mountain Trout Hotel," a well-kept house, where everything is scrupulously neat—the food being plainly, but well cooked. At this house, the traveler will find regular Chinese waiters, dressed in Chinese costume, quick, polite and attentive, and you can here gratify your curiosity by seeing and talking with them. Game and trout will usually be found on the tables, in their season. The proximity of this eating-station, and the one kept at Green River, to the great trout-fishing regions of the Rocky Mountains, creates an expectation on the part of the traveler, that he will usually find the speckled beauties served up at these stations, nor is he often disappointed, in the proper season of the year.

The town has good schools, three or four churches and an excellent court-house. A daily and weekly newspaper—" *The Evanston Age*," is published here. Bear River, which runs through this place, rises in the Uintah Mountains, on the south, and runs in a general northerly direction to the great soda springs in Idaho, about 120 miles directly north of Echo City. It then turns to the south-west and empties into Great Salt Lake, near Corinne. Its valley is pretty well settled by Mormons, and others, all the way round its great bend. Near the location of these soda springs, and at the northern extremity of Bear River Mountains, evidences of volcanic action are everywhere visible, and extinct craters are no uncommon thing.

Evanston is built mostly on the left side of the track, as you enter the town, the valley rising into the hill behind it. This hill, were it not for the hard winds and deep snows of winter, would afford some very fine building spots, and for summer residences must be delightful. In winter, however, some of the little houses that skirt the hill on the western borders of the place, are literally covered with snow which drifts over the hills from the south. The agricultural prospects of the valley, lower down, are said to be flattering —the Mormon farmers producing fine crops. Near Evanston there are a number of cattle ranches where hay is cut, and cattle have to be fed and sheltered during the winter. There have also been some successful experiments in raising potatoes, cabbages, turnips, parsnips, radishes, lettuce, onions and other "garden truck," while oats, barley and wheat can undoubtedly be raised in favorable seasons. Notice the altitude of this place, and then the traveler can form the best opinion as to whether agriculture, as a steady business, can be made successful. Candor compels us further to say that frosts may happen during every one of the summer months.

LAKE LAL, OR MOORE'S LAKE, HEAD OF BEAR RIVER.

Sporting.—Evanston, however, possesses all the attractions which delight the sportsman. The mountains to the north and south, and the high hills in the immediate vicinity, are full of game, while Bear River is renowned for its trout. The streams flowing into Bear River, on either side, both north and south of the town, are full of trout, and afford excellent sport in those seasons of the year when their catching is not prohibited by law, while

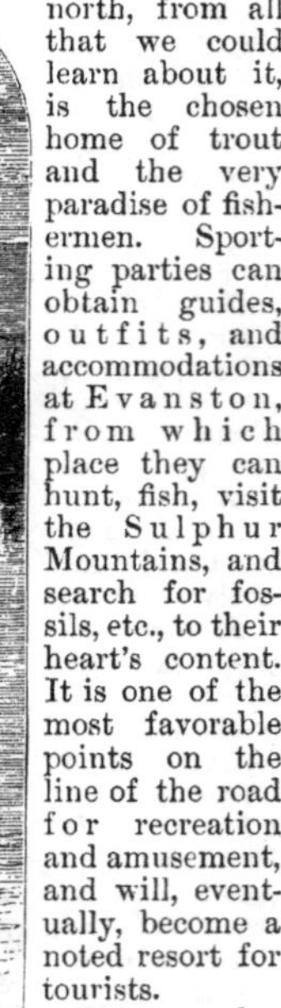

Bear Lake, some sixty miles north, from all that we could learn about it, is the chosen home of trout and the very paradise of fishermen. Sporting parties can obtain guides, outfits, and accommodations at Evanston, from which place they can hunt, fish, visit the Sulphur Mountains, and search for fossils, etc., to their heart's content. It is one of the most favorable points on the line of the road for recreation and amusement, and will, eventually, become a noted resort for tourists.

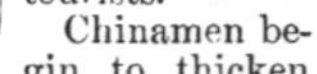

Chinamen begin to thicken as you proceed west. At Evanston they have quite a settlement, the shanties and buildings on the right of the track and opposite the depot being "China Town." Here they have their "Joss" house, saloons and residences. *Ah Say*, their head man, speaks very good English, has his Chinese wife with him, and with the exception of the inevitable "cue," dresses and appears like the Americans, with whom he has now lived for about fifteen years.

About three miles from Evanston, on the east side of Bear River, is Alma, the coal miners' town. Here coal mines belonging to the Central Pacific, the Union Pacific, and to S. H.

Winsor are worked. Mr. Winsor is just opening his mine—which is nearest to Evanston—while the other mines have been worked for some time. "The Rocky Mountain Coal Company," is the name of the corporation which supplies the Central Pacific with coal. In 1875, this company mined 98,897 tons, or 9,890 cars of coal. They have three mines open. In one year, not long since, they mined about 150,000 tons, or 15,000 cars. The Union Pacific having other mines along their road do not, of course, mine as much here as does the Rocky Mountain Company.

A Mountain on fire.

Do not be startled at this announcement, yet this is a genuine fact; the companies operating these mines, have been put to immense labor and expense to keep under control an immense fire in their coal veins. These mines took fire from spontaneous combustion in this way. They perhaps took out too much coal in the first place, that is, did not leave pillars enough to support the overhanging walls; what is called "slack"—coal that has crumbled by action of air—was also allowed to accumulate in the mine. The vein of fire clay next above the vein of coal fell down on this slack, and caused spontaneous combustion of the coal underneath it. A fire with a perpetual supply of fuel is rather a hard thing to master, and in a coal mine generally awakens no small amount of anxiety. In fact, it is very dangerous. As soon as it was discovered, and its location fixed, the company immediately began to wall around it; they ceased all operations in its immediate vicinity, and with rock, lime and sand, made their air-tight walls along "the slopes," between "the rooms" and across "the air passages," until the outside air was completely shut out, and the fire entirely shut in, and awaited further developments. Occasionally it breaks out over a piece of this wall, and then they begin farther back and wall again. But the fire is not extinguished and probably never will be. Water will not quench it, its action on the fire clay only increases the difficulty. Inside of these fire walls, pillar after pillar of the coal left standing to support the roof has been consumed, and the earth and rocks above have fallen into the cavity, leaving great craters on the side of the mountain, and the rock-ribbed pile itself has seamed and cracked open in places above the burning fires. Air has thus got in and the rains and melting snows of spring run into these fissures and craters, dissolving the fire clay, and thus add to the extent of the burning mass. But everything goes on around the mine without excitement, and as though nothing had happened. Watchmen are kept on duty all the time, and the first appearance of the fire near the walls is detected and a new wall built. And thus while the smouldering fires are burning up the coal in one part of the mine, men are taking it out unconcernedly in another part, to supply the locomotives with the power to generate steam.

How long the fire will burn no one can tell. It will only stop when the fuel upon which it feeds is exhausted, and this can only be cut off by mining all around it, taking out the full thickness of the vein—26 feet—and thus exhausting the supply. It will then cave in and the rest of the mine can be saved. Coal mining has its dangers, not the least of which are "slack and waste" which result in fires. In Mine No. 1, of the Rocky Mountain Coal Company, the fire is confined in a space 250 by 600 feet. In Mine No. 2, owned by same company, it is confined by a space 175 by 1,100 feet.

A Valuable Coal Mine.—Leaving Evanston, in about two miles the branch to Alma turns off to the right, and the town with hoisting works of the coal companies can be plainly seen, together with a beautiful view down the Bear River Valley. On what is called Twin Creek, down this valley, the Wyoming Coal & Coke Company, have discovered and located a coal mine 41 miles due north from Evanston. The mine is on the east side of Bear River. This company has what it claims to be a mountain of coal. The veins on the ground level are four and one-half feet thick, above it there are about six feet of slate; then a ten foot vein of coal; then sandstone about five feet thick—what miners call "Winn rock;" then three feet of fire clay; then two feet of coal; then alternate layers of fire clay and coal 26 feet; then 125 feet of solid fire clay; then sandstone, limestone, etc., to the summit, it being about 400 feet above the level surface around it. A shaft has been sunk from the ground level, and another vein of coal struck ten feet below the surface. We are minute in giving this description of this coal mine, because it is claimed that the coal it furnishes will coke, that it will give 50 per cent. coke, and coke is the great demand of the smelting furnaces in the mining regions of this part of the Continent. It is claimed that the tests which have been applied to this coal, establish conclusively its coking qualities and ovens for coking purposes have been put in. The work of the present year will, satisfactorily determine the question whether coking coal can be found in the Rocky Mountains. The history of rich mineral-producing regions is that the metals are usually (because cheaper) brought to the fuel instead of carrying the fuel to the metal. Hence if these coal mines are proved to produce good coke, a town of smelters must spring up near by.

Wahsatch,—a telegraph station, on the divide between Bear River Valley and Echo Canon. It

ROCKS NEAR ECHO CITY.

1.—Bromley's Cathedral. 2.—Castle Rock. 3.—The Great Eastern. 4.—Hanging Rock.

is 968 miles from Omaha, and reported to be 6,879 feet above the level of the sea. The road here crosses a low pass in the Wahsatch Range of Mountains. As you ascend the beautiful valley leading to this station, the grim peaks of the Uintahs tower up in the distance on your left, while the adjoining hills shut out the higher elevations of the Wahsatch Range, on the north. Leaving Evanston, the road turns abruptly to the left, and the town and valley are soon lost to sight. Four miles out, on the left side of the track, the traveler will notice a sign put up on a post—the east side of which reads, "Wyoming," the west side, "Utah." Wahsatch was formerly a terminus of a sub-division of the road, and contained the regular dining-hall of the company, with roundhouse, machine and repair shops, etc. The water in the tank is supplied from a mountain spring near by, and a "Y" for turning engines, and a small house to shelter one, is about all that is left of a once famous town.

Artesian Wells.—It has been our candid opinion that the great plains, basins and alkali deserts which lie between the Rocky Mountains and Sierras can all be reclaimed and soil made fertile by the sinking of artesian wells. The entire Humboldt Valley can be made productive by this means alone. As a proof of the success of sinking artesian wells, we can mention several along the Union Pacific Railroad. Commencing at Separation and terminating at Rock Springs, a distance of 108 miles, the Union Pacific Railroad has sunk successfully six artesian wells:

One at Separation, 6,900 feet above sea level, is 1,180 feet deep, the water rising to within 10 feet of the surface.

At Creston, 7,030 feet elevation, the well is only 300 feet deep, furnishing abundant supply of water at that point.

At Washakie, 6,697 feet elevation, the well is 638 feet deep. The water rises 15 feet above the surface, and flows at the rate of 800 gallons per hour.

At Bitter Creek, 6,685 feet elevation, the well is 696 feet deep, discharging at the surface 1,000 gallons per hour, and with pumping, yields 2,160 gallons per hour.

At Point of Rocks, elevation 6,490 feet, the well is 1,000 feet deep, and the supply of water abundant, although it does not rise to the surface nearer than 17 feet.

At Rock Springs, at an elevation of 6,280 feet, the well is 1,156 feet deep, and discharges at the surface 960 gallons per hour, or at 26 feet above the surface, 571 gallons per hour.

As the elevation of all these places is 2,000 feet or more above the Salt Lake Valley, and also the Humboldt Valley, there is every probability that the sinking of artesian wells in these valleys would result in an immense flow of water.

Chinese Workmen.—The Chinese are emphatically a peculiar people, renowned for their industry and economy. They will live comfortably on what the same number of Americans would throw away. Their peculiarities have been so often described that a repetition of them to any great extent is not needed here. Nevertheless a sight of them always awakens a curiosity to know all there is to be known concerning their customs, habits, social and moral relations, etc. A great deal that they do is mysterious to us, but perfectly plain and simple to them. In their habits of eating, for instance, why do they use "chopsticks" instead of forks? "Same as 'Melican man's fork" said one as we watched its dextrous use. Their principal articles of diet seem to be rice and pork. They reject the great American fashion of frying nearly everything they cook, and substitute boiling instead. In the center of a table, or on a bench near by, they place a pan filled with boiled rice. To this each one of the "mess" will go and fill his bowl with a spoon or ladle, return to the table and take his "chopsticks"—two slender sticks, about the length of an ordinary table knife, and operate them with his fingers as if they were fastened together with a pivot, like shears, lifting the bowl to his mouth every time he takes up the food with the "chopsticks." The pork for a "mess" will be cut into small pieces and placed in one dish on the table from which each one helps himself with these "chopsticks." In other words "they all dive into one dish" for their pork. They are called "almond-eyed celestials"—but did you ever notice how much their eyes resemble those of swine?

The first gang of Chinamen you meet with on the road are employed near Table Rock; formerly they extended to Rawlins, but they are inefficient laborers, although industrious, especially in the winter. We shall see more of them by the time we reach the Pacific Coast. Rock Springs as a town is mostly composed of dugouts, shanties, holes in the ground, etc., occupied by miners, including Chinamen, together with a few substantial buildings, such as the company's store, a good school-house, two or three ordinary hotels and the customary saloons. The importance of the town is wholly due to the coal trade, otherwise it would be nothing.

ECHO AND WEBER CANONS.

And now, with full breath and anxious heart, repressed excitement and keen zest,—we anxiously scan the scenes from car windows or platforms, and prepare for one grand, rushing descent into the glories of Echo Canon. The writer will never forget the feelings of overwhelming wonder and awe, as with the seal of admiration in both eye and lips, the ride through this famous canon was enjoyed. Rocks beside which all eastern scenes were pigmies, rose up in astounding abruptness and massiveness—colossal old Titans of majestic dimensions, and sublimely soaring summits, and perpendicular sides,—succeeded each other for miles, and the little company of spectators, seemed but an insignificant portion of the handiwork of the Almighty. The train of cars, which, on the plain, seemed so full of life, and grand in power, here was dwarfed into baby carriages; and the shriek of the whistle, as it echoed and resounded along the cliffs and from rock to rock, or was hemmed in by the confines of the *amphitheatre*, appeared like entering the portals to the palace of some *Terrible Being*. Into the short distance of sixty miles is crowded a constant succession of those scenes and objects of natural curiosity, which form the most interesting part of the road, and have made it world-wide in fame. It seems hard, after nearly a week of expectation and keen anxiety for a glimpse of such scenes of grandeur, and after more than two days of steady riding over the smooth surface of the rolling upland plain, to find all the most magnificent objects of interest crowded into so short a space, and passed in less than three hours.

Travelers must remember, however, that the scenes witnessed from the railroad are but a very little portion of the whole. To gather true refreshing glimpses of western scenery, the tourist must get away from the railroad, into the little valleys, ascend the bluffs and mountains, and views yet more glorious will greet the eye. Echo Canon is the most impressive scene that is beheld for over 1,500 miles, on the overland railroad. The constant succession of rocks—each growing more and more huge, and more and more perpendicular and colossal in form—make the attractions of the valley *grow upon the eye* instead of decrease.

The observer enters the canon about on a level with the top of the rocks, and even can overlook them, then gradually descends until at the very bottom of the valley the track is so close to the foot of the rocks, the observer has to elevate his head with an upward look of nearly 90°, to scale their summits. Let us now prepare to descend, and brace ourselves eagerly for the exhilaration of the ride, the scenery of which will live with you in memory for years.

Entering Echo Canon.—Leaving Wahsatch we pass rapidly down grade, into the canon, and we will point out, in detail, all objects of interest as they are passed, so that travelers may recognize them. From Wahsatch, especially, you want to look with all the eyes you have, and look quick, too, as one object passes quickly out of sight and another comes into view. About a mile from Wahsatch, you will notice what is called the "Z" canon where the road formerly zigzagged down a small canon, on the left, and passed through the valley of the creek to near Castle Rock Station, where it united with the present line. Two miles farther on, over heavy grades and short curves, you enter tunnel No. 2, which is 1,100 feet long. Passing through the tunnel, the high reddish rocks, moulded into every conceivable shape, and frequent side canons cut through the walls on either side of the road. You reach at last

Castle Rock Station,—about eight and one-half miles from Wahsatch, 976.4 miles from Omaha with an elevation of 6,290 feet. It is so called from the rock a little east of the station which bears the same name. Notice the arched doorway on one corner of the old castle just after it is passed, with red colored side pieces, and capped with gray. In close proximity are some needle rocks—sharp-pointed—one small one especially prominent. Still nearer the station is a shelving rock on a projecting peak. Opposite the water tank are rocks worn in curious shape. Further on, about half a mile, is a cave with rocks and scattering cedars above it. Next comes what is termed "Swallows' Nest," because of the numerous holes near the top, chiseled out by the action of both water and wind, and in summer sheltering a large number of swallows. Toward it in summer months,

"The Swallows Homeward fly."

Then comes a honey-combed peak with a shelving gray rock under it, after which we pass through, what the railroad boys call "gravel" or "wet cut"—the sides being gravel, and springs breaking out in the bottom by the track. Then Phillip's Canon juts in from the right with yards for cattle at its mouth. See the curious formations along the side of this canon as you pass it. About four miles from the last station, are other castle rocks similar in appearance to those already passed, and rocks with caps and slender little spires like needles. Then comes a singular perpendicular column jutting out in front of the ledge, with outstretched wings as if it would lift itself up and fly, but for its weight.

This is called the "Winged Rock." If there was a projection in front to resemble a neck and head, the rock would appear very much like an eagle or some other large bird, with pinions extended just ready to fly. A little below this, are the "Kettle Rocks" huge gray-looking boulders, nearly to the top of the ledge, looking like immense caldron kettles. Behind them are some sharp-pointed projections like spires. These rocks are capped with red, but gray underneath. Then comes "Hood Rock" a single angular rock about half way to the top of the ledge, worn out in the center, and resembling the three-cornered hoods on modern ulster overcoats. About a mile before reaching the next station, the rocks are yellow in appearance and rounding a point you will notice sandstone layers with a dip of more than 45 degrees, showing a mighty upheaval at some period in the remote past.

Hanging Rock,—a little over seven miles from Castle Rock, and 983.7 miles from Omaha; elevation, 5,974 feet. The descent has been very rapid since we struck this canon. This station is wrongly named. All books and guides which represent the rocks of Echo Canon overhanging the railroad, are erroneous. Nothing in the shape of a hanging rock can be seen, but as you pass the station, you will notice how the elements have worn out a hollow or cavity in one place, which is bridged by a slim gray rock, nearly horizontal in position, forming a natural or hanging bridge across the cavity, about 50 feet in depth. It can be seen as you pass around a curve just after leaving the station. Going a little farther, you notice what is called "Jack-in-the-Pulpit-Rock," at the corner of a projecting ledge, and near the top thereof. A round gray column, flat on the surface, stands in front; this is the pulpit, while in close proximity rises the veritable "Jack" himself, as if expounding the law and gospel to his scattering auditors. Then comes the

North Fork of Echo Canon,—down which more water annually flows, than in the main canon. Now bending around a curve, if you look forward, it seems as though the train was about to throw us directly against a high precipice in front, and that there was no way of escape; but we keep onward and finally pass safely on another side. We now approach what are called "the narrows." The rocky sides of the canon seem to draw together. Notice the frame of an old rickety saw-mill on the left, and a short distance below, still on the left, see a huge, conical-shaped rock rising close to the track. We are particular in mentioning these, because they are landmarks, and will enable the traveler to know when he is near the ledge on the right of the track, upon which the Mormons piled up stones to roll down on Gen. Albert Sidney Johnson's army, when it should pass here, in 1857. The canon virtually becomes a gorge here, and the wagon road runs close to the base of the high bluffs, (it could not be made in any other place) —which the Mormons fortified after a fashion. Now you pass these forts; high up on the top, on the outer edge or rim you will still see small piles of stones which they gathered there for offensive operations, when the trains and soldiers of the army went by. They look small—they are so far off, and you pass them so quickly—not larger than your fist—but nevertheless they are there. They are best seen as they recede from view.

At the time we speak of, (1857) there was trouble between the Mormons and the United States authorities, which led to the sending of an army to Salt Lake City. It approached as far as Fort Bridger, where — the season being late—it went into winter quarters. It was expected to pass through this canon, however, that same fall, and hence the preparations which the Mormons made to receive it. Their army—the Nauvoo Legion, *redivivus*, under the command of Gen. Daniel H. Wells, had its camp near these rocks, in a little widening of the valley below, just beyond where you pass a "pocket" of boulders, or detached parts of the ledges above, which have sometime, in the dim past, rolled into the valley. The rocky fort being passed, with the pocket of boulders and the site of the old camp, the traveler next approaches "Steamboat Rock," a huge red projection like the prow of a big propeller. A little cedar, like a flag of perpetual green, shows its head on the bow, while farther back, the beginning of the hurricane deck is visible. It slopes off to the rear, and becomes enveloped in the rocky mass around it. By some, this is called "The Great Eastern," and the one just below it, if anything, a more perfect representation of a steamer, is

SENTINEL ROCK, ECHO CANON.

called "The Great Republic." They are really curious formations, and wonderful to those who look upon them for the first time. "Sentinel Rock" comes next. It is within a cove and seems withdrawn from the front, as though shunning the gaze of the passing world, yet in a position to observe every thing that goes by. If the train would only stop and give you more time—but this cannot be done, and your only recourse

ROCK SCENES NEAR ECHO CITY.

1.—Witches Rocks. 2.—Battlement Rocks. 3.—Egyptian Tombs. 4.—Witches Bottles. 5.—Needle Rocks, near Wahsatch.

is to pause at Echo and let it pass, while you wait for the one following. This will give you ample opportunity to see the natural wonders congregated in this vicinity. We have almost reached the mouth of Echo Creek, and the Weber River comes in from the left, opposite "*Bromley's Cathedral*," in front of which stands "*Pulpit Rock*," on the most extended point as you turn the elbow in the road. This "Cathedral" is named in honor of J. E. Bromley, Esq., who has lived at Echo since 1858, and who came here as a division superintendent of Ben Holladay's Overland Stage and Express Line. It extends some distance—a mile or more—around the bend in the mountain, and has numerous towers and spires, turrets and domes, on either side. "Pulpit Rock" is so called from its resemblance to an old-fashioned pulpit, and rises in plain view as you go round the curve into Weber Valley. It is a tradition among a good many people, that the "Prophet of the Lord," who now presides over the church of "The Latter Day Saints," in Salt Lake City, once preached to the assembled multitude from this exalted eminence; but, while we dislike to spoil a story that lends such a charm to the place, and clothes it with historic interest, nevertheless, such is not the fact. The oldest and most faithful Mormons we could find in Echo, know nothing of any such transaction. Our cut is a faithful representation of this remarkable rock. It is estimated to be about sixty feet high—above the track. You will desire to know how high the ledges are, which have been so rapidly passed. We are informed that Mr. S. B. Reed, one of the civil engineers who constructed this part of the railroad, stated that the average height of all the rocks of Echo canon, is from 600 to 800 feet above the railroad.

PULPIT ROCK, ECHO CANON—LOOKING WESTWARD.

As you approach the elbow referred to, there is an opening through the mountains on the left, and in close proximity to "Pulpit Rock," the waters of Echo Creek unite with those of Weber River, which here come in through this opening. If not the southernmost point on the line of the road, it is next to it. You have been traveling in a south-westerly direction since leaving Evanston; you now round the elbow, turn toward the north-west, and arrive at

Echo,—a beautiful spot—a valley nestled between the hills, with evidences of thrift on every hand. This station is nearly nine and a half miles from Hanging Rock, 993 miles from Omaha, and 5,315 feet above the level of the sea. The town and the canon are rightly named, for the report of a gun or pistol discharged in this canon will bound from side to side, in continuous echoes, until it finally dies away. "Bromley's Cathedral" rears its red-stained columns in rear of and overshadowing the town, while opposite is a lofty peak of the Wahsatch Range. To the right the valley opens out for a short distance like an amphitheatre, near the lower extremity of which, "The Witches," a group of rocks, lift their weird and grotesque forms. They are about half way to the summit of the ledge behind them. Weber Valley, from its source to the Great Salt Lake, is pretty thickly settled with Mormons, though quite a number of Gentiles have obtained a foothold in the mines and along the line of the railroad.

Upper Weber Valley.—From this station there is a narrow gauge railroad up the Weber Valley to Coalville, seven miles in length. The town has two or three stores, hotels, saloons, etc., and a school-house is to be built this year. Accommodations for fishing parties, with guides, can here be obtained. The Echo and Weber Rivers, with their tributaries, abound in trout, while there is plenty of game, elk, deer, bear, etc., in the mountains. Richard F. Burton, the African explorer, visited this canon and Salt Lake City in 1860, and wrote a book called "City of the Saints," which was published by the Harpers, in 1862. He speaks of the wonders of this valley as follows: "Echo Kanyon has but one fault; its sublimity will make all similar features look tame."

PULPIT ROCK AND VALLEY.—LOOKING SOUTHWARD.

Weber River rises in the Wahsatch Mountains, about 50 miles in a south-eastern direction from Echo, flows nearly due west to Kammas City, when it turns to the north-west and passes in that general direction into the Great Salt Lake, not far from Ogden. Going up this river from Echo, Grass Creek flows in about two and a half miles from the starting point. This creek and canon runs very nearly parallel to Echo Creek. Very important and extensive coal mines have been discovered from two to four miles up this canon. It is not as wild or rugged in its formation as Echo Canon. The mines are soon to be developed. Two and a half miles above the mouth of Grass Creek is

Coalville,—a town of about 600 people, with a few elegant buildings, among which are the Mormon bishop's residence and a fine two-story brick court-house, which stands on an elevation near the town, and can be seen for a long distance. The town is situated on the south side of Chalk Creek where it empties into Weber River. This creek also runs nearly parallel with Echo Canon, and rises in the mountains near the head of the Hilliard Lumber Company's flume. It is called Chalk Creek from the white chalky appearance of the bluffs along its banks. Coalville is a Mormon village, and its inhabitants are nearly all employed in mining coal from two to three miles above the town where the railroad ends. This road is called the Summit County Railroad, and is owned by some of the wealthy Mormons in Salt Lake City. Four miles farther up the Weber, and you come to Hoytsville, another Mormon village. It is a farming settlement. The town has a grist-mill. Four miles still farther is located the town of Wanship, named after an old Ute chief. It has about 400 inhabitants, with a hotel, stores, grist-mill, saw-mill, etc. It is located at the junction of Silver Creek with the Weber. Still going up the Weber, in about three miles there is another Mormon settlement called Three Mile. It has a "co-op" store, bishop's residence, and a tithing office.

Peoa.—Leaving Three Mile, and pursuing the course still up one of the most beautiful valleys in the country, the tourist will reach Peoa, a nice little farming town, in five miles travel. Evidences of thrift and of the successful cultivation of the soil, are visible all along the valley, but it is a wonderful matter to eastern

SCENE AT MOUTH OF ECHO CANON.

men who know nothing of the characteristics of the soil, and see nothing but sage brush and greasewood growing thereon, how crops can be raised amidst such sterility. Irrigation has done it all. The labor to accomplish it has been immense, but thirty-five to forty bushels of spring wheat to the acre attest the result. The soil has been proved to be very prolific.

Kammas City.—Next on this mountain journey comes Kammas City, eight miles beyond Peoa, on Kammas Prairie. This is an elevated plateau about four miles by ten, and affords some very fine grazing lands and meadows. It is nearly all occupied by stockmen. Here the Weber makes a grand detour; coming from the mountains in the east, it here turns almost a square corner toward the north, and then pursues its way through valleys and gorges, through hills and mountains to a quiet rest in the waters of the Great Salt Lake. Above this prairie the river cuts its way through a wild rocky canon, lashing its sides with foam as though angry at its confinement, out into the prairie where it seems to gather strength for its next fearful plunge in the rocky gorges below. In the lofty peaks of the mountains, east of Kammas Prairie, in the frigid realms of perpetual snow, the traveler will find the head of Weber River, and the route to it will give him some of the grandest views to be found on the American Continent.

Parley's Park.—The old stage road to the "City of the Saints," after leaving Echo passed up the Weber to Wanship, at the mouth of Silver Creek; thence nine miles to Parley's Park, a lovely place in summer, where a week or two could be whiled away in the beauty of the valley and amidst the grandeur of the mountains. There are three things in nature which make a man feel small—as though he stood in the presence of Divinity. These are the ocean, with its ceaseless roar; the mighty plains in their solitude, and with their sense of loneliness; and the mountains in their towering greatness, with heads almost beyond the ken of mortal vision, and crowned with eternal snows. Parley's Park is nearly round in shape, about four miles in diameter, and almost surrounded by the rocky domes of the Wahsatch Range. The old stage road leaves Park City to the left, and reaches the summit on the west side of the divide; thence, it follows down Parley's Canon to Salt Lake City, forty-eight miles, by this route, from Echo. The mountain streams along this road abound in trout, while elk, deer and bear, will reward the hunter's toil. There are ranches and small farms by the way, which will afford abundant stopping places for rest and food; there are mines of marvelous richness, to reward one's curiosity, if nothing else will do it; and, in fact, there is probably nothing which can be gained along the line of the Union Pacific, which will afford so much gratification, at so little expense, of either money or time, as a leisurely jaunt of a week or two up the river and its tributaries from Echo.

Characteristics of Echo and Weber Canons.—The massive rocks which form Echo Canon, are of red sandstone, which by the steady process of *original erosion* and subsequent weather, have worn into their present shape. Their shapes are exceedingly curious, and their average height, 500 to 800 feet. At the amphitheatre, and the Steamboat Rock, the height is fully 800 feet to the summit. There is a bold projection in the wall of rock near the Pulpit, called Hanging Rock; but it is composed of a mass of coarse conglomerate, which is easily washed away, and is not very easily noticed. Pulpit Rock overlooks Echo City and the valley of the Weber, through which flows a pure beautiful mountain stream. In one of our illustrations is shown a railroad train passing through this valley and descending to the entrance of Weber Canon just below. This is the sketch of the special excursion train of the New York and Eastern Editorial Excursion Party of 1875, who, at this part, the center of the valley, midway between the two canons, were profuse in their exclamations of delight at the scene of beauty.

A curious feature of Echo Canon is that its scenery is entirely on the right or north side, and that the Weber Canon has, also, upon the

MONUMENT ROCK.—ECHO CANON.

same side, its wildest and most characteristic scenery. The entrance and departure from each canon is distinguished with great abruptness and distinctness. Travelers who can enjoy the fortunate position of the lowest step on the platform of each car, can witness all the scenes of Echo and Weber Canons, to the best advantage. The view is particularly fine,—as when the train describes the sharp turn, under and around Pulpit Rock, the view from the last platform includes the whole length of the train on the curve,—and overhead the jutting point of the rock, and, farther above, the massive Rock Mountain, the overlook to the entire valley. Just as the train rounds at Pulpit Rock, passengers

THE CLIFFS OF ECHO CANON, UTAH.

BY THOMAS MORAN.

on the south side of the train, will have a pretty little glimpse of the upper portion of Weber River, with its green banks and tree verdure—a charming relief to the bare, dry plains, so constant and even tiresome. A curious feature of this little Weber Valley, are the *terraces.* Near Echo City is a low, narrow bottom, near the river; then an abrupt ascent of 30 feet; then a level plain or bottom of 200 to 400 yards; then a gentle ascent to the rock bluffs.

The Weber River is exceedingly crooked in its course,—originally occupying the entire width of the little space in the canon—and in constructing the railroad at various points, the road-bed here has been built directly into the river, to make room for the track. The average angle of elevation of the heights of Weber Canon is 70 to 80 degrees,—and the height of the summits above the river is 1,500 to 2,000 feet. In this canon is found a thick bed of hard, red sandstone, of great value for building stone,—which can be wrought into fine forms for culverts, fronts of buildings, caps, sills, etc. Emerging from the mouth of Weber Canon—and turning to the right, every vestige of rugged canon scenery vanishes, and the scene is changed into one of peace and quietness of valley life. Here the Weber River has a strong, powerful current—with heavy and constant fall over beds of water-worn stones, and fallen rocks of immense size. In the spring and summer months, it is swollen by the melting of snow from the mountains, and is of great depth,—though usually it averages but four to six feet in depth and its width, at the mouth of the canon, is usually 120 feet.

The remainder of its course to the Great Salt Lake, is through a large open bottom of increasing breadth, along which gather little villages, grain fields, meadows, brilliant with flowers of which the Indian Pink, with its deep scarlet clusters, is most luxuriant. The hills are smooth in outline, and as we approach Ogden, the grand summit of the Wahsatch Mountains, with snowy peaks, arise behind, in front, and northward, around us bold and impressive. This is the range of mountains which border the east side of the Salt Lake Valley, and will accompany us, as we go southward to Salt Lake City.

Rocks of Weber Canon.—Returning to the road; after leaving Echo you will soon notice, on the north side of the track, two curious formations. The first is a group of reddish-colored cones of different sizes and varying some, in shape, but on the whole remarkably uniform in their appearance. These are known as Battlement Rocks. They are about one mile, perhaps not that, below Echo. Next come the wierd forms of "The Witches"—looking as though they were talking with each other. These are gray, and about this place it seems that the formation changes—the red-colored rocks disappearing—dark gray taking their place. How these columns were formed will ever be a question of interest to those who are permitted to see them. One of the Witches especially looks as though she was afflicted with the "Grecian bend" of modern fashion, a fact which does not at all comport with the dignity or character of a witch. Worn in fantastic shapes by the storms of ages, and capped with gray, they stand as if "mocking the changes and the chance of time." Four miles below Echo, we round a rocky point, nearly opposite to which lies the little Mormon Village of Henniferville, on the left side of Weber River, with its bishop's palace—the largest brick building in sight—and school-house, also of brick, nestled under the mountains which lift up rugged peaks in the background. The valley now narrows to a gorge, and we approach Weber Canon proper. It has high bluffs on the left, with a rocky castle towering up on the right. If Echo Canon was a wonderful place in the mind of the traveler, wonders, if possible more rugged and grand, will be revealed to his gaze here. High up on the face of a bluff to the left, as you pass through the gorge, see the little holes or caves worn by the winds, in which the eagles build their nests. This bluff is called "*Eagle nest Rock.*" Every year the proud monarch of the air finds here a safe habitation in which to raise his young. It is beyond the reach of men, and accessible only to the birds which fly in the air. Passing this home of "Freedom's Bird," before we have time to read these lines hardly, we are at the

Thousand Mile Tree, Devil's Slide, &c.,—on the left side of the track. There it stands, spreading its arms of green, from one of which hangs the sign which marks the distance traveled since leaving Omaha. It is passed in a moment, and other objects of interest claim your attention. High upon rocks to the right, as you peer ahead, see how the winds have made holes in projecting points through which the light and sky beyond can be observed; now looking back see another similar formation on the opposite side—one to be seen looking ahead, the other looking back. Now we come to *Slate Cut*—where photograph rocks without number are found. The rocks are so called from the pictures of ferns, branches of trees, shrubs, etc., which are seen traced in them. They remind one of moss-agates, only they are a great deal larger—magnified a thousand times, and are not in clear groundwork like the agates. *Lost Creek Canon* now puts in from the right, and around the curve you can see the houses of the little Mormon Town, Croyden. It is only seven miles from Echo. This canon runs parallel with Echo Canon for quite a distance, and is said to be rich in the scenery characteristic of this region, with a narrow valley of great fertility when cultivated. But right here on the left side of the road, pushing out from the side of the mountain, is the "*Devil's Slide*"—one of the most singular formations to be seen on the entire route from ocean to ocean. It is composed of two parallel ledges of granite, turned upon their edges, serrated and jutting out in places fifty feet from the mountain side, and about 14 feet apart. It is a rough place for any one; height about 800 feet.

Weber Quarry,—1,001.5 miles from Omaha, and 5,250 feet above the sea. It is a side track where fine reddish sandstone is obtained for building purposes, and for the use of the road. The sandstone is variegated, and is both beautiful and durable when cut, or polished. The gorge still continues, and devils' slides on a smaller scale than the one noticed, are visible on both sides of the road. A little below this station, *Dry Creek Canon* comes in on the right. The road now passes round short curves amidst the wildest scenery, when it is suddenly blocked to all human appearance; yet tunnel No. 3 gives us liberty. Crossing a bridge observe the terraced mountain on the right, and by the time it is well in view, we enter and pass through tunnel No. 4, after which comes *Round Valley*, where a huge basin in the mountains is formed, and where man again obtains a foothold. On the right of the mountain, as you enter this valley, there is a group of balanced rocks, that seem ready to topple over into the valley below. Still rounding another point farther down, and we arrive at

THOUSAND MILE TREE.—WEBER CANON.

Weber,—1,008.5 miles from Omaha, an elevation of 5,130 feet. It is a telegraph station in a thrifty looking Mormon village. The valley here widens out—the narrows are passed—and scenes of surpassing beauty, especially in the summer, enchant the eye. To the left the mountains gradually recede, and *East Canon Creek*, which takes its rise in Parley's Park, before mentioned, cutting its way through the rocky hills, comes into the valley of the Weber. This station is the nearest point on the Union Pacific Road to Salt Lake City. The town and cultivated farms in the valley seem like an oasis in the midst of a desert. Here, for the first time on the road, the traveler will see the magic sign, "Z. C. M. I.," which, literally translated, means "Zion's Co-operative Mercantile Institution," where all the faithful are expected to purchase their dry goods, groceries, notions, etc. The Mormon name for this station is Morgan City. As you leave this station, the same query broached before, rises in the mind of the traveler—how are we to get out? We seem entirely surrounded by hills and mountains, and, while there is a depression visible off to the right, it does not seem low enough for a railroad to pass over. But we follow the river down, and notice the result. Bending first to the right, then to the left, and again to the right round a curve like an elbow, and nearly as short, we reach

Peterson,—1,016.4 miles from Omaha; elevation, 4,963 feet—another telegraph station, near which a wagon bridge crosses the river on the left. It is convenient to a Mormon village called Enterprise, near by, and within a few miles of another, called Mountain Green. Just below Peterson, *Cottonwood Creek* puts in from the right, while immediately in front, Devil's Gate Mountain rears its snowy crest. You now begin to see where we are to get out of the basin. A huge gap in the mountains opens before you. It is the *Devil's Gap* with the *Devil's Gate* and several other odd characteristics about it. It is one of the most remarkable places on the line of the road. The waters of Weber River, as if enraged at their attempted restraint, rush wildly along, now on one side of the road, and now on the other, and now headed off completely by a projecting ledge before them, turn madly to the right, determined with irresistible strength to force their way through the mountain; foiled in this, they turn abruptly to the left, still rushing madly on, and at last find their way out to the plain beyond. If Echo was grand, and the narrows grander—this Devil's Gate pass is surely grandest of all. Just before you enter the deep cut, you will notice the old wagon road winding along the bed of the stream, cut out of the mountain's side in some places, and, in others, walled up from the river. In the midst of all this majestic grandeur, the train passes, but seldom stops at a station appropriately named

Devil's Gate,—1,020.4 miles from Omaha, and 4,870 feet above the sea,—and so we pass rapidly on. The gap begins to open in the west, and we soon emerge from one of the grandest scenes in nature, into the lovely valley below, reclaimed by the hands of men from the barren waste of a desert, and made to bud and blossom as the rose. We have now passed the Wahsatch Range of mountains, though their towering peaks are on the right, and recede from view on the left, as we leave their base and get out into the plain. We are now in the Great Salt Lake Basin, or Valley; and, though the lake itself is not in sight, the mountains on its islands are. These mountains, back of Ogden, are almost always crowned with snow, and frequently have their summits enveloped in clouds. They are storm-breeders—every one, and the old Storm King sometimes holds high carnival among them, when

> "From peak to peak, the rattling crags among,
> Leaps the live thunder."

The winds and storms of winter occasionally fill the craggy gap through which we have passed with snow, to such an extent that it slides like an avalanche down over the track, and in the river below, where the rushing waters give it a cordial greeting, and where it soon melts in their embrace.

Uintah,—1,025.3 miles from Omaha; elevation, 4,560 feet. This was formerly the stage station for Salt Lake City, but the completion of the Utah Central Railroad from Ogden, took away its glory. While it was the stage terminus it was a lively place, though it never possessed indications of being a town of any great size. Approaching the town, the valley opens out like a panorama, and neat little houses with farms and gardens attached, greet the eyes of the traveler in a wonderful change from the scenes through which he has just passed. Looking off to the left you will notice the first bench of land across the river, with a higher bench or terrace in the rear. Upon this first bench, the Morrisite massacre took place in 1862, an account of which we shall give in another place. Leaving Uintah, the road pursues its way in a general northerly direction along the base of the mountains, till it arrives at

Ogden,—the western terminus of the Union Pacific Railroad, 1,033.8 miles from Omaha, and 4,340 feet above the level of the sea. By agreement between the two roads, it is also the eastern terminus of the Central Pacific Railroad. The place is one of considerable importance, being the second city in size and population in the Territory of Utah. It is regularly laid out, is the county-seat of Weber County, has a court-house of brick, which, with grounds, cost about $20,000, two or three churches and a Mormon tabernacle. The town may properly be divided into two parts — upper and lower Ogden. The upper part is pleasantly situated on an elevated

DEVIL'S SLIDE.—WEBER CAÑON.

SCENES IN WEBER CANON.

1.—Ogden, Utah. Wahsatch Mountains in the distance. 2.—Devil's Gate and High Peaks of Wahsatch Mountains. 3.—Heights of Weber Canon. 4.—Tunnel No. 3, Weber Canon.

bench adjoining the mountains. This bench breaks rather abruptly, and almost forms a bluff, and then begins lower Ogden. The upper part is mostly occupied for residences, and has some beautiful yards with trees now well grown. The lower portion—that which is principally seen from the railroad, is mostly occupied by business houses. One peculiarity of the towns in these western or central Territories, is the running streams of water on each side of nearly every street, which are fed by some mountain stream, and from which water is taken to irrigate the yards, gardens and orchards adjoining the dwellings. Ogden now has fully 6,000 people, and has a bright future before it. It is not only the terminus of the two great trans-continental lines before mentioned, but is also the starting-point of the Utah Central and Utah Northern Railroads. These four companies have united in the purchase of grounds, on which a large Union depot will soon be built, nearly east of the present building, and nearer the business portion of the city. It is the regular supper and breakfast station of the Union Pacific and Central Pacific Railroads—passengers having one hour in which to take their meals and transfer their baggage. The Central Pacific Road has numerous machine and repair shops here which are wooden buildings of a temporary character, and which will soon be replaced by more permanent structures. In addition to their freight depots the Union Pacific has only a roundhouse for the shelter of engines—their buildings for the sub-division of the road being located at Evanston.

Ogden is the last town on the Weber River before it empties into the Great Salt Lake. This river takes its name from an old mountaineer and trapper, who was well known in these parts during the early days of the Mormon settlement. The town is named for Mr. Ogden, another old mountaineer who lived and died near or in the city. Ogden is destined to become a manufacturing town of no small importance. Vast quantities of iron ore can be obtained within five miles of the city, and iron works on a large scale have been commenced, but owing to want of proper foresight, the company ran short of means before their works were completed. An effort is now being made to resuscitate them, and with additional capital carry them on to completion. The freight on all iron brought into the Territory is so large in amount, that an iron manufactory here, with coal and iron ore bearing 60 per cent. of pure iron of an excellent quality, near by, will prove a paying investment and materially facilitate the development of the Territory. Discoveries of silver have also been made on the mountains back of the city, but the mines have not, as yet, been developed. These discoveries have been made up in Ogden Canon, about five miles from the city.

On the mountain directly east of the town, excellent slate quarries have been discovered and worked to some extent. It is said to be equal to the best found in the Eastern States.

Ogden River rises in the Wahsatch Range of Mountains, some 40 miles east of the city. It has three forks—north, middle and south—all of which unite just above the canon and fairly cut their way through one of the wildest and most romantic gorges on the Continent.

Ogden Canon.—This lovely little canon contains views quite as pretty as either Weber or Echo Canons. Visitors should stay over at Ogden and spend a day in a drive hither.

A fine creek, about 30 feet wide, and three to five feet deep, has cut through the mountain and its ridges. As it comes out of the mountain on the west side, it opens into a broad, grassy valley, thickly settled with farmers, and joins the Weber River about five miles distant. The scenes, as the traveler passes through the narrows of the canon, are wild in the extreme. The rocks rise from 500 to 2,000 feet almost perpendicularly, and the width averages less than 100 feet for a long distance. In this canon, geologists have found evidence sufficiently satisfactory to indicate that the entire Salt Lake Valley was once a huge fresh water lake, whose surface rose high up on the sides of the mountains, even covering the highest terrace.

Five miles up the canon, which runs eastward, there is a beautiful little valley, with table-like terraces, 30 to 50 feet above the bed of the creek, wherein a little Mormon village is located. The situation is a lovely one—the sides of the hills which enclose the valley, are 800 to 1,000 feet high, smoothly rounded and sloping, covered with coarse bunch grass and small bushes.

In addition to the railroad hotel before spoken of—which, by the way, is a first-class house and popular with the traveling public—Ogden has several hotels, prominent among which are the Utah Hotel, an up-town establishment, convenient for commercial men, and the Beardsley House which caters for railroad travel. It is also supplied with two newspapers, the *Daily Junction*, a small seven by nine sheet—the organ of the church, and published by one of the bishops, a Mormon poet, etc. The other is a weekly, styled the *Ogden Freeman*, the organ of the opposition. The city water-works are supplied with water taken from Ogden River, at the mouth of Ogden Canon. The road through the canon is a dugway along the stream, and sometimes built up from it, while the wall rocks on either side tower up thousands of feet. The water in the river goes rushing madly on over huge rocks and boulders lying in the bed of the stream, as though it would push them out of the way. In some places the rocks almost hang over the road, and as you round some point they seem as though they would push you into the stream. In some places the formation and dip of the rocks is very peculiar. They seem to be set up on end, in thin layers, and with a slight dip, while the wash of ages has worn out a channel for the river. About two miles up the canon, Warm Spring Canon comes in on the right. It is not much of a canon, but high up on the mountain side, near its source, are warm springs from which it takes its name. About half a mile farther are some hot sulphur springs, on the left side of the river, in the midst of a little grove of trees. This is a charming resort for the tourist, and he will never cease admiring the wild and rugged in nature, as exhibited in this canon. The canon is about six miles long, and the stream which runs through it is filled with "the speckled beauties" which are so tempting to the fisherman and so satisfactory to the epicure. As you look to the top of the mountain you will see pine trees that appear like little shrubs. These trees are from 50 to 80 feet in height, and are cut and brought down to the valleys for their timber. Accommodations for pleasure parties for visiting this wonderful canon, and for fishing and hunting, can be obtained in Ogden, and no excursion party from ocean to ocean should fail to visit it. Beyond the mountains, before the river gorges through, there is a fertile valley pretty well settled, and the road through the canon gives the people living there an outlet to the town. This road was built several years ago, and required a great deal of time and labor, and fitly illustrates the persevering industry of the Mormon people.

NARROWS OF OGDEN CANON.

Fruit-growing is very common in the vicinity of Ogden, and a large quantity of the best varieties grown in the Territory are produced in this region of country. Utah apples, peaches and pears are finer in size, color and flavor than any grown in the Eastern or Middle States.

Hot Springs. — Northward from Ogden, about a day's ride, is a very interesting locality, known as the *Hot Springs.* Here is a group of warm springs, forming, in the aggregate, a stream three feet wide, and six to twelve inches deep; the surface, for a space of 300 to 400 yards in extent, is covered with a deposit of oxide of iron, so that it resembles a tan-yard in color. The temperature is 136°. They flow from beneath a mountain called Hot Spring Mountain, which is about five miles long and three wide. The elevation of the lake is 4,191 feet. The water of the spring is clear as crystal, containing great quantities of iron, and the supply is abundant. As there are plenty of cold springs in the vicinity, there is nothing to prevent this from being a noted place of resort for invalids. The medicinal qualities of this water are excellent for rheumatism, skin diseases, dyspepsia, and the climate is unsurpassed.

The Territory of Utah.

When the Mormons first located in Utah, in 1847, it was territory belonging to Mexico, but by the treaty of Guadaloupe Hidalgo, in March, 1848, it was passed over to the United States with New Mexico and the whole of upper California. The government of the United States was not very prompt in extending its jurisdiction over the newly-acquired Territory, and in

WILHELMINA PASS, WEBER CANON.

BY THOMAS MORAN.

the absence of any other government the Mormons set up one for themselves, which was called the State of Deseret. This was done in the spring of 1849. On the 9th of September, 1850, Congress passed a bill which ignored the State government of the Mormons, and organized the Territory of Utah, and on the 28th of that same month, Millard Fillmore, President, appointed Brigham Young, Governor of the Territory with a full complement of executive and judicial officers. Since that time the area of the Territory has been diminished, but it is still large enough for all practical purposes. It now extends from the 37th to the 42d parallels of north latitude, and from the 109th to the 114th degree of longitude, embracing over 84,000 square miles or over 54,000,000 of acres. The national census of 1870 showed a population of about 90,000, and a fair estimate would give the Territory about 125,000 people at the present time. The climate, as a general thing, is salubrious and healthy, and violent extremes of either heat or cold are seldom experienced. The area of land susceptible of cultivation is small as compared to that included in the whole Territory, and a large quantity of even desert land is now unproductive because of the presence of alkali and mineral substances. While all kinds of grain can be grown with more or less success—depending upon local causes—wheat is the great staple, and in favorable seasons and localities monstrous crops of the great cereal have been produced.

It may astonish eastern readers, but it is nevertheless a fact, that whole fields, producing from fifty to sixty bushels per acre of as fine wheat as was ever grown, are no uncommon thing in Utah. The land, of course, is irrigated, and there is no great danger of loss by rains during the harvest season. The average yield, it is true, is a great deal less than this, amounting to about twenty-five bushels per acre. On account of the high altitude and cool nights, corn will not do as well, though fair crops are raised. Vegetables of all kinds grow to an astonishing size, and are superior in quality. Corn will, as a general thing, do better in the valleys in the southern part of the Territory, where cotton is also grown to a limited extent, and some kinds of tropical fruits. The climate and soil are especially adapted to the production of apples, pears, peaches, plums, currants, strawberries, raspberries, blackberries, etc. It must constantly be borne in mind, that successful agricultural pursuits can only be carried on here with irrigation, and that, as a general thing, it costs no more to irrigate land here, nor as much, as it costs to drain and clear it in many of the Eastern States. The market for most of the products raised in this Territory, is at the mining camps and settlements, and in Nevada, Idaho and Montana. The explorations in the southern half of the Territory, have resulted in the discovery of vast deposits of iron, coal, copper, silver, gold and lead. In the Strawberry Valley, coal veins over twenty feet thick, of excellent quality, have been discovered. In San Pete Valley, other magnificent coal deposits have been found, from which coke for smelting purposes has been made. East of the Wahsatch Range, in San Pete County, are the remains of the Moquis Village, of which much has been written. Iron County, still south, is so named from the vast deposits of this material found within its limits; and, in the spring of 1876, the most wonderful discoveries of silver were made near St. George, in what has been called the Bonanza District. There is horn silver around a piece of petrified wood in a sandstone formation. A part of this petrifaction was coal. The discovery of silver in such a formation, has upset many of the geological theories heretofore prevalent in the country. Ore from surface mines to the value of over fifty thousand dollars, has already been taken out. This discovery is one of the wonders of the country. A correspondent of the *Salt Lake Tribune*, recently spoke of these mines as follows: "The mines are in the rear of Bonanza City, and are certainly a new thing in the theory of geology and the mining world. Those in Silver Flat are found under and in sandstone, lying flat and about six to eight inches in width, showing rich chlorides, horn silver and sulphurets, carrying some mica. The manner of working the same has the appearance of quarrying rock." Judge Barbee, the discoverer of these mines, found several pieces of petrified wood ore, containing chlorides and horn silver. The specimen that we saw, said to have been brought from these mines, was carbonized to a certain extent—one side distinctly showing a thin vein of coal. There are two main ranges of mountains in Utah, running nearly parallel to each other. The easternmost range is the Wahsatch, and that farther west, the Oquirrh. Still farther to the west are broken ranges, parallel with those above named. Nearly all of these, so far as they have been prospected, are mineral bearing; and, in our judgment, the time is not far distant, when mines greater even than the Comstock, will be developed in Utah. They only await capital and the extension of railroads for their development. The Emma mine, which has filled the public prints, is thought to be one of the richest mines on the Continent, to-day, by the leading business men of Utah, who are familiar with the characteristics of the district in which it is located. In fact, Utah alone, has all the resources of an empire; and if it were only under a safe, stable and peaceful political local government, she would become the richest and brightest star in the coronet of the nation. It were well if certain pages in her eventful history could be forever obliterated.

Utah Central Railroad.—Ogden is the

northern terminus of this road. It is the pioneer line of Utah proper, though the Union Pacific and Central Pacific Roads were completed first through the magnificent generosity of the people of the United States. Early in May, 1869, the iron rails which bound the Continent together were joined near Promontory, some 50 miles west of Ogden. One week after this was done, work on the Utah Central began. The company was organized on the 8th of March previous, Brigham Young being president. A large quantity of material for building railroads was left on hand, when the Union Pacific was finished to Promontory, and this was purchased by the Utah Central Company. Brigham Young had entered into a contract for grading the former road, from the head of Echo Canon to Ogden, and successfully accomplished the work. If this had not been done, that road would have failed in its race across the Continent, and the Central Pacific would have built the greatest part of the trans-continental line. His contract was sublet to John Sharp and Joseph A. Young, the eldest son of the Mormon prophet. They crowded it with all possible speed, and obtained that experience in railroad building then, which has been of great advantage to the people of Utah since. In less than eight months from the time ground was broken for this new line of road, the last rail was laid, and on the 10th day of January, 1870, the first through train from Ogden, arrived in Salt Lake City. As elsewhere stated, this company is to unite with others in the erection of a Union depot at Ogden, work upon which will probably begin the present year. Their road now crosses the Central Pacific in Ogden, at nearly right angles, and their depot and freight houses are north of the Pacific Roads. Arriving at Ogden from the east, the traveler, looking ahead to the right, will see the engine and train of cars ready to take him to the City of the Saints. Entering elegantly furnished cars at about 6 o'clock P. M., and turning your back upon Ogden and the lofty mountain peaks behind it, you will soon be off. In less than a quarter of a mile, the road passes over the Weber River on a new and elegant iron bridge, just put up by the American Bridge Company of Chicago. It is a suspension bridge, 150 feet span, each end resting on a solid abutment of masonry. This bridge is so constructed that it will contract by cold or expand by heat as one body, one end being placed on rollers to allow self adjustment by the action of heat or cold. The bridge crossed, the road passes through a cut, and rises upon a bench or terrace of land from which, off to the right, the traveler obtains the first view of the Dead Sea of America—the Great Salt Lake. The general direction of the road is due south, and you pursue your way along the base of the foot hills and mountains, which form the first line looking east, of the Wahsatch Range. As far as Kaysville, the road passes over a comparatively unsettled country, though in the dim distance on the right, the farming settlements of Hooper may be seen near the mouth of Weber River. We soon arrive at

Kaysville,—16 miles from Ogden. It is a telegraph station surrounded by a farming settlement, with its "co-op" store, blacksmith-shop and the usual buildings of a small country town. In entering and leaving, the road crosses several little creeks that flow down from the mountains, the waters of which are nearly all drank up by the dry earth in the processes of irrigation. Passing on, the traveler will notice a few houses and settlements, toward the lake and mountains, sometimes nearer the mountains; arriving at

Farmington,—the next station, 21 1-4 miles from Ogden. It is the county-seat of Davis County, and has, besides a court-house, the usual store and shops. This town is also located in the midst of a farming region, and nearly overshadowed by the mountains on the east. Davis County slopes to the west toward the lake, has a warm rich soil, and when irrigated, produces luxuriant crops of vegetables, melons, grain, etc., for the Salt Lake market. Leaving this station the road draws near to the side of this great inland sea, to

Centerville,—25 1-2 miles from Ogden,—a little farming town with its store, etc. Between the lake on one side and the mountains on the other, and the thrifty farms with orchards and gardens now on either side and all around him, the traveler will be kept pretty busy.

Wood's Cross—is the next station, 27 3-4 miles from Ogden. It is about midway between the mountains and the lake, and is located in what is called the best portion of Davis County. It is a telegraph station with usual side tracks, etc. The country gradually slopes into the lake toward the west with an occasional drift of sand near the shore, covered with the inevitable sage brush which we have had since leaving Laramie River. The cosy farm houses and the evidences of thrift everywhere visible, the growing crops and ripening fruits, if in the summer—all conspire to make a pleasant landscape, upon which the traveler can feast his greedy gaze, while the shadow of the mountains grows longer, and the twilight deepens into night as we arrive at

Salt Lake City,—the southern terminus of the road, 36 1-2 miles from Ogden. But of this city, more in another place.

The Utah Central has been a paying road from the start, and its business, as the years pass by, is destined to make it better still. We have not all the data at hand to show what it has done, but will give one or two illustrations. In 1873, its tonnage was as follows. Freights received, 233,533,450 lbs. Freights shipped, 55,387,754 lbs. In 1874, there was a slight falling off,

SALT LAKE CITY AND WAHSATCH MOUNTAINS.

though it was not as large as expected from the business done in 1873, because of general depression of the mining interest of the Territory. In 1875, its business was as follows: Freights received, 184,158,526 lbs. Freights shipped 54,189, 929 lbs. Its gross earnings for 1875 were $407,000. Its operating expenses were $162,000. This last sum does not of course include dividends on its stock of $1,500,000, nor the interest on its bonds amounting to $1,000,000. The passenger fare, first class, from Ogden to Salt Lake is $2. The controlling interest in this road is at present owned by stockholders in the Union Pacific, and it is one of the best paying roads in the country. The above figures prove it.

SALT LAKE CITY.

Its Discovery.—When Brigham Young, with his weary band of pioneers arrived here, in 1847, it was a dreary waste, nevertheless a beautiful site so far as location is concerned, for a city. It lies on a bench or gradual slope from the Wahsatch Mountains, which tower up behind it on the east, to the River Jordan, which bounds it on the west. It is recorded that when the pioneers came within a few days' march of the place, Orson Pratt and a few others went ahead of the party "to spy out the land" and select a place for camping, etc., convenient to wood and water. On the 22d day of July, 1847, he rode over this valley with his companions, and returning to the main body, reported the results of their observations. On the morning of July 24, 1847, this body arrived at the top of the hill, overlooking the site of the city, and the valley beyond, and were enchanted with the scene. They gave vent to their joy in exclamations of thanksgiving and praise to Almighty God, firmly believing they had found the land of promise, though it did not flow with "milk and honey," and the "Zion of the Mountains" predicted by ancient prophets. The Mormons are great on literal interpretation. Figurative language and expressions as viewed by them are realities. The Bible means exactly what it says with them. They had reasons, however, for being enchanted. From the canon through which they entered the valley, the view is simply magnificent. The Great Salt Lake glittered like a sheet of silver in the rays of the morning sun; the towering peaks of the mountain ranges, crowned with clouds and snow, lifted themselves high up toward the sky, and the valley, though a desert, was to them as lovely as a June rose. The party camped on a small stream south-west of the Tabernacle, and proceeded to consecrate the entire valley to the "Kingdom of God." On the 28th of the same month, the ground for the temple was selected—a tract of 40 acres, and a city two miles square was laid off. Streets eight rods wide were staked out, and the blocks contained ten acres each. Orson Pratt took observations, and determined the latitude and longitude of the city. A large number of this pioneer party, after planting their crops returned for their families, and the last expedition for that year arrived on the last day of October, when they were received by those that remained with demonstrations of great joy. Brigham Young went back with the returning party, and did not find his way again to "Zion" until the next year. After the city had been founded, emigration from foreign countries, which had been suspended, was re-organized and came pouring into the Territory in masses. The city grew and the people spread out over the Territory, settling every available spot of land, thus contributing to its prosperity.

Beauty of Position.—The main portion of the city lies off to the left, as it is approached by the traveler, and presents a pleasing appearance. Its streets are wide, with streams of water coursing their way along the sides, while rows of beautiful shade trees line the walks; and gardens, and yards filled with fruit trees of various kinds, everywhere greet the eye. The city is now nearly thirty years old, and in that time, the tourist can see for himself what wonderful changes have been made. The desert truly buds and blossoms as the rose, and the waste places are made glad. The city is admirably located for beauty, and at once charms its visitors. The first practical thing, however, with the traveler, is to select his stopping place, during his visit. Of hotels there are two first-class houses that are popular resorts with the traveling public. These are the Townsend House and the Walker House. The latter is a four story brick structure with 132 rooms. It is located on the west side of Main Street, has a frontage of 82 feet and a depth of 120 feet. It is well finished and nicely furnished. The Townsend House is on the corner of West Temple and South Second streets. It has 150 rooms, elegantly furnished. It is two stories high, with piazzas on its entire front, and beautiful shade trees with a grassy plat, which make a delightful resort in the heat of the day, or when the evening shades appear. Both of these hotels face eastward, both are lighted with gas, and both are supplied with all modern conveniences and luxuries. Mr. Townsend owns his house and takes a natural pride in it. Those who have experienced the effects of the hot sun of this country in the summer, will kindly appreciate the cooling shade of the trees and the grassy plat, upon which water from fountains is continually sprinkling. There are, also, other good hotels in the city, but they are not considered first-class, though they are largely patronized.

Sights for Tourists.—Having selected a stopping place, the next thing is a visit to the warm sulphur springs, for a bath. The street

OFFICES AND FAMILY RESIDENCE OF BRIGHAM YOUNG.

cars, running by nearly all the hotels, will take you there.

Warm Springs.—These are, to invalids, the most grateful and delightful places of resort in the city. Exceedingly valuable either for rheumatic or dyspeptic complaints, they are excellent in general invigorating properties, and specially efficacious in skin diseases. They are but about one mile from the hotel, reached either by horse-cars or carriage. Even a pleasant walk is preferable. Best times to enjoy them are early in the morning before breakfast, or immediately before dinner. Should never be taken within three hours after a meal. The springs issue from the limestone rock near the foot of the mountains, and the curious character of the rock is seen in the stones used for either fences or the foundation of the buildings. The following analysis has been made of the water by Dr. Charles S. Jackson of Boston, and is generally posted on the walls of the bathing-house.

"Three fluid ounces of the water, on evaporating to entire dryness in a platine capsule, gave 8.25 grains of solid dry saline matter.

Carbonate of lime and magnesia,	0.240	1.280
Peroxide of iron,	0.040	0.208
Lime,	0.545	2.907
Chlorine,	3.454	18.421
Soda,	2.877	15.344
Magnesia,	0.370	2.073
Sulphuric Acid,	0.703	3.748
	8.229	43.981

It is slightly charged with hydro-sulphuric acid gas, and with carbonic acid gas, and is a pleasant, saline mineral water, having the valuable properties belonging to a saline sulphur spring.

The temperature is lukewarm, and, being of a sulphurous nature, the effects are very penetrating; at first the sensation is delicious, producing a delightful feeling of ease and repose; but if the bather remains long, over fifteen minutes, there is danger of weakness and too great relaxation. These baths are now under control of an experienced gentleman, and fitted up with every modern convenience. Here are Turkish baths, Hot Air baths and Russian baths, in addition to the natural bath. The warm sulphur-water can be enjoyed in private

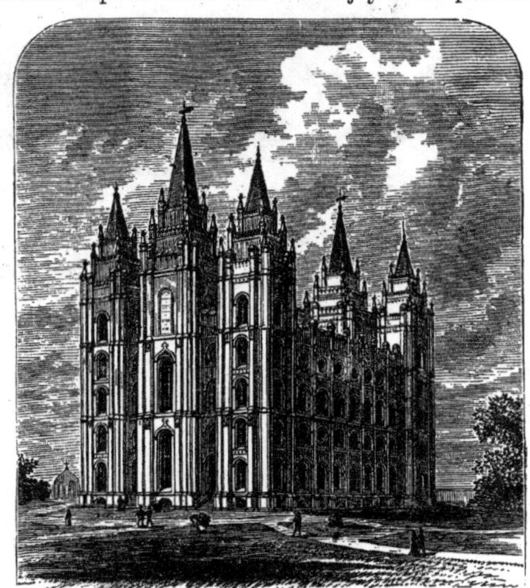

NEW MORMON TEMPLE.

rooms, or in the large plunge or swimming bath. Separate rooms for ladies and gentlemen, and a smaller building near by is fixed up for the boys, where they can frolic to their heart's content.

Hot Springs.—The tourist should take a

carriage, and, after visiting the Warm Springs and enjoying the bath, drive a mile farther north to where the mountain spur juts out to the very railroad—and, right at its base are situated the "*Hot Springs*," which are the greatest natural curiosity of the city. The water boils up, with great force, from a little alcove in the limestone rocks, just even with the surface of the ground. If you dare to thrust your hand in it, you will find it boiling hot, apparently with a temperature of over 200°. The finger can not be retained in the water for the best part of a minute; yet the sensation, as it is withdrawn, is so soft and cooling, you will like to try it again and again—and, strange to say, rarely with any danger of scalding. If meat is dropped into this boiling water, it is soon cooked, (though we cannot guarantee a pleasant taste) and eggs will be boiled, ready for the table, in three minutes. Often a dense volume of steam rises from the spring, though not always. A very large volume of water issues forth from the little hole in the rock—scarcely larger than the top of a barrel—about four feet wide and six to twenty inches deep. Immediately near the rock is a little pool, in which the water, still hot, deposits a peculiar greenish color on the sides, and coats the long, wavy grass with its sulphurous sediment. Flowing beneath the railroad track and beyond in the meadows, it forms a beautiful little lake, called Hot Spring Lake, which, constantly filling up, is steadily increasing its area, and, practically, destroying all agriculture and vegetation for hundreds of yards within the vicinity. This lake is also supposed to be supplied, to some extent, by other hot springs beneath the surface. Strange as it may seem, the hot water does not prevent the existence of some kinds of excellent fish, among which have been seen some very fine large trout.

Analysis of Hot Sulphur Spring:

Chloride of Sodium,	0.8052
" " Magnesium,	0.0288
" " Calcium,	0.1096
Sulphate of Lime.	0.0806
Carbonate of Lime,	0.0180
Silica,	0.0180
	1.0602

Specific gravity, 1.1454.

The Museum—is located on the south side of South Temple street, and directly opposite the Tabernacle. Professor Barfoot is in charge, and he will show you specimen ores from the mines, precious stones from the desert, pottery-ware and other articles from the ruins of ancient Indian villages, the first boat ever launched on the Great Salt Lake by white men, home-made cloths and silks, the products of the industry of this people, specimen birds of Utah, a scalp from the head of a dead Indian, implements of Indian warfare and industry, such as blankets white people cannot make, shells from the ocean, and various articles from the Sandwich Islands, and other things too numerous to mention.

Formerly there were quite a number of living wild animals kept here, but some fiend poisoned

INTERIOR OF OFFICE OF BRIGHAM YOUNG.

VIEW OF SALT LAKE CITY, LOOKING WESTWARD ACROSS THE JORDAN VALLEY.

the most of them. There are now living, however, a large horned owl, a prairie dog, and the owls that burrow with him, together with the rattlesnake; also other birds and reptiles which need not be named. This institution is the result of the individual enterprise of John W. Young, Esq., and for which he is entitled to great credit. A nominal sum, simply, is charged for admission, which goes for the support of Professor Barfoot, who has the care and direction of the Museum. Across the street, behind a high wall, is the Tabernacle, and near by it, on the east, enclosed within the same high wall, are the foundation walls of the new Temple. We shall not attempt a description of either, as a personal inspection will be far more satisfactory to the visitor. We advise every tourist to get to the top of the Tabernacle, if possible, and get a view of the city from the roof. Within the same walls may be found the Endowment house, of which so much has been written. In this building both monogamous and polygamous marriages take place, and the quasi-masonic rites of the church are performed. On South Temple street, east of Temple block, is the private residence of Brigham Young, also enclosed in a high wall which shuts out the rude gaze of passers-by, and gently reminds the outsider that he has no business to obtrude there. Nearly opposite to this residence is a large and beautiful house which is supposed to belong to the Prophet's favorite wife, Amelia — familiarly called *Amelia Palace*, probably the finest residence for 500 miles around. Returning to East Temple or Main street, we behold a large brick building with iron and glass front, three stories high, with a skylight its

SIGN OF MORMON STORES.—SALT LAKE CITY.

entire length. This is the new "co-op" store, 40 feet wide and 300 feet long, with all the modern improvements, steam elevator, etc. Nearly opposite this store is Savage's picture gallery, where fine photographs of views along the road may be obtained; also of the prominent Saints and some who are not so prominent. Continuing on the same street south, and the elegant building of the Deseret National Bank greets our gaze, on the north-east corner of East Temple and First South streets. Diagonally across the street from this is the emporium of William Jennings, Esq. But it is needless to enumerate all the buildings in the city, be they public or private. We must not omit, however, the elegant private residence and beautiful grounds of Mr. Jennings, on the corner east of the depot. They are worthy of a visit, and so, also, is the elegant private residence of Feramor Little, directly east of the Deseret National Bank. The theater is open occasionally in the evening, where may be seen many of the leading Mormons and their families.

The city is supplied with gas, water, and street railroads. The water is brought from City Creek Canon, through the principal streets, in iron pipes, though in some seasons the supply is rather short.

INTERIOR OF MORMON TABERNACLE.—THE GREAT ORGAN.

Scenery Near the City.—North of the city, Ensign Peak lifts its head, the Mountain of Prophecy, etc. Its crown is oval in shape, and the mountain, etc., is said to have been seen in a vision by some of the Mormon dignitaries long before it was beheld by the naked eyes of the present settlers. The sight from this peak, or others near at hand, is grand and impressive. Under your feet lies the City of the Saints, to the west the Great Salt Lake, to the south the valley of the river Jordan, the settlements along the line of the railroad, and the mountains on either side. Though the way to the summit requires a little toil, and will expand one's lungs to the fullest extent, yet the reward, when once the summit is reached, will amply pay for all the toil it has cost.

In the summer months only, the Tabernacle is open, and the services of the Mormon church are then held there nearly every Sabbath. Behind the rostrum or pulpit is the great organ, made in the city, and said to be the second in size on the Continent.

East of the city there seems to be a withdrawal of the mountains and a part of a circle, formed like an amphitheatre. About two miles east is Camp Douglas, established by General Connor during the late war. It is beautifully located on an elevated bench commanding the city, and at the base of the mountains. New buildings have been erected, and it is now considered one of the finest and most convenient posts the government has. It is supplied with water from Red Butte Canon, and has a great many conveniences.

Below Camp Douglas, Emigration Canon next cuts the mountains in twain. It is the canon through which Orson Pratt and his companions came when they first discovered the valley, the lake, and the site for a city—through which Brigham Young and the pioneers came, and was the route by which nearly all the overland emigrants arrived, on coming from the East. Below this, as you look south, is Parley's Canon, through which a road leads to Parley's Park and the mining districts in that region. Then comes South Mill Creek with its canon, through the towering peaks, and then the Big Cottonwood Creek and Canon. Between it and Little Cottonwood Canon, next on the south, is the mountain of silver—or the hill upon which is located some of the richest paying mines in the Territory. Here is the Flagstaff, the North Star, the Emma, the Reed & Benson, and others worth their millions. The Emma mine has become notorious in the history of mines, but there is not a practical miner in Utah who doubts the existence of large bodies of rich ore there, and, if it had been practically worked, would, in the opinion of many, have equaled, if not exceeded, the celebrated Comstock lode before this.

No visitor to Salt Lake should leave the city without a trip to the lake and a ride on its placid bosom—a trip, also, to the southern terminus of the Utah Southern Railroad, the mountains and canons along its line, and to the mountains and mines of Stockton, Ophir, Bingham, and above all, the Cottonwood districts. If you are further inclined to improve the opportunity, ride up to Parley's Park, go to Provo and spend a week, or a month even, in visiting the wonderful canons near there, and in hunting and fishing in the mountain streams and in Lake Utah. A trip to the summit of old Mount Nebo would afford you good exercise, and very fine views. With Salt Lake for headquarters, all these places can be taken in, and your only regret will be that you did not stay longer, travel farther, and see more of this wonderful land.

NEW RESIDENCE OF BRIGHAM YOUNG.—AMELIA PALACE.

Gardening Irrigation.—The city was originally laid out in large ten acre blocks, which were, in time, subdivided into house lots, most of which, having been liberally planted with fruit trees, have since grown with great luxuriance, and the city seems a vast fruit orchard and garden. Through all the streets run the little irrigating streams, and every part of the city has its chance, once or twice a week, to get a supply of pure water to wet the soil and freshen the vegetation.

The city is divided into wards. Every ward has its master, and he compels all the inhabitants to turn out and work on public improvements. There is no shirking. Every one has a responsibility to guard and watch his own property, take care of his own irrigating ditches, and keep his ward in perfect order. The city is one of perfect order and quietness.

Through all the streets of the city there is a universal and luxuriant growth of shade trees. These have been planted profusely, and grow with amazing rapidity. The locust, maple and box-elder, are the greatest favorites, the former, however, being most planted. In many cases the roots have struck the alkali soils, which contain an excess of soda and potash, and their leaves have turned from a bright or dark green to a sickly yellow—and often trees may be noticed, half green and half yellow.

This alkali has to be washed out of the soil by irrigation, and gradually grows less positive year by year. In nearly all the gardens are splendid apples, pears, plums and apricots, growing with exceeding thrift, and covered with the most beautiful blushing colors. Apricots which in the East are almost unknown, here have been so abundant as often to sell as low as $1.00 per bushel, and we have seen them as large as eastern peaches, from four to six and eight inches round.

Flowers are very abundant, and vegetables are wonderfully prolific. In the gardens of William Jennings, may be seen growing out doors on trellises, grapes, the Black Hamburgh, Golden Chasselas and Mission grape, varieties which are only grown in a hot-house in the East. Through all the gardens can be seen an abundance of raspberries, gooseberries and currants. In Mr. Jennings's garden, in summer, may be seen a pretty flower garden, 150 feet in diameter,—within the center of which is a piece of velvety lawn—the finest and most perfect ever seen—while from it, southward, can be caught a specially glorious view of the Twin Peaks of the Wahsatch Mountains, capped with unvarying snow.

Future of Salt Lake City.—The future of Salt Lake depends upon two things—the mines and the railroads. If the mines are developed and capital is thus increased, it will have a tendency to cause an immense amount of building in the city, and a corresponding advance in real estate. It is claimed that the city now has a population of 30,000 souls, but we think 22,000 a closer estimate. Many parties owning and operating mines make the city their place of residence, and some have already invested in real estate there. We heard the opinion of a wealthy capitalist—a gentleman operating in mines—to the effect that in ten years Salt Lake would number 250,000 people, but he was a little enthusiastic. If the Utah Southern is extended to the Pacific Coast, it will add largely to the wealth, population and influence of the "City of the Saints." The silent influence of the Gentiles and the moral power of the Nation has already had an effect upon the Mormons of the city, which will soon be felt throughout the Territory. The discovery and development of the mines will largely increase the Gentile population throughout the Territory, and their influence will then be each year more powerfully felt, and we question if Mormonism will be strong enough to withstand them.

Newspapers.—The press of Salt Lake is exceedingly peculiar. The *Daily News* is the recognized church organ; the *Daily Herald* is more lively. It is the organ of the so-called progressive Mormons. The *Daily Tribune* is a stinging, lively journal—the leading organ of the opposition to the priesthood and the theocracy. The *Mail* is an evening paper under Gentile influences, but not as bold or belligerent as the *Tribune.* The *Utah Weekly Miner* is a paper devoted to the development of the mineral resources of the Territory. There is another little evening paper called the *Times*, under church influences. Fortunes have been expended upon newspaper enterprises in Salt Lake, but with the exception of the three papers first mentioned, none have succeeded. The ground is now, however, fully occupied, and further efforts should be directed toward improving those already established, rather than in new and costly experiments.

The Utah Southern Railroad.—This road is really a continuation of the Utah Central. It was begun on the 1st day of May, 1871, and completed to Sandy that same year. In 1872 it was extended to Lehi, about thirty miles from Salt Lake City. In 1873 it was extended to Provo, and its present terminus is at York, a little place just across the divide between Lake Utah and Juab Valley. It will probably be extended from a hundred to a hundred and fifty miles the present year. York is 75 miles from Salt Lake City, and 16 miles from Nephi, the next town on its proposed line of any importance. The stockholders of the Union Pacific Road, own a controlling interest in this, as also in the Utah Central. It will probably be extended to the Pacific Coast sometime. The following is the record of freight received and forwarded at the Salt Lake City Station for the year 1875. Freight received, 70,916,527 lbs. Freight forwarded, 71,969,954 lbs. Its gross earnings for same period, were $188,987.60,—and its operating expenses, were $120,650.87. The great bulk of its business is between Salt Lake City and Sandy, though travel and traffic are gradually increasing on the balance of its line, and will rapidly double up as soon as the road shall have reached the rich mining districts in the southern portions of Utah, which are at present comparatively undeveloped. Its general direction is southward from Salt Lake City, up the Jordan Valley to the Valley of Lake Utah, and thence across the divide as before mentioned. Travelers visiting this Territory should not fail to visit the towns, valleys and mountains on this line of road. The Valley of Lake Utah especially, entirely surrounded by mountains lofty and rugged, will compare favorably, so far as magnificent scenery is concerned, with anything of a similar character to be found either in Europe or America. Leaving Salt Lake City, we slowly pass through the limits of the corporation where cultivated fields and gardens, with farm houses and fine orchards of all kinds of fruit trees, giving evidences of thrift on every side, greet our gaze. Streams of water are constantly running through the irrigating ditches, and the contrast between the cultivated lands and the sage brush deserts, sometimes side by side, is wonderful. On our left, the everlasting mountains, with their crowns of snow almost always visible, stand like an impenetrable barrier to approaches from the east, or like eternal fingerboards, and say as plainly as words can indicate —"go south or north; you cannot pass us." On the right, the river Jordan winds its way to the waters of the great inland sea, while beyond, towering into the sky, are the peaks of the Oquirrh Range. You will need to keep your eyes wide open, and gaze quickly upon the rapidly changing scenes as they come into view, or swiftly recede from your vision; for, between the scenes of nature and the works of man in reclaiming this desert, you will hardly know which to admire the most, or which is the most worthy of your attention. Passing on, we arrive at the first station—

Little Cottonwood,—7 miles from the city. It is a way station at which trains do not stop unless flagged, or the signal is given from on board the train. All the canons and ravines in the mountains supply more or less water, which is gathered into canals and distributed through ditches as required for the fields, meadows and orchards. The well cultivated fields continue until we arrive at

Junction,—12 miles from Salt Lake City, where the Bingham Canon & Camp Floyd Railroad intersects the Utah Southern. Passengers here change cars for Bingham Canon and the mining districts in that vicinity. This road is about twenty-two miles long and is extensively used in transporting ore, bullion, coke, coal and charcoal to and from the mines and smelting works and railroad. It is a narrow gauge (three feet) road and is now doing a fine business.

SNOW SLIDE MOUNTAIN.—LITTLE COTTONWOOD CANON.

Sandy,—13 miles from the city and the point of intersection of the Wahsatch & Jordan Valley Railroad,—narrow gauge (three feet). This road turns off to the left and goes up Little Cottonwood Canon, which can now plainly be seen from the cars. The Big Cottonwood Canon is also in sight. There they are, with the mountain of silver between them. There is silver enough in that mountain to pay the national debt of the United States, with enough left to pay for a huge fourth of July celebration. This road has some very heavy grades, and, on the upper end of it, horses, instead of engines, are employed to haul the empty cars. These two narrow gauge roads are now under one management. The Little Cottonwood Road is about eighteen miles in length. Sandy is a flourishing little town. It has several smelters, or reduction works, where crude ore is converted into bullion. The celebrated Flagstaff mine has its smelting works here; its ore is brought down from the mine on the Wahsatch & Jordan Valley Railroad. Every visitor to Utah, who is at all interested in mines, or metallurgy, will obtain a great deal of information, and be amply repaid for the time and expense of a visit to its more celebrated mining districts. A visit to the Bingham and Little Cottonwood Districts, certainly should not be neglected. Leaving Sandy, we enter into a desert country again; the farmhouses are scattering, though the land on the right, toward the immediate vicinity of the Jordan, is still pretty well settled. The next station is

Draperville,—17 miles from Salt Lake City. It is an unimportant station, convenient to a little Mormon settlement. Leaving this station we soon cross South Willow Creek, and then follow the outer rim of the hills around the valley toward the right, like a huge amphitheatre. We have been going up hill, and, as we turn to the right, to get through a pass or gorge in the mountains, the valley below us with Sandy, Salt Lake City, Salt Lake itself, its islands, the mountains beyond and a vast scope of country is suddenly unrolled, like a beautiful panorama, to our view — a magnificent spectacle which never fails to excite and satisfy the beholder. Turning to the left again, we near the narrows, and, looking to the right, the river Jordan winds along beneath us; then, passing through a deep cut, we suddenly emerge into the valley of Lake Utah, and at once become enchanted with the lovely view now spread out before us. The valley, cities and towns we have just left, are entirely shut out from our vision, and, in their stead, new wonders invite our attention. There is Lake Utah, with little villages and settlements between its shores and the base of the mountains, and those mountains thousands of feet in height, piercing the very clouds, around it. With an elevation about 500 feet higher than that of the Great Salt Lake, it lies nestled down among the lofty peaks, as though it would hide its beauty and shun the gaze of the outside world. But iron arms have forced their way through the rugged defiles, and now hold it in long and lasting embrace. Henceforth it will receive the homage of thousands, and become a place of worship to the multitudes who shall see in it and its surroundings, the Mecca of their pilgrimages—the gratification of their desires and the satisfaction of every hope. This is strong language, and the tourist himself shall be the judge of its truthfulness. This lake is virtually the head of the river Jordan. It winds its way, like a ribbon of silver, through the valley, passes through the gorge we have entered and becomes lost to view. Down into the valley of the lake we go and arrive at

Lehi,—the next station, 31 miles from the City of the Saints. It is located on Dry Canon Creek, though the creek furnishes water sufficient to irrigate the thrifty farms bordering the little village. A large portion of the bottom-lands around the lake are cultivated and irrigated with the water that flows down the mountain streams.

American Fork,—34 miles from Salt Lake City, is now reached. It is named from the creek and canon back of the town, which has cleft the mountains in twain, and left on their ragged edges the marks of the heroic and victorious struggle. From this town another narrow gauge railroad has been built up the canon to Deer Creek, some twelve miles, to accommodate the necessities of the mines which have been opened there. It will be extended whenever the increased productions of these mines shall demand it. Of the grand scenery of this noted canon we shall speak in another place. The town is about six miles from the mouth of the canon, and has every appearance of the industry which usually characterizes Mormon towns.

Pleasant Grove,—37 miles from the city, is the next station. It is a thriving farming settlement, and similar to all the little villages in the Territory. It was formerly called Battle Creek because of a fight which early settlers had with the Ute Indians. Leaving Pleasant Grove we soon arrive at

Provo,—48 miles from Salt Lake City, and the third town in size in Utah Territory, having a population of about 5,000 souls. After leaving the last station, off to the left, Provo Canon is visible, with Provo or Timpanogos River flowing through it. This river rises in the western spur of the Uintah Mountains, flows along the southern part of Kammas Prairie and then turns to the south-west, entering what is called Provo Valley, which lies east of the range of mountains on our left, and finally cutting through this range into the valley of Lake Utah. Observe, as you approach the town, how the strata of rocks in the mountains on each side of the canon dip toward each other. An immense body of water flows down this river, annually—more than passes through the river Jordan, the surplus being taken up by evaporation or drank by the thirsty soil. We cross the river as we approach the town, and for the first time since leaving Salt Lake, see small bodies of timber, mostly cottonwood, and a thick undergrowth of brush, etc.

Sporting.—Between the town and lake are low marshes and meadows which render this place a paradise for ducks, which fact the sportsman will do well to note. The streams which flow into the lake abound in fish, and the lake itself is full of trout, chub, suckers, etc. It is no unfrequent matter to catch trout here weighing from seven to ten pounds, though from two to five pounds is their usual weight. The trout ascend the streams in the proper season to deposit their spawn; the suckers follow to devour it, and sometimes they almost choke the river, so vast are they in numbers, and are caught in large quantities. The streams sometimes fall so rapidly that they are left in shallow places and die there as the water recedes. Measures should be taken to prevent this wholesale raid on the spawn of the trout, or it will soon be destroyed—at least materially lessened. If the suckers are masters of the situation, so far as the spawn is concerned, the reverse holds true with the trout in the lake, for there they attack the suckers without mercy, and the old adage that "the big fish eat the little ones," proves literally true. It is evident that the young suckers are highly relished by the larger trout in this lake.

The town of Provo is regularly laid out, has numerous school-houses, stores, grist-mill, tanneries, woolen factory, etc. Brigham Young has a private residence here, which he frequently visits, and which is occupied by one of his so-called wives. It has finely cultivated gardens, yards, orchards and small farms adjacent.

Springville,—53 miles from Salt Lake City. The little town lies back under the mountains, and will probably be the initial point of a narrow gauge railroad to the extensive coal fields in Strawberry Valley, some 60 miles east. This coal possesses coking qualities, and as a large amount of coke is now imported from Pittsburg, Pa., for the use of the numerous smelting works in the Territory, it at once becomes an object to manufacture it nearer home. Coke made from coal found in the San Pete Valley is already shipped from this point. Still rounding the eastern rim of the valley, we soon arrive at the next station, which is

Spanish Fork,—58 miles from Salt Lake City. To the left, the traveler will observe the canons and gorges which have cut their way through the mountains, and the lofty peaks of Mount Nebo, now nearly in front. Hobble Creek courses a canon through the range back of Springville, and now Spanish Fork does likewise. There is more of a depression in the mountain, however, where this river canons through. It has two main branches on the other side of the range—upon the northern, the proposed Denver Railroad comes in, while the southern branch heads in the divide that crosses San Pete Valley, east of Mount Nebo. Near Wales, in this valley, coking coal has been discovered, ovens erected, and the manufactured article is now delivered at Springville, being hauled nearly 60 miles by wagons. The projected railroad from Springville, will pass up the valley of the Spanish Fork River. The town is located on this river, a little distance from the road. We cross the river soon after leaving the station. A little village called Pontoun, is seen on the left at the base of Mount Nebo.

Payson,—66 miles from the City of the Saints. Iron ore is shipped from here to the smelters, where it is used for fluxing purposes in the reduction of ore. It is hauled some 14 miles by wagons. It is said to bear 60 or 65 per cent. of iron, and is known as brown hematite. At this station and the next, ore and bullion are hauled from the East Tintic Mining District, which is about 22 miles away. To our right, a mountain rises from the level plain around it, while the lake puts out an arm, as if to clasp it in fond embrace. Between this mountain and Mount Nebo, the road finds its way, and a little farther on, this arm of the lake can be seen west of the mountain.

Santaquin—is the next station, 71 miles from Salt Lake City. This station is also an outlet for the mining district referred to, and for one or two little villages nestled down at the base of the mountains on the left. The road now passes through a low depression or valley, which divides the Wahsatch and Oquirrh Ranges, and across the divide between Lake Utah and Juab Valley, by easy grades, and we soon arrive at

York,—75 miles from the northern terminus, and the present southern terminus of the Utah Southern Railroad. The town is of no particular importance, and will lose its present significance as soon as the road is extended. In fact it is no place for a town, and there is no country around it to support one. Farther down the valley, streams from the mountains come in, water for irrigation can be obtained, and the desert, under the manipulations of labor, is made to bud and blossom as the rose. When the road is extended to Nephi, 16 miles, the traveler can pass into a beautiful and highly cultivated valley, and behold the towering form and giant outlines of Mount Nebo, from the south. It is one of the highest peaks in the Wahsatch Range of the Rocky Mountains, and its lofty head whitened by eternal snows, is frequently obscured by clouds. The elevation of the summit of this mountain, is given by the Engineer Department of the United States Army, at 11,922 feet. Froiseth's map of Utah places it at 12,000 feet, but the difference is so slight as to be scarcely worthy of notice. It is a grand old mountain, and worthy of a visit from the remotest parts of the globe.

AMERICAN FORK CANON.

Of this canon, no less a writer than the late Charles Kingsley, Canon of the English Church in London, England, has given the most enthusiastic expression, and declares it "*The rival of the Yosemite.*"

It is by far the most wonderful of all the canons which are within convenient access to the Pacific Railroad, and tourists who value sights of grandeur and sublime rock scenery, must not omit it in their overland tour. In interest, beauty, and as a delightful pleasure trip, it will surpass either Echo, Weber, or Humboldt Canons, and not a little of the joy is attributable to the novel mode of ascent and descent.

Taking the cars of the Utah Southern Railroad at Salt Lake City, proceed southward to American Fork Station; there a little train is in waiting with narrow gauge cars and locomotive. If the party is large enough for a picnic, so much the better, as often flat cars are added, neatly trimmed with evergreen boughs. The railroad, after leaving the station turns directly toward the mountain range, and gradually ascends for the first six miles, a steady grade of 200 feet to the mile, until just before the mouth of the canon it reaches 296 feet. Nothing can describe the apparent desolation of sage brush and dry sterile appearance of the soil, but here and there whereever the little mountain brook can be diverted from its course, and its water used to irrigate the land, the richest of fruit trees, grass and grain spring up and give abundant crops. The little stream, with its rapid fall, follows us up the entire length of the canon. The upward ascent of the grade seems hardly noticeable, of so uniform a slope is the surface of the country, and it is not till the base of the mountains is reached, and the tourist looks back, he realizes his height,

AMERICAN FORK CANON.

BY THOMAS MORAN.

and sees in the distance the clear surface of Utah Lake considerably below him. Gathering now on the flat cars—where the scenery can be best observed—the little train slowly enters the canon. Scarcely 500 feet are passed over before there bursts upon the eye views of rock scenes of the most rugged character. The little valley is scarcely 100 feet broad, and in its widest part not over 200 feet, but from the very track and little stream, the rocks loom up into heights of startling distinctness and almost perpendicular elevation.

The color of the rocks is uniformly of very dark red and brown granite, apparently having once been heated in a terrible furnace, and then in melting had arranged themselves into rugged and fantastic shape more than mortal could conceive.

At the beginning of the canon, the rocks average about 800 feet in height, then, as the route ascends, the sides become more and more bold and erect,—the height greater, and the summits sticking up in jagged points seem like heaven-reaching spires,—often 1,500, 2,000, and 2,500 feet above the observer.

No pen can picture the sensations of the observer, as he passes slowly through these scenes —which are constantly shifting. Each turn in the road brings forward some new view, more entrancing than the last,—and on either side, front and rear, the vision is superb in the highest degree. We could not term these scenes better than to call them "*Rock Kaleidoscopes.*" For in this short distance of 12 miles, there is a constant succession of castellated heights, titanic monsters, spires, rock mountains of increasing height, sublime form and piercing altitudes, meeting us, crossing our path, and shooting up above and around us the entire distance,—it seems like a succession of nature's castles, far more rugged and picturesque than the castle covered rocks of the Rhine. Rocks of endless form and beauty, vistas of rocks, sky towering summits, bold crags, and flinty points jutting out from the mountain sides in most profuse, rugged, yet charming positions and combinations, that those eyes which once had no admiration for rocks—here confess with extreme enthusiasm, that there is beauty beyond the wildest imaginations.

While passing upward, the train is very slow, scarcely passing more than four or six miles per hour,—the traveler will see some rocks of curious formations at the left hand, about one-third of the way up; on the summit of one of the highest crags, will be seen a sharp-pointed rock, and in it a large distinct hole, through which can be seen the sky beyond. The contrast of the dark brown rock, and the clear blue of the sky is intense. This is familiarly called the *Devil's Eye.*

Farther up, the track passes under the jutting edge of a rock mountain with a sharply cut alcove in its base. This is *Hanging Rock*—the roof of the rock which projects over the railroad, being about 20 feet outward.

Near the upper part of the canon, just before reaching the junction of two little valleys, the track reaches a huge rock mountain overlooking a little wilderness of trees and vegetation, in the center of which is located the *Old Mill.* It is now entirely useless, once used for sawing timber and ties for the railroad, but though it has left its field of usefulness behind,—it has remained to add a far more important help to art. The scene as viewed in our illustration, is one considered the most lovely and picturesque, not only of the entire canon, but also of all the Territory. In all that grand reach of country, of 2,000 miles from Omaha to the Sierras, not a single view is the equal of this delightful scene of the Old Mill. The dense growth of trees, the rippling water, the bold rock at the side, the soft shades of light in the distance, the luxuriant bushes along the stream, and the little silent deserted mill, situated exactly in the most beautiful site, make up a view which artists of keenest taste admit with rapture is unparalleled in beauty.

Beyond this, as the track ascends the canon, it is bordered with more shrubbery and trees,—and the rock views partially ceasing—the tourist will find his best vision looking backward, with a good view of the tallest mountain of the canon, *Lone Mountain*, or *Mount Aspinwall.*

At last the end of the track is reached at *Deer Creek*, though the canon continues six miles or more to the *Silver Lake Mine.* At Deer Creek, there is a little village with a comfortable inn and store, and a large collection of charcoal kilns. This business is quite large, there being ten pits of brick, which reduce each about 1,100 bushels of charcoal, for which the proprietor gets 25 cents per bushel,—a business of about $50,000 per year is done.

The Miller Mine has been estimated exceedingly rich, and is owned largely by New York capitalists, who work it steadily. It is said to yield, with lead, over fifty ounces of silver per ton. The American Fork Railroad was built originally to facilitate the carrying of ores, as well as the charcoal, but the grandeur of the scenery has given it a celebrity among tourists, far beyond that of any railroad in Utah.

At Deer Creek is a lovely picnic grove, pure spring water, and for those of good wind and lovers of adventure,—an opportunity for mountain climbing.

The total length of the canon to this point, is 12 miles, and the total length of the railroad, is 16 miles,—cost about $400,000, and the most solidly built narrow gauge railroad in the United States. The total ascent in elevation for the whole railroad, is nearly 5,000 feet, and

SCENES IN AMERICAN FORK CANON.

1.—Mt. Aspinwall, or Lone Mountain. 2.—Rock Summits. 3.—Picnic Grove, Deer Creek. 4.—A quiet Glen. 5.—Hanging Rock. 6.—Rock Narrows.

the average grade of the railroad is 200 feet. The maximum grade is 296 feet. This is the steepest railroad grade in the United States, and the only grade over 200 feet ascended by a locomotive.

Tourists who have enjoyed so fine and glorious a ride up the canon hither, will perhaps expect that the return will be tame. They will be most pleasantly surprised and disappointed, for it is *the grandest of all railroad scenes they will ever witness.*

Detaching the locomotive from the train, the conductor stands at the little brake, and without a signal or help, the little cars of the train quietly start on their downward journey, alone. Gliding down with increasing speed, rounding the curves with grand and swinging motion, the breeze fanning your face, and the beautiful, pure mountain air stimulating your spirits to the highest limits of exhilaration, your feelings and body are in an intense glow of delight, as the rock scenes, crags and mountain heights come back again in all their sublimity, and your little car, securely held, glides swiftly down the beautiful valley. In no part of the country is there a scene to be compared with this. The entire being is fascinated, and when, at last, the little car turns swiftly into the broad plain, the tourist feels he has left behind him a land of delight. The little cars occupy but one hour in making the descent, and the writer has made the trip in forty minutes. This canon was first brought to the notice of the traveling public and pleasure travelers of the East, by the editor of "THE PACIFIC TOURIST," who conducted over it, in 1873, the first body of editors which had ever visited the locality. Since that time, while its value as a road for mining purposes has become less valuable, yet the canon has become so noted as a resort of grand and remarkable scenery, that the steady crowd of pleasure travelers, give it now a large and valuable custom. Tourists can purchase excursion tickets at a great reduction from single prices. No one who crosses the Continent, should omit a sight of this most wonderful locality.

Lake Utah.—This beautiful sheet of water lies between the Oquirrh and Wahsatch Ranges of Mountains. These ranges and their foot hills come closely together between Drapersville and Lehi, and the River Jordan cuts through them there in a narrow gorge or canon. The lake and valley then suddenly burst upon the view of the traveler, and admiration grows into enthusiasm as he contemplates the lovely picture before him. The lake is about thirty miles long and six miles wide, is triangular in shape and composed of fresh water. Its elevation is about 4,482 feet, or nearly 300 feet greater than that of the Great Salt Lake. The railroad goes around the eastern side of the lake, turning an obtuse angle at or near Provo. The lake is fed by Provo River, American Fork, Hobble, Spanish Fork, Peteetneet, Salt and a few other small creeks. Its outlet is the River Jordan which empties into Great Salt Lake, and supplies water for irrigating the numerous farms in its valley. As before stated the lake abounds in fish, and on its eastern and northern sides, has a large quantity of arable land. Its western shore is not very well watered, only one or two little creeks putting down into it from the Oquirrh Range of Mountains. It is well worthy of a visit from the tourist, or sportsman.

The Utah Western Railroad. — This road was first chartered on the 15th of June, 1874, with a capital stock of $900,000. The company is mostly composed of Utah men having their residence in Salt Lake City; John W. Young, a son of Brigham Young, being President, while Heber P. Kimball is Superintendent. The same year it was chartered, twelve miles were completed and opened for business on the 12th day of December, and, on the 1st of April, 1875, it was completed to Half-Way House, thirteen miles farther. An extension of fourteen miles is now under contract, which will doubtless be completed the present year. This last extension will take the road to within one and a half miles of Stockton, a prosperous mining town on the western slope of the Oquirrh Range of Mountains. Its business on twenty-five miles of completed road, for the year beginning February 10, 1875, and ending February 9, 1876, both days inclusive, was as follows: Freights received, 15,284,636 lbs.; freights forwarded, 5,276,619 lbs., one of the smelting works near Stockton, alone forwarding over 7,000,000 lbs. of bullion, ore, etc. The cash receipts for the same time were as follows: $49,186, and the operating expenses of the road, also, for the same period, were nearly $16,000. It is a narrow gauge road, (three feet) and has prospects for an extensive business in the future. Its general route is westward until it passes the southernmost point of the Great Salt Lake, and then southward, along the western base of the Oquirrh Range, and into the rich mining districts which have been developed on the western slope of those mountains. Leaving Salt Lake City, on a heavy downward grade of ninety-five feet to the mile, but which is short, the road crosses the River Jordan on a common pile bridge, and then over a barren sage brush country, until it reaches

Millstone Point,—near the base of the mountains, and 11 1-2 miles from Salt Lake City. This place is named from the fact that the first millstones used in grinding grain in Utah, were quarried from the mountains near this point. The old overland stage road from Salt Lake City to California passes along the line of the road, as does one line of the Western Union Telegraph Company, to the present terminus of the road. The station is of no partic-

THE OLD MILL, AMERICAN FORK CANON.

ular importance, and beyond the incident mentioned, is without a history. We are now at the base of the Oquirrh Range, and the first station of the Old Stage Company where they changed horses is pointed out to the traveler on the south side of the road. Beyond Millstone Point, about two miles on the south side of the track, is a large spring, which furnishes a good supply of water, and which has been utilized by a dairyman. A little beyond this spring on the same side of the track, there is, in the first point of rocks, quite an extensive cave which a shepherd uses as a shelter for his sheep, during the inclement season of the year. A rail fence with gate surrounds the entrance to the cave, and it is said to be large enough to turn a four horse team and wagon without difficulty. The extent of the outer part of the cave is about 40 feet, where a huge fallen rock precludes further access without inconvenience. The lake and its mountain islands, and the ranges beyond, now come grandly into view on the north side of the track. The next station is

Black Rock, —17 1-2 miles from Salt Lake City,—a station named from a rock, dark enough to be called black, rising in the lake about 100 yards from the shore. It is nearly flat on the top, and with a little effort can be easily ascended. Jutting out from the shore, and a short distance from the station, is "Lion's Head" Rock. Beyond this is "Observation Point," from which the Goose Creek Mountains, 145 miles north, can be seen in a clear day, with their white peaks glistening in the sunlight. The northern point of the Oquirrh Range here comes close to the lake, and what seems to be a few scattering trees, or groves of trees, high up on the mountain, contain millions of feet of pine lumber, if it could only be made available. Right under "Observation Point," on the very edge of the lake shore stands a stone house, formerly kept as a hotel for pleasure seekers, but now the private property of John W. Young, Esq. Whoever occupies it hereafter, can very nearly be "rocked in the cradle of the deep," or, at least, be lulled to sleep by the murmur of the restless waves. Standing upon "Observation Point," before you, a little to the left, rises the rock from which the station is named; beyond and to the left still, Kimball's Island rises out of the sea twenty-two miles away; while off to the right is Church Island, 14 miles away: they do not look half the distance, but the rarified atmosphere of these elevated portions of the Continent is very deceptive as regards vision and distance. Promontory Point on the north shore of the lake is also visible at a distance of about eighty miles.

LIONS HEAD ROCK.—GREAT SALT LAKE.

Lake Point, —20 miles from the city is the next station and the great resort for excursion parties and tourists in the summer. Near this station is "Giant's Cave" from which stalactites may be obtained, and other relics, said to be remains of Indians who were conquered and penned in until they died. A personal examination will satisfy the tourist as to the probable truth of this tradition. The company has a large hotel at Lake Point containing 35 rooms for guests, besides other necessary appurtenances to a good hotel. A wharf has been built into the lake, beside which, when not employed, the stern wheel steamer, "General Garfield," is moored. This steamer is employed for excursion parties and for transporting ore from the islands, and the west side of the lake, to the railroad. A bathing-house has been erected on the wharf, where conveniences for a salt water bath are kept. The waters of the lake are very dense, and it is almost impossible for bathers to sink. In former times three barrels of water would make by evaporation, one barrel of salt; now four barrels of water are required to effect the same result. A company has been organized in Salt Lake City, to manufacture salt from the waters of this lake near Millstone Point, and vats are to be erected the present year. An excellent quality can be made and sacked—ready for market for $4.50 per ton.

Half-Way House,—25 miles from Salt Lake City, is the next station, and present terminus of the road. Stages leave here for the mining camps on the western slope of the mountains, and a large amount of freighting is done with teams, to and from the mines. The station will lose its importance as soon as the road passes beyond it. There are large springs of fresh water near the station, which supply a flouring mill and woolen factory with power. Twelve miles from Half-Way House is Grantville, one of the richest agricultural towns in Utah. On the left side of the track, before you reach the station, is "E. T. City"—the initials being those of E. T. Benson, who was interested in the town. It is simply a settlement of Mormon farmers, nestled under the mountains. The woolen factory alluded to is a long, low stone structure, with approved modern machinery, about one and three-fourths miles from the station, north of the track. This route must prove very attractive to travelers, and one which will amply reward them in the pleasures it will afford. The rich mining districts of Rush Valley, Ophir and others, are reached by this line of road. The Hidden Treasure and other mines in these districts have already acquired a reputation and standing among the first mines in the country.

Social Life Among the Mormons.—Beyond the limits of Salt Lake City the uniform character of Mormon families is of exceeding plain ways of living, almost all being of very modest means, and even poor. What the better families have gained has been by the hardest and most persistent labor. It is said that when the city was first settled, there was not found over $1,000 in cash for the whole community, and for a long series of years thereafter money was little used, and the people lived and paid for their wants by barter, and a writer facetiously says: "A farmer wishes to purchase a pair of shoes for his wife. He consults the shoemaker, who avers his willingness to furnish the same for one load of wood. He has no wood, but sells a calf for a quantity of *adobes*, the *adobes* for an order on the merchant, payable in goods, and the goods and the order for a load of wood, and straightway the matron is shod.

"Seven water-melons purchased the price of a ticket of admission to the theater. He paid for the tuition of his children, seventy-five cabbages per quarter. The dressmaker received for her services, four squashes per day. He settled his church dues in sorghum molasses. Two loads of pumpkins paid his annual subscription to the newspaper. He bought a '*Treatise on Celestial Marriage*' for a load of gravel, and a bottle of soothing syrup for the baby, with a bushel of string beans."

In this way, before the advent of the railroad, fully nine-tenths of the business of the Mormon people was conducted. Now barter has given place to actual circulation of money.

While there is not what may be called distress or abject poverty in any part of the Mormon settlements, yet with many, especially the new emigrants, their means are so limited, and the labor so hard, it would be exceedingly discouraging to exist, but for the *grand confidence* all have in the joys to come promised by their religion and their leader.

Except in the cities there is little or no form of amusement, and the Sabbath is mainly the great day of reunion, when the population turn out *en masse* to the Tabernacle or other places of worship.

In the church services no one knows, until the speaker arises, who is to preach from the pulpit, or what may be the subject.

The subjects of sermons, addresses and exhortations are as wide as there are books. A writer has laughingly said: "In the Great Tabernacle, one will hear sermons, or advice on the culture of sorghum, upon infant baptism, upon the best manure for cabbages, upon the perseverance of the Saints, upon the wickedness of skimming milk before its sale, upon the best method of cleaning water ditches, upon bed-bug poison, upon the price of real estate, upon teething in children, upon the martyrs and persecutions of the Church, terrible denunciations of Gentiles and the enemies of the Mormons, upon olive oil as a cure for measles, upon the ordination of the priesthood, upon the character of Melchisedec, upon worms in dried peaches, upon abstinence from plug tobacco, upon the crime of fœticide, upon chignons, twenty-five-yard dresses, upon plural marriages, etc."

Portions of this are doubtless the extravagance of humor, yet it is true every possible thing, secular or spiritual, is discussed from the pulpit which the president thinks necessary for the instruction of the flock. We attended personally one Sunday a Sunday-school celebration in the Tabernacle, where the exercises were enlivened with a spirited delivery of "*Marco Bozarris*," "*Gay Young Lochinvar*," the singing of "Home, Sweet Home," and the gallery fronts were decorated with gay mottoes, of which there shone in great prominence, "*Utah's best crop, children.*"

REPRESENTATIVE MORMONS.

1.—W. Woodruff. 2.—John Taylor. 3.—Mayor Daniel H. Wells. 4.—W. H. Hooper. 5.—President Brigham Young. 6.—Orson Pratt. 7.—John Sharp. 8.—George Q. Cannon. 9.—Orson Hyde.

The city Mormons are fond of the theater and dancing, and as their president is both the owner of the theater and its largest patron, the Saints consider his example highly judicious and exemplary, so the theater is crowded on all occasions. We were present, on one occasion, in 1869, when we witnessed over thirty of the children of one of the Mormons sitting in a row in the dress circle, and the private boxes filled with his wives. The most striking event of the evening was when one of the theatrical performers sung this ditty:

"If Jim Fisk's rat-and-tan, should have a bull-dog pup,
Do you think Louis Napoleon would try to bring him up?"

This elicited tremendous applause, and the performers, much to their own laughter and astonishment, had to repeat it.

A few years afterward, in witnessing a large body of Mormon children singing their school songs—we noticed the end of one of their little verses:

"Oh, how happy I ought to be,
For, daddy, I'm a Mormon."

As justifying their amusements, the Saints thus say, through one of their authorities:

"Dancing is a diversion for which all men and women have a natural fondness."

Dancing parties in the city are, therefore, quite frequent, and the most religious man is best entitled to the biggest amount of fun. Hence their religion should never be dull.

"As all people have a fondness for dramatic representations, it is well to so regulate and govern such exhibitions, that they may be instructive and purifying in their tendencies. If the best people absent themselves, the worst will dictate the character of the exercises."

Therefore every good Mormon, who can get a little money, indulges in the theater.

The Religion of the Mormons.—It is not the purpose of this *Guide* to express opinions of the religious aspect of Mormonism; but, as all visitors who come from the East, seeking either from curiosity to gain reliable information, or, having prejudices, expect to gratify them with outbursts of indignation, we can only stand aloof, and explain, calmly and candidly, a few facts as we have found them by actual contact and experience with both Mormons and Gentiles, and leave each reader to judge for himself the merits of this vexed question.

So thoroughly and implicitly have the masses of the Mormon people been led by their leader, that no one must be surprised to find that they are firm believers and obedient servants to all the doctrines and orders of the Church. *They believe just as they are told.*

Whatever, therefore, there is in their life, character and business, industry and enterprise, that is good and praiseworthy, to Brigham Young, their leader, belongs the credit. But for whatever there is wicked in their religion, life, faith, deeds and church work—and for whatever is lacking in good, to the same powerful mind and willful hand, belongs the fearful responsibility.

Whether Mormonism be a religion or not—yet candor must confess, that if it fails to give and preserve peace, contentment, purity; if it makes its followers ignorant, brutal, superstitious, jealous, abusive, defiant; if it lack gentleness, meekness, kindness, courtesy; if it brings to its homes, sadness and discontent, it cannot be that *true religion*, which exists alone by sincere *trust in Christ* and *love for heaven*. If in all its doctrines, services, sermons, prayers, praise and church work, it fails to give the soul that seeks after rest, the refreshing, comforting peace it needs, it cannot be everlasting.

Mormonism has accomplished much in industry, and perseverance, in reclaiming Utah's waste lands and barren plains. It has opened a country, which now is teeming with riches inexhaustible and untold wealth is coming to a scene, once the very type of desolation. We give to the Mormons every worthy praise for their frugality, temperance and hard labor. No other class of people would have settled here. By patience they have reclaimed a desert,—peopled a waste, developed hidden treasures, have grown in thrift, and their lives bear witness to their forbearance, and complete trust and faith.

How The Mormon Church Influences Visitors.—The system of polygamy is not the only great question which affects the future of Utah. More than all things else, it is the *Power of the Rulers of the Mormon Church.* It is natural that they should make efforts to maintain it by every use of power; gentleness if that will do the work, *coercion* if not.

It is unfortunate that in the spiritual services of the Church, they fail to impress visitors with proper respect. Their sermons, all eastern travelers have uniformly admitted, were remarkable in the absence of spiritual power. The simple truths of the Gospel rarely ever are discussed, the life of Christ, the Gospel of the New Testament, the "Sermon on the Mount"—the Cross are all ignored,—the Psalms of David, the life of Daniel, Solomon, and the work of the twelve Apostles are rarely referred to; instead, visitors are compelled to listen to long arguments justifying Mormonism and plural marriage, and expressions of detestation for their enemies.

We heard three of the elders talk at one of their Sabbath meetings, during which the name of Jesus Christ as the Saviour of the world, was scarcely mentioned. One talked of the wonderful conversion as he claimed, and baptism of some Lamanites (Indians), not one of whom today, can give a single intelligent reason for the course he has adopted. Another told of the time he was a local preacher in the East, of the Methodist Church, and of the trials and persecution they had endured there. The third was quite belligerent in tone, and gave utterance to what might possibly be interpreted as treasonable sentiments against the government of the United States. In the meantime the audience accepted all that was said with apparent relish. We thought of the saying of one of the popular humorists of the day, to the effect that "*if that kind of preaching suits that kind of people, it is just the kind of preaching that kind of people likes.*" Their preachers will often take a text from the sayings of the prophets, and give it a literal interpretation that would grate harshly upon orthodox ears, while the listener would be amused at the ingenuity displayed in twisting the word of God—making it mean anything desired.

It is exceedingly unfortunate for the cause of the Mormons, that such exhibitions of nature are made, the only result of which is to increase the prejudice of all visitors, and tend to gradually change the minds of those who would gladly be cordial, but feel they can not. We speak in candor; the efficacy of a religion is judged by its purity of life and speech. A true religion wins admiration from even its enemies. But Mormonism seems never to have made a friend of an enemy, and only returns even deeper resentment.

A religion which does not do as Christ commanded, "*Pray for them which persecute you, bless and curse not,*"—but treasures its resentments and fulminates its curses continually—can it be any religion at all?

Inconsistencies. — Another circumstance, one very unfortunate for the Mormons, and always noticed by strangers, is the inconsistency of their history.

In the original revelation to Joseph Smith, there was not only no mention of polygamy, but in the Book of Mormon, such a practice was fiercely denounced. In the second chapter of the Book of Mormon, there originally appeared this warning to the Nephites:

"*Wherefore, hearken unto the word of the Lord, for there shall not any man among you have save it be one wife; and concubines he shall have none; for I the Lord God, delighteth in the chastity of woman.*"

The following comments and arguments based on the above, seem absolutely necessary, and impossible for any one to controvert:

1. *If Joseph Smith wrote this under the inspiration of the Holy Spirit, then present Mormon practices and doctrines, being wholly different, are not true nor worthy of confidence.*

2. *If Joseph Smith did* **not** *write this under the inspiration of the Almighty, then Joseph Smith did* **not** *receive a true revelation, was* **not** *a true Prophet, and what he has written has been entirely unworthy the confidence of his people.*

3. *If Mormonism since then has found a new revelation totally opposed to the first, then the first must have been false.*

4. *If the first revelation was false, then the Book of Mormon is wholly false and unreliable, and Joseph Smith was an impostor.*

5. *If the first revelation was true, then (as the decrees of the Almighty once given, never change), the second revelation is not true, nor ever was inspired by God.*

6. *As History proves that Joseph Smith received and promulgated both the first and second revelations—as one of these must be false—as no Prophet could ever be falsely led, if instructed by the Almighty—it follows that Joseph Smith never received a true inspiration, was not a true Prophet—that Mormonism is not a revealed religion.*

Another inconsistency, fatal to the claims of the Mormon religion, is the curious act of Joseph Smith at Nauvoo. On the 12th of July, 1843, Smith received the new revelation. When it was first mentioned, it caused great commotion, and many rebelled against it. A few elders attempted to promulgate it, but so fierce was the opposition that at last, for peace, Smith officially made public proclamation *against it* in the Church paper as follows:

NOTICE.—As we have lately been credibly informed that an elder of the Church of Jesus Christ of Latter Day Saints, by the name of Hiram Brown has been preaching polygamy and other false and corrupt doctrines in the County of Lapeer and State of Michigan,

This is to notify him, and the Church in general, that he has been cut off from the Church for his iniquity, and he is further notified to appear at the special conference on the 6th of April next, to make answer to these charges.

JOSEPH SMITH,
HYRUM SMITH, } *Presidents of the Church.*

QUERY.—*What is the world to think of a religion, or a people, when their Prophet falsifies his own record, and denies his own revelation?*

Subsequent history shows that in less than three years from the publication of the above notice, the Mormon leaders were living in open and undisguised polygamy.

Would a Prophet who ever received a true revelation deny it, punish his followers for observing it, and then practice it for himself?

How appropriately the answer is given to this question when one takes up the Mormon Hymn Book, and finds among its verses, used in their church services, the following leading lines:

1. "The God that others worship is not the God for me."
2. "A church without a Prophet is not the church for me."
3. "A church without Apostles is not the church for me."
4. "The hope that Gentiles cherish is not the hope for me."
   "It has no faith nor knowledge; far from it I would be."
5. "The heaven of sectarians is not the heaven for me."

Mormon Courtesies.—The leading members of the Mormon Church we met during our stay, were gentlemen, treated us very courteously, and apparently offered us every facility for obtaining information, and they will treat all strangers in the same way. We feel under

VIEW OF GREAT SALT LAKE, FROM THE WAHSATCH MOUNTAINS.

BY THOMAS MORAN.

especial obligation to many of them for their kindness and courtesy. And we are greatly mistaken if they do not respect any one for a free, manly and frank expression of opinion concerning them and their institutions, more than they would a fawning sycophant, or gushing twaddler in reference to the course they have chosen to follow, or the work they have done. Neither their institutions nor their practices are thrust into the faces of travelers. If knowledge concerning them or their customs is desired, it must be sought after. They have a special hostility for those whom they call apostates, and though a man may be moral and upright in his life before he leaves their church, he is nothing but concentrated meanness afterwards. His course of life may not be changed in the least, and the fact that he is just as honorable and upright as before is of no consequence. Godbe, Lawrence, Harrison and others, all pure men in private life, become, according to Mormon account, the princes of liars and scoundrels as soon as they leave the church. In fact, to attack and destroy an apostate's character is their favorite, and hitherto most successful mode of destroying his influence. In this respect the Mormons can not tolerate freedom of opinion. They would much prefer open attacks by Gentiles than the more vital thrusts of apostates.

The Great Salt Lake.

In many respects this is the most wonderful body of water on the American Continent. It is the chief object of interest in the physical geography of the great basin in which it is located. Its waters are saline and brackish, unfit for use, and uninhabited by representatives of the finny tribes.

Its Discovery.—In his report on this lake, Captain Stansbury speaks of a French explorer, with an unpronounceable name, who left the western shores of the great lakes sometime in the seventeenth century, and proceeded westward for an undefined period, and made extensive discoveries on the Mississippi, Missouri, and other western rivers, and either saw, or heard from the Indians, of the Great Salt Lake. His accounts, however, are somewhat mixed, and not at all satisfactory. It is reported that John Jacob Astor fitted out an expedition, in 1820, to cross the Continent, meet a vessel he had sent round Cape Horn, and at some point on the Pacific Coast, form a town which should be to it what New York was to the Atlantic Coast, the greatest commercial emporium of that part of the country. This expedition, it is said, crossed the Rocky Mountains, near Fremont's Peak in the Wind River Range, and after reaching the Tetons separated into small parties, each one exploring on its own account. One of these, consisting of four men and commanded by a Mr. Miller, hunted around the vicinity of Snake River and the Soda Springs, finally crossing into Cache Valley, a little north-west of Corinne. It is further reported that Miller, in one of his rambles, ascended the mountains south of this valley, and here, for the first time, beheld the waters of the great inland sea spread out before him. He returned to his party, and with them proceeded to the lake, and on further inspection concluded it was an arm of the ocean. This was its first discovery by white men. The next recorded visitation is that of John Bedyer, in 1825, and the next was by Captain Bonneville, in 1831, who saw it from the Red Buttes in the Wahsatch Range, and whose account was written up by Washington Irving. In 1832, Captain Walker first attempted to explore it with a party of forty men. He traveled around the northern and western boundaries, but was compelled to abandon the undertaking for want of water for his animals and men. Captain Stansbury afterwards explored it, and his report contains the only reliable information concerning this remarkable lake that has been published from official sources, though subsequent observation has revealed many facts and phenomenon concerning it which would be highly interesting if they could be collected and given to the world in tangible form. General Fremont also visited this lake, and has given some information about it.

Analysis.—The only analysis of its waters that we have been able to obtain is that given by Dr. Gale and recorded in Captain Stansbury's report. We quote: "It gives the specific gravity, 1.170; solid contents, 22.422 out of 100 parts. The solid contents when analyzed gave the following components:

Chloride of sodium,	20.196
Sulphate of soda,	1.834
Chloride of magnesium,	0.252
Chloride of Calcium, a trace.	
	22.282
Loss,	0.140
	22.422

A remarkable thing about this analysis is that the specific gravity, as here given, corresponds exactly with the mean of eight different analyses of the waters of the Dead Sea of Palestine, which is largely above that of the water of the ocean. This analysis reveals what is now generally known, that here is a source from which salt enough can be obtained to supply the Continent. When it is considered, however, that all the streams flowing into this lake are fresh water, draining the water-shed of a large area of country, and discharging from the springs, melting snows and rains of the great basin, an immense volume of water, the puzzling question very naturally arises as to the source of this abundant supply of saline matter. The various saline incrustations, however, at various points on the surrounding shores, indicate clearly that some portion of the earth is saturated with this ingredient. Still this lake is without any visible outlet, and with all the great influx of fresh water, annually, why does it remain so salty? The inference naturally follows that it washes some vast bed of rock salt or saline deposit in the bottom of the lake, hitherto undiscovered. Without facts, however, even this is a supposition which may or may not be true. The shores of this lake, especially toward the city bearing the same name, have now been settled nearly thirty years, and it would be strange indeed if the changes which have been gradually going on in this lake should not have been noticed. The elevation of the lake is given at 4,200 feet above the level of the sea. The elevation of Salt Lake City is given at 4,351 feet above the sea—difference of 151 feet. The figures here given as the elevation of the lake, we think, are based upon observations and calculations made several years ago, perhaps by Captain Stansbury. The observation of the old settlers is, that it is not correct—that the lake is from ten to fifteen feet higher now than it was in 1850, and that in proportion as the water rises it becomes less salty. Reliable citizens have informed us that in 1850, three barrels of water evaporated would make one of salt; now, four barrels of water are required for the same result. This fact leads to the opinion that the humidity of the atmosphere in this region of the Continent is increasing—in consequence of which there is less evaporation—evaporation being greater and more rapid in a dry than in a moist atmosphere—and the failure of evaporation to take up the surplus waters discharged into this lake has not only increased its volume and extent, but lessened its saline character. Since the settlement of this Territory, there has been a great increase of rain-fall, so much so that it is noticed and remarked upon by very many of the inhabitants, and the belief is very generally entertained that the Territory is gradually undergoing a great climatic change.

Speculations as to the Result.—The evaporation of the water in the lake growing gradually less, it will, of course, continue to rise and overflow its banks in the lowest places, but no fears need be entertained for the safety of any considerable portion of the country, or the inhabitants thereof. Notice the elevation of Salt Lake City, as herein given, being about 151 feet greater than the lake itself. If the rise continues it will be slower as the covered surface of the adjoining land becomes greater, on the principle that the larger end of a vessel fills more slowly with the same stream, than the smaller end. If it reaches a height of 15 or 20 feet above its present surface, it will first overflow a low, sandy and alkali desert on its western shore, nearly as large as the lake itself. In this case, its evaporating capacity will be nearly doubled in extent—a fact which will operate to retard its rise. But if it continues to rise in the years to come until it must have an outlet to the ocean, that outlet will be the Humboldt River, and a cut of 100 feet or less in the low hills of the divide, will give it. When, however, this event transpires, it will be—unless some convulsion of nature intervenes to hasten it—after the last reader of this book shall have finished his earthly labors and been quietly laid away to rest.

Boundaries and Extent.—Looking from Observation Point at the south end of the lake, to the north, it seems to be pretty well divided. Promontory Mountains on Antelope Island, those on Stansbury Island and Oquirrh Mountains are evidently parts of the same range—running from north to south, parallel with the Wahsatch Range. Their continuity is only broken by the waters in the lake or sink of the great basin. Promontory Mountains divide the northern end of the lake into two parts, or arms, the eastern being called Bear River Bay, and the western, Spring Bay—the latter being considerably the largest. The lake has numerous islands, both large and small. Fremont Island lies due west of the mouth of Weber River, and is plainly visible from the cars of the Utah Central Railroad. South of it and nearest to Salt Lake City, is Antelope Island. West of Antelope, and north-west from Lake Point, is Stansbury Island. A little north-west of this, is Carrington Island. North of these still, and in the western part of the lake are Hat, Gunnison and Dolphin Islands. Nearly south of Gunnison Island is a high promontory jutting out into the lake called Strong's Knob; it is a prominent landmark on the western shore of the lake. Travelers on the Central Pacific Road can obtain a fine view of this great inland sea, near Monument Station. The extreme length of the lake is about 80 miles, and its extreme width, a little south of the 41st parallel of latitude, is about 50 miles. Promontory Mountains project into the lake from the north about 30 miles. Nearly all the islands we have named are rich in minerals, such as copper, silver, gold and iron. Excellent quarries of slate have also been opened, but neither it nor the mines have been developed to any great extent, because of the want of capital.

Incidents and Curiosities.—When Colonel Fremont first explored the lake in 1843, it is related by Jessie, his wife, that when his boat first touched the shore of Fremont Island, an oarsman in the bow of the boat was about to jump ashore, when Kit Carson, the guide, insisted that Colonel Fremont should first land and name the island,—"Fremont Island."

Tonic Properties.—A bath in the water of the Great Salt Lake, is one of the greatest delights a tourist can seek. We have personally indulged in its pleasure, and it is beyond question a splendid recreation. Upon the wharf near Lake Point, is a cozy bathing-house, wherein are bathing-suits, and large tubs filled with fresh water; donning the suits, you descend the steps and jump into the water. You are surprised at the buoyancy of it. The most vigorous effort and plunge will not keep your body under the surface. Clasping your hands and feet in the water, you can sit on its bosom with head and shoulders projecting above the surface,—and even then for but a short period, as the buoyancy of the water soon has a tendency to tip you over on your side. It is impossible to stand erect in the water, no matter how straight or rigid you place your limbs,—in a moment over goes your head, and up come your feet. Lying on your back, or side, or face, in any position —still you will always keep at the surface. But beyond this curious feature of impossibility of sinking, there is the better quality of the *toning and invigorating properties of the bath.* These are beyond all question, the finest of any spring along the Overland Route. In some warm summer day, take your bath in the lake,—spend, say half an hour in its water, and then returning to your bath-house, cleanse your skin from all saline material, which may adhere, by plentiful ablutions of pure water from the tubs, wash the hair and face thoroughly, then dress and walk up and down the wharf, or the cool piazza of the hotel,—and you are astonished at the wonderful amount of strength and invigoration given to your system, and with greater elasticity than ever you have possessed before, it seems like the commencement of a new life. Invalids should never fail to visit this lake, and enjoy its bath. Tourists who omit it,—will leave behind them the greatest curiosity of the Overland Tour, and it is no great effort of the imagination to conceive this fully the rival of the great ocean in all that can contribute to the attractions of sea-shore life. The cool breeze and delicious bath are all here.

In the summer time the excursion rates from Salt Lake City, are $1.50 per ticket, which includes passage both ways over the Utah Western Railroad, a ride on the steamer on the lake, and the privilege of a bath,—the cheapest and most useful enjoyment in the entire Territory.

The only life in or near the lake, is seen in the summer time by immense masses of little insects (*astemia fertiliso,*) which live on the surface of the lake, and thrive on its brine. These masses stretch out in curious forms over the surface. Sometimes, when small, they appear like a serpent, at other times like rings, globes, and other irregular figures. A gentle breeze will never disturb them, for their presence keeps the water a dead calm as if oil had been poured upon it. If disturbed by a boat passing through the mass, millions of little gnats or flies arise and swarm all over the vessel—anything but agreeable. Professor Spencer M. Baird, of the Smithsonian Institute, Washington, believes the lake may yet sustain fish and other animal life. There seems to be plenty of insect food always on the surface,—occasionally with high winds, the surface of the lake is driven into waves, which dashing against the shore, shower the sage brushes near with salty incrustations, which, when dried in the sunlight, give a bright, glittering and pearly appearance, often furnishing splendid specimens for mineral cabinets.

Atmosphere.—The atmosphere which surrounds the lake, is a curiosity, always bluish and hazy—from the effects of the active evaporation, —in decided contrast to the purity and transparency of the air elsewhere. Surveyors say that it is difficult to use telescopes, and astronomical observations are imperfect.

The solid ingredients of the water have six and one-half times the density of those of the ocean, and wherever washed upon the shore, the salt dried, after evaporation, can be easily shoveled up into buckets and bags.

Burton describes a beautiful sunset scene upon the lake. "We turned our faces eastward as the sun was declining. The view had memorable beauties. From the blue and purple clouds, gorgeously edged with celestial fire, shot up a fan of penciled and colored light, extending halfway to the zenith, while in the south and southeast lightnings played among the darker mist masses, which backed the golden and emerald bench-lands of the farther valley. The splendid sunset gave a reflex of its loveliness upon the alkaline barrens around us. Opposite rose the Wahsatch Mountains, vast and voluminous, in stern and gloomy grandeur, northward the thin white vapors rising from the hot springs, and the dark swells of the lake."

The Great Desert West of Salt Lake City.—The overland stage, which traversed westward, followed a route immediately south of Salt Lake, and passed for several hundred miles through a desert, beside which the Humboldt Valley had no comparison in tediousness and discomfort. Captain Stansbury, an early explorer, in describing this section, describes large tracts of land covered with an incrustation of salt:

"The first part of the plains consisted simply of dried mud, with small crystals of salt scattered thickly over the surface; crossing this, we came upon another portion of it, three miles in width, where the ground was entirely covered with a thin layer of salt in a state of deliquescence, and of so soft consistence, that the feet of our mules sank at every step into the mud beneath. But we soon came upon a portion of the plains where the salt lay in a solid state, in one unbroken sheet, extending apparently to its western border. So firm and strong was this unique and snowy floor, that it sustained the weight of our entire train without in the least giving way, or cracking beneath the pressure.

REPRESENTATIVE MEN OF THE CENTRAL PACIFIC RAILROAD.

1.—E. B. Crocker. 2.—C. P. Huntington. 3.—Leland Stanford. 4.—Charles Crocker. 5.—Mark Hopkins.

Our mules walked upon it as upon a sheet of solid ice. The whole field was crossed by a net-work of little ridges, projecting about half an inch, as if the salt had expanded in the process of crystallization. I estimated this field to be, at least, seven miles wide and ten miles in length. The salt which was very pure and white, averaged from one-half to three-quarters of an inch in thickness, and was equal in all repects to our finest specimen for table use. Assuming these data, the quantity that here lay upon the ground in one body, exclusive of that already dissolved,—amounted to over 4,500,000 cubic yards, or about 100,000,000 bushels." And even this small area, is but a very little portion of the whole region, farther northward and westward.

The Central Pacific Railroad.

The record of the building of the Central Pacific Railroad is a description of one of the greatest trials of courage and faith the world has ever seen, and the actual results are, beyond doubt, the greatest marvel in engineering science, ever known in the United States. The heroic strength of character, the magnificent power and endurance, the financial intrepidity and the bold daring which defied all obstacles, overcame all difficulties, and literally shoved the mountains aside to make room for their pathway, are not equaled by any other achievement of the century. If ever an American can feel and express just admiration, it is to those *Samsons of the Pacific Coast*, who have hewn their way with the ponderous strength of their arms, and with invincible fortitude opened to the world the treasures of industry in the mountains and valleys of the Far West and the Pacific Coast. To one man, more than all others, is due the credit for the conception, survey and actual beginning of the great Trans-Continental Line. Theodore D. Judah—yet he did not live to see the completion of the railroad up the Sierras—and his successor Mr. S. S. Montague carried it through with great energy and success, and to them the nation and all California owe a debt of gratitude.

For years this brave and accomplished engineer had the subject of the road in his mind. It occupied his thoughts by day and was the subject of his dreams by night. The idea took a firm hold upon him, and he became completely absorbed in it. It energized his whole being and he was persistent and hopeful to the end. Sacramento, then a much smaller place than now, was the home of C. P. Huntington and Mark Hopkins, the former now Vice-President and the latter now Treasurer of the company, then hardware merchants under the firm name of Huntington & Hopkins. Their store became the headquarters of the little company that used to meet Judah there and talk over the enterprise. Judah's ideas were clear, his plans seemed practicable and his enthusiasm was contagious. The men who associated with him were led to make contributions for the purpose of partial payment toward a preliminary survey, and, in 1860, Judah and his assistants wandered over the gorges and canons of the Sierra Nevadas in search of a line for a railroad. The results of his summer's work were in every way encouraging—so much so that other contributions and subscriptions were obtained for work the following year. The summer of 1861 again found Judah and his party in the mountains. The work of the previous year was extended and further examination renewed the hope of the engineer and quickened the zeal of his followers. Success was certain if they could only enlist capital in the enterprise.

But right here was the difficulty. While the great majority of the people of California believed that the road would be built some day—it would not be done in their time. Some generation in the future might accomplish it, but it would be after they were all dead. The subject was broached in Congress, and finally, in 1862, the bill was passed. Huntington and Judah went to Washington with maps and charts, and rendered invaluable assistance to the friends of the measure in both houses of Congress, and the day of its passage was the day of their triumph. The news was sent to California with lightning speed, and caused great rejoicing among the people. The beginning of the end could now distinctly be seen. Though great difficulties had been surmounted, a comparatively greater one lay in the way. Capital which is proverbially timid, must now be enlisted in the enterprise. Forty miles of road must be built and accepted by the government, before the aid could be secured. Finally, with what local help they could get, and the assistance of New York capitalists and bankers, the work was begun at Sacramento, and the first section carried the line high up toward the summit of the Sierras. Their financial agents in New York, put their bonds on the market, and the funds for the further extension of the road were rapidly forthcoming. Leland Stanford, then as now President of the company, inaugurated the work at Sacramento, and also drove the silver spike, which completed the union of the two roads at Promontory on the 10th day of May, 1869. The progress of the road during each year, from the time of its commencement until its completion, is given as follows: In the years 1863–4–5, the company completed 20 miles each year. This might be called preliminary work. They were learning how, and their severest difficulties were to be overcome. In 1866 they built 30 miles, and the next year 46 miles. Now the rivalry between the two great corporations may be said to have commenced in earnest. In 1868, they built 364, and in 1869, up to May 10th, they closed the gap with 191 miles.

Difficulties, Discouragements and Labor.—Few travelers realize, as they pass so easily and pleasantly over this railroad,—what is represented by these long, smoothly-laid rails, nor do they know of the early days of labor, and intense energy.

Everything of every description of supplies had to be shipped by water from New York, *via* Cape Horn—to San Francisco, and then inland to Sacramento. Thus months of delay occurred in obtaining all needful material.

Even when the project was under full discussion at the little office in Sacramento, where gathered the six great brains which controlled the destiny of the enterprise, (these were Governor Leland Stanford, C. P. Huntington, Mark Hopkins, Charles Crocker, E. B. Crocker, and T. D. Judah), everybody predicted its failure, and few or none looked for its success. Very little was known of the country it was to traverse,—and that not satisfactory, and one prophesied that this, the western end of the Great Trans-Continental Railroad, would be run up into the clouds, and left in eternal snows.

Scores of friends approached Huntington in those days and said, "*Huntington, don't go into it; you will bury your whole fortune in the Sierra Nevadas.*"

Outsiders called it, after the first 40 miles were built, "*The Dutch Flat Swindle*;" and the project was caricatured, abused by the newspapers, derided by politicians, discountenanced by capitalists, and the credit of every one was impaired who was connected with it.

Thus nobly did the Californians help this the greatest enterprise of the State, and how much more noble have they since been!

In a speech before the Senate Committee of Congress by C. P. Huntington, he says:

"I suppose that it is a fact, the mercantile credit of my partners in business and myself, was positively injured by our connection with this enterprise.

"The difficulties which confronted us then, are now nearly forgotten, but they were intensely vivid and real then. There were difficulties from end to end; difficulties from high and steep mountains; from snows; from deserts where there was scarcity of water, and from gorges and flats where there was an excess; difficulties from cold and from heat, from a scarcity of timber and from obstructions of rock; difficulties in supplying a large force on a long line; from Indians and want of laborers."

Of the princely subsidies voted by the United States in its government bonds to aid the road—what was the real case? From the individual and private means of the five capitalists, they were compelled to support a force of 800 men one year—at their own risks—build 40 miles before they were entitled to the government bonds, and then were eleven months delayed in receiving what was their due. To build the first section of the road to the mountains, they were obliged to call in private means, which out on loan was yielding them two per cent. interest in gold, per month—invest in the road and wait for reimbursement. When the government bonds were at last received, they vested into gold at the high rate of premium then prevailing, (often taking $2 in bonds to buy $1.00 in gold) to pay for labor and expense of construction, which, too, were excessively high for gold prices.

The personal dangers of the builders were great. The very surveyors ran the risk of being killed by Indians, and some of them were; the grading parties, at times, could only work under military guard; at all times all the track-layers and the train hands had to be armed, and even after construction the trains were often attacked.

The first 100 miles was up a total ascent of 7,000 feet, requiring the most skillful engineering and expenditures of vast sums of money in excavation. At the height of 5,000 feet, the snow line was reached, and 40 miles of snow galleries had to be erected, at an additional expense of $20,000 to $30,000 per mile, and for a mile or more, in many places, these must be made so strong that avalanches might pass over them and yet preserve the safety of the track. Even after passing the Sierras, the railroad descended into a vast plain, dry, sere and deserted, where there was not a sign of civilized life, nor any fuel. For over 600 miles of the route, there was not a single white inhabitant. For over 100 miles at a stretch, no water could be found for either man or machinery; and, even at the present day, in many places the railroad company is obliged to bring its water in artificial pipes for distances of one to fifteen miles for the use of the engines.

Labor was almost impossible to get, and when attained was almost impossible to control, until the Chinese arrived, and to them is due the real credit of the greatest help the road possessed. Powder was one of the heaviest items of expense, which before the rise in prices of the war, could have been had for $2.25 per keg—but then was obtained with difficulty at $5.00. Locomotives, cars, tools, all were bought at double prices. Rails, now worth but $40.00 to $50.00 per ton, then cost $80.00 to $150.00.

Every bar of iron and every tool had first to be bought and started on a sea voyage round Cape Horn, some four or six months before it was needed.

Insurance on the sea voyages rose from 2 1-2 to 10 per cent.—freights increased from $18.00 to $45.00 per ton.

Of the engineering difficulties of the construction on the Sierras, none can form a possible idea. A culvert would be built, the beginning of which was on the grade, while the other end would be 50 feet or more below. At another place is a bank 80 to 100 feet in height, covering a culvert 250 feet in length, then comes a bridge leaping a chasm of 150 feet in depth.

Next a cut of hardest granite, where, in the short space of 250 feet, would be working 30 carts and 250 workmen, thick as bees—while a little beyond is an embankment built up 80 feet, from whose top you can look down 1,000 feet.

The famous Summit Tunnel is 1,659 feet in length, cut through solid granite, and for a mile on either side there are rock cuttings of the most stupendous character, and the railroad is cut directly in the face of a precipice. The powder bill alone for one month was $54,000. Blasting was done three times per day, and sometimes of extraordinary execution. A hole of eight feet was once drilled and fired, and 1,440 yards of granite were thrown clear from the road-bed. Several more holes of same depth were drilled into a seam in the rock, which were lightly loaded and exploded until a large fissure was opened, when an immense charge was put in, set off, and 3,000 tons of granite went whirling down the mountain, tearing up trees, rocks, etc., with fearful havoc. One rock, weighing 70 pounds, was blown one-third of a mile away from its bed, while another of 240 pounds was blown entirely across Donner Lake, a distance of two-thirds of a mile. At one place, near Donner's Backbone, the railroad track is so constructed that it describes a curve of 180°, and runs back on the opposite side of the ridge only a few feet parallel to the course it has followed to the point, all at a grade of 90 feet to the mile.

But it is impossible to tell all the wonders of engineering, or the feats of skill; let active eyes watch the scene as the traveler passes over the railroad, and then give due credit and admiration to the pluck, skill, persistence and faith which has accomplished so much, and been productive of so much good.

The little beginning, in 1860, has now given place to the most astonishing enterprise of modern times. The pay-roll of the Central Pacific Railroad Company now exceeds 7,000 names of employes. The Southern Pacific Railroad, another grand enterprise, controlled in part by some of the same company, is building its road rapidly, with a force of 5,000 men, toward the fields of Arizona and New Mexico. All the important railroads and steamboats of California are now controlled by these gigantic corporations, and from the latest reports we quote figures of this financial capital of the greatest corporations in the United States:

CENTRAL PACIFIC RAILROAD COMPANY.

Capital stock actually paid in,	$54,275,500
Funded debt,	53,069,095
United States subsidy bonds,	27,855,680
Land grants of 11,722,400 acres at $2.50,	29,306,000
Value of lands in San Francisco, Oakland, and Sacramento,	7,750,000
Total value,	$172,256,275

SOUTHERN PACIFIC RAILROAD COMPANY.

Authorized capital stock,	$90,000,000
First mortgage bonds, authorized,	46,000,000
12,000,000 acres land grants, at $2.50,	30,000,000
Total value Southern Pacific Railroad Company,	$166,000,000
Total capital of Central Pacific and Southern Pacific Railroads,	$338,256,275
Number miles constructed and in operation by Central Pacific Railroad,	1,213
Number miles built and being built by Southern Pacific Railroad,	1,160

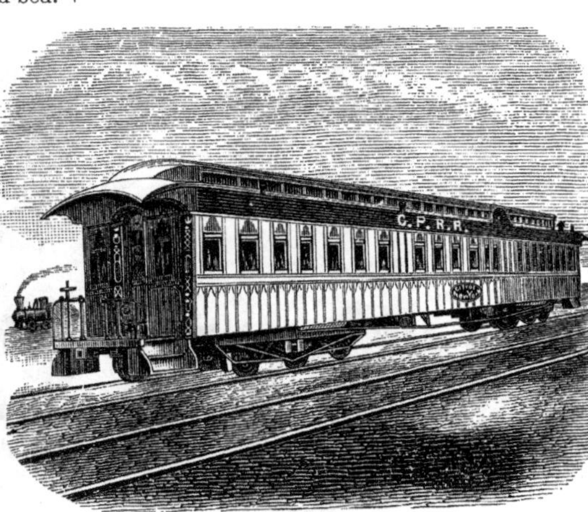

SILVER PALACE CAR, C. P. R. R.

Westward to San Francisco.

Travelers from the East, after dining at Ogden and having an hour in which to re-check their baggage, will board a train of silver palace cars belonging to the Central Pacific, in the evening, as the trains now run, and will soon be whirling away across the Great American Desert. As we pass out of the suburbs of Ogden, we cross Ogden River on a pile bridge, and leave it to pursue its turbulent way to the lake. We soon arrive at the point of junction before alluded to, but find no magnificent hotel, or other buildings, or any evidence of any. "Union Junction" is therefore a myth, and exists only in the fertile imagination. The land, such as it is, however, is there, and we soon pass the steaming Hot Springs on the right of the road and close to the track. These springs are said to be both iron and sulphur, and from the red sediment which has been deposited over quite an area of surface near by, we judge that the iron springs predominate. Since leaving Weber Canon we have come nearly north and will continue in that direction until we approach Corinne. On our right are the towering peaks of the Wahsatch in close proximity. On our left are the irrigating ditches that supply the farms with water, an increasing growth of underbrush off toward the lake, and Fremont's Island in the distance with a towering rock, looking like a huge castle, upon one extremity of it. We soon pass a little town called North Ogden, at a canon through the mountains, which is sometimes called Ogden Hole, or North Ogden Canon. Before the road was built through Ogden Canon proper, this was the nearest source of communication with the valley the other side of the mountains. There are about nine miles of straight track here and we soon arrive at

Bonneville—871 miles from San Francisco, with an elevation of 4,310 feet. It is merely a side track. The Mormons have some fine farms in this vicinity, and between the railroad and base of the mountains there are many cultivated fields and fine orchards of apple and peach trees. There are frequent canons through the range, at the mouth of which are little settlements or villages; the creeks from the canons supplying the water which irrigates their fields, gardens and orchards. The largest of these settlements or villages are called Willard City and Brigham City, and their business is now done almost exclusively with the Utah Northern Railroad, which runs parallel with the Central Pacific between Ogden and Corinne and nearer the base of the mountains. The next station is

Brigham,—862 miles from San Francisco; elevation, 4,220 feet. A side track for the passing of trains. It is the station for Brigham City, which is some three miles away, though it does not look half that distance. Leaving this station we cross some alkali marshes near, and cross an arm of the lake or small bay, with the eastern part of the Great Salt Sea in full view, with Promontory Mountains beyond. Approaching Corinne we enter the celebrated Bear River Valley, crossing the river on a pile bridge and reach

SHOSHONE INDIAN VILLAGE.

Corinne,—857 miles from San Francisco, with an elevation of 4,294 feet. It is the largest Gentile town in the Territory, and if not hated is cordially and effectually let alone by most of the Mormons in the surrounding settlements. The natural location is excellent, and when the thousands of acres of fertile lands in the Bear River Valley are settled, as they surely will be in time, Corinne will be the center of trade and influence to which her location entitles her. On the completion of the railroad through here—before it came, even—the Gentiles had taken possession of the town and determined to maintain an ascendency. From that time it has been an object of defamation by the Saints; and the lands in the broad valley which surround it, as rich as any in the Territory, are left with scarcely a settler. To-day these lands are open and in the market, and if enterprising farmers in the East desire farms in a healthful climate, near a good market, with short winters and those seldom excessively cold, with the salt water breezes fresh from the lake, and in a country where the finest kind of fruit can be grown, we advise them to stop here, inform themselves as best they can, look the ground over thoroughly and decide for themselves, the question of choosing this place for a new home. This is one side of the picture. The other is want of water. All crops in this valley are raised by irrigation. A ditch has already been dug from Malad River, which supplies some farms on its line, and the town with water. A large flouring-mill is also supplied with water from this ditch.

Some of the finest wheat we ever saw was raised near Corinne, on irrigated land. It was

UTE SQUAW AND PAPPOOSE.

spring wheat and produced at the rate of nearly 50 bushels to the acre. The spring wheat of Utah far excels in quality, the best winter wheat produced in Eastern States. It has a large, plump, hard, white berry, and will rank as A No. 1 in any wheat market in the country.

Corinne in its early history, was "a rough town;" but the roughs have passed on, or sleep in unknown graves. The town now has three churches, a good school, a large flouring-mill, several commission and forwarding houses, stores of various kinds, etc. It is the natural freighting point to eastern Idaho and Montana, and before the Utah Northern, with which it is connected by a short branch, was completed to Franklin, its present terminus, nearly all the freighting business of the last named Territory was done from this point, and a large share of it still comes here.

Corinne is about seven miles from Great Salt Lake. A railroad company has been chartered to build a road direct to Montana, with favorable prospects of being put through at an early day. At some point on or near the Snake River, it will form a junction with the proposed Portland, Dalles and Salt Lake Road, the southern terminus of which will be at this city. The Central Pacific have also considered a railroad project around the Bear River Valley, by way of the Soda Springs, to the newly discovered coal fields north of Evanston.

There are quite a number of hotels and public boarding-houses, for the accommodation of guests, the leading house, a brick structure, being the "Central." Bear River abounds in fish, and in the proper season the sloughs and marshes bordering the river near the lake, are almost covered with ducks and wild geese, thus offering fine sport for the hunter and fisherman. The water-lines of the lake become, as we pass westward toward the mountains of the Promontory Range, visible high up on the side of the mountains. There are three distinct water-lines to be seen in some places near Ogden, and each one has left a bench or terrace of land or rock by which it may be traced. The great basin is full of wonders, and no richer field on the Continent awaits scientific examination than this. We soon pass

Quarry,—a side track, with a huge, rocky, black castle on the right and back of it. Trains do not stop here, nor is the station down on the advertised time-cards. The mountain on our right is called Little Mountain, and rises solitary and alone out of the plain. As we pass beyond and look back, an oval-shaped dome rises from its northern end as the turret of a castle. Salt Creek rises in the valley above, and sinks into the sand on its way to the lake.

Blue Creek,—838 miles from San Francisco, with an elevation of 4,379 feet. It is a telegraph station with a side track and turn-table. If we have a heavy train a helper engine is here awaiting our arrival, and will assist in pulling us up the hill to Promontory. Between this and the next station, are some very heavy grades, short curves and deep rocky cuts, with fills across ravines. Blue Creek comes rushing down from the mountains, and furnishes water for several stations along the road. Leaving this station we begin to climb around a curve and up the side of the Promontory Range, the road almost doubling back on itself. The old grade of the Union Pacific is crossed and recrossed in several places, and is only a short distance away.

As we wind into the depressions and round the points, gradually ascending to the summit of the divide, the view of the lake, Corinne, Ogden and the Wahsatch Mountains, is grand. The grade for a short distance, is said to be 110 feet to the mile. We pass the rock cuts where each road expended thousands of dollars, and where Bishop John Sharp, now President of the Utah Central, exploded a mine which lifted the rock from the grade completely out, and gave a clear track after the rubbish was cleared away.

Promontory,—804 miles from San Francisco; elevation, 4,905 feet. It is about 9 miles from Blue Creek, and in the first seven miles we ascend over 500 feet. While the road was under construction, this little place was quite lively, but its glory has departed, and its importance at this time, is chiefly historic. It has a very well-kept eating-house for railroad and train men, and large coal-sheds with a three-stall round-house and other buildings for the convenience of employes. The water used here is brought from Blue Creek. It is located between two peaks or ridges of the Promontory Range, one of which on the left, is covered with cedars, and a portion of the year crowned with snow.

This place is well known as the meeting of the two railroads.

The highest point on the left, is called "Peak" on Froiseth's Map of Utah, and from its summit a magnificent view of the lake and surrounding country can be obtained.

The Great Railroad Wedding—Driving the Last Spike.

American history, in its triumphs of skill, labor and genius, knows no event of greater, thrilling interest, than the scene which attended the driving of the last spike, which united the East and West with the bands of iron. The completion of a project so grand in conception, so successful in execution, and likely to prove so fruitful and rich in promise, was worthy of world-wide celebrity.

Upon the 10th of May, 1869, the rival roads approached each other, and two lengths of rails were left for the day's work. At 8 A. M., spectators began to arrive; at quarter to 9 A. M., the whistle of the Central Pacific Railroad is heard, and the first train arrives, bringing a large number of passengers. Then two additional trains arrive on the Union Pacific Railroad, from the East. At a quarter of 11 A. M., the Chinese workmen commenced leveling the bed of the road, with picks and shovels, preparatory to placing the ties. At a quarter past eleven the Governor's train (Governor Stanford) arrived. The engine was gaily decorated with little flags and ribbons—the red white and blue. The last tie is put in place—eight feet long, eight inches wide, and six inches thick. It was made of California laurel, finely polished, and ornamented with a silver escutcheon, bearing the following inscription:

"*The last tie laid on the Pacific Railroad, May* 10, 1869."

Then follow the names of the directors and officers of the Central Pacific Company, and of the presenter of the tie.

The exact point of contact of the road was 1,085.8 miles west from Omaha, which allowed 690 miles to the Central Pacific Railroad, for Sacramento, for their portion of the work. The engine Jupiter, of the Central Pacific Railroad, and the engine 119 of the Union Pacific Railroad, moved up to within 30 feet of each other.

Just before noon the announcement was sent to Washington, that the driving of the *last spike* of the railroad which connected the Atlantic and Pacific, would be communicated to all the telegraph offices in the country the instant the work was done, and instantly a large crowd gathered around the offices of the Western Union Telegraph Company to receive the welcome news.

The manager of the company placed a magnetic ball in a conspicuous position, where all present could witness the performance, and connected the same with the main lines, notifying the various offices of the country that he was ready. New Orleans, New York and Boston instantly answered "Ready."

In San Francisco, the wires were connected with the fire-alarm in the tower, where the heavy ring of the bell might spread the news immediately over the city, as quick as the event was completed.

Waiting for some time in impatience, at last came this message from Promontory Point, at 2.27 P. M.:

"*Almost ready. Hats off, prayer is being offered.*"

A silence for the prayer ensued; at 2.40 P. M., the bell tapped again, and the officer at Promontory said:

"*We have got done praying, the spike is about to be presented.*"

Chicago replied: "*We understand, all are ready in the East.*"

From Promontory Point. "*All ready now; the spike will soon be driven. The signal will be three dots for the commencement of the blows.*"

For a moment the instrument was silent, and then the hammer of the magnet tapped the bell, *one, two, three,* the signal. Another pause of a few seconds, and the lightning came flashing eastward, 2,400 miles to Washington; and the blows of the hammer on the spike were repeated instantly in telegraphic accents upon the bell of the Capitol. At 2.47 P. M., Promontory Point gave the signal, "*Done*;" and the great American Continent was successfully spanned. Immediately thereafter, flashed over the line, the following official announcement to the Associated Press:

Promontory Summit, Utah, May 10.—THE LAST RAIL IS LAID! THE LAST SPIKE IS DRIVEN! THE PACIFIC RAILROAD IS COMPLETED! *The point of junction is* 1,086 *miles west*

THE GREAT RAILROAD WEDDING.

1.—Driving the last Spike. 2.—Union of the East and West. 3.—First Whistle of the Iron Horse.

of the Missouri River, and 690 *miles east of Sacramento City.*

LELAND STANFORD,
Central Pacific Railroad.

T. C. DURANT,
SIDNEY DILLON,
JOHN DUFF, } *Union Pacific Railroad.*

Such were the telegraphic incidents that attended the completion of the greatest work of the age,—but during these few expectant moments, the scene itself at Promontory Point, was very impressive.

After the rival engines had moved up toward each other, a call was made for the people to stand back, in order that all might have a chance to see. Prayer was offered by Rev. Dr. Todd of Massachusetts. Brief remarks were then made by General Dodge and Governor Stanford. Three cheers were given for the Government of the *United States*, for the Railroad, for the Presidents, for the Star Spangled Banner, for the Laborers, and for those respectively, who furnished the means. Four spikes were then furnished,—*two gold* and *two silver*,—by Montana, Idaho, California, and Nevada. They were each about seven inches long, and a little larger than the iron spike.

Dr. Harkness, of Sacramento, in presenting to Governor Stanford a spike of pure gold, delivered a short and appropriate speech.

The Hon. F. A. Fritle, of Nevada, presented Dr. Durant with a spike of silver, saying: "*To the iron of the East, and the gold of the West, Nevada adds her link of silver to span the Continent and weld the oceans.*"

Governor Stanford, presenting another spike, said: "*Ribbed in iron, clad in silver, and crowned with gold, Arizona presents her offering to the enterprise that has banded the Continent and welded the oceans.*"

Dr. Durant stood on the north side of the tie, and Governor Stanford on the south side. At a given signal, these gentlemen struck the spikes, and at the same instant the electric spark was sent through the wires, east and west. The two locomotives moved up until they touched each other, and a bottle of wine was poured, as a libation on the last rail.

A number of ladies graced the ceremonies with their presence, and at 1 P. M., under an almost cloudless sky, and in the presence of about *one thousand one hundred people*, the greatest railroad on earth was completed.

A sumptuous repast was given to all the guests and railroad officers, and toward evening the trains each moved away and darkness fell upon the scene of joy and triumph.

Immediately after the ceremonies, the laurel tie was removed for preservation, and in its place an ordinary one substituted. Scarcely had it been put in its place, before a grand advance was made upon it by the curiosity seekers and relic hunters and divided into numberless mementoes, and as fast as each tie was demolished and a new one substituted, this, too, shared the same fate, and probably within the first six months, there were used as many new ties. It is said that even one of the rails did not escape the grand battery of knife and hack, and the first one had soon to be removed to give place to another.

A curious incident, connected with the laying of the last rails, has been little noticed hitherto. Two lengths of rails, 56 feet, had been omitted. The Union Pacific people brought up their pair of rails, and the work of placing them was done by Europeans. The Central Pacific people then laid their pair of rails, the labor being performed by Mongolians. The foremen, in both cases, were Americans. Here, near the center of the great American Continent, were representatives of Asia, Europe and America—America directing and controlling.

It is somewhat unfortunate that all the scenes which characterize this place of meeting are passed over by the railroad trains at night, and travelers can not catch even a glimpse.

Leaving Promontory, a sugar-loaf peak rises on our right, and, as we near it, the lake again comes into view, looking like a green meadow in the distance. About three miles west of the station, on the left side of the track, a sign-board has been erected, stating that 10 miles of track were here laid in one day. Ten miles farther west a similar sign-board appears. This track was laid on the 29th of April, 1869, and, so far as known, is the largest number of miles ever laid in one day. (For a full description, see page 8.)

Rozel,—an unimportant station, where trains meet and pass; but passenger trains do not stop unless signaled. The lake can now be seen for a long distance, and in a clear day, with a good glass, the view is magnificent. Still crossing a sage brush plain, with occasional alkali patches, closing in upon the shore at times, we soon arrive at

Lake.—There is an open plain to the north of these two stations, and north of Rozel especially, are salt wells. Between these two stations the second sign-board close to the track, showing the western limit of the 10 miles of track laid in one day, is seen. North of Lake Station about three miles, are Cedar Springs, which was quite a place during the construction of the road, and a great deal of wood, etc., was obtained near them, for use of the road. Leaving this station we pass across flats and marshes, with the old Union Pacific grade still well preserved, on our left. In places, however, it is partially washed away by the waves of the lake. Next comes

Monument,—804 miles from San Francisco;

SALT LAKE FROM MONUMENT POINT. MONUMENT POINT FROM SALT LAKE.

elevation, 4,227 feet. An isolated rock rises, like a monument, in the lake on the left, while the hill on the right is crowned with turrets and projecting domes. You have here a grand view of the lake, its islands and shores, with promontories, etc., which is correctly represented by our artist. The station itself is a mere side track and "Y," for the convenience of the road. When the strong south wind blows, the waves, dashing against the rocks on the shore, and the rolling white caps in the distance, form a beautiful view which the tourist, after passing the dreary waste, will appreciate. The road now turns to the right, and the view of the lake is shut out by a low hill that intervenes. On the west side of this hill are the Locomotive Springs which puff out steam at times, and which give them their name. A Mormon brother has a ranche at the springs, and seems to enjoy life as best he can with three wives.

The Overflow of the Great Salt Lake—Another theory as to its outlet.—Parties who profess to be well posted as to the nature of the country surrounding this great body of salt water, do not agree with the views elsewhere expressed, that in case its rise continues, its waters will flow into the Humboldt River. They assert that north of Monument Rock is an extensive arm of the lake, now dry, and that the divide between the northern extremity of this arm and the Raft River, a tributary of Snake River, is not more than from 50 to 75 feet high; and that, if the lake rises, this divide will be washed out—or a channel may be cut through it into Raft River, and the surplus waters of the lake thus drained into the Pacific Ocean, through the Snake and Columbia Rivers. Next we pass

Seco,—which is an unimportant station in the midst of sage plains, and soon arrive at

Kelton,—790 miles from San Francisco, with an elevation of 4,223 feet. There have been no very heavy grades between this and Promontory. The town is located at the north-west corner of Salt Lake, and about two miles from it, with low marshes and sloughs intervening. This is a stage station, and passengers for Boise City and other points in Idaho, and points in Oregon as far as Dalles, will here leave the train and secure seats in the coaches of the stage line. The shipping of freight for Idaho, and the fact that it is the terminus of the stage line, are the principal causes for the growth and business of this place. It has a fair hotel, several stores, the usual number of saloons, and corrals for stock used in freighting. In 1875, 6,000,000 pounds of freight were shipped from this place to Idaho, or about 3,000 tons. The freighting business has gradually increased from year to year, and will continue to do so as the mines of the Territory are developed, and until the Portland, Dalles and Salt Lake Railroad is pushed forward into the Territory. Seven miles north of the town, at the foot of the mountains, are springs of clear, fresh water, from which water is conveyed for the use of the railroad and inhabitants. There is a good deal of stock grazed in the vicinity of this station, which feed on sage brush in the winter and such grass as they get, but find good grazing in the summer. The surplus cattle are shipped to the markets on the Pacific Coast.

Tourists will also bear in mind, that this is the station nearest to the great Shoshone Falls. These falls are 110 miles from Kelton. Passengers from the east will arrive at about 10 o'clock P. M., and stay all night. Passengers from the west will arrive at about two o'clock A. M. The next morning they will take the stage run by the North-western Stage Company, 100 miles to Rock Creek Station, which are made over good roads in twelve hours. Here you will stay over night, and take a team the next morning for the falls; distance ten miles over a lava plain, with stinted sage brush. No sign of the great falls is seen, until you reach a point one mile from them, when they suddenly burst upon the eye with a grandeur and magnificence truly bewildering.

Travelers to the main falls can reach them on foot very easily from the upper ridge. It will abundantly repay visitors to go to the edge of the river, and contemplate their silent grandeur. A pathway or trail leads from the point where wagons stop, and the distance is about one mile.

The Great Shoshone Falls.

BY CLARENCE KING.

In October, 1868, with a small detachment of a United States Geological Survey, the writer crossed the Goose Creek Mountains, in northern Utah, and descended by the old Fort Boise Road to the level of the Snake Plain. After camp and breakfast, at Rock Creek, mounting in the saddle we headed toward the *Canon of the Shoshone.* The air was cold and clear. The remotest mountain peaks upon the horizon could be distinctly seen, and the forlorn details of their brown slopes stared at us as through a vacuum. A few miles in front, the smooth surface of the plain was broken by a ragged, zigzag line of black, which marked the edge of the farther wall of the Snake Canon. A dull, throbbing sound greeted us. Its pulsations were deep and seemed to proceed from the ground beneath our feet.

Leaving the cavalry to bring up the wagon, my two friends and I galloped on, and were quickly upon the edge of the canon wall. We looked down into a broad, circular excavation, three-quarters of a mile in diameter, and nearly seven hundred feet deep. East and north, over the edges of the canon, we looked across miles and miles of the Snake Plain, far on to the blue boundary mountains. The wall of the gorge opposite us, like the cliff at our feet, sank in perpendicular bluffs, nearly to the level of the river. A horizon as level as the sea; a circling wall, whose sharp edges were here and there battlemented in huge, fortress-like masses; a broad river, smooth and unruffled, flowing quietly into the middle of the scene, and then plunging into a labyrinth of rocks, tumbling over a precipice two hundred feet high, and flowing westward in a still, deep current, disappear behind a black promontory. Where the river flowed around the western promontory, it was wholly in shadow, and of a deep sea-green. A scanty growth of coniferous trees fringed the brink of the lower cliffs, overhanging the river. Dead barrenness is the whole sentiment of the scene.

My tent was pitched upon the edge of a cliff, directly overhanging the rapids. From my door I looked over the edge of the falls, and, whenever the veil of mist was blown aside, I could see for a mile down the river. At the very brink of the fall a few twisted evergreens cling with their roots to the rock, and lean over the abyss of foam with something of that air of fatal fascination which is apt to take possession of men.

In plan, the fall recurves up-stream in a deep horseshoe, resembling the outline of Niagara. The total breadth is about seven hundred feet, and the greatest height of a single fall about one hundred and ninety. Among the islands above the brink are several beautiful cascades, where portions of the river pour over in lace-like forms. The whole mass of the fall is one ever-varying sheet of spray. In the early spring, when swollen by the rapidly melted snows, the river pours over with something like the grand volume of Niagara, but at the time of my visit, it was wholly white foam. The river below the falls is very deep. The right bank sinks into the water in a clear, sharp precipice, but on the left side a narrow, pebbly beach extends along the foot of the cliff. From the top of the wall, at a point a quarter of a mile below the falls, a stream has gradually worn a little stairway down to the river: thick growths of evergreens have huddled together in this ravine. Under the influence of the cool shadow of the cliffs and the pines, and constant percolating of surface-waters, a rare fertility is developed in the ravines opening upon the shore of the canon. A luxuriance of ferns and mosses, an almost tropical wealth of green leaves and velvety carpeting line the banks. There are no rocks at the base of the fall. The sheet of foam plunges almost vertically into a dark, beryl-green, lake-like expanse of the river. Immense volumes of foam roll up from the cataract-base, and, whirling about in the eddying winds, rise often a thousand feet into the air. When the wind blows down the canon, a gray mist obscures the river for half a mile; and when, as is usually the case in the afternoon, the breezes blow eastward, the foam-cloud curls over the brink of the fall, and hangs like a veil over the upper river. The incessant roar, reinforced by a thousand echoes, fills the canon. From out this monotone, from time to time, rise strange, wild sounds, and now and then may be heard a slow, measured beat, not unlike the recurring fall of breakers. From the white front of the cata-

SHOSHONE FALLS.

ract the eye constantly wanders up to the black, frowning parapet of lava. The actual edge is usually formed of irregular blocks and prisms of lava, poised upon their ends in an unstable equilibrium, ready to be tumbled over at the first leverage of the frost. Hardly an hour passes without the sudden boom of one of those rock-masses falling upon the ragged *debris* piled below.

After sleeping on the nightmareish brink of the falls, it was no small satisfaction to climb out of the Dantean gulf and find myself once more upon a pleasantly prosaic foreground of sage. Nothing more effectually banishes the melotragic state of the mind than the obtrusive ugliness and abominable smell of this plant. From my feet a hundred miles of it stretched eastward. A half-hour's walk took me out of sight of the canon, and as the wind blew westward, only occasional, indistinct pulsations of the fall could be heard.

I walked for an hour, following an old Indian trail which occasionally approached within seeing distance of the river, and then, apparently quite satisfied, diverged again into the desert. When about four miles from the Shoshone, it bent abruptly to the north, and led to the edge of the canon. Here again the narrow gorge widened into a broad theater, surrounded as before by black, vertical walls, and crowded over its whole surface by rude piles and ridges of volcanic rock. The river entered it from the east through a magnificent gateway of basalt, and, having reached the middle, flows on either side of a low, rocky island, and plunges in two falls into a deep, green basin. A very singular ridge of the basalt projects like an arm almost across the river, inclosing within its semi-circle a bowl three hundred feet in diameter and two hundred feet deep. Within this the water was of the same peculiar beryl-green, dappled here and there by masses of foam which swim around and around with a spiral tendency toward the center. To the left of the island half the river plunges off an overhanging lip, and falls about 150 feet, the whole volume reaching the surface of the basin many feet from the wall. The other half of the river has worn away the edge, and descends in a tumbling cascade at an angle of about forty-five degrees.

The cliffs around the upper cataract are inferior to those of the Shoshone. While the level of the upper plain remains nearly the same, the river constantly deepens the channel in its westward course.

By dint of hard climbing I reached the actual brink in a few places, and saw the canon successively widening and narrowing, its walls here and there approaching each other and standing like the pillars of a gateway; the river alternately flowing along smooth, placid reaches of level, and then rushing swiftly down rocky cascades. Here and there along the cliff are disclosed the mouths of black caverns, where the lava seems to have been blown up in the form of a great blister, as if the original flow had poured over some pool of water, and the hot rock, converting it into steam, had been blown up bubble-like by its immense expansion. I continued my excursions along the canon to the west of the Shoshone. About a mile below the fall, a very fine promontory juts sharply out from the wall, and projects nearly to the middle of the canon. Climbing with difficulty along its toppling crest, I reached a point which I found composed of immense, angular fragments piled up in dangerous poise. Looking eastward, the battlemented rocks around the falls limited the view; but westward I could see down long reaches of river, where islands of trachyte rose above white cascades. A peculiar and fine effect is noticeable upon the river during all the midday. The shadow of the southern cliff is cast down here and there, completely darkening the river, but often defining itself upon the water. The contrast between the rich, gem-like green of the sunlit portions and the deep-violet shadow of the cliff is of extreme beauty. The Snake River, deriving its volume wholly from the melting of the mountain snows, is a direct gauge of the annual advance of the sun. In June and July it is a tremendous torrent, carrying a full half of the Columbia. From the middle of July it constantly shrinks, reaching its minimum in midwinter. At the lowest, it is a river equal to the Sacramento or Connecticut.

Near the "City of Rocks" Station, in the Goose Creek Mountains, are found the "Giant Rocks," and over the little rise is the place that gives the name to the station. Dotting the plains are thousands of singular rocks, on which the weary pilgrims of 1849, have written their names in cart-grease paint. The old California road is still seen, but now overgrown with rank weeds. The view as you descend from the summit is sublime. Far away in the distance loom up the Salmon River Mountains, distant 125 miles, and in the intervening space winds the valley of the Snake River.

Kelton has from 250 to 300 inhabitants, nearly all supported by the Idaho trade, though it will eventually have some mining trade, as the recent discovery of mines in the Black Pine District, 25 miles north, will have an influence in this direction. Kelton is the nearest railroad station to these mines, and parties desiring to visit them will leave the cars here.

Idaho Territory.—This is one of the smallest of the Territories, as now constituted, and claims a population of about 15,000 people. There are three public lines of conveyance which lead into the Territory, or rather two, as one of them passes entirely through it. The stage line from Kelton passes the City of Rocks, and within ten miles of the Great Shoshone Falls, to Dalles in Oregon, by way of Boise City, 250 miles out; thence to Baker City, Oregon, 400 miles; to Union, 435 miles; to La Grande, 450 miles; to Unatilla, 510 miles, and to Walla Walla, 530 miles. At Boise City the line connects with stages for Idaho City, Centerville, Placerville and Silver City. Boise City is the territorial capital, a city said to contain 3,500 people, and located on the Boise River. There is not much agricultural land in the Territory, but a few of the valleys are cultivated and produce excellent crops of wheat, barley and oats, with potatoes and all kinds of vegetables. Crops are raised by irrigation. Boise Valley, the settled portion of it, is about 60 miles long and four miles wide, and is the most thickly settled of any of the valleys in the Territory. The nights are so cool and the altitude of the valleys is so great that experiments in corn raising have not, thus far, turned out very well. The second line of public conveyance spoken of, runs from Winnemucca to Silver City.

It is claimed that this town is equal in population to Boise City. It is sustained by the mines located near it. At Rattlesnake Station there is also a connecting stage line for Rocky Bar, a mining camp, near which placer and gulch diggings have been discovered. There are quite a large number of Chinese in the Territory, mostly engaged in placer and gulch mining. They are industrious and frugal and will frequently make money from claims that have been abandoned as worthless by white men. So far as developed, the Territory has some rich mines, and those in the Atlantic District are becoming somewhat noted. It is claimed that the richest known gold mine in the country at present, is in this district. In addition to the supplies, etc., shipped from Winnemucca, over 6,000,000 pounds of freight were shipped from Kelton Station to this Territory in 1875, and more than this amount will be shipped the present year. Much of it has been, and will be, mining machinery. A railroad through the Territory is much needed, will aid greatly in the development of its mines, and will be a paying investment from the start, or, at least, in a very short time after its completion. The Snake and Salmon Rivers are among its principal streams. The Snake River rises in the mountains of the Yellowstone Region, and flows entirely through the Territory from east to west, and forms one of the tributaries to the Columbia River of Oregon. The scenery along its valley is varied, but in some places is grand. Idaho also has immense ranges where a large number of cattle are grazed both winter and summer, without hay. The stock

VIEW LOOKING DOWN THE SHOSHONE FALLS.

interest is rapidly becoming one of the principal features of the Territory. Its future prosperity, however, depends largely upon the development of its mining interests.

Leaving Kelton, the road soon turns to the left, and, rising a heavy grade, reaches the divide between the Great Salt Lake and the valley beyond. The mountains for a distance are on our right, while, from the left, a magnificent view of the western arm of the lake can be obtained. Between the road and the lake are extensive salt plains, which in the sun glisten like burnished silver, while beyond are the green waters of this inland sea. Going up this grade, you will notice a ledge of rocks on the left side of the track, the lower end of which has been tunneled by the wind, forming a natural aperture like an open arch. We soon turn to the right, leave the lake behind us and wind along the side of the mountain. A dreary salt marsh or alkali plain is now seen on the left, and the low, isolated hill on the shore, which for a time obscured our vision is passed, giving us another view of the lake in the distance, and the mountains of the Wahsatch and Oquirrh Ranges beyond, as far as the eye can reach. Passing through a rocky cut from a projecting spur of the range we are passing, and looking to the right, a beautiful conical dome rises up, as a grim sentinel to guard the way.

Ombey,—simply a side track in the midst of a heavy gravel cut, 778 miles from San Francisco, with an elevation of 4,721 feet. At Kelton we were but little above the elevation of Salt Lake, 4,223 feet, and we are 500 feet higher here than when we left that place, the distance between the two being about 11 miles. From the frequent views of the Great American Desert which the traveler can obtain while passing over this portion of the road, he can form some idea of its utter barrenness and desolation, and the great sufferings of those who have attempted to cross it without adequate preparation, and the consequent burning thirst they and their animals have endured.

Matlin,—only a side track, 768 miles from San Francisco; elevation, 4,597 feet.

Terrace,—a railroad town on the edge of the Great American Desert. It is 757 miles from San Francisco, with an elevation of 4,544 feet. Here is a ten-stall roundhouse, and the machine and repair shops of the Salt Lake Division of the Central Pacific Railroad. Mr. R. H. Pratt, with headquarters at Ogden, is Superintendent of this Division, which extends from that place to Toano in Nevada. The town has about 300 people, which includes not only the railroad men and their families, but those who are here for the purpose of trade and traffic with them. The water tank here, as at a good many stations on this road, is supplied with water brought through pipes from the springs in the mountains.

The town has two or three stores, saloons and an eating-house, where railroad men and emigrants take their meals. It depends wholly on its local trade at present; but the discovering and opening of the Rosebud Mines, about 10 miles north, will tend to increase its business, if they are developed. Terrace is the railroad station for the mines in the Newfoundland District, some 18 miles south. Miners for either of the above named districts, will leave the cars at this station. There are no stage lines to them, as yet, but private conveyances can be readily obtained. The desert with its dreary loneliness—a barren waste—still continues.

Leaving Terrace we have over 20 miles of straight road over which we soon pass. A spur of the Goose Creek Range of Mountains puts down on our right, while Silver Islet Mountain rises out of the alkali plain on our left, and Pilot's Peak, one of the lofty mountains of Nevada, and a noted landmark for many a weary pilgrim across the desert, looms up in the southwest.

Bovine,—an unimportant station, with side track for the convenience of passing trains, 747 miles from San Francisco, with an elevation of 4,347 feet. On our right are broken mountains, while there is an isolated peak one side of which seems to have settled away from the other, leaving it very rough and ragged. Next we come to

Lucin,—734 miles from San Francisco, with an elevation of 4,486 feet above the sea. Beyond Lucin, a short distance, we strike Grouse Creek, which rises in the hills north. This creek usually sinks in the sandy desert, and no water in it crosses the railroad, except in the spring when the snows are melting. On the right, east of the hills, and north of Lucin about 4 1-2 miles, are the Owl Springs which have an abundance of water. As we enter the pass in this low range of hills, we lose sight of Silver Islet Mountains, and the range close to the track is called the Pilot Range, or by the miners, Buel Range, after Buel City. Leaving Grouse Creek on our right, the road leads to the left again, and we enter the Thousand Spring Valley. It virtually unites with the Grouse Valley, though its waters usually sink in the sand before they reach those of the creek mentioned. As we near Tecoma, the traveler will notice a small granite monument on the left side of the track, near the summit of the grade, supported by a heap of stones. This monument marks the Nevada State line and passing it, we enter the land of the "big bonanzas."

Tecoma,—Nevada, 724 miles from San Francisco, with an elevation of 4,812 feet. This is the nearest railroad station to the celebrated Tecoma Mines, one owned by Howland & Aspinwall of New York, and the other owned by a London company,—both mines bearing the same name. Tecoma is the railroad station for Lucin Mining District, and stages leave here every morning for Buel City, the mining town of the district, six miles south, in the foot hills of the range. It is the nearest railroad station also, to the Deep Creek District, 90 miles due south. The Goose Creek and Delano Districts have recently been opened about 35 miles north of this place and are said to contain rich prospects. The formation, however, is very much broken, and affords strong evidences of a mighty upheaval sometime. Within a mile or two of the town, north, a good view of the Thousand Spring Valley is obtained with its pasturage and hay lands. Tecoma has two or three stores, saloon, dwellings, etc., and will soon have a smelting works. It has a population of from 50 to 100; and the most of its business is with the mines and cattle men. Stock-yards convenient for shipping cattle have been erected here. There is a fine grazing country off to the north, where large herds of cattle are kept, and this has come to be a prominent business of this part of the country. As we approach Tecoma, on our left a bluff peak with perpendicular walls closes the northern end of Pilot Range, while Pilot Peak towers up to the heavens at the southern extremity. It is 20 miles from Tecoma to the base of this peak, though it does not seem half that distance. Tecoma is also the railroad station for the Silver Islet Mining District, and if the mines in its immediate vicinity are developed, it will become a place of considerable importance. Leaving Tecoma the railroad continues over a sage brush and greasewood plain to the left of the valley, with a part of the old Union Pacific grade on the right, and as we approach the next range of hills or mountains, we have a fine broadside view of grand old Pilot Peak, and do not wonder at its prominence, or the great regard in which it was held by the emigrants across this dreary desert.

Montello,—715 miles from San Francisco, with an elevation of 5,010 feet. At this station is a large water-tank supplied with water from a spring in the mountains on the right, some ten miles away. The mountain ranges this side of Ogden run from north to south, parallel with each other, and the railroad crosses them over low divides or passes, while the plains of the desert lay between them. To our right a point of the Pequop Range approaches the track, and shuts out our view of the Old Pilot, as we pass up the grade, and into the narrow defile.

It is generally understood that the mines of the Pilot Range are quite extensive, and that the ore, though of rather low grade, is nevertheless to be found in large quantities and is quite accessible. Buel City has a smelter erected which has reduced considerable ore.

Loray,—nearly on the summit of the divide. It is 704 miles from San Francisco, with an elevation of about 5,960 feet. It is a station of no particular importance to travelers. Wood and timber, cut in the mountains for the use of the road, is delivered here.

Toano,—698 miles from San Francisco, with an elevation of 5,973 feet—the western terminus of the Salt Lake Division of the Central Pacific, and nearly 183 miles from Ogden. Toano has a roundhouse with six stalls and an adjoining shed where two engines can be sheltered. It has the usual side tracks, coal-sheds and buildings for the transaction of the business of the company. The town has about 250 people.

The following mining districts are tributary to this place, and transact the most of their business here: Silver Zone, distant 20 miles, mines mostly milling ore; Dolly Varden, 55 miles; Cherry Creek, 100 miles; Egan Canon, 105 miles; Shellburn, 110 miles; Mineral City, 130 miles; Ward, 140 miles. They are all south of the railroad, and connected with Toano by a good wagon road, though there are no mails carried by this route. A great deal of freight is carried to the mines, and ore and bullion hauled back. The road is destitute of water for a considerable part of the way, and wells, at a great expense, have been dug in some places, from which water is sold to freighters. The ore from some of the mines in these districts is very rich. Twenty cars of ore from the Paymaster Mine in the Ward District were shipped from here in January, 1876, nineteen of which averaged about $800 per ton, and one car averaged a little over $1,000 per ton, net. Not only the Ward, but others in this region are regarded as prosperous mining camps. In 1875, from 800 to 1,000 tons of base bullion were shipped from this place, the product of these mines. The valleys south have good ranges for stock, and some of them, as the Steptoe Valley, produce excellent crops of small grain and vegetables. The Toano Range of Mountains runs from north to south, and heads near this place. On the road to Pioche, about 180 miles from Toano, and about half a mile from the road, is the Mammoth Cave of Nevada. It has been partially explored, but its extent is not known. Beautiful specimens of stalactites and crystals have been found here, and the tourist would be highly interested in a visit to this cave, which in a short time must become a place of public resort.

North of Toano, the Goose Creek Range of Mountains, which divides Goose Creek and Thousand Spring Valley, are plainly visible. The Salmon Falls copper mines, on Salmon Falls River, are about 60 miles north, and are known to be rich in copper.

About 20 miles south of the town, a road to the Deep Creek Mining District branches off from the Pioche road, and part of the business of that mining camp is done here. The country immediately around Toano is barren and desolate in appearance—not very inviting to the traveler or settler.

On leaving Toano we have an up grade to Moore's Station, about 30 miles. In the winter great difficulty is experienced with snow over this distance, and in the summer the route is extremely beautiful and picturesque. Just west of the town, on the right, the low hills are covered with a scattering growth of scrub pines and cedars. The Pequop Range juts up to the town on the south, while on the north may still be seen the mountains of the Goose Creek Range. The road between this point and Wells is undulating, and full of short curves and heavy grades. Six snow sheds are passed, in rapid succession. As we look off to the right, the hill seems to descend into a large valley, with a range of mountains beyond. It is a dry, sage brush valley and continues in sight until we pass Independence.

Pequop,—689 miles from San Francisco, with an elevation of 6,184 feet. It is simply a side track, at which passenger trains do not stop. Passing this, we next reach the Otego telegraph station, which is only used in winter, to give notice of snow-blocked trains, etc.

Dead Man's Spring.—About five miles from Pequop, in the low hills off to the right of the track, is a spring which bears the above suggestive title. In the spring of 1873, the body of a dead man was found near it, with a bullet hole through his skull. The decomposition of the body had advanced so far that it was past recognition, and the questions as to who he was, and how he came to be killed, were not likely to be solved. In short, the man and his tragic end were wrapped in great mystery. The old adage, however, that "murder will out," was again verified in this case. It seems that a large drove of cattle came into this region of country, in the fall of 1872, and that two of the herders employed—one a Mexican, and the other a white man, were paid off near Wells, and started back for Colorado, where they were first employed. They camped together one night at this spring, and the next morning one was left cold and stark upon the bosom of mother earth, while the other, the Mexican, went on and in due time arrived in Denver, Col. He had murdered his companion, robbed him of his money, his watch and his horse, and with his plunder, with no one to witness the deed, thought himself secure. But a brother of the murdered man lived in Denver, and hearing nothing from the absent one for a long time, became somewhat alarmed about him, and began to institute inquiries and to search for his companion. His efforts were soon rewarded, and in a short time he heard that the Mexican,—who was known to have accompanied his brother in driving the herd to Nevada,—had returned, and had been seen in Denver. Furthermore, it was supposed that he had not left that city, and could be found somewhere in its immediate vicinity. His trail was finally struck, and followed until he was found. His account of the missing man was so confused, and his different stories so conflicting and improbable, that he was arrested and searched. The search revealed the watch and other trinkets of the murdered man, which were at once recognized by his brother. His horse was also found. The Mexican, now thoroughly suspected, was closely questioned, and the evidence against him was so strong, that, while confined in jail, he confessed the crime. This so exasperated the friends of the murdered man that they determined upon vengeance, and immediately organized to secure the death of the culprit. The villain was taken from his cell in the jail one night, and found the next morning hanging to a telegraph pole. Thus was the spring named.

Otego,—station and side track, which is 688 miles from San Francisco, with an elevation of 6,154 feet. The tourist may enjoy a magnificent view of hills and mountains, valleys and dales, as we pass on over some of the reverse curves in the road. The old Union Pacific grade is still seen in patches, on our right. Pequop Range, with Independence Valley, now looms grandly into view on our left, as we arrive at

Independence,—676 miles from San Francisco, with an elevation of 6,007 feet. We are now crossing a low divide between the valley on our right, above spoken of, and Independence Valley on our left. This station is on a heavy down grade, and trains going west seldom stop. The water tank is supplied from springs in the low hills off to the right, and the side track is a little beyond it. We now pass to the right around an isolated mountain that seems to guard the entrance to Independence Valley,—and then to the left, and as we turn to enter the pass in the mountains a lovely view of this beautiful valley is again obtained stretching away as far as the eye can reach. It is a great stock range, and thousands of cattle annually feed upon its rich nutritious grasses. Turning again to the right we enter what is called Cedar Pass. Passing a section-house at which there is a winter telegraph station for use of snow-bound trains, we soon reach the summit of the divide between Independence Valley, and the valley of the Humboldt, at

Moore's,—669 miles from San Francisco, with an elevation of 6,166 feet. It was formerly quite a town for wood-choppers and frontier men, when the railroad was being built; but its glory has departed and the stakes and posts of a few houses are all that remain to mark the spot. Down the grade we go into the far-famed Humboldt Valley, passing Cedar, a side track, where a camp of wood-choppers in the mountains on our left, deliver their wood.

Wells,—661 miles from San Francisco, with an elevation of 5,629 feet. Just as we enter the town, we pass the mountain spur on our left, and Clover Valley bursts into view. Its name is significant as it abounds in the natural clover so well known in the Eastern States. The town has about 100 inhabitants, with roundhouse for three engines, a hotel, stores, saloon, etc. The railroad water tank formerly supplied with water pumped from the wells, a little west of the town, is now filled from a mountain spring four miles away.

Humboldt Wells as they are called, give celebrity to this place. They are really springs about thirty in number, situated mostly in a low basin half a mile west of the station. There are no evidences of volcanic action about them as we could perceive, nor does a crater in this low place seem at all probable. They are very probably natural springs and from the nature of the porous soil around them, they do not rise and flow away as similar springs do in a more compact soil. The water, by residents here, is not considered brackish at all, nor is it particularly warm, though the springs have never been known to freeze over. They are also called bottomless, but no accurate knowledge has yet been published in regard to their depth. They are simply deep springs, but the opinion is here entertained that a lead and line would soon touch bottom in them. It was the great watering place in times of the old emigrant travel, and at least three of these roads converged to this point and united here. These were the Grass Creek, the Thousand Spring Valley and the Cedar Pass Roads. Emigrants in those days always rejoiced when they had passed the perils of the Great American Desert, and arrived at these springs where there was plenty of water, pure and sweet and an abundance of grass for their weary and worn animals. Hence it was a favorite camping ground. Visitors approaching these springs in the summer, and springing on the sod can fairly shake the adjoining springs, a fact that leads to the opinion entertained by some, that they are really openings of a lake, which has been gradually covered over by the accumulation of grass and grass roots and other luxuriant vegetation, which abounds along and around the basin. The fact that the ground around these springs is so elastic, and the known incidents in history, where luxuriant vegetation has frequently caused islands in rivers and lakes, confirms this opinion in our mind, and we believe a thorough investigation will establish this theory as correct. There is then in this basin simply a covered lake, and the springs are openings to it. The conformation of the land around the basin also tends to convince us of the truth of this theory. The basin is the receptacle of the drainage of a large water-shed, and there are high mountains nearly all around it. These springs abound in fish—the little minnows that are so common in the brooks and small streams in the Eastern States. Other kinds there may be, but these only have been caught. The apertures differ in size, and the openings to some are much larger than the openings in others. If they were on a side-hill every body would call them springs, but inasmuch as they are in a low basin, they are called wells. Their depth and surroundings also convey this impression.

Mr. Hamill, a merchant of Wells, says that he took a piece of railroad iron and tied some lariat ropes to it (about 160 feet), and could find no bottom in the deepest springs which he sounded with that length of rope. He further says that a government exploring party, under command of Lieutenant Cuppinger, visited Wells in 1870 and took soundings of the springs to a depth of from 1,500 to 1,700 feet and found no bottom. These soundings were of the largest springs or wells, and while his statement may be true, even soundings to this depth does not render them bottomless.

How to see them and know where they are, is the next thing of consequence to the traveler. As you pass west of the station, notice the end of a piece of the old Union Pacific grade; next the graves surrounded by painted fences; then off to the right a heap of stones, where the engine-house was built—the engine being used to force water from the well, which is just beyond this heap of stones, to the tank along side of the track. The heavy growth of grass around the place will indicate where this well is in summer, and the accumulated deposits of this grass has raised a little rim around this particular well,—and the same is true of others in its immediate vicinity.

Travelers will take notice that a mail and express stage line leaves Wells tri-weekly—Mondays, Wednesdays and Fridays—in the morning, for Sprucemont, 40 miles, and Cherry Creek, 95 miles distant. At Cherry Creek this line connects with stages for Egan Canon, on the line of the old overland stage route, Mineral City (Robinson District) and Hamilton, the county-seat of White Pine County. At Mineral City, conveyances can be easily obtained for Ward's District, 20 miles distant. The Spruce Mountain Mining District is said to contain some very good mines, and a company has recently been organized in San Francisco, to continue the work of development. Sprucemont is the mining town of the district, and is beautifully located on an elevated bench in the midst of groves of pines and cedars. It has a population of from 50 to 100, according to the season.

There are estimated to be about 40 ranches in Clover Valley, and as many in Ruby Valley. These ranchemen are engaged in agriculture and stock growing. They raise wheat, barley, oats, and splendid vegetables. Wells has extensive stock-yards, to accommodate the large shipments of cattle, annually made from these ranches. The valley in this immediate vicinity is the scene of the annual "round-ups," every spring. Cedar Pass Range is the range on our left, as we come through by Moore's Station. West of this range and south of Wells, is Clover Valley. The tourist will see "Castle Peak" on the further side of this valley as the train pauses at the station, and this peak is on the northern end of Ruby Range, and it is always covered with snow. Ruby Valley is nearly due south of the "Castle" which you see in the mountain, and is divided from Clover Valley by a spur of this range, which turns into it like a hook. Ruby Range is about 150 miles long, and we only see its northern extremity at Wells.

North of Wells, across the first range, lies the Thousand Spring Valley—then across another low divide, you will strike a valley whose waters flow north-west through the Columbia River, to the Pacific Ocean. Fishermen will bear in mind that salmon trout are caught in this valley in the spring of the year. The stream is a branch of the Salmon Falls River, which empties into Snake River, about 120 miles north of this station.

A proposed railroad has been talked of, to connect this point with Callville, on the Colorado River, and the route is said to be very feasible. Wells is also the connecting point for a direct "cut off" to Salt Lake City, should such a road be built.

It may be well to remark here, that the mountain ranges in Nevada, as in Utah, generally extend from north to south—and the only exception to this rule, is where there are broken or detached ranges, or isolated peaks. Leaving Wells, the foot hills on our left, in a short distance, obscure a view of the high peaks in the Ruby Range; but they soon reappear as we pass down the valley, and are our constant companions, only a short distance away, until we leave Halleck. Between the Humboldt River and the base of these mountains, there is an elevated bench covered with the usual sage brush and greasewood, while in the valley and along the borders of the stream, grass land predominates. An extensive stock-dealer, when asked about the qualifications, etc., for growing cattle, said that "there was about one acre of grass to seventy-five acres of sage brush," and a limited observation of this part of the State, at least, proves that he was not far out of the way. As we descend the river, however, a gradual increase in grass lands will be observed, while in places, the greasewood which, so far as we know, is entirely useless, grows in astonishing luxuriance.

Tulasco,—654 miles from San Francisco, with an elevation of 5,482 feet. The valley seems to widen out as we descend it, and bushes grow in bunches along the banks of the stream as if the old earth, under the most favorable conditions, was trying to produce trees to beautify and adorn these barren plains. Soon Bishop's Valley can be seen on our right. Looking to the left, we see the canon in the mountain side, down which rushes Trout Creek, when the snows are melting in the spring and early summer. This creek abounds in "speckled beauties," and unites with the Humboldt about a mile and a half below Bishop's Creek, which we soon cross, through a covered bridge.

Bishop's—is another side track station, but on we glide through the valley as it widens out into magnificent proportions. It is 649 miles from San Francisco, and has an elevation of 5,412 feet. Another little creek and valley now appear on our right, and we soon arrive at

Deeth,—642 miles from San Francisco; elevation, 5,340 feet. It is a telegraph station, and has a few buildings around it. The valley seems very broad as we approach this station, and evidences of settlement and cultivation begin to appear. The bushes and willows along the banks of the stream increase, and it is a paradise for ducks and geese.

Halleck—is the next station, 630 miles from San Francisco, with an elevation of 5,230 feet. It is named from Camp Halleck, which is located at the base of mountains, 13 miles from the station, and across the river. A few troops are usually kept here—two or three companies,—and all the freighting and business of the post is done from this station. The town itself has a post-office, hotel, a small store and the usual saloons where "lingering death," or "blue ruin," the common terms for whisky, is doled out to soldiers, and others who patronize them. It is probable that good crops of wheat, barley and oats could be raised here by irrigating the land, but it is mostly occupied as stock ranges. Camp Halleck is not plainly seen from the railroad, though a few buildings a little removed from it, will point out its locality. A regular mail ambulance runs daily between it and the station. Leaving Halleck, Elko Mountain seems to rise on our right close to the track, but the road soon turns and we pass this landmark on our left. The Ruby Range which we have seen away to the left, from Wells to the last station, is now left in the rear as we turn westward again, and pass down one of the Humboldt Canons. The camp is delightfully located, well watered and is surrounded with thriving groves of cottonwood trees.

Peko—is the next station, merely a side track, and section-house at the head of the first canon on the river. It is 626 miles from San Francisco, with an elevation of 5,204 feet. We are now at the head of the Humboldt Canon, the first one through which the river passes. It is not wild and rugged but nevertheless sufficiently so to make it interesting. A short distance below Peko, the North Fork of Humboldt comes in. It is about as large as the main body and is a peculiar stream. It rises nearly north of Carlin, some distance west of this point, and runs to the north-east for a distance, then nearly east, and finally turns toward the south-west, and unites with the Humboldt at this point. The road through this canon is full of short curves, and winds like a serpent through the hills. Now it seems as though the train would be thrown into a heap at the base of the hill we are approaching, but a turn to the right or left saves us from such a calamity. Once or twice before we reach Osino, the valley opens out between the hills, and where the North Fork enters there is an abundance of grass which is monopolized by a rancheman. At the next station,

Osino,—614 miles from San Francisco, with an elevation of 5,132 feet,—a mere side track, we enter upon an open valley, and for about nine miles pass over a nearly straight track. The valley is all taken up by ranchemen and farmers, and good crops are raised by irrigation. The water is taken from the Humboldt above, brought down in a ditch, from which it is taken and distributed among the farms.

Elko,—606 miles from San Francisco, with an elevation of 5,063 feet. It is the regular breakfast and supper station of the road, and passengers get an excellent meal in a neat, well-kept house. In the midst of a game and fish country, the table is generally supplied in the proper season. Passengers have half an hour for their meal.

Elko is the county-seat of Elko County—the north-eastern county of the State. It has a population of about 1,200, and is destined to become one of the important commercial and educational centers of the State. It has a large brick court-house and jail, one church, an excellent public school, and is the seat of the State University. This institution has 40 acres of ground on a bench of land overlooking the city, in plain sight of the cars on the right, just before reaching the town. Its buildings have thus far cost about $30,000, and it was first opened in 1875. The money paid for freights consigned to this place and the mining districts which are tributary to it, in 1875 amounted to nearly $400,000, and the first year the railroad was completed ran up to over $1,000,000. The town has numerous retail stores and two or three wholesale establishments, with a bank, a flouring mill, brewery, hotels, etc. Water taken from the Humboldt River some 17 miles distant, and brought here in pipes, supplies the city. It has three large freight depots, for the accommodation of its railroad business, and is the location of the United States Land office for the Elko Land District. The city is rapidly improving, brick and wooden structures taking the place of the canvas houses that were formerly prevalent. Altogether it has a bright and promising future. Indians, mostly the Shoshones, of all sizes and of both sexes, hover around the town and beg from the trains of cars. They still bedaub themselves with paint, and strut around with feathers in their hats in true Indian style.

Elko is destined to become famous as a watering place. About one and a half miles north of the river, and west of the town, are a group of mineral springs that are already attracting the attention of invalids. There are six springs in this group, three hot, and three cold. The hot springs show 185° Fahrenheit, and one of them, called the "Chicken Soup Spring," has water which, with a little salt and pepper for seasoning, tastes very much like chicken broth. We regret that no analysis of the waters of these springs has been made, which we could furnish to our readers. Tourists in search of wonderful curiosities will not fail to visit these springs and observe the craters of those which are now extinct. The sediment or incrustations formed by the water into some kind of porous rock, accumulated around the apertures until at length they were raised, in one instance, about three feet above the surface of the ground, with a hollow basin, at least one foot in diameter on the top. Other extinct springs are not as high as this one, but show the same formation and have the same peculiarities. Of the hot flowing springs—said to be white sulphur—two are quite large, and one of them is said to contain a large solution of iron. A bathing-house has been erected a short distance away, to which the water is conducted, and in which there are private bathing-rooms supplied with both hot and cold water from the springs. There is also a large swimming bath near by, with dressing-rooms adjoining. A large hotel is to be erected the present year for the accommodation of guests. There is a public conveyance running between the city and the springs for the accommodation of visitors. In the absence of an analysis of the waters we will simply state that they are claimed to be a certain cure for rheumatism and all diseases of the blood; to have a remarkable effect in paralytic cases; to have a good effect on consumptives, when the disease is not too far advanced; to cure fevers of all kinds, and the leaded cases of miners who become poisoned with the lead disease, by working among antimonial ores. The uniform temperature of the hot springs has been further utilized in hatching chickens, and the experiment, if carried to perfection, will beat all the setting hens in the country. Poultry breeders will make a note of this fact. A competent physician who is a good judge of temperaments and diseases should be located at the springs, and additional facilities for the accommodation of invalids will make it a place of great resort.

The following mining districts are tributary to Elko, and will in the future, far more than in the past, contribute to its growth and prosperity: Lone Mountain, 30 miles distant; Tuscarora, 50 miles; Grand Junction, 55 miles; Cornucopia, 70 miles; Aurora, 80 miles; Bull Run, lately changed to Centennial, 80 miles; Cope, 100 miles; Island Mountain placer diggings and quartz mines, 75 miles; Bruno, 80 miles; Hicks, 110 miles; Mardis, 100 miles. Nearly all the business done in these mining districts is transacted through Elko, and adds not a little to its bustling activity. These districts are north of the town, and located mostly in the ranges of mountains that border or lie between the forks of the Owyhee River, a stream that flows into the Snake River of Idaho. Lieutenant Wheeler, in his report of the United States Exploring Expedition, which made a partial survey of the lands and features of Nevada, describes this mineral belt as about 160 miles long, and as one of the richest in the country. It has been but partially prospected, however, and we believe the developments which are now in progress and which are hereafter to be made, will astonish the nation as to the unparalleled richness of the mines of Nevada. Up to the spring of 1876, greater developments had been made in the mines in Tuscarora and Cornucopia Districts than in most of the others. Tuscarora is the principal town in the mining district of the same name. It has about 500 inhabitants, and by September of the present year is anticipated to have 1,500. The principal mines of this district are Young America, Young America North, Young America South, Lida, De Frees, Star, Grand Deposit, Syracuse and others. The most work thus far done, is on the Young America, Young America South, and De Frees. On the first named of these three there is an inclined shaft of 190 feet, and carries free ore from surface to end of development. In sinking, levels have been run to full extent of the ground, 800 feet, and the ledge is from 20 inches to five feet wide.

It is easily worked, no explosions being required, and the ore is said to average from $80 to $106 per ton in gold and silver, without assorting.

The development on the De Frees Mine is as follows: A tunnel has been run from side of hill and ledge struck, about 40 feet from the surface; an incline shaft has been sunk from level of this tunnel to a depth of 95 feet, showing fine ore all the distance, the extreme bottom showing the best ore. This ore has averaged from $90 to $150 per ton, in gold and silver. Steam hoisting works have been erected on the Young America, and a twenty-stamp mill will soon be finished, for the reduction of the ores from this mine. A twenty-stamp mill will soon be finished for the De Frees Mine, and it is expected that these mills will do some custom work for the mines being developed in the vicinity. Other mines in the district are said to be very promising. The mines in the Tuscarora and Cornucopia Districts are in a porphyry formation, with free milling ore; those in the Bull Run or Centennial District are in porphyry and lime, and the ores have to be roasted before they are milled.

Cornucopia District is about 25 miles north of Tuscarora District, and contains a population of 500. Its mines are upon the same range of mountains as the Tuscarora. The principal mines in this district are the Leopard; the Panther, the Tiger, the Hussey, and the Consolidated Cornucopia. Principal developments are on the Leopard and Hussey. The former has been largely opened, and has been running a twenty-stamp mill for the past year or more, producing about $1,000,000. The ore is said to average about $150 per ton, all silver.

The Centennial District has a population of about 200. Its principal mine is the Blue Jacket, which supplies a twenty-stamp mill with ore. A Buckner furnace for roasting is also used in connection with the mill. The ore is said to average $70 per ton, and the vein is very large, frequently 20 feet between the walls. Other districts are said to contain promising mines, but miners and those interested in mines, are always so full of hope—always expecting to strike something rich—and nearly always having a good thing in the "prospects" already found, that it is extremely difficult to determine, in a short investigation, which is the most promising district, or where are the best undeveloped mines. In a developed mine the daily product of bullion will show what it is worth.

Elko has a daily stage route north, which carries the mail and express and supplies the following places: Taylors, Tuscarora, Independence Valley, Grand Junction, Cornucopia, Bull Run and Cope. These places are generally north and north-west of Elko. At Cope, the route ends. There is a weekly mail, stage and express line to the Island Mountain District, 75 miles due north. This is a placer gold field, discovered in 1873, and it is estimated that $100,000 in gold-dust, were taken out in 1875. Three miles north of the Island Mountain District, is the Wyoming District, where valuable silver mines are said to have been discovered. The chief lode is known as the Mardis, which is owned by a Chicago company. A stamp mill is now being erected there. The mineral belt before alluded to, begins at the north end of the Goose Creek Range, and runs south-west about 160 miles. It is about 60 miles wide. Tuscarora is also somewhat noted as a placer field, while Aurora, a new district west of Cornucopia, is said to be very promising. It is 10 miles from the last named place to Aurora.

In the vicinity of the mining districts spoken of, there are rich agricultural valleys where all kinds of grain, but corn, are extensively raised,

MOUNTAIN SCENE IN THE RUBY RANGE.

and vegetables and melons grow to a great size and excellence. There are, also, vast stock ranges—all of which are tributary to Elko.

South from Elko there is a semi-weekly stage, mail and express route to Bullion City, the town of the Railroad Mining District. This town has about 150 people, and is distant 25 miles from Elko. The ores of this district are smelting ores, and the town has two large furnaces for the reduction of this ore. The principal mines are owned by the Empire Company of New York.

There is also a weekly stage line into the South Fork and Huntington Valleys—two rich agricultural valleys, which are thickly settled with farmers and stockmen. In addition to the two valleys last named, there are the Star, Pleasant and Mound Valleys, all rich agricultural districts, and all tributary to Elko. Elko has one daily and two weekly papers which are well supported. The *Post* is a weekly, Republican in politics, and the *Independent*, daily and weekly, is Democratic in politics—though party ties do not seem to be drawn very tightly, and men, regardless of their personal political affiliations, frequently receive the support of all parties.

We will now take leave of this city, and, refreshed with food and rest, renew our journey westward. The valley of the Humboldt continues to widen as we leave Elko for a few miles, and if it is winter or cool mornings of spring or autumn, we will see the steam rising in clouds from the Hot Springs across the river near the wagon bridge, on our left. The pasture and meadow lands, with occasional houses are soon passed, and we arrive at

Moleen,—594 miles from San Francisco, with an elevation of 4,982 feet. It is simply a side track station, with no settlements around it, and trains seldom stop. The same general appearance of the valley and low ranges on either side continue to this place. Occasionally as we have glanced to the left, the high peaks of the Ruby Range have lifted themselves into view, overtopping the nearer and lower range that borders the river on the south.

Passing Moleen, the valley begins to narrow, and the river gorges through the Five Mile Canon. Close to the bluffs we roll along and suddenly, almost over our heads, the beating storms of ages have washed out the softer and more porous parts of the ledges, leaving turrets and peaks, towers and domes standing along in irregular order. We could not learn that this peculiar formation had any local name; they are known in this vicinity as the "Moleen Rocks," and with this name we must be satisfied. The road curves to conform to the line of the earth now one way and now another. The scenery here is not grand and sublime, but just enough peculiar to be interesting. The towering ledges in this canon or, in the one below, are not a thousand or fifteen hundred feet high,—for accurate measurements have placed them at about 800 feet. This canon is soon passed and the valley opens out again. We soon cross Susan's Creek, and then Maggie's Creek, then Mary's Creek, and we are at

Carlin,—585 miles from San Francisco, at an elevation of 4,897 feet. It is a railroad town, the terminus of a freight division of the road and the location of the roundhouse, machine, car and repair shops of the Humboldt Division of the Central Pacific Railroad. It is the headquarters of Mr. G. W. Coddington, the Division Superintendent. The division extends from Toano to Winnemucca, and this place is about half way between them. The town has no business outside of the railroad shops and employes, and numbers about 200 people. The roundhouse has 16 stalls for engines, and the repair shop, six pits. It is in Elko County. The old emigrant road divided just before reaching Carlin, one branch going south of the river, and the range of mountains bordering the same, and the other going north of the hills on the north side of the river. These two roads came together below, near Gravelly Ford. In the vicinity of Carlin the four little creeks come in from the north. In the order in which they are crossed, they are called Susie, Maggie, Mary and Amelia. Tradition says in regard to these names, that an emigrant was crossing the plains with his family at an early day, and that in this family were four daughters in the order given, and that as the party came to these streams, they gave the name of each one of the daughters to them—a very appropriate thing to do, and their names have been perpetuated in history. Just east of Moleen Station, the tourist looking off to the left, will notice the break or gorge through the low hills, on the south side of the river. Through this gorge the South Fork of the Humboldt comes in. This stream rises in the Ruby Range of Mountains and flows in a general westerly direction, uniting with the main river at this point. We will here state that nearly all the people in the vicinity, call the range of mountains last alluded to "Ruby," and we have followed the custom; but Lieutenant Wheeler's Map speaks of it as the Humboldt Range, and according to the custom of the people along this valley, nearly every range of mountains in sight, from one side of the State to the other, is called "Humboldt Range," or "Humboldt Mountains." As to the fertility of these and other valleys in this part of the State, it all depends upon irrigation. A sage brush plain indicates good soil, but water must be obtained to raise a crop. An effort has been made to make Carlin the shipping point to the mining districts on the north, but without much success thus far. The iron horses are changed here, and with a fresh steed we pass down the valley. It is quite wide here, but will soon narrow as we enter the Twelve Mile Canon. Like the former, the road winds around the base of the bluffs and almost under the ledges, with the river sometimes almost under us. The peaks and ledges seem to have no local name, but some of them are very singular. In one place, soon after entering the canon, the ledges on the right side of the track seem to stand up on edge, and broken into very irregular, serrated lines,—the teeth of the ledge being uneven as to

SCENES IN THE HUMBOLDT DESERT.

1.—The Sink of the Humboldt. 2.—Mountain Scene near Deeth. 3.—Group of Piute Indians. 4.—Humboldt River. 5.—Great American Desert, East of Elko. 6.—Wadsworth.

length. The height of the bluffs and of the palisades below, is about the same as in the former canon—800 feet. In some places the palisades are hollowed out like caves or open arches, and the debris that has crumbled and fallen from their summits during the ages, obscures their full form and height from view.

Twelve Mile Canon, in the Palisades, was graded in six weeks by the Central Pacific Railroad Company, one cut herein containing 6,600 cubic yards. Five Mile Canon just eastward, was graded in three weeks, with a force of 5,000 to 6,000 men.

With the perpendicular walls rising on each side of us, we glide around the curves, and in the midst of these reddish lines of towering rocks, arrive at

Palisade,—576 miles from San Francisco, with an elevation of 4,841 feet. It is the initial point of the Eureka & Palisade Railroad, is a growing little place between the wall rocks of the river, and has a population of from 150 to 200 souls. It has one or two hotels or lodging-houses, stores, saloons, two large freight depots, and the machine and repair shops of the Eureka & Palisade Railroad. This road is a three feet gauge, and we shall speak of it more fully hereafter. A new station-house, ticket and telegraph office has been constructed here,—the finest on the road—to be occupied and used by both the Central Pacific and Eureka & Palisade Roads.

The town is located about half the distance down the canon, and the rocky, perpendicular walls give it a picturesque appearance. The lower half of the canon is not as wild and rugged, however, as the upper half. All freight, which is mostly base bullion, that is shipped from Eureka and other points on this branch road, has to be transferred here, and the traveler may sometimes be surprised, in passing, at the immense piles of bullion which may here be seen on the platform of the railroad companies. On a hill to the right is a wooden reservoir supplied by springs, from which the water used in town is taken. The canon above was not used for the purposes of travel before the passage of the Central Pacific Road—not even a horseman venturing through it.

Shoshone Indian Village.—Just below the town is what Fenimore Cooper would doubtless call an Indian Village, but it requires a great stretch of the imagination on the part of the practical American, or live Yankee, now-a-days, to see it. A dozen or so tents, discolored with smoke and besmeared with dirt and grease, revealing from six to ten squalid beings covered with vermin, filth and rags, is not calculated to create a pleasing impression, or awaken imaginary flights to any great extent. Between Ogden and Battle Mountain, the Indians now seen on the line of the road are mostly Shoshones. Their reservation proper, for this part of the country, is at Carlin, but very few of them are on it. For some reason, best known to themselves, they prefer to look out for themselves rather than receive the small annual amount appropriated by the government for their maintenance. They are all inveterate gamblers, and a group of squaws will sit on the ground for hours, around a blanket stretched out, and throw sticks. There are usually five of these flat sticks, from four to six inches in length, one side of which is colored slightly. Each one has a rock, a piece of coal, or some other hard substance by her side, and slightly inclined toward the blanket. She will then gather the sticks in her hand and throw them upon this rock so that they will bound on to the blanket, and the point of the game seems to be, which side of the sticks, the colored or plain, comes up in falling. It seems to be a perfect game of chance, and the one who throws so that the sticks all fall colored side up, seems to have some advantage in the game. There is said to be some improvement in their methods of living during the last fifteen years; some of them have been employed on ranches, and some of the squaws are employed in doing the plainest kinds of housework; the children and younger members of the tribe are most all becoming acquainted with the English language, and all, so far as they are able, are gradually adopting the civilized customs of dress, etc., though they invariably, thus far, paint their faces.

Leaving Palisade, the traveler will notice the railroad bridge, a short distance out, on which the narrow gauge crosses the river on its way south as it enters Pine Valley. We soon enter gorges in the canon, and on the left side of the river a high bluff rises. After passing this, and looking back about half way up the side, a column is seen jutting out in front of the bluff, and crowned with what appears like a finger. We have called it "Finger Rock." The channel of the river has been turned from its bed by a heavy embankment—a work rendered necessary to avoid a short curve, and on we go over a very crooked piece of road for nearly six miles, when we cross the river and the valley again opens. We have now passed through the Twelve Mile Canon, and soon arrive at

Cluro,—a way-station 565 miles from San Francisco, with an elevation of 4,785 feet. Trains do not stop unless signaled. The valley becomes wider, the hills more sloping and less high as they border the valley, but away to the left are the higher peaks of the Cortez Mountains. We now enter an open basin, and on the right we see the old emigrant road making up the hill from Gravelly Ford. One branch of this road, leading to the same ford, we also cross, but the old roadway, plainly visible from the cars, up the hill on the north side of the river, marks the locality of the ford itself. The river here spreads over a wide, gravelly bed, and is

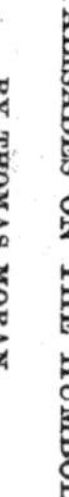

THE PALISADES ON THE HUMBOLDT.

BY THOMAS MORAN.

always shallow so that it is easily crossed. The emigrants, in the days of ox and mule trains, took advantage of this crossing to send letters, either one way or the other, by outward bound or returning trains. They would split a willow sprout by the side of the road and put their letters in it, which would be taken out by some one in the first train and carried to the nearest post-office on the route.

In 1858, it is said, that an Indian massacre took place here, in which 18 emigrants were killed; and other skirmishes with the gentle red men, were frequently in order. The old emigrant road is fairly lined with the graves of emigrants, who perished on their way to the land of gold, or in returning from the same. There are, also, many of the Shoshones and Piutes now living, who have been made cripples in these battles and skirmishes with the emigrants. They will talk about them with their acquaintances, and say "heap of white men killed there," but can seldom be induced to say how many Indians were slain in the same conflict. Indeed, parties representing each side of the contending forces have become well acquainted, and now frequently meet each other on friendly terms. There is a disposition, also, among these old plainsmen "to spin yarns," equal to any old navigator that ever lived, and one has to be extremely cautious as to what he believes. These old story-tellers are like old Jim Bridger—they will tell a lie so often and so earnestly, that they finally come to believe it themselves; and this may account for the many wonderful stories that have been palmed off on some book-makers, and by them, in turn, hashed up for the traveling public. Travelers can always hear all they choose, but it is well to be a little cautious about believing all they hear.

ENTERING HUMBOLDT CANON.

The Maiden's Grave.—There is hardly an old resident on this coast, but who has some incident to relate in reference to Gravelly Ford. It was not only an excellent crossing place, but it was also a fine camping place, where both man and beast could recruit after the weary days on the dreary plains. There were wide bottom-lands that offered excellent grazing for stock, and the small brush along the banks of the stream gave excellent shade and firewood. On a low point of land that juts out toward the river on the south side of the track, and just below this ford, is the Maiden's Grave. Tradition has it that she was one of a party of emigrants from Missouri, and that, at this ford, while they were in camp, she sickened and died. Her loving friends laid her away to rest in a grave on this point of land, in plain sight of the ford and of the valley for miles in either direction. But while her remains were crumbling into dust, and she, too, was fading from the memory of all, perhaps, but her immediate relatives, the railroad builders came along, and found the low mound, and the decayed head-board which marked her resting-place. With that admiration of, and devotion to woman, which characterizes American citizens of even humble origin, they made a new grave and surrounded it with an enclosure—a picket fence, painted white—and by the side of it erected a cross, the emblem of the Christian's faith, which bears on one side, this legend—"The Maiden's Grave"—and on the other, her name, "Lucinda Duncan." All honor to the men whose respect for the true woman led them to the performance of this praiseworthy act—an act which would have been performed by no race under the heavens, but ours; and not by them, indeed, to the remains, under similar circumstances, of a representative of the sterner sex. The location of this grave is near Beowawe, and the point is now used as a burial ground by the people living in the vicinity. Passing the point where the grave is located, an extended valley comes in from the left, south of which extends the Cortez Range of Mountains. We now arrive at

Beowawe,—556 miles from San Francisco, with an elevation of 4,695 feet. It has a hotel, a few dwellings, and is the station where the business of the Cortez Mining District is transacted. There is no regular stage line to this district, but private conveyances may be obtained. The mines are reported looking well—are mostly individual property. They are 30 miles from the station and a tri-weekly mail is carried by some parties who are interested in the matter. A reduction mill has been erected there, which is producing bullion regularly. There is a beautiful signification attached to the name of this station, which will be more fully realized after the station is passed, than before. It means "gate," or "the gate," and as you look back from below, the conformation of the hills on either side of the valley is such, that the station seems to stand in an open gateway, up the Humboldt Valley to the canon beyond. The valley is occasionally dotted with farm-houses, or ranches, and besides stock raising, which is one of the principal features of this part of the country, there is considerable done in the way of agriculture, barley being the chief crop—yielding immensely when the land is properly irrigated and the crops taken care of. At Beowawe an immense stretch of valley land can be seen away to the right, with a range of mountains, which seems to be an extension of the Reese River Range, north of the Humboldt, west of it. As the river bends northward to meet these valleys, it receives the waters of Boulder and Rock Creeks, which come in from the north and northeast. These creeks open up a vast country, which is well occupied by ranches and stockmen. Leaving Beowawe, we cross a large valley and sage brush plain—the valley coming in from the south. A few miles out, we notice, if the weather is at all cool, steam rising from the side of the mountain, while colored streaks, caused by the sediment of the springs, can clearly be seen from the passing train. This steam comes from the Hot Springs on the mountain side, and the sediment marks their locality. The water in some of these springs is boiling hot, and partakes strongly of sulphur. We could not learn that any analysis had been made, nor could any one inform us of the exact temperature. There is a vast field for geological exploration in this State, and the general government should enter upon the work at once. The springs also are impregnated with iron, but no one knows the quantity, nor just in what proportion these mineral waters are mixed. To the inhabitants in this immediate vicinity, of course, they have ceased to be a wonder; but to the majority of travelers, they will ever be clothed with interest. A creek of alkali water comes down from the springs and we cross it on the flat alluded to, and the wide valley off to the right is still better seen as we approach and pass

Shoshone,—546 miles from San Francisco; elevation, 4,636 feet. It is simply a side track station. Rock Creek, before spoken of, comes into the Humboldt nearly opposite this place, and the broad valley continues, on the right of the road. The station is called Shoshone Point by the people in the valley, because a mountain, or high ridge, pushes out into the valley, like a promontory. This is one of the landmarks on the dividing line between the Shoshone and Piute tribes of Indians; but the line we consider purely imaginary, from the fact that Indians, as a general thing, go where they please in this country, lines or no lines. The wide basin spoken of, continues below and off to the right of this station, and, as we pass on, a long line of board fence will be noticed stretching, from a point high up on the mountain, across the track and valley toward the Humboldt River, on the right. This is the eastern line of Dunphy & Hildreth's stock ranche. In seven miles we shall pass the western line, or fence. We have before spoken of Iliff, as the cattle king of the plains, and, while this is true east of the Black Hills of Wyoming, he will have to yield the crown to some of the cattle kings of the Pacific Coast. This firm has 20 miles of fencing in these two lines: They have over 20 thousand acres fenced in. Their fences, made of redwood posts and Oregon pine boards, cost them a little over $900 per mile. They have, altogether, about 40,000 head of cattle, mainly in two herds—one here and the other north, on the Snake River. They have purchased of the State, government and Central Pacific Railroad and now own about 30,000 acres of land. Most of their cattle are shipped to, and find a market in San Francisco.

The immense range fenced in at this point is occupied by a select herd of graded stock, and some of the best blooded animals in the country are annually purchased to improve the grades.

The system they have adopted for grading up their herds, is such that in a very few years they will have the largest herd of high graded stock in the country. They also cut large quantities of hay on the meadow lands near the banks of the Humboldt, which they feed to all their weak cattle, and to those which they intend for late winter, or early spring market. The Humboldt Valley and its tributaries constitute the best part of the State for stock ranges. The snow seldom falls very deep; does not stay long, and the grass makes its appearance early in the spring. The purchase of large tracts of land by these foresighted cattlemen, will give them a monopoly of the business in the future.

Argenta,—535 miles from San Francisco; elevation, 4,548 feet. It is simply a side track station, where considerable hay is shipped. This station is immediately surrounded by alkali flats, near the base of the Reese River Mountains. The road continues for a few miles along the base of these mountains, when, suddenly, a broad valley opens out, on the left. It is the valley of Reese River. We turn to the right, cross the valley and the river—all there is left of it—and arrive at

Battle Mountain,—524 miles from San Francisco, with an elevation of 4,511 feet. It is located at the junction of the Reese River and Humboldt Valleys. The mountain which gives it its name is about three miles south of the station, where there are magnificent springs from which water is conducted to the town, supplying the railroad and inhabitants with water. Battle Mountain is the regular dinner station on the line of the road, and the passenger will dine at a very cosy and attractive place. In the midst of a surrounding desert he will observe the flowing fountain and patches of green grass which will here greet his eyes, together with the evident taste and care which is manifested about everything connected with the house. Travelers will occasionally have a great deal of fun in listening to the talk of the Chinese waiters.

The town is mostly on one street south of the railroad. It has several quite extensive stores, a public hall, an excellent school-house, two large freight depots, a first-class hotel. It has an extensive and rapidly increasing trade with the surrounding country, and newly developed mining districts in its neighborhood. It is the business center of a large number of stockmen, and the trading point for a large number of mining districts—districts considerably scattered over quite a large part of the State. The town is located in Lander County, but is not the county-seat. Austin, 90 miles away, claims that honor.

Daily stages, carrying the mail and express, leave here for Austin, Belmont and other places south, immediately on the arrival of the trains from the west. The distance to Austin, 90 miles, is made by about 6 o'clock on the morning of the day after departure, and, of course, takes in an all night stage ride. Belmont, about 90 miles from Austin, is reached in the evening of the day after departure.

The following mining districts, south of the railroad, are more or less tributary to Battle Mountain: commencing on the east side of the Reese River Range, first is the Lewis Mining District, 16 miles distant from Battle Mountain. It is located on the northern extremity of the range. At the southern extremity of this range is the Austin District. The mountain range between these two districts, is said to contain mines, but it has not been thoroughly prospected. Austin, the head-quarters of the Austin District, is a very nice town with a population of about 3,000 souls. It is said to possess a good deal of public spirit, and is active and enterprising. It has a fine court-house, three churches, a large brick public school building, some elegant residences, and other appearances of thrift. The Reese River Valley is about 160 miles long, traversed its entire length by the river of the same name, though it cannot be called much of a river where the railroad crosses it, near Battle Mountain. The upper portion of the valley, about 50 miles in length, is a very fine agricultural district, is quite well settled, and is tributary to Austin. The valley is also settled in places where mountain streams come into it, between Battle Mountain and Austin. The Manhattan Company, composed of New York capitalists, own and operate nearly all the mines in the Austin District. They are reported to possess some excellent mines with milling ore, some of which is high grade. There are other mining districts around Austin, and tributary to it—such as the Jefferson, Ione, Belmont, etc., which are favorably spoken of.

On the west side of the Reese River Valley, and immediately south of Battle Mountain, are the following districts: Battle Mountain District, 7 miles distant; Galena District, 16 miles; Copper Canon, 18 miles, and Jersey, 55 miles. The copper mines are owned by an English company—which is now putting in concentrating machinery—and are said to be rich. The Jersey District produces smelting ore, and has one or two furnaces already erected which are turning out bullion.

North of Battle Mountain are the Cornucopia and Tuscarora Districts which are said to do some business from this place, and are regarded as tributary to it. Several stations on the line of the road are competing for the trade of these mining districts, and all claim it, and also claim to be the nearest railroad point, with the best wagon roads, etc.

Battle Mountain—not north of the Humboldt River, but about three miles south of the station—is reported to have been the scene of a conflict between a party of emigrants camped near the springs heretofore spoken of, and a band of redskins who had an innate hankering after the stock of the said party of emigrants. The losses of this battle are said to have been quite severe on both sides, considering the numbers engaged. It is generally conceded, however, that the redskins got the worst of it, though they say "A heap white men killed there."

The opening, or valley directly opposite and north of Battle Mountain, is without water in its lower portion, and is a desert of sand and sage brush. The range of mountains at whose base the town is situated, and south of it, on the west side of Reese River Valley, is sometimes called the Battle Mountain Range, and sometimes the Fish Creek Range, from a creek that rises in it about 25 miles south of Battle Mountain, and runs into Reese River Valley.

About 25 miles south of Battle Mountain, are some very fine hot springs. There are nearly 60 of them, covering about half a section of land. The largest one is about 60 feet long by 30 feet wide, and at times rises and falls from three to five feet. These springs are on the stage road to Austin, and are something of a wonder to travelers in that direction.

How Ore is Reduced.—We visited the reduction works of the Lewis District, and to those who are not familiar with the way in which ores are handled, the following account may be of some interest. The ore from the mine in this district is neither free milling nor smelting ore. It has to be dried before it can be milled, and then roasted before it can be separated and amalgamated. The following is our account of the process in taking the silver from the ore: The ore, as it comes from the mine, is first run through a crusher—a machine which has two heavy pieces of iron coming together like the human jaws in chewing. It is then passed either onto drying pans, heated by a fire from some furnace, or into a revolving dryer where all the moisture is extracted. From this dryer it passes through a large iron tube or pipe into the milling hoppers below. These hoppers, holding the crushed and dried ore, are similar to those seen in old fashioned gristmills, and from them the ore runs on to the stamp mill. The stamp mill is a series of upright iron shafts with a heavy iron or steel hammer on the lower end of each shaft. By machinery, these shafts are lifted up very rapidly and dropped—a process repeated by each one from sixty to ninety times per minute. As they fall, they stamp or crush the ore to powder. In fact it leaves this mill pulverized like dust, and is conveyed by a horizontal screw to an adjoining room, where it is taken by elevators, just like those used in flouring mills to a bin or tank above. In the room where this elevator and bin are, is the cylindrical roaster and furnace. From the tank the pulverized ore is taken as required, through an iron pipe into a large horizontal revolving roaster. About one and one-half tons of ore dust are required to charge the roaster, to which is added from eight to ten per cent. of salt. The heat and fire from the furnace pass through this roaster as it slowly turns around, the ore now mixed with salt, falling of course, from side to side at each revolution, across and through the flames. It is kept in this place about seven hours, or until it is supposed to be thoroughly chloridized. It is a sulphuret ore as it comes from the mine, but becomes a chloride ore by passing through this process. It comes out of the roaster at a white heat, is then wet down and cooled, and taken to an amalgamating pan which is agitated with a muller, which revolves in the pan from 60 to 70 times per minute—in other words, it is a stirring apparatus. One and a half tons of ore are put into these pans, to which is added about 350 lbs. of quicksilver. Water is then turned in and the mixture stirred a little, to the consistency of thick paste. Then hot steam is let in upon the mass, and while in process of agitation it is heated to a boiling heat. The pulp, as it is now called, is kept in this pan and constantly agitated or stirred for about seven hours. A plug is then drawn from the bottom of the tank or pan, and the pulp passes into "a settler" or "separator" where it is again agitated in water—the amalgam, meanwhile, settling to the bottom of the "settler," the quicksilver—with the silver—being drawn into a little receiver, from which it is dipped into sacks and strained. The quicksilver being thus nearly all taken out, the balance is called dry amalgam, and this is taken to an iron retort, cylindrical in shape, about five feet long and 12 inches in diameter. This cylinder is charged with about 900 lbs. of this dry amalgam, then thoroughly sealed, after which it is heated from a furnace underneath. The quicksilver remaining in the amalgam, volatilizes under the action of heat, and passes through an iron tube surrounded by cold water, where it is condensed and saved. The quicksilver being expelled by the action of the heat, leaves the crude bullion (silver in this case) in the cylinder. The dry amalgam remains in the retort some six or seven hours,—requiring two or three hours additional to cool. The base bullion is then taken out, cut into small pieces and placed in a black lead crucible, and melted over a charcoal fire. While in this crucible the dross of course rises to the surface of the molten metal and is skimmed off. In the crucible it is thoroughly stirred with a long iron spoon, and a sample poured into cold water for assaying purposes. This is done just before the hot metal is poured into the molds and becomes bars. The assay determines its fineness and value, which is stamped upon it, and it is then shipped and sold. It goes into the mill ore from the mine, and comes out silver in bars.

The Great Plains and Desert.

BY JOAQUIN MILLER.

Go ye and look upon that land,
That far, vast land that few behold,
And none beholding, understand;
That old, old land, which men call new,
That land as old as time is old:

Go journey with the seasons through
Its wastes, and learn how limitless,
How shoreless lie the distances,
Before you come to question this,
Or dare to dream what grandeur is.

The solemn silence of that plain,
Where unmanned tempests ride and reign,
It awes and it possesses you,
'Tis, oh, so eloquent.

The blue
And bended skies seem built for it,
With rounded roof all fashioned fit,
And frescoed clouds, quaint-wrought and true:
While all else seems so far, so vain,
An idle tale but illy told,
Before this land so lone and old.

Lo! here you learn how more than fit,
And dignified is silence, when
You hear the petty jeers of men,
Who point, and show their pointless wit.
The vastness of that voiceless plain,
Its awful solitudes remain,
Thenceforth for aye a part of you,
And you are of the favored few,
For you have learned your littleness.

Some silent red men cross your track;
Some sun-tann'd trappers come and go;
Some rolling seas of buffalo
Break thunder-like and far away,
Against the foot hills, breaking back,
Like breakers of some troubled bay;
But not a voice the long, lone day.

Some white tail'd antelope flow by,
So airy-like; some foxes shy,
And shadow-like shoot to and fro,
Like weaver's shuttles as you pass—;
And now and then from out the grass,
You hear some lone bird chick, and call,
A sharp keen call for her lost brood.
That only make the solitude,
That mantles like some sombre pall,
Seem deeper still, and that is all.

A wide domain of mysteries,
And signs that men misunderstand!
A land of space and dreams: a land
Of sea, salt lakes and dried up seas!
A land of caves and caravans,
And lonely wells and pools.

A land
That hath its purposes and plans,
That seem so like dead Palestine,
Save that its wastes have no confine,
Till pushed against the levell'd skies.

How the Piutes Bury their Dead.—There seems to be a very irregular custom in practice among this tribe of Indians, in reference to the disposition they make of their dead. When one of their number is sick, the services of a Medicine Man, as he is called, are made available, and all his arts and skill are exhausted to effect a recovery if possible. The Medicine Man comes, and goes through a system of contortions, which would rack the frame of a white person till it was unjointed, makes passes with the hands over the body of the sick one, and keeps up a continual howl that must grate very harshly upon the nerves of a sensitive person. Amidst these motions and groans and passes, the victim to disease lingers, until death puts an end to his sufferings. When the final dissolution has occurred, the body hardly has time to become cold, before it is wrapped in a blanket, or old cloths, and preparations are made for the burial. This is done in secret, and, strange as it may appear, though many have died since the advent of the whites into this country, not a single person, so far as we could learn, knows of the burial place of a Piute Indian. The Indians will scatter in small parties, some of whom, it is supposed, will dig a grave, or perhaps several of them; and though their actions may be closely watched, they somehow manage to spirit away the body and conceal it in its final resting-place so completely, that its location is unknown. Whether the immediate relatives of the deceased are made acquainted with the burial place, we could not learn, but judge not, from the fact that all traces of the grave are obliterated from human view. This custom of concealing their dead, so very strange to us, is said to be universal among this tribe. Another singular custom among them, is to remove the tent, or wick-ee-up, at once, as soon as the body is taken away. They claim that an evil spirit has cursed the spot, and that it would be dangerous for them to remain in the "wick-ee" longer, or on the ground where it stood. They hasten into this work as if actuated by the greatest fear, and, ever afterwards, seem to regard it with suspicious awe.

How the Piutes Catch Fish.—Nearly all the Indians seen on the line of the road between Battle Mountain and Reno, are Piutes. They are great rabbit-hunters, and very successful in fishing. They make hooks from rabbit bones and greasewood, which are certainly superior to the most improved article made by the whites. This hook is in the shape of what might be called the letter "V" condensed; that is, the prongs do not spread very far. A line, made of the sinews of animals, or the bark of a species of wild hemp, is attached to this hook at the angle, and baited with a snail or fresh water bloodsucker. Several of these hooks are tied to a heavier line, or a piece of light rope, one above the other, so far that they will not become tangled or snarled. A stone is then tied to the end of the heavy line, and it is cast into the stream. The fish take the bait readily, but Mr. Indian does not "pull up" when he feels one fish on the line. He waits until the indications are that several fish are there—one on each hook—and then he pulls out the heavy line, with fish and all. It seems that the hooks are so made that they can be swallowed easily enough with the bait, but as soon as the fish begins to struggle, the string acts on both prongs of the hook, pulling it straight, the ends of the letter "V" hook, of course, piercing its throat. It can neither swallow it, nor cast it forth from its mouth. The more it pulls and struggles, the more straightened the hook becomes. Besides the superiority of this hook, one fish being caught, others are naturally drawn around it, and seize the tempting bait upon the fatal hook. In this way an Indian will catch a dozen or so fish, while a white man, with his fancy rod and "flies" and "spoons," and other inventions to lure the finny tribes and tempt them to take a bait, will catch not one.

Leaving Battle Mountain we have a straight track for about 20 miles, across a sage brush plain, the river and a narrow strip of bottom-lands, on our right.

Piute,—519 miles from San Francisco, with no elevation given, and

Coin,—511 miles from San Francisco, are simply side track stations where trains meet and pass, but of no importance to the traveler. There was no Indian battle fought near Piute, nor does the Reese River sink into the valley here. What battle there was, was fought, as before stated, about three miles south of Battle Mountain Station, and what the sands in the valley do not absorb of the waters of Reese River, may be seen—a little alkali stream—flowing across the railroad track, east of Battle Mountain, to effect a junction with the Humboldt River.

Stone House,—504 miles from San Francisco, with an elevation of 4,422 feet. This was not an old trading post, but a station in former times of the Overland Stage Company, and the house, built of stone near some very fine springs, was one of the eating-houses on their line, where travelers could relish square meals of bacon and coffee with safety. There is no particular ravine near the old ruins which the traveler would notice as an impregnable fortress. Quite a number of skirmishes are reported to have taken place near this station, however, and the graves yet distinguished in its vicinity tell of the number who were killed near this place, or died here on their journey to the golden shores of the Pacific. Stone House Mountain, as it is now called, rears its head just back of the crumbling ruins, and from its summit a most extensive and beautiful view of the neighboring valleys and surrounding country can be obtained. On the western slope of this mountain, and about seven miles from the station, are some hot springs similar to others found in the Great Basin. But these springs are no more peculiar than those found at Golconda, a few miles below, nor different from those found near Beowawe, which have already been mentioned. A gentleman who camped four days near them, while in pursuit of a marauding party of Indians, informs us that there are four springs at the place alluded to, that they vary in temperature, and that only one is boiling hot, from which steam simply rises in the cool mornings of the season. The waters of this particular spring are very fine for drinking, when cooled. These springs are not in sight from the railroad, nor can the steam therefrom be seen. About the only way one can become scalded is to tumble into it. In such a case, something more than "simple cerate and the prayers of friends" will be required. During the passage of the Humboldt Valley we cross several dry valleys, between ranges of mountains, that seem to be cut in twain by the river. These valleys are mostly covered with sand and sage brush; occasionally have streams flowing down from the mountains which soon sink in the sands. There is a wide valley of this description north of the track as we approach

Iron Point,—491 miles from San Francisco; elevation, 4,375 feet. This station is near the point of a low ridge, with barren sides and rocky summit; the rocks a little reddish, indicating the proximity of iron. It is a shipping point for cattle, and has extensive stock-yards, though there are no other accommodations near by. This ridge was formerly considered the boundary line between the Shoshones and Piutes, and a trespass by either party has been the cause of many an Indian war. The wasting away of these tribes, however, renders the line simply imaginary, and the rights of either party to exclusive privileges on either side are no longer regarded. The valley now narrows, and we pass through a sort of a canon, with high bluffs on both sides of the road. We wind round numerous curves, and after the canon is passed, we shall see the remains of an old irrigating ditch that was started here by a French company to take water from the Humboldt and carry it down the valley quite a distance for irrigating and mill purposes. A great amount of labor and money was expended upon this enterprise, but it was finally abandoned. We believe a small outlay, comparatively, would now make it a success. The ditch began at an adobe house, just as we are through a short canon and as the valley again begins to widen. This pass was called Emigrant Canon in the days of wagon travel.

Golconda,—478 miles from San Francisco, with an elevation of 4,385 feet. The little town here has one or two stores, a hotel, several adobe houses and the usual railroad conveniences. Golconda is favorably located, as regards two or three important mining districts, and will eventually do considerable business with them. It is also the location of some eight or ten hot mineral springs, which are passed on the right side of the track, just after leaving town. These springs vary in temperature from cool, or tepid water, to that which is boiling hot. The swimming bath —an excavation in the ground—is supplied with tepid water, and is said to be very exhilarating. The Boiling Spring — exact temperature and analysis unknown—is utilized by the farmers in the valley in scalding their swine. The water is said to be hot enough to boil an egg in one minute. Here clouds of steam can be seen when the weather is cold, rising from the hot water and warm soil surrounding.

One of the springs near this station is also a curiosity, and should be visited by tourists. It is conical in shape, like an inverted tea-cup, four or five feet high, with a basin about three feet in diameter on the top. Formerly, the water came in at the bottom of this basin and bubbled over the rim; but a few years since, it was tapped from below, and the water now flows out at the side, leaving the basin and cone as it was formed, by the sedimentary incrustations and deposit. The water flowing from the hot spring is used for irrigating purposes, and the owners of the spring have a monopoly of early vegetable "garden truck," raising early radishes, lettuce, onions, etc., before their season, by the warmth produced from the hot water. It is expected that the springs will be improved this year by the erection of a suitable bathing-house and hotel for the accommodation of guests.

Gold Run Mining District, south of Golconda, is tributary to the place. The mines are reported rich in large bodies of ore, but not of a very high grade. They are, however, easily accessible, and not more than 10 or 15 miles from the railroad, with good wagon roads the entire distance. The ore in this district is both smelting and milling—but requires roasting if it is to be milled. Three prospects are now being worked. About three miles from town is a small four-stamp mill, which is running on ore from this district.

Paradise District of gold and silver mines, is about 18 miles north of Golconda. The ore is said to be a rich milling variety, but the prospects are not yet sufficiently developed to determine the true value of the district.

Tule,—530 miles from San Francisco, with an elevation of 4,313 feet. It is simply a side track of no importance to travelers, and trains seldom stop. After leaving Golconda, we look toward the north and see the opening of Eden Valley. East of this valley, and to our right, is the Soldier's Spring Range, a broken range of mountains. Eden Valley extends north to the Little

Humboldt River. In fact, this river flows through the upper portion of the valley, and rises in the range just named, and flows in a south-westerly direction through Paradise Valley and unites with the Humboldt, nearly opposite, north of Tule. Paradise Valley is a fine agricultural basin, thickly settled, about 30 miles north. Paradise Valley is the name of the post-office—a semi-weekly line of mail stages connecting it with Winnemucca, the county-seat of Humboldt County. This valley is shaped like a horseshoe, and produces superior crops of barley, wheat, rye and all kinds of vegetables. It seems to have a depression in the center, and, while it is nearly all cultivated, the best crops are raised on the slopes toward the mountains. The soil is a black, gravelly loam, and sage brush grows on the slopes to enormous size. Experiments in fruit culture have been tried, but, thus far, with indifferent success. Paradise Valley has a flouring-mill, store and dwellings, and gives every indication of thrift. Its name indicates the high esteem in which it is held by the settlers. It is nearly surrounded by mountains, and the numerous streams flowing down from them, afford ample water for irrigation. Most of these streams sink in the ground before they reach the Little Humboldt. Five miles beyond Tule, we reach

Winnemucca,—463 miles from San Francisco; elevation, 4,332 feet. It is named in honor of the chief of the Piute tribe of Indians. The name itself means "chief," and is given to any member of the tribe who holds that office. The Piutes are divided into several bands, each under a chief they call "Captan," thought here to be derived from the Spanish, and to mean the same as our English word, "captain." Winnemucca is now about 70 years old, and lives on the Malheur Reservation, in Oregon—a reservation occupied by the Piutes and Bannocks. He is very much respected—almost worshiped by his dusky followers.

The town is the county-seat of Humboldt County, and has a population of about 1,200 people, among whom are some Indians, and quite a number of Chinamen. It is the western terminus of the Humboldt Division of the Central Pacific, has a large roundhouse, two large freight depots and the usual offices, etc., for the accommodation of the railroad business. An elegant brick court-house has been erected, together with several stores, hotels, shops, a large flouring-mill, a foundry, a ten-stamp quartz mill, with a capacity for crushing ten tons of ore every 24 hours, and other public improvements completed, or in contemplation. The town is divided into two parts—upper and lower; the latter being built on the bottom land near the river, and the upper, on a huge sand-bank, adjoining the railroad. Most of the buildings are frame, though a few are built of brick, or adobe, which, in this western country, are called "dobe," for short.

There is a school-house with accommodations for about 150 pupils—two apartments, and no churches. It is also quite a shipping point for cattle and wool. About 9,000 head of cattle were shipped to the San Francisco market from this place, in the months of January and February of the present year. In the spring of 1875, over 500,000 lbs. of wool were shipped to New York and Boston markets. It is also the shipping point to Camp McDermott, near the northern line of the State; to Silver City and Boise City, Idaho; and to Baker and Grant

WINNEMUCCA, THE NAPOLEON OF THE PIUTES.

Counties, in south-eastern Oregon. The stage lines are as follows: Daily stage and mail line to Silver City and Boise City, Idaho,—distance to Silver City, 210 miles, extension to Boise, 65 miles farther. The same line supplies Camp McDermott, 85 miles distant. Semi-weekly line, Mondays and Fridays, to Paradise Valley, 45 miles. Weekly line—soon to be made daily and to carry the mail to Jersey, 65 miles, (south) leaving at present every Wednesday. There is also an immense freighting business done with the mining districts in the vicinity, and with Idaho Territory. Regular freight lines are on the road between this place and Silver City.

The following mining districts are tributary

to Winnemucca and located in Humboldt County: beginning north of the railroad—there are placer mines west of Paradise Valley and settlement; at Willow Creek about 60 miles distant from Winnemucca. Bartlett Creek Mines, gold and silver, 100 miles distant. Varyville is the town of this camp. It has about a hundred inhabitants, and is north-west of this city. Two quartz mills are in operation there, controlled by a Chicago company. Pueblo District—copper mines, about 100 miles distant. Winnemucca District—silver, two miles west of town, mines owned and operated by the Humboldt Mining Company, which has a ten-stamp quartz mill in town, supplied in part with ore from their mine, and run on custom ore at times. The ores in this vicinity have to be roasted, and this mill has a drop furnace—the ore dropping through the flaming fire instead of being turned in a revolving heated cylinder.

Central District in Eugene Mountain, south-west of town, produces silver ore and has a quartz mill.

South of the railroad there is Jersey District and town, 65 miles distant. The business of this mining camp is divided between Battle Mountain and this place—both claiming it. The town has about 200 people. The ore is argentiferous galena, rather above the average grade, and is found in large quantities. A smelting furnace has been erected and a considerable amount of base bullion has been turned out. The smelter has a capacity of 25 tons per day. The shaft in the mine has been sunk to a depth of 130 feet, and levels run about 300 feet. It is claimed to be a very promising mining district.

Antimony District is 80 miles due south of Winnemucca. Slabs of that mineral, weighing three tons, and averaging 70 per cent. pure antimony, can be obtained in this district. Near it is the Humboldt Salt Marsh, where salt, 95 per cent. pure, can be shoveled up by the wagon-load. This salt deposit is very extensive, and the supply seems to be exhaustless. Underneath the surface deposit, rock salt, or salt in large cakes or slabs, is taken out, in the driest part of the season, by the ton.

In the valley leading to the above-named district are some very fine hot springs, but they are so common here as to be no curiosity. Twelve miles out, in the same valley, is a rich agricultural district, thickly settled, where not only grain and vegetables have been successfully cultivated, but the experiments in fruit culture have also proved successful. At the county fair, held in this city during the fall of 1875, fine specimens of apples, peaches, pears and plums were exhibited which were raised in this valley.

Bolivia District, silver ore, 70 miles away. Ore from this district is shipped to various points; some to the mill here that is claimed to average $500 per ton. Comminsville Camp, in Sierra District, produces gold and silver ore. A ten-stamp mill is erected there.

As the tourist walks the platform at this place, looking across the river to the right, he will see Winnemucca Mountain, but a short distance away, overlooking the town. To the left, he will observe the peaks of the Franklin or Sonoma Range. To the east, and somewhat distant, are the ragged summits of the Soldier's Spring Range, while a little to the south-west, but apparently in front, Eugene Mountain lifts itself up as a landmark to guide the traveler on his way. This mountain will be passed on our left as we continue the journey.

Winnemucca has two newspapers, *The Daily Humboldt Register* and the *Daily Silver State*. Both are energetic little sheets, and fitly illustrate the enterprise of these western towns. Across the river, over a wooden bridge, is located the cemetery, in which the remains of the dead are enclosed. It is on an elevated, sandy bench, the second terrace or step from the river level. By it winds the stage road to Idaho and the north. The Piutes have their tents scattered on all sides of the town, to which the euphonious name of "Wick-ee-ups" is given. They serve to remind one of the departing glory—if they ever had any—of the Indian race. In this tribe, to their honor be it said, licentiousness among their women is very rare, and virtue is held in high esteem. But very few half-breed Indians can be found, or are they known in the State. This tribe, with the Bannocks, were especially hostile to the whites in an early day, and fought for many years with desperation and cruelty to prevent the settlement and development of this country. Their courage and deadly enmity has been displayed on many a hard-fought field, and if there are families in the East, or on the Pacific Coast, who still mourn the loss of missing ones, who were last heard of as crossing the plains, some Indian warrior, yet living, might be able to explain the mystery which has enveloped their final doom. For a number of years, with ceaseless vigilance, they hung around the trains of emigrants, eager to dispatch a stray victim, or upon the borders of settlements, ready to strike down the hardy pioneer at the first favorable opportunity. At present, overpowered by numbers, they live upon the bounty of their former enemies, and are slowly, but surely learning, by example, the ways of civilization. As a class, however, they are still indolent, dirty and covered with vermin. But they begin to learn the worth of money, and know already that it has a purchasing power which will supply their scanty wardrobe, and satisfy their longing appetites.

The mines on the top of Winnemucca Mountain are plainly seen, and the road that leads to them, from the cars, and the tourist from this will be able to understand something of the difficulties attending the process of getting out ore.

As we pass westward, a grand view of a distant range is obtained between Winnemucca and Black Butte. The last named mountain is an isolated peak, and stands out like a sentinel on guard. As we approach the higher peaks of the East or Humboldt Range, we pass

Rose Creek,—453 miles from San Francisco, with an elevation of 4,322 feet. It is an unimportant station, with side track, etc. You will have to look sharp to see the creek, or the roses, and, by way of variety, you will discover plenty of sage brush. It is a staple article, in this country. The river still winds its way along our right, and there is an occasional ranche on the mountain slope, where the water from some spring, or little creek, can be obtained for irrigation.

Raspberry,—443 miles from San Francisco; elevation 4,327 feet. If roses were few and far between, at the last station, raspberries are less frequent here. But these names are tantalizing and suggestive in the places they are applied to. Having turned the point of East Range, we bear off to the left. Eugene Mountain is now on our right, across the Humboldt River.

Mill City,—435 miles from San Francisco, with an elevation of 4,225 feet. This was once a town with great prospects. It was to be the terminus of the irrigating ditch, which we have seen beyond Winnemucca and Golconda, and this ditch, by a small expenditure of money, could now be made available, as far as Winnemucca. The Humboldt Mining Company, owning the stamp mill at that place, already alluded to, also own this ditch. The French capitalists, who put their money into the enterprise, long since abandoned it. Mill City, in their imagination, was to be the seat of empire—a mighty city of the plains, of influence and power. The banks of the canal they partially dug, were to be lined with factories and mills. The mineral bearing ore of the State was to be brought to these mills, for reduction. Their ideas were grand, and could have been made successful, under other circumstances; but they were in advance of the times—ahead of the age in which they lived. In the mutations of time, the town has become a great shipping-point for cattle—100 cars being shipped last year—a number which is greatly exceeded in some years. It has a steam foundry in operation,—mostly employed in the manufacture and repair of mining machinery,—and is the railroad point where the business of several mining districts is done. Ore from Dun Glen, Unionville and Star City, comes here for shipment, and, once per week, bullion comes over from Unionville. This last place was formerly more lively than at present. It is a town of about 300 people—has four quartz mills in operation, and is connected with Mill City by a daily stage line, which passes by Star City—distance to Unionville, 20 miles; to Star City, 10 miles; to Dun Glen, 8 miles. The general course of the railroad being east and west, these places are all south of it. The mining districts, including the towns named, which are tributary to this place, are Unionville, Star and Indian Districts—all tributary to Mill City. Mill City has a neat little hotel, a livery stable and several dwellings. It may possibly be the junction of a railroad to Oregon—surveys of which have been, and are now being made.

R. R. STATION, HUMBOLDT, NEVADA.

Leaving Mill City, we pass rapidly by an opening or gap in the mountains on our left, while a broad extent of valley opens out on our right, as Eugene Mountain sinks into the plain. The river recedes from our view, and winds along across an alkali flat some six or seven miles away. Through this opening on our right, the proposed branch railroad to Oregon will pass.—

Surveys have already been made, and it is supposed the men in the Central Pacific Company will build it, and the junction with this road will be either here or near here. Through this gap travelers in the old emigrant times, turned off to go by the Honey Lake Route to Northern California and Southern Oregon. A natural road with easy grades is claimed for this route. In coming down this valley from Mill City, we pass a high mountain on our left,—said to be the highest peak in Nevada—8,000 feet high. It is called Star peak. The elevation given is the common rumor in the vicinity. It is certainly a high mountain, and its lofty towers are nearly always covered with snow. Opposite this mountain is

Humboldt,—423 miles from San Francisco, with an elevation of 4,236 feet above the sea,—nearly the same as the Great Salt Lake. We have been coming down hill all the way from Wells, and yet we are no lower than when we left Ogden. We have now arrived at

An Oasis in the Desert.

The traveler from the East, will be especially delighted with this spot. It will remind him of things human, of living in a land of cultivation again. The first growing trees since leaving Ogden will be seen here, with green grass, shady bowers and flowing fountains. Humboldt House is a regular breakfast and supper station, at which all passenger trains stop for meals. The proprietors have been here quite a number of years, and seem to delight in making their house, and surroundings beautiful and attractive to the traveling public. A fountain surrounded with an iron fence, springs up in front of the house, while gold-fish swim around in the basin below. East of the house, trees, locusts and poplars are growing finely, while the ground is covered with a thick matting of blue-grass. At first this lot was sown to alfalfa, which grew very rank and strong. Blue-grass seed was afterwards sown, and now it has rooted everything else out and grows luxuriantly. A field south of the road toward the mountain, has produced 18 tons of alfalfa at one cutting, and has been cut from five to seven times a year. In the garden north of the house, toward the valley, all kinds of vegetables grow luxuriantly. The average yield of potatoes is 300 bushels to the acre, of the very best quality. We were, however, particularly interested in the experiments made in fruit growing. Here in the midst, almost, of the Great Nevada Desert, with barrenness and desolation spread out on every hand—with a high rocky mountain on one side, and a huge alkali flat on the other, nestled under the towering cliffs as though it would claim shelter and protection, is this Oasis in the desert,—this reminder of more genial climes and a more kindly soil—this relief from the wearisome, dreary views, which have everywhere met our gaze, over the largest part of the journey. The experiments so successful here prove, beyond a doubt, that the desert can be reclaimed and "made to bud and blossom as the rose." Grit, labor and above all, water, will do it. Here is an orchard of apple trees five years old, bearing not only fruit as beautiful to the eye as that raised in California, but superior in flavor—in fact retaining the flavor of eastern apples. These apple trees of all varieties are prolific bearers, and the same is true of the peaches, pears, plums and cherries. In the orchard and opposite the water tank, is a fish-pond some 25 or 30 feet in diameter. In it are trout, great speckled fellows, very thick and very shy. Rocky coves have been built for them in the bottom and center of the basin, and here they hide—seeking shade from the rays of the hot summer's sun, and also from those of the silvery moon. The experiments first made with these fish were costly, but have at last proved successful. This place and its surroundings cause the traveler not only to rejoice over the scene which here greets his gaze, but serves to remind him of home—of "God's country" either in the far East or, at this point, in the nearer West.

In the fish-pond mentioned, there are a couple of wild geese, and a Mandarin duck said to be from Japan. It is a beautiful little creature with tufts of feathers on each side of its head, and finely colored plumage. The proprietors of the Humboldt House, seem to strive to offer attractions to their guests in both their indoor accommodations, and outside arrangements.

The station has shipped a large number of cattle, and is the shipping point for the sulphur or brimstone, that is manufactured some thirty miles north-west of the place. The old emigrant road spoken of as leading to Northern California and Southern Oregon, winds around the base of Eugene Mountain and near a low butte, resembling a haystack, which can be seen in the distance across the alkali flats. This road was laid out by General F. W. Lander, who was killed in the war of 1861, and is said to be one of the best wagon routes to the regions named. The Humboldt House is the place of resort for tourists who desire to visit the sulphur mines, Star Peak, or the mining districts in the Humboldt Range, Eugene Mountain, and the Antelope Range. The latter is a low range on our right, beginning as we leave this station. In front and south-east of the Humboldt House, is the Humboldt Mining District, four to six miles distant. Humboldt Canon opens in the mountain side, in which was formerly located Humboldt City. Mines were first discovered in the rocky gorges of this range in 1861, and there was a great rush here from all parts of the country. The "City" sprang up as if by magic, and at one time contained about 500 people. Several substantial buildings were erected, a few of which still remain. The mines were diligently prospected, but not rewarded with immediate success, the expenses of living and building being very great, together with the determined hostility of the Indians, the people left it as suddenly as they came. The district remained idle until 1874–5, when work was again begun by a few individuals, and the mines are now being re-opened with rich developments and every prospect of success. The ore is gold, silver and argentiferous galena.

Antelope District is 16 miles away, in a westerly direction; Geneva District is 21 miles distant, in a north-westerly direction; both of these are but little developed.

TWO BITS TO SEE THE PAPPOOSE.

The sulphur mines are 30 miles away, in a north-westerly direction. Very large deposits of native sulphur are found in these mines which will average nearly 75 per cent. pure. There are two mines opened. One called the McWorthy Mine, located and developed by Mr. McWorthy, is now operated by a San Francisco company. The product of this mine is refined by retorts, three in number, which are now in active operation, and which are capable of producing about three tons per day of twenty-four hours. The mines of the Pacific Sulphur Company are about one and one-half miles distant from the McWorthy Mines. They were formerly known as the Wright and Egbert Mines. This company have a new patented process for refining the crude ore, which they claim has a capacity of ten tons per day, and producing an article which they further claim is superior to that manufactured by any other process yet known. The ore, as it comes from the mine, is a mixture of sulphur, clay, gypsum, water, etc., and the trouble has heretofore been to separate them perfectly and cheaply. This company fuses the crude or mixed ore by heat, and then separates them by a chemical process which is claimed to be very simple, producing the "brimstone" of commerce, nearly 100 per cent. fine. The deposits lie in the hills, and are found from 20 to 100 feet thick. They are also found in some of the adjoining valleys, but are not as pure in the valleys as in the hills. They are covered with ashes and mixed with extraneous matter. In fact, wherever these deposits come to the surface, they are covered with ashes, nearly white in color, indicating that at some period, they were on fire, and that the fire was extinguished—smothered—by the accumulation of these ashes. When "the elements shall melt with fervent heat," the vast sulphur deposits of Nevada will add fuel to the flames and greatly accelerate the melting process. Humboldt is the business center of the mining districts named, and has bright prospects for the future.

The Oregon branch of the Central Pacific Railroad, which was surveyed in 1875, will leave the main line of the Central Pacific, between Mill City and Humboldt, cross the Rabbit Hole Mountains, Mud Lakes, thence northerly to Goose Lake, then on to Klamath Lake, and across the Cascade Mountains near Fort Klamath, to intersect the completed railroad in Oregon. This road is to be constructed by an Oregon company, is not a part of the Central Pacific Railroad, but will be a feeder to it, and it is understood that some of the principal owners of the Central Pacific Railroad are giving it some of their support. It is expected to be in progress next year, and completed between Humboldt and some point on the California and Oregon Railroad, near Eugene City, a distance of 450 miles, within five years.

Immediately to the north-west of these mines, and in close proximity around them, is a vast alkali desert covering a large area of ground. Of all the dreary wastes to be seen in this section of the country, this desert is one of the most forbidding and desolate.

About half a mile west of Humboldt, on our right, is a sulphur deposit. It seems to be near the remains of what was once, evidently, a sulphur spring, long since dried up. It is not worked for the reason of its impurities—a far better article of crude is being obtained elsewhere. The river, still on our right, seems to have cut a deeper channel in the valley, and is seldom seen from the cars. On our left are the towering peaks of the Humboldt Range. The valley itself becomes more undulating, but still retains its dull monotony.

A Vigilance Committee Incident.—The following incident which happened in one of the Nevada mining towns, is vouched for by Clarence King:

Early in the fifties, on a still, hot summer's afternoon, a certain man, in a camp of the northern mines, which shall be nameless, having tracked his two donkeys and one horse a half mile, and discovering that a man's track with spur marks followed them, came back to town and told "the boys," who loitered about a popular saloon, that in his opinion some Mexican had stolen the animals. Such news as this demanded, naturally, drinks all round.

"Do you know, gentlemen," said one who assumed leadership, "that just naturally to shoot these greasers aint the best way? Give 'em a fair jury trial, and rope 'em up with all the majesty of the law. That's the cure."

Such words of moderation were well received, and they drank again to "Here's hoping we ketch that greaser."

As they loafed back to the veranda, a Mexican walked over the hill brow, jingling his spurs pleasantly in accord with a whistled waltz.

The advocate for the law said in an undertone, "That's the cuss."

A rush, a struggle, and the Mexican, bound hand and foot, lay on his back in the bar-room. The camp turned out to a man.

Happily such cries as "*String him up!*" "*Burn the doggoned lubricator!*" and other equally pleasant phrases fell unheeded upon his Spanish ear. A jury was quickly gathered in the street, and despite refusals to serve, the crowd hurried them in behind the bar.

A brief statement of the case was made by the *ci-devant* advocate, and they showed the jury into a commodious poker-room where were seats grouped about neat green tables. The noise outside, in the bar-room, by and by died away into complete silence, but from afar down the canon came confused sounds as of disorderly cheering. They came nearer, and again the light-hearted noise of human laughter mingled with clinking glasses around the bar.

A low knock at the jury door, the lock burst in, and a dozen smiling fellows asked the verdict. A foreman promptly answered, "*Not guilty.*"

With volleyed oaths, and ominous laying of hands on pistol hilts, the boys slammed the door with "*You'll have to do better than that.*"

In half an hour the advocate gently opened the door again.

"Your *opinion*, gentlemen?"

"Guilty."

"Correct, you can come out. We hung him an hour ago."

The jury took theirs next, and when, after a few minutes, the pleasant village returned to its former tranquility, it was "*allowed*" at more than one saloon, that "Mexicans'll know enough to let white men's stock alone after this." One and another exchanged the belief that this sort of thing was more sensible than "nipping 'em on sight."

When, before sunset, the bar-keeper concluded to sweep some dust out of his poker-room back-door, he felt a momentary surprise at finding the missing horse dozing under the shadow of an oak, and the two lost donkeys serenely masticating playing-cards, of which many bushels lay in a dirty pile. He was then reminded that the animals had been there all day.

Rye Patch.—411 miles from San Francisco, with an elevation of 4,257 feet. In early days, in the canons that put down from the mountains near here and along the banks of the little creeks flowing through them, there were large patches of wild rye, from which the station took its name. The increase, however, in the herds of the stockmen has destroyed its native growth, and it is now seldom seen. It is a small station with a store and saloon, freight-house, side track, etc. It is the location of a ten-stamp mill owned by the Rye Patch Mill and Mining Company, and which is supplied by ore taken from the company's mine in the mountains on our left. This mine is about four miles distant from the station. The Rye Patch Mining District, and the Eldorado Mining District, six miles away, are tributary to this place. The train stops but a moment, and as you look to the mountains, on the left, two high peaks are seen—the left one being Stark Peak, and the right one Eldorado Mountain. This is the best view of these mountains that can be obtained. Leaving this station, the mountains of the Humboldt Range gradually dwindle into hills, and a conical or isolated little peak across the range is seen. It seems fully as prominent as a wart on a man's nose. It is called Black Knob—a very appropriate name—and near it is Relief Mine and mill. There is no stage to this mining district, and its principal business point is

Oreana,—400 miles from San Francisco, with an elevation of 4,181 feet. The descent from Humboldt has been quite rapid, and we will soon be at the lowest elevation in this great basin. The Antelope Range continues on the north-west, and the Humboldt Range on the left, though the peaks in these ranges grow smaller as we pass this place. Oreana is the railroad and business point for the following mining districts: in the Antelope Range is the Trinity District, seven miles away, ore principally milling. The Governor Booth Mine has the most development thus far, though other prospects are said to be looking well. Some of the ore found in this district is claimed to be very rich. Adjoining this is the Arabia District, five miles from the station; it has smelting ore. Three miles from the mine and two miles from the station, on the Humboldt River, which has been dammed at this point, are the smelting furnaces, where the ore is reduced to base bullion. There is also a small stamp mill at this point. The principal mines thus far developed in this district are the Vanderbilt, Montezuma and Hurricane, and the ore is said to average 33 per cent. metal,—lead, antimony and silver. South of the railroad first comes the Sacrament District, seven miles away. It has milling ore but the prospects are not yet developed. Spring Valley District is next, 12 miles distant. The ore is gold and silver, and the Eagle Mine has a fifteen-stamp mill in operation reducing the ore. Relief District follows, 16 miles from Oreana. It has milling ore and a five-stamp mill. At the south end of this district, is a very superior mine of antimony, the ores of which are brought to this station and shipped to San Francisco. Bolivia District is 40 miles away, and abounds in copper ore. Tidal Wave is the name of the principal mine; Kellogg's Mine is next in importance. Conveyances to these mining districts can be obtained at Oreana. The region round about the station is occupied by stockmen, and large numbers of cattle and horses are grazing upon the extensive ranges in the vicinity. No traveler will be able to see what they live on, but stockmen claim that they relish the white sage which abounds here, and that they will grow fat upon it. The face of the country, however, is very uninviting.

Leaving Oreana, we pass round a curve where the Humboldt River bends in toward the hills on our left, and soon cross the river which makes its way into Humboldt Lake. After crossing the river, the large growth of sage brush and greasewood shows that the soil in this vicinity is very rich and that, properly cultivated and well supplied with water, it will produce immense crops.

Lovelock's,—389 miles from San Francisco, with an elevation of 3,977 feet. It is a side track station with a telegraph office, a store, post-office and a few adjoining buildings. The Humboldt River near here, spreads out over considerable territory—a fact which renders irrigation comparatively easy. It has also caused the formation of a large body of natural meadows, from which immense quantities of hay are cut and shipped to different points along the line of the road. It is also a fine grazing region and large herds of cattle are fattened here upon the rich native grasses and the white sage. There are three varieties of the sage brush to be found on the plains and on the deserts. The largest kind is used as fuel for the engines at several stamp mills; white sage is considerably smaller and affords grazing for both cattle and sheep; the clover sage, still smaller, is not as plentiful as the former kinds, but is highly relished by sheep. Thus we have at last found the uses to which this shrub is applied. Even greasewood, when it first starts up in the spring, and before it hardens, is a favorite food with sheep and swine.

There is quite a settlement of farmers near Lovelock's. The station itself is named after a gentleman who lives near it, and who is an old settler in this part of the country. Farms are being cleared of sage brush and greasewood, irrigating ditches are being dug, and the success which has hitherto attended the growing of barley and potatoes, induces quite a number to engage in the business, and a black, rich soil gives every promise of encouragement. Before the railroad came, the meadow or pasture lands here were renowned among the emigrants, parties of whom recruited their stock after the wearisome journey across the plains. The meadows are off to the left of the road, as you pass, and are not conspicuous from the cars. After leaving Rye Patch, the Humboldt Mountains on our left dwindle considerably, and are neither ragged nor formidable after reaching this place. The same is likewise true of the

Trinity Range on our right They are low, barren, tinged with reddish brown; the evidences of volcanic action become more apparent as we pass, and the broken lava of the desert, the cinders and *scoriæ*, visible in places, speak of the time when the mountain ranges near here, were seething volcanoes and vomited forth smoke, flames, fire and lava with great profusion. Passing Lovelock's we soon arrive at a point, where a glimpse can be obtained of the waters of Humboldt Lake, just under the mountain ridge on our left. We have also passed by the richer soil that surrounds the last station, and entered upon the barren desert again.

Granite Point,—380 miles from San Francisco, with an elevation of 3,918 feet. Approaching the sink in this great basin, it will be seen that our elevation is decreasing, but this will only last for a short distance, and then it will be up hill again. On the right of the station, which is merely a side track, there is a ragged, broken mountain, which undoubtedly gives the place its name. It is the only thing curious or interesting to be seen from the cars. As we leave this place the lake comes into full view—a beautiful sheet of water with white, salty incrustations all around it, like a cloud fringed with a silver border. The waters on the shore nearest the road, are said to be far more brackish and saline in character than those on the farther side. The channel through the lake is on that side, and probably the cause of the difference. The lake abounds in fish but they are mostly in the fresh water channel, and at the proper season it is a great resort for pelicans, wild geese and ducks. We approach nearer the shore as we pass to

Brown's,—373 miles from San Francisco, with an elevation of 3,929 feet. It is a coaling station, and engines sometimes take water from the tank, pumped from the lake, though it is poor stuff to make steam with. Above the nearer range of mountains, just across the lake, can be seen the tops of a farther and higher range in the distance. This higher range runs south of the Humboldt and Carson Sink, and looms into view as the nearer range gives way. Humboldt Lake was not as large formerly as now,—in fact it was a simple widening of the river as it entered the gateway of the sink below. At the foot of the lake a ridge of land extends nearly across the valley, and there was something of a gorge through which the outlet passed. The opportunity to build a dam was thus improved, and what was formerly a little widening in the river, has now become a lake about 35 miles long and from 16 to 18 miles wide in the widest places. It is filled with islands caused by this rise, and the head or volume of water thus accumulated serves to run a stamp mill, located a few miles below the station and under a reddish bluff across the valley. Ore for this mill has been found in the mountains near it, and some is brought from the range on the north. You will notice an island nearly opposite the station, and may be interested to know that it was part of the main land before the dam was built. The mountains on each side of the track, now become high hills though, occasionally, a ragged peak is seen, to relieve the monotony of the journey. We pass over the ridge of land before spoken of, and fairly enter upon what is the beginning of the Humboldt and Carson Sink. We pass down on the low alkali flats which are whitened with salt, and which extend for miles as far as the eye can reach, off to our left.

White Plains,—361 miles from San Francisco, with an elevation of 3,894 feet—the lowest point we reach in this great basin. The place—a side track, is appropriately named for it is surrounded by a white alkali desert, covered in places with salt and alkali deposits.

The evidences of volcanic action and a lava formation are everywhere visible in the hills and on the plains in this vicinity. Though the plains immediately adjoining the station are white with alkali or salty deposits, yet the ridge and uplands to the right are covered with the reddish, porous rocks and finer blackish sand which always accompany this formation. At White Plains we have reached the lowest elevation on the Central Pacific, east of the Sierras. We are, in fact, almost in the sink itself of the Humboldt and Carson Rivers. The low flats stretching away to our left, are usually more or less covered with water in the season of floods, and the two rivers virtually unite in this great valley or basin. There is no visible outlet to these streams, or rather to this basin, and the immense drainage of these two rivers sinks in the sand and is taken up by evaporation. The oldest settlers in this region of country, hold to the opinion that the water is taken up by evaporation, and say that at certain seasons of the year this process is very rapid—large bodies of land covered with water becoming thoroughly dry in a few days.

Leaving White Plains, we again begin to go up a grade. We have to cross a divide between White Plains and the Hot Spring Valley. This divide is reached at

Mirage,—355 miles from San Francisco, with an elevation of 4,247 feet. It is simply a side track with no habitation near it but a section-house—and is near the summit of the divide. This place, like many others, is named from some peculiarity of location or from some characteristic of the country. The wonderful optical delusions that are apparently seen here, have given it a suggestive name. When the conditions of the atmosphere are favorable, wonderful visions of lakes, mountains, trees, rivers, etc., can be seen. It is reported that many a weary emigrant in the days of old, was deceived by the optical illusions that here seemed so real, and wondered why he did not reach the cooling lakes and spreading shade that seemed so near and was yet so far away. The heat of summer on these plains is almost intolerable. The dust, sometimes blowing in clouds, is suffocating, and without water, one can easily imagine how tantalizing such visions must be to those weary with travel and desiring especially the rest so comforting beneath the shade of trees and by the side of some pure lake. The country on either side of the station is broken, and on the left we have the low hills or isolated peaks of the Hot Spring Mountains.

Crossing the low divide, in what may be called the terminus of the Antelope Range, we whirl over a down grade, and in a few moments arrive at

Hot Springs,—346 miles from San Francisco, with an elevation of 4,072 feet. This is a telegraph station with side track, section-houses, etc. Great efforts have been made here to sink artesian wells in order to obtain fresh water for the use of the road. First a depth of 800 feet was reached, then 1,000 feet, and lastly 1,300 feet, but all without success. In some portions of work very rapid progress would be made—95 feet having been made in one day—then some hard, flinty rock would be struck, and progress of less than one foot per day would be the result.

The station is in the midst of a desert, and is named from the Hot Springs, whose rising steam can readily be seen about half a mile from the track on the left. There are quite a number of them boiling hot. They formerly extended along the base of the hill, still farther to the left, and nearer the track, but while they seem to have dried up in one locality, they have broken out in another. These springs are now owned by a German company, who have a dwelling-house, and works for producing borax, erected near by. They were badly "sold" by sharpers who induced them to believe that borax, in large quantities, could be obtained here. They sent out an expert who was induced to make a favorable report to the effect that there were inexhaustible quantities of the mineral to be found near here. As a consequence, they invested large sums of money in the purchase of the mines and in the erection of works. We believe some 60 boxes of the manufactured article was all that was ever turned out, and then the mine suddenly gave out, the production ceased, of course, and the company, after an expenditure estimated at about a quarter million of dollars, ceased operations, their property remaining idle. These springs are said to be a sovereign remedy for rheumatism and kindred diseases, and the property may yet be utilized as an infirmary or watering-place for invalids. The erection of a bathing-house would be all that is at present required. The steam from these springs can be seen for quite a distance in the cool mornings of the winter, and in the spring and fall months. Looking off to the right, as far as the eye can reach, almost, is a valley coming in from the north-east—a dreary waste of sage brush and alkali, which extends across the track, over low hills, to the sink of the Carson. We move out through a gap in the hills, and in about two miles come to the salt works. Buildings have been erected, side track put in, and large platforms built where the salt is stored preparatory to shipping. The whole face of the country, in this vicinity, is nearly white, the saline water rising to the surface and evaporating, leaves the white incrustations to glisten in the sun. The salt obtained here is produced by solar evaporation, and is said to be nearly 99 per cent. pure. Formerly vats were tried, but they were found to be useless and unnecessary. Vats are now dug in the ground and the salt water pumped into them. It soon evaporates, and after a sufficient quantity has accumulated, it is shoveled out, drawn to the station, ground and sacked, when it is ready for the market. We are now passing over one of the most uninviting portions of the desert. The range of mountains directly in front are those through which the Truckee River comes, and the valley, both north and south, extends beyond our vision. Away off to the left we can see the mountains south of the Carson Sink and River. The aspect of the desert becomes more dreary as we approach

Desert,—335 miles from San Francisco; elevation, 4,018 feet. It is only a side track, rightly named, and passenger trains seldom stop. The winds that sweep the barren plains here heap the sand around the scattering sage brush like huge potato hills. Now we turn toward the right approaching the base of the adjoining hills, while boulders of lava, large and small, greet the eye. The hill on our right, dwindles into the plain; we round it, toward the right, and arrive at

Two-Mile,—329 miles from San Francisco; elevation, 4,156 feet. The gap, in the mountain range in front, now opens and we see where the Truckee River comes tumbling down. The valley extends, on the right, till it is lost in Pyramid Lake. We pass rapidly on, and in a short distance pitch down a steep grade into the valley of the Truckee, where green grass, green trees and flowing water, God's best gift to man, again greet our vision.

Rabbit drives and Rabbit Robes.—The Piutes have a very clever way of catching rabbits, by a method called "rabbit drives" in this country. They make some long, narrow nets like fish-seines from the bark of the willow, or from wild hemp, and hold them up on edge by means of sticks, which they fasten in the ground at intervals; the part of net next to the ground is held there by weights—just as seine is managed. These nets they spread in the shape of the letter "V," with the arms extended to receive the game when it shall be driven in. One Indian crouches in the enclosure for a purpose which will be explained hereafter. The nets are woven coarsely, so that a rabbit's head, once through the meshes, is tight. Late in the fall or early in the winter, when a light snow has covered the ground, the Indians will set their nets generally across some valley and prepare for the "drive." From twenty-five to sixty of them, the more the better, will start out and go quietly away from the net some ten or twelve miles. This company is composed of Indians, squaws, and children armed with sticks, old sacks or blankets which they can flourish in the air, and when they have arrived where they propose to commence the drive, they spread out in a semi-circular form, and begin to hoot and yell, swinging their rags around their heads, and beating the sage brush with their sticks. The rabbits, very much frightened, run in the only direction open for them, while the Indians press forward to the net and gradually draw in toward it. The rabbits continue their flight until they are fairly within the arms of the nets, with the Indians close upon them. The Indians, perhaps two or three of them—who have remained in the net perfectly still until the frightened rabbits surround them, suddenly rise up with a shout, and the frantic creatures wildly rush hither and thither and finally dash into the meshes of the net, which holds them by the neck so that they cannot escape. Then follows "the slaughter of the innocents." The Indians pass along and tap the rabbits over the head, the squaws secure the game, and the whole drive results in a big feast, wherein the course begins and ends with rabbit *ad libitum.* Our informant stated that he had known from 500 to 1,000 rabbits to be caught in this way, in one drive.

About Rabbit Robes.—The traveler has doubtless noticed the gray fur robes, which adorn the persons of a large number of the Indians seen on the road west of Ogden. These robes are a curious piece of workmanship in some respects. They are not made of whole rabbit-skins sewed together, as wolf and coon-skin robes are made. When the rabbits are skinned, their hides are at once cut into narrow strips with the fur on. These strips are sewed together until the right length for a robe is secured, and then they are twisted like a rope—in fact, become fur ropes. These are used the same as "filling" in woolen or cotton cloth, as distinguished from the "warp." You can press your fingers through these robes at pleasure—the threads of the "warp" being from one to three inches apart. This warp is made from the sinews of animals, from the bark of willows, or from the wild hemp which the Indians gather for this purpose. It is very stout and very durable, and is not perceptible as you casually examine one of these robes. The Indians value a rabbit-skin robe very highly, and much prefer them to blankets, though it takes a good deal of time and patience to make one. This work, however, is all done by the squaws, and is taken as a matter of course by the "bucks" of the tribe.

Wadsworth,—328 miles from San Francisco; elevation. 4,077 feet. It is a little village of about 400 inhabitants, nestled down in the valley of the Truckee and overshadowed by the range of mountains beyond. The railroad has a twenty-stall roundhouse, 65 feet deep, with over 500 feet of circular length. The machine shop has six working stalls where engines are repaired, and is 75 by 130 feet. Engines are here entirely rebuilt. At one end of this shop a piece of ground has been fenced in, a fountain erected, trees planted, and alfalfa and blue-grass sown. It affords a refreshing sight to the mechanics here employed, and strangely contrasts with the barren desert surrounding the place. The engines used on that part of the division between Winnemucca and this place, have very large tenders, the tanks in them holding 3,800 gallons of water. They run 70 miles without taking water on the line of the road. Other shops for the convenience of the road are located near by. The huge water tank in which water is stored for use of shops and engines, has a capacity of 60,000 gallons. Hydrants have been erected, connected with it by pipes, and hose supplied by which the water may be quickly applied in case of fire, to any part of the buildings. The road passes from Wadsworth to Sacramento through a mountainous region of country, where there is plenty of timber and, hence, wood is used for fuel on the engines between these two places. Between Ogden and this place coal taken from the mines north of Evanston, on the Union Pacific Road, is used. West of Sacramento, coal from Oregon and Washington Territory is used. Between Wadsworth and Truckee some trouble has been experienced with snow, and in some places huge boulders roll down on the track which are knocked out of the way by the snow-plows on the engines. This is a novel use for snow-plows. In addition to the machine shops, there is a large freight building and other offices for the convenience of the company. The town has several large stores, hotels, saloons, with China houses, *ad libitum*, and is, altogether, the place of considerable trade. Huge freight wagons, from two to four attached together, are here loaded with freight for the mining districts south. These large wagons, with their teams attached, are quite a curiosity to eastern travelers, and fully illustrate how western men do their freighting.

The following mining districts do business at this station: Columbus, borax mines, 130 miles distant; Teal's Marsh borax Mines, 140 miles away; the Pacific Borax Works are 20 miles south-east of Columbus still; the Bellville Mining District, 140 miles distant. In this district the celebrated Northern Bell Silver Mine is located, also the General Thomas and others less prominent. Silver Peak Mining District is 110 miles distant. These districts, and others not named here, are all south of Wadsworth. Rhodes' Salt Marsh, an immense salt deposit, is about 130 miles distant. There is salt enough in this deposit to preserve the world, if reports as to its extent, etc., prove true.

there are three bodies of water which travelers will more fully understand by an explanation. Humboldt Lake proper, into which flows the Humboldt River, we pass at Brown's Station. A little south-west of this lake is the Humboldt and Carson Sink — the waters from the lake seeping through a channel or slough into the sink. The dam at the foot of the lake is across this outlet or slough. The waters from Carson Lake flowing nearly east, find their way into this sink through a similar outlet. Thus the waters of the two rivers, the Humboldt

PYRAMID LAKE.

From Wadsworth to Carson Lake, south, the distance is about 40 miles. This lake is named from the river of the same name, which flows into, or rather through it. Directly south of Carson Lake is Walker Lake into which flows Walker River. The lake last named has no visible outlet, and is one of the sinks of the great basin east of the Sierras. South of the railroad,

and Carson, each flowing through a small lake, finally meet in the same sink. To this sink there is no visible outlet, and the vast amount of water which is poured into this basin through these two rivers is undoubtedly taken up on its way, or after its arrival into this common sink, by evaporation.

The Humboldt River, though it has a length

of 500 miles, and has several tributaries constantly flowing into it, yet does not increase in volume, throughout its length, as do most rivers. After passing Winnemucca it diminishes to a small stream, finally spreads into a marsh and "sinks" out of sight.

In addition to the mining districts south of the railroad, the Soda Lakes and refining works must not be forgotten. These are now in active operation, and the results are the frequent shipments from this place.

North of Wadsworth about 21 miles is Pyramid Lake, and east of it, separated by Lake Range of Mountains, which can plainly be seen from Wadsworth,—is Winnemucca Lake, 26 miles distant. Both of them are sinks, and have no visible outlet. Both of them receive the waters of Truckee River, and the latter is said to be rising,—being several feet higher now than it was ten years ago.

Curiosities of Pyramid Lake.—In 1867 a surveying party visited this lake, which they found to be 12 miles long and 30 miles wide. The lake takes its name from a remarkable rock formation, a *pyramid* which towers above the lake to a height of more than 500 feet, and presents in its outlines the most perfect form. Upon visiting this pyramid, the party found it occupied with tenants who were capable of holding their ground against all intruders.

From every crevice there seemed to come a hiss. The rattling, too, was sharp and long-continued. The whole rock was alive with rattlesnakes. Even in the party those who had been champion snake exterminators, and had demolished them on all previous occasions, now found the combat beyond their power to carry on, and abandoned the island with all hope of victory.

The water of Pyramid Lake is clear, sparkling. In it are said to be fish, principally among which is the *couier*, very sprightly, with flesh the color of salmon. The weight of the fish ranges from 3 to 20 pounds. There is also said to be an abundance of trout.

Winnemucca Lake is also stated to be some 200 feet lower than Pyramid Lake, its basin being on the east side of Lake Range of Mountains. The Truckee River and these two lakes are great resorts for ducks, geese and pelicans. The latter abound here in large numbers in the spring. An island in Pyramid Lake is a great resort for them and there, undisturbed, they rear their young. These birds are very destructive to the fish of the river and lake. They will stand in the shallow water of the entrance to the lake for hours, and scoop up any unwary fish that may happen to pass within their reach. They are apparently harmless, and of no earthly use whatever. The huge sacks on their under jaws, are used to carry food and water to their young. These waddle around before they fly—a shapeless, uncouth mass, and easily destroyed because unable to get out of the way. A man with a club could kill thousands of them in a day, without much difficulty.

North of Pyramid Lake is Mud Lake, another sink of this great basin, and a little north-east of Winnemucca Lake is the sink of Quin's River and other streams. In fact, they lose their identity in flowing across the desert,—are swallowed up by the thirsty sands.

On the north, Pyramid Lake Mining District is 15 miles away. This is a new district, and said to contain good "prospects." Mud Lake District, similar in character, is 75 miles due north from Wadsworth. Black Butte District on the east side of Winnemucca Lake, is about 28 miles distant.

The Piute reservation, or rather one of them, begins about seven miles north of the town. The reservation house, which is supposed to be the place where the government officers reside, is 16 miles away. There is another reservation for these Indians south, on Walker River. They have some very good land near the lake, and some of them cultivate the soil,—raising good crops.

There is considerable good bottom-land on the Truckee River, between Wadsworth and Pyramid Lake. That which is not included in the Indian reservation is occupied by stockmen and farmers, much of it being cultivated and producing excellent crops of cereals and vegetables. The experiments thus far tried in fruit growing have been successful, and in a few years there will be a home supply of fruit equal to home demand.

The arrival at Wadsworth is a great relief to the tourist weary with the dull, unchanging monotony of the plains, the desert and bleak desolation which he has passed. The scenes are now to change and another miniature world is to open upon his view. There is to be variety—beauty, grandeur and sublimity. If he enters this place at night, the following day will reveal to him the green fields and magnificent landscapes of California, and in less than 24 hours, he will be able to feast his greedy eyes upon a glowing sunset on the Pacific Coast.

Leaving Wadsworth we cross the Truckee River and gaze with delight upon the trees, the green meadows, the comfortable farm-house, and well-tilled fields of the ranche on our left, just across the bridge. Like everything else lovely in this world, it soon fades from our vision, as we rapidly pass into the Truckee Canon. The mountains now come down on either side as though they would shake hands across the silver torrent that divides them. The valley narrows as if to hasten their cordial grasp, and to remove all obstacles in their way. Now it widens a little as though it was not exactly certain whether these mountains should come together or not, and wanted to consider the matter. But

SCENES ON THE TRUCKEE RIVER.—BY THOMAS MORAN.
1.—Truckee Meadows, Sierras in the distance. 2.—Pleasant Valley. 3.—Truckee River, near State Line
4.—Red Bluff, Truckee River. 5.—Bridge at Eagle Gap. 6.—Truckee River Rapids.

leaving this question to the more practical thoughts of our readers, we hasten on, winding around promontories and in and out of "draws" and ravines, through rocky cuts, and over high embankments with the river rolling and tumbling almost beneath our feet, and the ragged peaks towering high above us, passing

Salvia,—a simple side track, six miles from Wadsworth. Now we have something to occupy our attention; there are new scenes passing by at every length of the car, and we have to look sharp and quick, or many of them will be lost forever. Soon we make a short turn to the right, and what the railroad men call "Red Rock" appears in front, then to our right, and finally over our heads. It is a huge mountain of lava that has, sometime, in the ages of the past, been vomited from the crater of some volcano now extinct; or it may have been thrown up by some mighty convulsion of nature that fairly shook the rock-ribbed earth till it trembled like an aspen leaf, and in which these huge mountain piles were thrown into their present position. Presently, amidst the grandeur of these mountains, a lovely valley bursts upon our view. We have arrived at the little meadows of the Truckee, at a station called

Clark's,—313 miles from San Francisco, with an elevation of 4,263 feet. This station is named from a former proprietor of the ranche here. It is a beautiful place with mountains all around it, and the only way you can see out, is to look up toward the heavens. The narrow bottom on either side of the river is fenced in, producing excellent crops of vegetables and hay, and affording excellent grazing for the stock that is kept here. As we arrive at this station, we pass through a cut of sand which seems just ready to become stratified, and which holds itself up in layers, in the sides of the cut. Occasionally, as we look over the nearer peaks in front, we can catch a glimpse of the snow-crowned Sierras in the distance. Now a creek comes in from a canon on our left, and through this canon is a wagon road to Virginia City, and now a butte is passed between us and the river—the river being on our left since we crossed it at Wadsworth. There are a few ranches scattered along its banks where vegetables for the 10,000 miners at Virginia City are grown. The mountains we have passed are full of variegated streaks of clay or mineral, some white, some red, some yellow, and some pale green. You will notice them as you pass

Vista,—301 miles from San Francisco; elevation, 4,403 feet. We are going up hill again. At this station we arrive at the Truckee Meadows. It is like an immense amphitheatre, and the traveler rejoices again in the presence of farm-houses and cultivated fields—in the scene of beauty that spreads out before him. Beyond the level plain, we see in front of us Peavine Mountain and at the base of the hills to the farther side of the valley, lies Reno. To our left Mt. Rose lifts its snow-covered head; to the left of Mt. Rose is Slide Mountain.

Letters.—Throughout the Territories and the Pacific Coast,—*letter days*, when the Pony Express, Mail Coaches or Steamer arrived, the local population was wrought up to its most intense excitement, and expectation of news. In the Territory of Montana letters could not be obtained from any direction by regular mails, and the inhabitants depended upon the good offices of traders, who journeyed at long intervals back and forth, who brought with them letters and newspapers, for which, gladly, every receiver paid $2.50 gold. Letters in California were received only by steam *via* the Isthmus of Panama, fully 30 days being occupied in the trip from New York, and fully 90 days' time was necessary to send a letter from San Francisco to any point in the East, and receive a reply. Whenever the semi-monthly steamer arrived at San Francisco, the event was celebrated by the firing of guns, and the ringing of bells, and an immediate rush for the post-office. The letter deliveries from the post-office, were often from a window opening directly upon the public street, and a long line of anxious letter-seekers would quickly form—extending often half a mile in length. Here were gathered the characteristic classes of California life, the "*gray shirt brigade*" of miners, many of whom in their rugged life had not heard from home for a full year; next anxious merchants whose fate depended upon their letters and invoices, and on approaching the office, had only a feeling of dismay at the terrible length of the line, with little hope of approaching the window for hours. At last they were compelled to offer sums for purchases of place from some fortunate one *in the line*. It used to take five hours or longer, on ordinary occasions, to get to the window, and there were lots of idlers who had no friends, nor ever expected a letter, who from pure mischief, took their places in the line, and then when near the window sold out again. From $5 to $20 were the average prices for fair places, but $50 to $100 were often paid for a good position near the window. Prices were in proportion to the length of the line or the anxiety of the individual. The expression of countenance of some of those paying highest rates, when forced to leave the window without a letter, is beyond description. "*Selling out in the line,*" soon became a trade, and many a loafer made his $10 to $20—three or four times a day. Cases have even been known, where over-anxious individuals in search of letters, would take their positions at the post-office window, *one or two days* before the arrival of the expected steamer, often passing the entire night standing and watching at the window, and only leaving it when forced to seek food and drink. It often happened that while temporarily absent from their post a few minutes, the steamer's gun would fire, and with a break-neck race of a few minutes back again, their disgust was immense to be compelled to attach themselves to the extreme end of a line, from one-fourth to one-half a mile in length, so quickly had it formed.

Ah Ching's Theology: a Belief in the Devil.—A traveler encountered once Ah Ching, a Chinese laundryman, at one of the San Francisco hotels, who spoke some English and had some intellect, of whom he asked the question, whether he believed in the devil.

"Hallo, John, do you believe in him?"

"*Ah, velley, Mellica man, me believe him.*"

"All Chinamen believe in him?"

"*Oh, China like Mellica man, some believe him sahvey, some tink him all gosh damn.*"

Firing off the Devil.—At one of the Chinese festivals, conducted by the Chinese priests, a large figure representing the devil was brought forward, and at the close of the play a torch was applied to him. The figure, which was full of fire-crackers, "went off" in brilliant style till nothing was left, apparently, but the hideous head and backbone; these, then, shot upward, like a huge Roman candle, leaving a trail of blue fire, and exploded, high in the air, with a loud report followed by a shower of sparks and insufferable stench, and that was supposed to be the last of the devil for another year.

The apparent reason for paying so much attention to the devil is contained in the answer made by one of the worshipers: "*If God good, why pray? 'Tend to the devil.*" Hence the ceremony of getting rid of him at regular intervals.

Curious Names Given by Miners.—Placerville was, in 1849, called *Hangtown* because it was the first place where any person was hanged by lynch-law.

Tin Cup was so named, because the first miners there found the place so rich that they measured their gold in pint tin cups.

Pine Log is so named because there was once a pine log across the South Fork of the Stanislaus River in such a position as to offer a very convenient crossing to miners.

The following are among the other oddities which have, through miners' freaks and fancies, been used to denote settlements and camps and diggings, small or large:

Jim Crow Canon,
Red Dog,
Jackass Gulch,
Ladies' Canon,
Miller's Defeat,
Loafer Hill,
Rattlesnake Bar,
Whisky Bar,
Poverty Hill,
Greasers' Camp,
Gridiron Bar,
Hen-Roost Camp,
Lousy Ravine,
Lazy Man's Canon,
Logtown,
Git-Up-and-Git,
Gopher Flat,
Bob Ridley Flat,
One Eye,
Push Coach Hill,
Christian Flat,
Rough and Ready,
Ragtown,
Sugar-Loaf Hill,
Paper Flat,
Wild-Cat Bar,
Dead Mule Canon,
Wild Goose Flat,
Brandy Flat,
Yankee Doodle,
Horsetown,
Petticoat Slide,
Chucklehead Diggings,
Plug Head Gulch,
Ground Hog's Glory,
Bogus Thunder,
Last Chance,
Greenhorn Canon,
Shanghai Hill,
Shirt-Tail Canon,
Skunk Gulch,
Coon Hollow,
Poor Man's Creek,
Humbug Canon,
Quack Hill,
Nigger Hill,
Piety Hill,
Brandy Gulch,
Love-Letter Camp,
Blue Belly Ravine,
Shinbone Peak,
Loafer's Retreat,
Swellhead Diggings,
Poodletown,
Gold Hill,
Centipede Hollow,
Seven-by-Nine Valley,
Gospel Swamp,
Puppytown,
Mad Canon,
Happy Valley,
Hell's Delight,
Devil's Basin,
Dead Wood,
Gouge Eye,
Puke Ravine,
Slap-Jack Bar,
Bloomer Hill,
Grizzly Flat,
Rat-Trap Slide,
Pike Hill,
Port Wine,
Snow Point,
Nary Red,
Gas Hill,
Ladies' Valley,
Graveyard Canon,
Gospel Gulch,
Chicken Thief Flat,
Hungry Camp,
Mud Springs,
Skinflint,
Pepper-Box Flat,
Seventy-Six,
Hog's Diggings,
Liberty Hill,
Paradise,
Sluice Fork,
Seven Up Ravine,
Humpback Slide,
Coyote Hill,
American Hollow,
Pancake Ravine,
Nutcake Camp,
Paint Pot Hill.

Tit for Tat.—When Hepworth Dixon was leaving California, he asked one of our newspaper men to write to him occasionally.

"Certainly," replied our knight of the paste-pot and shears, whom we will call plain Smith, "how shall I address you?"

"Simply Hepworth Dixon, England," replied the modest author of "The White Conquest."

"All right, Mr. Dixon," responded Mr. Smith, choking down his risibilities by a severe effort, "I trust to have the pleasure of hearing from you in reply."

"Certainly, Mr. Smith," replied Dixon, "how shall I address you?"

"Simply John Smith, America," triumphantly replied Mr. Smith.

Reno—is 293 miles from San Francisco, situated in the Truckee Meadows, the junction of the Virginia & Truckee Railroad, the first point reached from which there are *two daily* passenger trains to San Francisco, and the *best point* of departure for tourists going west to visit Lake Tahoe. The Meadows, about 15 miles long and eight wide, are mostly covered with sage brush.

WINTER FOREST SCENE IN THE SIERRA NEVADAS.

BY THOMAS MORAN.

The numerous boulders which also strew the meadows, are built into fences, and alfalfa seed sown after digging out the sage brush, and rich pasturage results on which sheep thrive. Eight or ten tons to the acre are cut in a single season, and farms make handsome returns. The boulders are most numerous along the river.

Reno has an altitude of 4,507 feet, and, although a railroad town only a few years old, is destined to be the prominent city of the State. It was named in honor of the fallen hero of South Mountain—has now 2,000 people, and is a county-seat with a $30,000 court-house, and is *the gate* to the West for all the State, and distributing point for a large portion of it. It has outrun Truckee in competing for the trade of California, east of the Sierras and among the beautiful and fertile valleys north of the railroad, for, from November to May, Truckee is shut in by deep snows, and its roads have steeper grades.

Sierra Valley, the Honey Lake Region, Long Valley, Camp Bidwell and Goose Lake Region, Surprise Valley, Indian Valley, Winnemucca Valley, the Pitt River Country, Fort Warner and South-eastern Oregon, all derive their supplies, wholly or in part, on wagons from this point. It is the healthiest place in the State and has the most stable population, being surrounded with an agricultural region.

It has five churches, Congregational, Methodist, Episcopal, Baptist and Catholic, and ground will soon be broken here for the erection of a Young Ladies' Seminary, under the care of Bishop Whitaker of the Protestant Episcopal Church, for which $10,000 were contributed by Miss Wolfe of New York City, $5,000 contributed elsewhere, and Reno has supplied the remaining $5,000 needed.

Nevada, by a State law, sets apart one-fourth of one per cent. of her tax for a building fund, out of which the Capitol was erected, at Carson City. About $100,000, since accumulated, has been spent on a State prison, the completion of which is yet in the future.

Here are the grounds of the State Agricultural Society and the finest speed-track in the State, two banks, one newspaper—the Nevada *State Journal*—and several factories, a steam fire department and a public library.

The benevolent orders are well represented, the Masons and Odd Fellows meeting in halls of their own. There are two hotels, the Railroad House, which is well kept, and the Lake House, on the bank of the Truckee River, a most desirable place for a few days' stay. A daily stage leaves for Susanville, in the California portion of the Sierra Nevadas.

The Pea Vine District is nine miles northwest, and about 1,500 feet above Reno, in which are valuable mines of dark sulphuret ore—the basest worked on the coast, and worked successfully only of late by the O'Hara process.

Virginia & Truckee Railroad.

Leaving Reno, the Red Mountain District is seen on the east, and the Washoe Range with Mount Rose, 8,200 feet high, on the west, and soon the cars pass a flume, 15 miles long, owned by Flood & O'Brien, running through a long canon to Evans Creek to convey lumber to the railroad. Huffaker's is six and one-half miles from Reno, the terminus of the Pacific Wood, Lumber and Flume Company's flume. The next stopping point is called

Brown's,—and is the terminus of the Eldorado Flume, owned by the Virginia & Truckee Railroad Company. This flume starts in White's Canon, and is about six miles long. The first important station is

Steamboat Springs,—11 miles south of Reno. They consist of many springs in two distinct groups, those of each group apparently connected with each other. Their escaping steam may be seen near the station on the rise to the right of the road, and the fissures, through which the water of 212° Fahrenheit gurgles up, vary from a narrow crack to a foot in width. Formerly they were more active than now, yet at times they spout the water to a height of ten feet. Sulphur abounds in the water, and remarkable cures of rheumatism and cutaneous diseases have been effected, but no reliable analysis of the water has been made.

The hotel is a popular resort, kept in first-class style with accommodations for fifty guests.

Steamboat Springs are fast becoming famous for mines of cinnabar and sulphur, of both of which this region seems to be full. Much of the sulphur is pure and beautifully crystallized. Cinnabar is found between strata of lava.

The railroad crosses Steamboat Creek, the outlet for Washoe Lake, and then enters Steamboat Valley, which contains about 6,000 acres of good soil with some natural meadow at the upper end.

South of Steamboat Valley is Washoe Valley, which is entered by passing through a narrow gorge with large conglomerate rocks, weather-beaten into castellated form. Emerging from the canon, one is in

Washoe City,—5 3-4 miles from Steamboat; it has a few dilapidated houses. Mount Rose, over 8,000 feet high, eternally snow-capped, is directly opposite the lower end of the valley.

On the left of the track may be seen the ruins of the old Ophir Mill—whose Superintendent was honored with a salary of $30,000 per annum, and a furnished house, while the mill employed 165 men.

On the left, at the foot of the mountains, overlooking the beautiful lake and valley, is Bower's Mansion—the favorite resort for picnics from Carson and Virginia City.

Franktown,—4 1-4 miles from Washoe, is an old Mormon colony, the terminus of another flume, and was the first place settled in this regularly formed and picturesque valley, twelve miles long by seven wide. The long promontories from the mountain side are denuded of timber, but numerous ice-cold crystal streams come down from the mountain side, and the valley produces considerable grain and fruit, and supports no little stock.

Mill Station,—3 miles from Franktown, is an old mill site at the upper end of the valley, from which Washoe Lake, ten miles long and six wide, may be clearly seen. Here is the end of still another flume for lumber and wood; next is Eagle Valley, reached by a short tunnel. At the summit, or

Lake View,—2 miles from Mill Station, commanding the finest view of Washoe Lake, the railroad crosses the large water pipe which supplies Virginia City from a lake on the western summit of the Sierras, above Lake Tahoe. Washoe and Eagle Valleys almost join, and on entering the latter, Carson City and the State Capitol are seen below.

Carson City—is 21 miles from Virginia City. It was settled in 1858, by Major Ormsby and others, has a population of 3,500, is regularly laid out, the streets coinciding with the cardinal points of the compass. Shade trees, the U. S. Mint, the Capitol, Court-house, and some neat private residences, four churches (Presbyterian, Methodist, Episcopalian and Catholic), the best school-house in the State, and good society, make it one of the most desirable places for residence in Nevada. It has two daily papers, the *Appeal* and *Tribune*. It is the center of a large trade for all parts of South-western Nevada and Mono and Inyo Counties of California.

It has three good hotels, the general offices and workshops of the Virginia & Truckee Railroad, and daily stages south to Genoa, 16 miles, Wellington and Aurora, 104 miles, connecting with stages for Benton, Cerro Gordo, Fort Independence and Los Angeles, and another line to Markleeville and Silver Mountain, and the line to Glenbrook on Lake Tahoe, leaving at 8.15 A. M., time two and one-half hours, 15 miles, fare $3.00.

The railroad from Carson City to Virginia City, is often spoken of as the Crooked Railroad, so full is it of curves and windings. There are many curves on it of 14°, and one of 19°, and on one portion of it for 16 miles, there is a continuous grade of 116 feet to the mile. This is believed to be the road of which it is said that an engineer, badly frightened at the approach of a red light, jumped from his engine, and soon saw that he had been scared by the rear end of his own train. It is fifty-one and three-quarter miles long, and has 35 miles of side track. Forty to fifty trains daily pass over it, and it is probably the best paying railroad in the country.

The railroad between Carson City and Virginia City is full of interest, passing along a continuous line of reducing works on the Carson River, and mines on the slope of Mount Davidson.

Proceeding through Eagle Valley to Virginia, there may be seen—off to the right; the State Prison, two and one-half miles from Carson, an edifice whose architectural appearance is befitting its purpose. Adjoining, as if it was the same building, are the Carson Warm Springs, a miserable hotel over one of the choicest spots for an attractive resort. The great volume of water boiling from the rocks, supplies a succession of large plunge baths for a distance of 160 feet. The first station from Carson is

Lookout,—2 1-4 miles from Carson, and next

Empire,—1 1-4 miles farther, the location of a quartz mill of the same name. Half a mile farther on is

Morgan,—named from the Morgan Mill, the only steam quartz mill along this end of the road, and another mile brings the train to

Brunswick,—another quartz mill. Cordwood will be seen filling the river here, floated down from the mountains, by different companies, to be caught and distributed.

Merrimac,—still another quartz mill, is only half a mile from Brunswick, and ***Eureka,*** i.e., Eureka Dump, is two and three-fourths miles farther. The mill is situated below, and the road turns almost directly away from the river, and rapidly ascends the side of the Mount Davidson Range, climbing to the lofty peak to which Virginia City clings. The peak and city are not far away, but the road makes many windings and curves, and it is long before the terminus is reached.

Mound House—is 1 3-4 miles from the Eureka Dump. Along here the road is without curves for a long distance for such a crooked railroad as this is. It is the depot of supply for Dayton and Sutroville, and after July, 1876, will have a new road opened to Columbus, *via* Walker's Lake, on which a steamer will be placed, thus saving four days' time for freight-wagons to Columbus, and making what will be the favorite route for passengers by a line of stages leaving the Mound House every morning, on arrival of the 4 P. M. train from San Francisco. At

Silver,—three miles from Mound House, there is a dump for ore which is caught in cars and carried on a narrow gauge horse railroad for two and one-half miles to mills at Silver City.

Scales,—a station for weighing ore. Silver City is to be seen down in the ravine, and the road makes a horseshoe curve around American Flat, on the farther side of which is seen the city of Gold Hill.

Gold Hill.—As the traveler approaches, he sees evidence of mining in every direction—

abandoned shafts, puffing engines, smoke issuing from gigantic stacks, huge mounds of earth dumped from the end of high trestle-work, the capacious buildings and the posts and stones that mark the undeveloped claims, or the loaded ore, need no explanation as to their origin or purpose.

Gold Hill follows the ravine of the same name, and the street is both steep and crooked. It has a population of 6,000 and is, in all respects, like Virginia City. The two are built up so as to be without marked separation. Gold Hill has a vigorous daily paper, the "*Gold Hill News*," a Catholic, a Methodist, and an Episcopal Church.

Virginia City and Gold Hill are connected by a line of omnibusses, making four trips every hour during the day, while the frequent trains of the railroad carry also many passengers. By rail the distance to Virginia City is two miles, in which several tunnels are passed through.

Virginia City—is one of the most interesting towns on the coast. One expects streets of gold and silver, and finds dust or mud. On October 26, 1875, it was almost wholly destroyed by fire, but the disaster has shown what energy there is in the people and it is nearly rebuilt. The completion of a first-class hotel has been delayed, but this will soon be accomplished, according to plans creditable to the city and the land of silver. Its narrow streets show with what difficulty sites are obtained for buildings, whether anchored to the rocks or perched in mid-air, and, while in the city but little of it is visible at a time, the dwellings are mostly low, and, therefore, unstable roofs do less damage when the Washoe zephyrs blow. It appears small, but is the most densely packed of all American cities. One-third its people are underground, where lighted candles glimmer faintly in subterranean passages, by day and by night. Bedrooms do double duty for hundreds or thousands, whose work never ceases. Miners are *shifted* every eight hours, and the men of two shifts may occupy the same couch.

STREET SCENE IN VIRGINIA CITY, NEVADA.

On many levels, down 1,500 feet, are thousands of busy, bustling, narrow streets, over which is the city proper. Tide-water is 6,205 feet below the banks, and perhaps it is best that it is no nearer, for now pumps are constructed to raise the water to the surface from 3,000 to 5,000 feet below, only seven of which are capable of raising 4,000 gallons every minute.

Dwellings on the side-hill overlook one another without any appearance of aristocratic pretensions, and steps and foot-ladders are continually at hand.

The streets present a busy appearance with men of all classes, and occasionally women, watching the indicator of the San Francisco stock-market as anxiously as a gambler reduced to the "bed rock" watches for the playing of the hand against him.

Saloons are numerous and crowded, and profanity fearfully prevalent.

It is a city of extremes in prices, speculations, character, activity, enterprise, debauchery and home life. The rich and the penniless are side by side. Every notion and *ism* is advocated—every nation represented by the worst and best of the race—except the horrible Celestial, who is always called bad, but is even somewhat like "the Englishman of character and the Englishman of no character to speak of." The lazy Indians that lounge about the street, rich with a loaf of bread, a blanket, a string of beads and some feathers, are no poorer than hundreds who will have nothing until they sober up, and at the other end are the owners of wealth incomprehensible by any system of counting—all glittering and golden-hued in a vast firmament of riches, as great as the reality of idlest dreams. Here the world has seen, not one, but at least four, richer than Crœsus; with lamps, rings and slaves better than Aladdin's; four Bonanza kings, each with a mountain of treasure greater to carry than the horrible Old Man of the Sea, but which no modern Sinbad would shake off with delight.

One says, "The gods here worshiped are heathen deities, Mammon, Bacchus and Venus. The temples are brokers' offices, whisky shops, gambling hells and brothels. There is wonderful enterprise, much intelligence, some refinement, not a little courtesy, and a sea of sin."

The view from the city is picturesque and sorrowfully beautiful. Off to the south and east the eye ranges over a waste of sage brush, and the face of the whole country appears like the waves of an angered sea, broken the more because they can go no farther.

The Carson River can be seen stretching off toward its sinking place in arid sands, and the twenty-six mile desert will deceive the unthinking, and add a faint lake-like look to the picture, of which the Walker and Sweetwater Ranges and endless mountains' rosy light and heaven's blue dome, all add their beauty.

But to enjoy the best view, make the ascent of Mount Davidson, about 2,000 feet above the city, and nearly 8,000 feet high. One need not climb, but may ascend it on horseback by following up the ravine from Gold Canon. When he reaches what seems from the street to be the top of the mountain, he sees another summit as far beyond, but the latter gained the view is magnificent.

Below, on the west, is a beautiful lake two or three miles in diameter, "glistening like the silver of the mountains which it covers." Reno, the Carson Valley, valleys, mountains, rivers, lakes, and deserts may be seen in every direction for a hundred miles.

Or, if it is too fatiguing to ascend, whoever is the fortunate possessor of a note of introduction to some mining superintendent, may prepare for a visit to the world below. Donning brogans, woolen socks and coarse flannels, he will step on the cage, holding his breath, his heart feeling gone, and as the water drips around him down the shaft, his feeble lantern will not remove the queer sensation of the descent. Once below, there are cuts, and cross-cuts, drifts, winzes, stopes and a maze of strange words, sights and sounds. Here is explained the use of the squared timbers seen by the car load, passing from the Sierras to Virginia City. As worthless rock or treasured ore is removed, the excavation must be replaced almost as solid as the rock itself. The huge timbers are mortised and fitted to each other with the utmost precision; ladders lead from level to level. Cars convey the ore to the shaft, and up and down the busy cages are always going. Every minute a loaded car ascends from a quarter of a mile below and is replaced by another. The engineer tells by an indicator the precise location of the cage at any moment, and by varying the signals to him, he directs the movements for passengers with greatly decreased speed.

If time permits, ride over to the Sutro Tunnel, six miles from Virginia City. It once promised well, may benefit the Comstock Lode more than its friends have ever dreamed, but from present appearances the real contest concerning it, was not in Congress, nor opposition from the mines it aims to tap, but has yet to come. As a specimen of engineering it will repay a visit. With indomitable energy it is pushed forward, and has now penetrated nearly three miles. The average progress is 90 feet per week, and tunneling was never done elsewhere, more speedily or successfully.

Mines of Virginia City.—The discovery of the Comstock Lode, was made in 1857, by men in pursuit of gold placers. They came upon some mineral new to them, which a Mexican recognized as silver ore. Comstock at an early day, was a middle-man in the purchase of an interest in the lode, and his name thus became attached to it. As explorations were made, very rich ore was found near the surface, and soon a great excitement was created, and vigorous operations commenced, which were crowned with wonderful success. The Ophir Mine, and the Gould & Curry, at an early day began to pay dividends, and continued to do so without interruption for several years. The Savage and the Hale & Norcross were later in becoming known, and their period of prosperity continued after the others had gone into decline. These are all Virginia City Mines. The Kentuck, Crown Point, Yellow Jacket, Chollar Potosi, and Belcher, which have all paid dividends and others less widely known, are in Gold Hill. Neither of them became successful as early as the Ophir and Gould & Curry. The original discoverers of these mines "located" them, as miners say, that is, posted upon the property a notice of claim in writing, of which they filed a copy with the recorder of the mining district. The regulations in reference to locating claims differed slightly in different districts. Usually not over 2,000 feet along the length of a vein could be located in one claim, and no one could claim over 200 feet except the discoverer, he being usually allowed 300, and sometimes 400 feet. Under the present United States Mining Law no single claim for over 1,500 feet can be made, whatever number of persons join in it, and the discoverer is accorded no advantage over others. Feet in length along a vein, are always stated and understood to carry all its depth, spurs and angles, that is, its whole *breadth* and *depth* be they more or less, for the length claimed. Veins are usually only a few feet wide, but sometimes extend miles in length. The Comstock Lode has been traced for five miles, but its greatest breadth so far as yet known, is between 300 and 400 feet, and no other silver vein in the State of Nevada approaches it in breadth, and some are worked which do not exceed 6 inches. In early days dealings in mines were by feet, and not by shares. The Ophir Mine comprised 1,400 feet for instance, and was sold on the stock-board by the foot. An owner of 100 feet owned a fourteenth of the mine. Gradually the selling by feet was abandoned, and only shares were dealt in, and those have been divided up very small, in order to bring speculation within the compass of persons of small means. The Ophir Mine has been divided so that each original foot is represented by seventy-two shares. The incorporations of all the mining companies on the Comstock Lode, and their offices have always been in San Francisco, and the men who live immediately over and about the mine, cannot buy or sell stock in them except by letter or telegraph to "The Bay."

In the development of this mineral lode, three distinct periods may be marked. For some time after its discovery, prosperity continually attended operations on it somewhere along its length, and often at all points. All the mines named above paid dividends, and very few assessments were made. The ore lying within 800 or 900 feet of the surface was finally exhausted along the whole vein, and dividends fell off, assessments became frequent, and great depression followed. This continued until patient exploration revealed, several hundred feet deeper, a rich ore body, in the Crown Point and Belcher Mines, which produced an amount of bullion hitherto unexampled in the history of the vein, dividends amounting to a million a month coming several months in succession. This body of ore was worked out in time, and depression followed again, until the discoveries in Consolidated Virginia, also at great depth, brought the vein once more into prominence. These surpass anything yet on record, in silver mining.

The Big Bonanza Mine.—For more than a year this mine has divided $1,080,000 monthly, and there is no sign of exhaustion. The following figures, which were furnished at the company's office, give a fair view of the operations of this mine: During 1875, and the three first months of 1876, the bullion receipts of this company were *twenty-four million eight hundred and fifty thousand, five hundred and twenty-four dollars and eighty-four cents* ($24,850,524.84).

In March, 1876, were worked 24,991 800–2,000 tons of ore, which produced $3,634,218.92 in bullion, the average product per ton being $145.40.

The above bullion weighed about 56 tons.

The bullion from this mine and others on the Comstock Lode is very pure, and on an average is about .045 fine in gold, and .950 in silver, leaving only about .005 of base metal. The proportion of gold to silver varies, and with it the value of the bullion per pound. A shipment, which represented a fair average, was of 50 bars of $186,998 stamped value, and weighing 5,741 lbs. avoirdupois, thus representing a value of $32.57 per lb. Had this been pure silver, it would have been stamped $18.81 per lb., and the excess above that, is for the gold in the bullion. It may surprise one to be told that silver bullion, carrying so large a portion of gold, shows no trace of it. A bar of gold and silver, in equal proportions, would scarcely differ in color from a pure silver bar. Its weight would, however, reveal the presence of the gold, at once. When six or seven-tenths are gold, its color begins to show.

The valuable product obtained from the ore was over seventy-two per cent. of its assay value during the month reported above. It is not usual to obtain a better result than this without roasting the ore before amalgamation. It will interest one, not familiar with mining, to notice how small in both bulk and weight the bullion product is when compared with the amount of ore handled. During the month referred to, four hundred and forty-six tons of ore, which would make a mass 10 feet high, 20 feet wide and 30 feet long, yielded only one ton of bullion, which could be melted into a solid cube 18 3-5 inches on a side, or 1,560 cubic feet of ore were worked to obtain one cubic foot of bullion.

Reduction of the Ores.—The ores at this place are worked without roasting by the pan process of American origin, first adopted on the Comstock Lode. It is suited admirably to ores which work kindly, requiring little chemical action or heat to make them part with their

LAKE ESTHER, SIERRA NEVADA MOUNTAINS.—FROM A PAINTING BY ALBERT B[illegible]

precious contents, to be taken up by amalgamation with quicksilver. Though it rarely yields as close a result as the Mexican patio process, or the furnace and barrel process of Freiberg, it is so much more expeditious and economical of labor, and so capable of being applied on a large scale, that, on the whole, it is unquestionably preferable. The other processes referred to have been thoroughly tried in Virginia City, and found utterly unsuited to the conditions existing there.

The first part of the process, is wet crushing of the ore, by stamps in iron mortars, a constant stream of water carrying off through a brass wire screen the pulverized portion as fast as reduced small enough. The screens are at the back of the mortar. Five stamps, weighing about 650 pounds each, are usually placed in a single mortar, and are lifted and dropped from five to eight inches about ninety times a minute. The feeder, standing in front, judges by the sound when and where to feed in the ore lying behind him. He is expected to feed two batteries of five stamps each, which are usually placed in one frame, and run by a single shaft. Some mills have twelve such batteries or sixty stamps. The amount crushed by a stamp in twenty-four hours—for work never stops day or night—varies with the fineness of the screen, the character of the ore, and the skill of the feeder, and is from one to two and a half tons a day. Automatic machinery for feeding batteries is now introduced in many mills.

The stream running constantly from the battery is received in a series of tanks and settled as much as possible, the deposit from it being coarse sand at first, and fine sediments at last. The fine sediments are called slums, and must be thoroughly mingled with the coarse sand in the after process, for though often containing the richest portion of the ore, the atoms are so impalpably fine, and adhere to one another so closely, as to elude the mechanical agencies employed to obtain the precious metal they bear, and, if worked by themselves, carry away nearly all they are worth with them. By mingling them with the sand in as nearly as possible the same proportion in which they come from the stamps, they become broken up, separated and distributed through the whole mass of pulp, and are persuaded to give up the most of the silver they hold. This silver is not in metallic form, but combined with sulphur, chlorine or antimony for the most part. Chlorides of silver easily and sulphurets more reluctantly part from the base with which they are united, and amalgamate with quicksilver.

Antimonial silver not only refuses to do this, but obstructs the process on the part of other silver compounds with which it may be associated, and is, therefore, dreaded by all silver millmen who do not roast their ores; but the compounds of silver at Virginia City, are chiefly chlorides, and antimonial silver ores, though they occur there, are found in small quantities only.

To effect this amalgamation of the silver in the ore with mercury, the crushed pulp is now placed in quantities of one to two tons, sometimes even more, in an iron pan, five or six feet in diameter and three to four feet deep, and ground and stirred by a revolving muller, till all the coarse sand is reduced fine. The muller is then raised and the grinding ceases, but the agitation is continued, and a large body of quicksilver is introduced, and steam is also let either into the body of the pulp, or a false bottom under the pan, so as to heat the whole mass, the amalgamator in charge standing by and testing it with his finger, thinning it with slums of water, thickening it with coarse sand, shutting off the steam or letting more on, as his judgment dictates, till the temperature and consistency suit. This process is continued from three to twelve hours, according to the richness and the kindly or refractory temper of the ore. Poor ores must be rushed through, that a large amount may be worked. Rich ores, after yielding handsomely, may still obstinately retain more value than some poor ones ever carried.

The pulp is kept thick enough to float minute atoms of quicksilver, and is made to roll over and over by wings on the sides of the pan and on the muller, until all the amalgamation that can be effected is accomplished, when the motion is diminished, and the charge in the pan drawn off into a large settler on a lower level, where it is diluted with a large volume of cold water, and slowly stirred, and the quicksilver atoms uniting, gather in a body at the bottom and are drawn off through a syphon. Meantime, a stream of water running through the settler, carries off the earthy contents, and finally, when quicksilver ceases to gather, the settler is drawn off nearly to the bottom and made ready for the contents of another pan. It is usual to have one settler for two pans, and give half the time to settling that is occupied in grinding and amalgamating.

The silver and gold, so far as they have been taken up, are now held by the quicksilver. This is strained through long, deep, conical, canvas bags, and the tough amalgam obtained is placed in close iron retorts, the quicksilver distilled out by fire; crude bullion results, which is melted in a crucible and poured into moulds, and when weighed, assayed and stamped with its value, is ready for market.

The discharged ore from the settler is called tailings, and is often caught in large reservoirs, and after lying months or years, as the case may be, is worked through the pans and settlers again, and this process is sometimes repeated several times, especially if ore becomes scarce. The practice of different mining companies as to the disposition of their tailings, varies exceedingly. So long as ore is plenty, no pains are taken to save them. They never have been worked so closely as not still to carry several dollars to the ton value in precious metal.

The process employed at Virginia City, is in use wherever silver is mined on the Pacific Coast, with such modifications as differences in the character of the ore demand. Some ores are so refractory as to require roasting. They are first dried thoroughly, then crushed dry, next roasted to expel sulphur, antimony, zinc, etc., and then treated in pans and settlers as if crushed wet without roasting. The process is expensive, but has some compensation in the closer percentage of assay value obtained, and smaller waste of quicksilver. The loss of this metal in amalgamating unroasted ores, amounts in various ways to from two to four pounds for each ton worked. Some of it combines with chlorine in the ore, and is converted into calomel. This is lost beyond recovery. Some of it is volatilized by the heat in the pans, and some escapes through the joints of the retorts, and this also is lost finally, and sometimes hurts workmen exposed to the fumes. Most of it is lost by not being gathered in the settler. It goes off in minute atoms, carrying gold and silver with it. This is partly recovered by working the tailings, or by running them over blankets in sluices which entrap enough of it to pay well for the cost of the process.

Sinks of the Great Nevada Basin.—One of the most wonderful natural features of that part of the Continent lying between the Wahsatch and Sierra Nevada Ranges of Mountains, is the Great Desert and its numerous sinks. The sink of the Great Salt Lake has already been alluded to. It is a great natural curiosity of itself. It receives the waters of an immense region of country, and, though gradually rising, is still confined to its banks, and gives off its surplus waters by evaporation. There is no evidence whatever that it has a subterraneous outlet. Between it and the sinks of the Nevada Desert, there is an elevated ridge and broken ranges of mountains, with gaps and valleys between them. This whole desert has evidently been a lake, or an inland sea, at some time, while the mountains have been islands in it. Passing the ridge, or low divide between the broken mountains, which separates the Great Salt Lake from the desert beyond, and we arrive at the sinks of the Nevada Basin. The first is the Humboldt Lake, which has been described. Then the Humboldt and Carson Sink, which, unlike the Great Salt Lake, receives the waters of both the Humboldt River and Lake and the Carson River and Lake, flowing from opposite directions; and, in the hot months of summer, when evaporation is greatest, is very nearly dry. On the other hand, in the spring, when the snows of the mountains melt, or when heavy rains occur in the winter and spring months, causing a large flow of water in the Humboldt and Carson Rivers, these lakes of the same name nearly always rise together, and the vast salty plain, in and around the sink, becomes a lake of great size. There is no evidence of any subterranean outlet to the waters that flow into this large sink. On the contrary, those who have noticed the rapidity with which water disappears from a tub or other vessel exposed to the sun and air in this region, have no difficulty in believing, in fact almost seeing, the process of evaporation going on, by which the waters are drunk up and scattered over the earth in clouds, to be again distilled in rain.

Walker Lake, which receives the flow of Walker River, is another one of these mysterious sinks. It is off to the south of Carson Lake. The river rises in the Sierra Nevadas and flows in a general easterly direction, till its waters are swallowed up by the sands of the desert, or lost through the same process mentioned elsewhere. There are also numerous streams rising in the mountains, assuming large proportions by the time they reach the valleys, but the sands of the desert soon drink them dry, and they are "lost to sight."

North of the Central Pacific, about 20 miles from Wadsworth, are the sinks of Pyramid Lake, Winnemucca Lake and Mud Lake, the latter being a considerable distance north of Pyramid Lake. These bodies of water at times quite large, are called fresh water lakes, though they are brackish and abound in fish. Northeast of Winnemucca Lake is Quin's River, quite a large stream near its source in the mountains of Idaho; but it becomes lost in the desert, on its way, apparently, to Winnemucca Lake. These lakes and the desert are the mighty sinks which drink up the water that is not evaporated, but sometimes evaporation gets the best of them. North-west of Mud Lake, over in California, is Honey Lake, another remarkable body of water. It is sometimes dry so that teams can be driven across its bed, and then again it is on the rampage. Its waters resemble soap-suds, and are admirably adapted for washing purposes. When lashed by the winds, its waters become a rolling mass of foam, and afford a magnificent spectacle to the beholder. If it only had permanent water of the character alluded to, it would be an excellent location for a huge laundry.

Stage Routes to Lake Tahoe.—A favorite route to Lake Tahoe is *via* Carson City. It may be more easily reached and seen on the westward tour, than to wait and include it on the eastward return.

After a visit to Virginia City, the tourist will return to Carson City, remain over night at a good comfortable hotel, the Ormsby House,—whose proprietor considers it "*the highest toned hotel in Nevada,*" and next morning, at 8.30 A. M., take Benton's Stage for Tahoe.

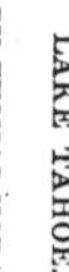

LAKE TAHOE.
BY THOMAS MORAN.

To visit and make the circuit of the lake, and return to Carson will require at least 18 hours, but most tourists will find it desirable to stop at the little hotel on the opposite side of the lake, and return *via* Truckee, thus seeing greater variety of scenery.

Tourists by this route to Virginia City, Carson and Tahoe, will be obliged to leave the Overland Western train at Reno, about 11.40 P. M., and a comfortable night's rest can be enjoyed at the Railroad Hotel. In the morning a train leaves at 6.15 A. M., and arrives at Carson at 7.30; after taking one hour for breakfast, the tourist can either proceed to Virginia City and spend the day, or take immediate departure for Lake Tahoe. Private team or special stage can be engaged at Benton's by any party, for a ride to the Lake at any special time.

On this route there is the best known of all California stage-drivers, who have reined kyuse or mustang horses,—the modest Hank Monk. His first fame was not on the platform of Faneuil Hall in oratory, but in the streets of Boston, with eight horses abreast, well trained to the voice and whip. He has driven stage in California and Nevada, since 1852, and made the distance between Carson and Virginia, 21 miles, in one hour and eight minutes. His appearance and gait do not indicate much energy, but he drove Horace Greeley 109 miles in 10 hours, fast enough toward the end of the journey, and as long as he can wake up his pets with a strong voice or far reaching whip, he will not fail to get his passengers through, "on time." But to the credit of others, it should be said, that California and Nevada have hundreds of drivers not less skillful and reliable than the favorite Monk.

The route to the lake lies first south, through the Carson Valley, toward Job's Peaks and Silver Mountain, always beautiful with snow. In the clear atmosphere, the first will appear only a few miles away, but it is still more than twenty miles distant. The stage road turns west, up Clear Creek Canon, through which comes the Twenty-one Mile (V shaped) Flume of the Carson & Tahoe Lumber Company, through which 700 cords of wood, or half a million feet of mining timber can be daily delivered at Carson City from the summits of the Sierras. Along the canon are many towering, sun-burnt rocks, weather-beaten and worn into weird and fantastic shapes, and these and the swift-descending timber, splashing the water up many feet at every turn, to sparkle in the sunlight, the Carson Valley spread out below, with the Pine Nut, Walker and Sweetwater Mountains on one side, and the Sierras opposite, always attract and delight the lover of bold mountain scenery.

Near the summit, the stage road joins the old Placerville Road, and at the summit ends a narrow gauge railroad from Glenbrook, eight miles long, used only for lumber. The distance by the stage road is only three and one-half miles. The railroad is worked only in the summer months—after much of it has been sought out and found with shovels, and is exposed to damage and destruction from avalanches of snow or rock which come thundering down the steep sides with resistless force. Near the summit it has the enormous grade of 201 feet to the mile. This passage over the eastern summit of the Sierras is made where the range is depressed and the view, though beautiful, is far too contracted to fully gratify the traveler. Below, lies Lake Tahoe, girt with everlasting pine-clad hills whose snowy masses and evergreen foliage mingle with the deep blue of an inland sea, yet only a small portion of its beauty can be seen.

Lake Tahoe.—This great body of fresh water, 22 miles long, on an average ten wide, about three-fourths in California, and one-fourth in Nevada, has an elevation of a mile and a quarter, and has been sounded to a depth of 1,645 feet. Through glacial action in past ages, ice must have been piled up in the valley of this lake 3,400 feet high. It never freezes, is smooth as glass and clear as crystal, permitting the trout to be seen or pebbles counted at a depth of 50 feet. Its water changes color to a beautiful emerald or almost indigo blue according to the depth, and when disturbed by the fierce mountain winds, its waves lash the shore with foaming fury.

At Glenbrook, four steamers will be found, three of which are employed for the mills, and the fourth, the "Stanford," will be ready to convey tourists not exceeding 200 in number, around the lake.

Glenbrook is the business center of the whole region that borders on the lake. It has four saw-mills with an aggregate capacity of five million feet per month, running 11 1-2 hours per day, also a planing mill.

Captain Pray, the oldest settler, is a large land-owner, and much of the 200 acres in the ranche on the shores of the lake, is covered with a beautiful sod of timothy and clover. In the State there is no finer land, and as the captain and other mill-owners will rent none for saloon purposes, Glenbrook, with a summer population of 500, is a temperance town. The Glenbrook Hotel, usually kept in first-class style, is usually open each season, if not, comfortable accommodations can still be found at the Lake House, for $20 a week, without extra charge for the use of boats.

Shakespeare Rock, a remarkable curiosity, is a bold, perpendicular rock on which the profile of the great poet's face is outlined with great accuracy.

From Glenbrook there is a charming drive on the old Placerville Road, past Cave Rock, and around the head of the lake to Rowlands or

Yank's. The road was constructed at great expense—a single mile near the rock, costing $40,000. The only other drive, of note, is from Tahoe City to Sugar Pine Point.

The whole of the lake is not visible until the steamer has run out a little distance from the shore. Then its generic name is rather fitting. "Tahoe," in the Indian, signifies "big water," and is the name for ocean. The shore slopes gently, in places, for two miles to a depth of from 30 to 50 feet, then breaks sometimes abruptly as at the Bluffs of Rubicon or Observatory Point, to a depth of 600 or 800 feet; and off Sugar Pine Point is the greatest depth yet found. The water is clear as crystal, and the temperature in summer, when taken from considerable depth, very near the freezing point. The fare across the lake is $2.50, and around, $5. The steamer must lie idle half the year, and reasonable fares may seem thus high. Leaving Glenbrook for a circuit around the head of the lake, the first object of interest is Cave Rock, three and one-half miles from Glenbrook, about 400 feet high. This appears in the engraving from Moran's sketch made from the point just south of Glenbrook, and looking south and west.

After passing the rock, and looking back, it resembles the Great South Dome of Yosemite, split in two, and the cavern, 30 feet in length, is seen about 100 feet above the ground. The line of solid masonry and bridge for the road can just be traced from the point where the artist stood. Leaving Cave Rock, Zephyr Cove is three miles south. Beautiful meadows afford fine pasturage, and being on the east side, the earliest vegetables are here grown. The mountain's wall shows plainly its broken but regular character. From the main ridge, a cross spur is thrown out, but this must again be broken into a succession of small canons and "divides."

Just south of the cave is the old Friday Ranche, well known by the pioneers who were "on the way to Washoe" and the Kingsbury Canon, through which the road crossed the mountain to Genoa. In other days, the toll receipts on the Kingsbury grade were $500 a day.

Rowlands,—14 miles from Glenbrook, at the head of the lake, on the Old Placerville Road, was the first place of resort on the lake and originally called the Lake House. It has greatly changed from the day when J. Ross Browne was a guest, and the host "seemed to be quite worn out with his run of customers,—from a hundred to three hundred of a night, and nowhere to stow 'em—all cussin' at him for not keepin' provisions, with but little to drink, except old fashioned tarantula-juice, warranted to kill at forty paces." It has now two stores and a post-office, with accommodations for tourists at moderate price. Lake Valley appears, from a distance, like a large, pine-covered flat. It is 14 miles long and six wide, partly covered with timber, and having much grazing land of the best quality. The stock that pastures in these fertile valleys of the lake, is all driven out before the winter snows begin. Between Rowlands and Yank's, is the terminus of Gardner's Railroad, a successful enterprise for lumbering. It will soon be extended from six to ten miles.

Yank's—is 4 miles from Rowlands, and at the south-west end of the lake, just west of and with convenient access to Lake Valley, and is situated on a grassy sward, in a beautiful grove of tamaracks interspersed with tall pines and quaking aspens, with a pebbly beach gently sloping from Tellac Point, commanding a view of the whole lake, with convenient access to Tellac Mountain, and only two miles from Fallen Leaf Lake, another beautiful sheet of water, three miles long and one and one-half wide, at the head of which are excellent Soda Springs. Tellac Mountain is easily recognized from its long, flat summit, and may be ascended *via* Fallen Leaf Lake and a steep canon. The view from the summit is one of the finest on the Continent.

To the east, looking across Lake Valley and the beautiful Tahoe, the eastern summits do not shut out the country beyond, for Carson Valley and much of Nevada are in sight. On the west, are the great valleys of central California, beyond them the Coast Range, and scattered among the countless snow and purple peaks of the Sierras, there nestle thirty-six lakes in sight, varying from the deep, dark blue of Tahoe to the brilliancy of silver beneath a noonday sun. Horses and boats are always to be had at Yank's. Twenty dollars per week is the price of board; boats are charged for at city prices for carriages. "Yank" is a *soubriquet* to mark the Green Mountain origin of the host, Mr. E. Clement. The tourist will need no further introduction, but should be informed that Yank spends his winters at the lake and *sees* snow come down the mountains and accumulate around his buildings. Of all places on the lake, none is more truly beautiful for situation, than *Yank's* and it is a favorite resort.

Leaving Yank's, the steamer heads north and proceeds four miles to Emerald Bay, passing two well-rounded peaks at the foot of which is a beautiful valley, in which lies Cascade Lake. This, too, is accessible from Yank's and is one of its attractions. The point just north of the entrance to Emerald Bay was long the home of America's pride among the birds, and is named Eagle Point.

Emerald Bay—is a gem of beauty—entered on the south side of a narrow strait, as shown on our title-page. It is two miles long by about three-fourths of a mile wide. The entrance is shoal, but the bay deep. Near the head of the bay is a little granite island, with a few small trees and shrubs, and the unfilled tomb of an eccentric tar—Captain Dick—who prepared the island for his own mausoleum, in which he intended to place himself on the approach of death, but his drowned body became food for the fishes, and the lonely cross marked an empty tomb.

This charming bay is owned by Ben Holladay, Jr. His summer residence is surrounded by a grove of willows and a stream fed by eternal snows, pouring down in three successive lofty waterfalls, which rival in grace and beauty some of the smaller in Yosemite, keeps the grassy sward always green, and plays in a fountain before the door.

The surrounding hills are so steep that they can be climbed only with great difficulty. Just opposite the island, on the north side, there is the mark of an avalanche of snow, that carried the tall pines before it like shrubs, and has left the mountain side completely bare.

Rubicon Point and Bay, and Sugar Pine Point are next passed, going north on the way to McKinney's, ten miles from Emerald Bay.

At McKinney's, there is no large house, but 13 cottages and pleasant surroundings. The road to Tahoe City, gives this the advantage of a pleasant drive. Board may be had at $20 a week.

Continuing north, the steamer passes Blackwood Creek, where some towering rocks are seen whose height is scarcely comprehended, because the trees and mountains beyond are on so great a scale. Small as they seem, they are two hundred and fifty feet high, and the trees at their base not less than 200 feet.

Ward's Bay lies north of the Creek, and Bawker's Peak, a sharp, high point, is back in the mountains.

Tahoe City—is eight miles from McKinney's, and one of the loveliest spots on the lake. It is at the source of the Truckee River, the only outlet of the lake, and has the "Grand Central," the largest hotel on the Sierras, with accommodations for 160 guests, and kept by those excellent hosts, Bayley & Moody. This is the most convenient point of access for tourists from California. The road to Truckee is down the beautiful canon of the Truckee River, through a noble forest of pines, invigorating and delightful at every step. Sail and row-boats of all kinds may be had at this point, and also carriages; but the prices should be agreed upon beforehand. No boats are kept for the use of the hotel.

Board at the Grand Central may be had, varying from $3.00 to $4.00 per day, according to rooms. The view of the lake from Tahoe City is not excelled, and equalled only at Yank's and the Hot Springs.

The hotel and other accommodations are superior to all others on the lake. Besides the Grand Central, there is the Tahoe House, kept by Captain Pomin.

Tourists who desire to spend only one day in visiting the lake, take stages at this point to Truckee, 12 miles down the river.

Trout.—At Tahoe City there is a trout establishment of much interest; and another, on a larger scale, on the river half way to Truckee Station. The water is admitted to a series of ponds, each pond being appropriated to trout of a different size. The eggs are taken during April, May and June, when the fish ascend the river and the creeks, to spawn. The eggs are stripped from the female and impregnated by stripping the male fish into the same vessel in which the eggs are contained, and then placed on inclined shelves or tables where about half an inch of water runs gently, but steadily over them. The temperature of the water affects the time of hatching, and the desire is to have the water as cold as possible at the expense of time to produce the hardier fish. One trout contains about 7,000 spawn. Twenty-five cents is charged for admission to the fishery, and the privilege of fishing in the ponds granted for twenty-five or fifty cents a fish, according to the size.

The fishing in the lake is done by trolling. Spoon-hooks are sometimes used, but early in the season it is necessary to have some shining device to attract attention besides a minnow on the hook. The fisheries have been quite successful in hatching fish, but not profitable. At first nearly all died; now nearly all are raised. The young fish are nourished for several days after birth by a portion of the egg from which they are hatched remaining attached to them till it is absorbed, and then are fed on mashed fish, the yolks of eggs and liver, and the large trout are fed on suckers and white fish caught in the lakes with seines. Of course no trout are caught in seines, for this is contrary to law.

After they have grown to weigh several pounds, they will increase at the rate of a pound a year. The quantity caught in a year can not be estimated. Many are never sent to market, and they are caught in both the lake and the river as well as in Donner Lake.

From the Truckee River alone, 170,000 pounds were caught last season, half of which were shipped to Virginia City.

In the lake there are at least four kinds, two of which are most commonly known. These are the silver trout and the black trout. The silver trout are most highly esteemed, are always taken in deep water, and attain a size of thirty-two pounds. The silver trout of Donner Lake grow from eight to ten pounds, and those in the river are not so large. The black trout run up the creeks sooner in the spring than the silver, but the latter can pass over greater obstacles than the former.

The white fish found in the lake are quite unlike those of the Great North American Lakes.

While the tourist who merely crosses the lake from Glenbrook to Tahoe or *vice versa*, or who desires to reach the Central Pacific Railroad, with the loss of one day only will not make the entire circuit of the lake; others will visit the north end, and some may prefer this alone. Continuing around from Tahoe City, Burton's or Island Farm is two miles from Tahoe City. It is a lovely spot, with summer green meadows and pebbly beach, and accommodates at reasonable cost, 25 or 30 people. It is a favorite resort for California clergymen needing rest.

Burton's is connected with Tahoe City by a carriage road, and is not too far to exercise at the oars of a small boat.

Passing around the north end of the lake, there is next, Observatory Point, where the great telescope of James Lick was expected to be erected, and beyond this is Carnelian Bay, and Carnelian Beach, so called from fine specimens of chalcedony here found. Here is Doctor Bournes' hygienic establishment.

Beyond this, are Agate bay and then Campbell's Hot Springs, ten miles from Glenbrook, and on Boundary Point, because it marks the dividing line between California and Nevada.

The water boils out in several places in great volume. The hotel is comfortable; the charge $3 a day; the entire lake is seen from the house, and the baths are an advantage to be had nowhere else on the lake. There is a stage from this point to Truckee, and the stages from Tahoe City will also carry passengers thence to the springs.

Fishing and boating and driving can be enjoyed at pleasure, and in the hills there are a few grouse, quail, deer, and bear, but game is not plentiful.

The Lumber and Trees of the Lake Region.—The logs which are brought down to the lake at various points are towed to Glenbrook in V-shaped booms, from 50 to 70 feet wide at one end, and about 150 feet long, averaging 200,000 feet of lumber.

The sugar pine is the most valuable, then the yellow pine. The black, or "bull" pine was long despised, but is now highly prized for its strength. It reaches, in California, a diameter of 15, and height of 200 feet; about the lake, a diameter of 10 feet. The leaves are of a dark green color, but the cones are enormous—sometimes 18 inches long. The wood is fine grained and solid, soft and clear.

The yellow pine is not quite so large, seldom exceeding 10 feet in diameter, and has bark furrowed into plate-like sections, six or eight inches wide, and from 12 to 20 inches long.

The "bull" pine is a favorite with the woodpecker for storing his acorns, not in the hollow trees, but by drilling holes in the bark, and fitting an acorn into each. Old woodmen say the bird never makes a misfit, and selects, the first time, a nut which will exactly fill the hole he has drilled. In the valleys of California, nearly all large trees are utilized in this way.

There are two kinds of fir, the white and the red. The latter called also the Douglass fir, is a good strong timber; the former is the least esteemed in the market.

Other pines of the Sierras are interesting, but notice of all must be omitted except the Nut or "Digger" pine, so called from a sweet or oily seed forming a staple article of food for the Indians, but it does not grow in the high Sierras. It is dwarfish and scraggy, without one main trunk, but dividing up into several. It is said that this is so liable to "draw" while seasoning, that miners who were compelled to use it for building their cabins, were not surprised to see them turn over two or three times in the course of the summer.

As two daily passenger trains leave Reno for San Francisco, one arriving *via* Vallejo in eleven and a quarter hours, and the other *via* Stockton in seventeen and a half hours, from the time of leaving Truckee, the tourist economizing time, will take the former, leaving Truckee at midnight.

By leaving at 3 A. M., daylight will soon follow in the summer months, and the fine scenery of the Sierras be more enjoyed.

To see the mountains, the best plan is to stop at the summit, where there is another of the first-class hotels of James Cardwell, and gain the views from the peaks near by, and then descend the mountain by a freight train, leaving the summit at 5.30 A. M., and reaching Sacramento the same evening, at 7.45. For this, one must be willing to exchange the Palace car for the caboose, and accept delay in exchange for the leisurely enjoyment of the most wonderful railroad scenery in the world.

The Great Nevada Flume.

A PERILOUS RIDE.

By H. J. Ramsdell, of The N. Y. Tribune.

A 15 mile ride in a flume down the Sierra Nevada Mountains in 35 minutes, was not one of the things contemplated on my visit to Virginia City, and it is entirely within reason to say that I shall never make the trip again.

The flume cost, with its appurtenances, between $200,000 and $300,000. It was built by a company interested in the mines here, principally owners of the Consolidated Virginia, California, Hale & Norcross, Gould & Curry, Best & Belcher, and Utah Mines. The largest stockholders are J. C. Flood, James G. Fair, John Mackey, and W. S. O'Brien, who compose, without doubt, the wealthiest firm in the United States.

The mines named use 1,000,000 feet of lumber per month underground, and burn 40,000 cords of wood per year. Wood here is worth from $10 to $12 a cord, and at market prices, Messrs.

Flood & Co., would have to pay for wood alone, nearly $500,000 per year.

Virginia City is not built in a forest. From the top of Mount Davidson, which is half a mile back from the city, there is not a tree in sight, except a few shade-trees in the city.

Going into the mines the other day, and seeing the immense amount of timber used, I asked Mr. Mackey where all the wood and timber came from. "It comes," said he, "from our lands in the Sierras, 40 or 50 miles from here. We own over 12,000 acres in the vicinity of Washoe Lake, all of which is heavily timbered."

"How do you get it here?" I asked.

"It comes," said he, "in our flume down the mountain, 15 miles, and from our dumping grounds is brought by the Virginia & Truckee Railroad to this city, 16 miles. You ought to see this flume before you go back. It is really a wonderful thing."

The Journey.—When, therefore, two days afterward, I was invited to accompany Mr. Flood and Mr. Fair to the head of the flume, I did not hesitate to accept their kind offer. We started at four o'clock in the morning, in two buggies, the two gentlemen named in one buggy, and Mr. Hereford, the President and Superintendent of the company (which is known as the Pacific Wood, Lumber and Flume Company) and myself in the other.

The drive through Washoe Valley, and along the mountains, up and down for 16 miles over a road which, for picturesqueness, is without an equal in memory, can not be described. Not a tree, nor bush, nor any green vegetation was in sight. Hills and mountains, well defined and separate in character, were in every direction. Sage brush and jack rabbits were the only living things in sight. That beautiful purple atmosphere or mist, which has a dreamy, sleepy effect in the landscape, overspread the mountains and extended through the valley.

The road we traversed swung round and round the mountains, now going nearly to the summit, and now descending to their base.

Both teams employed were of the best, and in less than an hour and a half we had accomplished the first part of our journey, 16 miles. Here we breakfasted and went to the end of the flume, a quarter of a mile distant. The men were running timber 16 inches square and 10 feet long through it. The trestle-work upon which the flume rested was about 20 feet from the ground. The velocity of the movement of the timber could scarcely be credited, for it requires from only twenty-five minutes to half an hour for it to float the entire length of the flume, 15 miles.

The flume is shaped like the letter V, and is made of two-inch plank nailed together in the above shape. Across the top it is about two and one-half feet in width. The ends are very carefully fitted, so that where the planks go together there may be no unevenness; for timbers going at the rate of 15 to 60 miles per hour must have a clear coast.

In this trough the water runs from Hunter's Creek, which is situated about 20 miles from the terminus of the flume.

Some idea of the swiftness with which the timber runs through the flume, may be had when it is stated that in the flume there floats 500,000 feet of lumber every day (about ten hours), or 500 cords of wood.

Near the terminus an iron break is placed in the trough, slanting toward one side, so that when the timber comes rushing down, 50 or 100 pieces, one after the other, each piece is turned toward the side, and the men at the break, with a dexterous use of the crowbar, send them bounding to the ground.

I climbed to the top of the trestle-work, before the timber began to come. It was like the rushing of a herd of buffalo on a party of hunters, and I preferred to view the flume, in active working, from a distance.

We changed teams upon resuming our journey, taking fresh horses for the mountain ascent. Horsemen in the East who have never seen the mountains of Nevada, Colorado and California, can have no idea of the amount of work a horse can do, and of the difficult places through which he will go, and of the load he will carry or draw.

How a pair of horses can pull a buggy and two men up a grade that seems half-way between the horizontal and the perpendicular, over stones and fallen trees, and through underbrush six feet high and very thick, is a question I can never hope to solve; at any rate, we reached the lower mill of the company, about 18 or 20 miles. This was several hours before noon.

The mill is situated in the lower belt of timber, and there are between 400 and 500 men at work. This number includes those engaged in cutting trees, hauling logs, and sawing the lumber. How the heavy machinery of the mills, and the engines which work them were brought from the city up the mountains and placed in position, is another mystery which I have not tried to investigate.

The amount of lumber turned out by the owner of these mills, the upper and the lower, the former being two and one-half miles farther up the mountain, is marvellous.

In five minutes' time, a log from two to four feet in diameter is reduced to lumber, planks, scantling, boards, and square timber, perhaps all from the same log, for it is cut in the most advantageous manner. Sometimes one log will give three or four different kinds of lumber. The lower mill is kept running night and day, and has a capacity of 50,000 feet per day of small stuff, and of 70,000 feet when working on large timber.

SUMMITS OF THE SIERRAS.

BY THOMAS MORAN.

The upper mill has less than half the capacity, being smaller, and being worked only 12 hours a day.

The Flume.—The flume is a wonderful piece of engineering work. It is built wholly upon trestle-work, and stringers; there is not a cut in the whole distance, and the grade is so heavy that there is little danger of a jam.

The trestle-work is very substantial, and is undoubtedly strong enough to support a narrow gauge railway. It runs over foot hills, through valleys, around mountains, and across canons.

In one place it is 70 feet high. The highest point of the flume from the plain, is 3,700 feet, and on an air line, from beginning to end, the distance is eight miles, the course thus taking up seven miles in twists and turns. The trestle-work is thoroughly braced, longitudinally and across, so that no break can extend farther than a single box, which is 16 feet; all the main supports, which are five feet apart, are firmly set in mud-sills, and the boxes or troughs rest in brackets four feet apart. These again rest upon substantial stringers. The grade of the flume is between 1,600 and 2,000 feet from the top to lower end, a distance of 15 miles.

The sharpest fall is three feet in six. There are two reservoirs from which the flume is fed. One is 1,100 feet long, and the other 600 feet. A ditch, nearly two miles long, takes the water to the first reservoir, whence it is conveyed 3 1-4 miles to the flume through a feeder capable of carrying 450 inches of water.

The whole flume was built in 10 weeks. In that time all the trestle-work, stringers and boxes were put in place. About 200 men were employed on it at one time, being divided into four gangs. It required 2,000,000 feet of lumber, but the item which astonished me most was that there were 28 tons, or 56,000 pounds of *nails*, used in the construction of this flume.

To the lower mill, as the road goes, it is about 40 miles from Virginia City. Although I had already ridden this distance, yet I mounted a horse and rode two or three miles to the top of the mountain, where I had one of the finest valley views that come to the lot of man. Miles and miles below, the valley was spread out with spots and squares of green crops growing, and barren wastes of sand and sage brush reaching in a long stretch to the base of another spur of the Sierras. The City of Reno occupied a little spot on the plain—from my mountain it seemed like a city of toy houses built on Nature's carpet.

A Ride in the Flume.—Upon my return I found that Mr. Flood and Mr. Fair had arranged for a ride in the flume, and I was challenged to go with them. Indeed, the proposition was put in the form of a challenge—they dared me to go.

I thought that if men worth $25,000,000 or $30,000,000 apiece, could afford to risk their lives, I could afford to risk mine, which was not worth half as much.

So I accepted the challenge, and two *boats* were ordered. These were nothing more than pig-troughs, with one end knocked out. The "*boat*" is built, like the flume, V shaped, and fits into the flume. It is composed of three pieces of wood—two two-inch planks, 16 feet long, and an end board which is nailed about two and one-half feet across the top.

The forward end of the boat was left open, the rear end closed with a board—against which was to come the current of water to propel us. Two narrow boards were placed in the boat for seats, and everything was made ready. Mr. Fair and myself were to go in the first boat, and Mr. Flood and Mr. Hereford in the other.

Mr. Fair thought that we had better take a third man with us who knew something about the flume. There were probably 50 men from the mill standing in the vicinity waiting to see us off, and when it was proposed to take a third man, the question was asked of them if anybody was willing to go.

Only one man, a red-faced carpenter, who takes more kindly to whisky than his bench, volunteered to go. Finally, everything was arranged. Two or three stout men held the boat over the flume, and told us to jump into it the minute it touched the water, and to "*hang on to our hats.*"

The signal of "*all ready*" was given, the boat was launched, and we jumped into it as best we could, which was not very well, and away we went like the wind.

One man who helped to launch the boat, fell into it just as the water struck it, but he scampered out on the trestle, and whether he was hurt or not, we could not wait to see.

The grade of the flume at the mill is very heavy, and the water rushes through it at railroad speed. The terrors of that ride can never be blotted from the memory of one of that party. To ride upon the cow-catcher of an engine down a steep grade is simply exhilarating, for you know there is a wide track, regularly laid upon a firm foundation, that there are wheels grooved and fitted to the track, that there are trusty men at the brakes, and better than all, you know that the power that impels the train can be rendered powerless in an instant by the driver's light touch upon his lever. But a flume has no element of safety. In the first place the grade can not be regulated as it can on a railroad; you can not go fast or slow at pleasure; you are wholly at the mercy of the water. You can not stop; you can not lessen your speed; you have nothing to hold to; you have only to sit still, shut your eyes, say your prayers, take all the water that comes—filling your boat, wetting your feet, drenching you like a plunge through the surf,—and wait for eternity. It is all there is to hope for after you are launched in a flume-boat. I can not give the reader a better idea of a flume ride than to compare it to riding down an old fashioned eave-trough at an angle of 45°, hanging in midair without support of roof or house, and thus shot a distance of 15 miles.

At the start, we went at the rate of about 20 miles an hour, which is a little less than the average speed of a railroad train. The reader can have no idea of the speed we made, until he compares it to a railroad. The average time we made was 30 miles per hour—a mile in two minutes for the entire distance. This is greater than the average running time of railroads.

Incidents of the Ride.—The red-faced carpenter sat in front of our boat on the bottom, as best he could. Mr. Fair sat on a seat behind him, and I sat behind Mr. Fair in the stern, and was of great service to him in keeping the water, which broke over the end-board, from his back.

There was a great deal of water also shipped in the bows of the hog-trough, and I know Mr. Fair's broad shoulders kept me from many a wetting in that memorable trip.

At the heaviest grade the water came in so furiously in front, that it was impossible to see where we were going, or what was ahead of us; but, when the grade was light, and we were going at a three or four-minute pace, the vision was very delightful, although it was terrible.

In this ride, which fails me to describe, I was perched up in a boat no wider than a chair, sometimes 20 feet high in the air, and with the ever varying altitude of the flume, often 70 feet high. When the water would enable me to look ahead, I would see this trestle here and there for miles, so small and narrow, and apparently so fragile, that I could only compare it to a chalk-mark, upon which, high in the air, I was running at a rate unknown upon railroads.

One circumstance during the trip did more to show me the terrible rapidity with which we dashed through the flume, than anything else. We had been rushing down at a pretty lively rate of speed, when the boat suddenly struck something in the bow—a nail, or lodged stick of wood, which ought not to have been there. What was the result? The red-faced carpenter was sent whirling into the flume, 10 feet ahead. Fair was precipitated on his face, and I found a soft lodgment on Fair's back.

It seemed to me that in a second's time, Fair, himself a powerful man, had the carpenter by the scruff of the neck, and had pulled him into the boat. I did not know that, at this time, Fair had his fingers crushed between the boat and the flume.

But we sped along; minutes seemed hours. It seemed an hour before we arrived at the worst place in the flume, and yet Hereford tells me it was less than 10 minutes. The flume at the point alluded to must have very near 45° inclination.

In looking out before we reached it, I thought the only way to get to the bottom was to fall. How our boat kept in the track is more than I know. The wind, the steamboat, the railroad never went so fast. I have been where the wind blew at the rate of 80 miles an hour, and yet my breath was not taken away. In the flume, in the bad places, it seemed as if I would suffocate.

The first bad place that we reached, and if I remember right, it was the worst, I got close against Fair. I did not know that I would survive the journey, but I wanted to see how fast we were going. So I lay close to him and placed my head between his shoulders. The water was coming into his face, like the breakers of the ocean. When we went slow, the breakers came in on my back, but when the heavy grades were reached, the breakers were in front. In one case Fair shielded me, and in the other, I shielded Fair.

In this particularly bad place I allude to, my desire was to form some judgment of the speed we were making. If the truth must be spoken, I was really scared almost out of reason; but if I was on the way to eternity, I wanted to know exactly how fast I went; so I huddled close to Fair, and turned my eyes toward the hills. Every object I placed my eye on was gone, before I could clearly see what it was. Mountains passed like visions and shadows. It was with difficulty that I could get my breath. I felt that I did not weigh an hundred pounds, although I knew, in the sharpness of intellect which one has at such a moment, that the scales turned at *two hundred.*

Mr. Flood and Mr. Hereford, although they started several minutes later than we, were close upon us. They were not so heavily loaded, and they had the full sweep of the water, while we had it rather at second hand. Their boat finally struck ours with a terrible crash.

Mr. Flood was thrown upon his face, and the waters flowed over him, leaving not a dry thread upon him. What became of Hereford I do not know, except that when he reached the terminus of the flume, he was as wet as any of us.

This only remains to be said. We made the entire distance in less time than a railroad train would ordinarily make, and a portion of the time we went faster than a railroad train ever went.

Fair said we went at least a mile a minute. Flood said we went at the rate of 100 miles an hour, and *my* deliberate belief is that we went at a rate that annihilated time and space. We were a wet lot when we reached the terminus of the flume. Flood said he would not make the trip again, for the whole *Consolidated Virginia Mine.*

Fair said that he should never again place himself on an equality with timber and wood, and Hereford said he was sorry that he ever built the flume. As for myself, I told the millionaire that

I had accepted my last challenge. When we left our boats we were more dead than alive.

We had yet 16 miles to drive to Virginia City. How we reached home, the reader will never know. I asked Flood what I was to do with my spoiled suit of English clothes. He bade me *good night*, with the remark that my clothes were good enough to give away. The next day, neither Flood nor Fair were able to leave their bed. For myself, I had only strength enough left to say, "*I have had enough of flumes.*"

RENO TO SAN FRANCISCO.

Proceeding from Reno, directly to San Francisco, the line of the railroad is along the Truckee River. The meadows grow narrower, and the mountains approach on either side, then widen again in Pleasant Valley.

Verdi—is 283 miles east of San Francisco, has three stores and a planing mill; derives its importance from the lumber trade, and its notoriety from the robbery of the express and mail cars, of an overland train.

The scenery is now becoming fine; Crystal Peak may be seen on the right, and winter moonlight nights will add charms to make the views more lovely and unique between this point and Truckee. Then the mountains, denuded at their base of all timber, and the shrubs and stumps buried in deep snow are of unbroken, silvery white, while the lofty pines, farther up the steep sides or on the rounding tops, form a veil of green, and above all irregular, fleecy clouds float fantastically by, as if a silvery mist in the valleys was rising over the dark peaks, mingling light of many shades, while exulting clouds, glide smoothly and silently along the azure sky.

SNOW SHEDS ACROSS THE SIERRAS.

The Truckee River foams, as its rapid waters battle with the rocks, and it is crossed and recrossed on Howe truss bridges, and the mountains, often precipitous, show their volcanic origin in masses of basaltic rock.

Essex,—282 miles from San Francisco, is a side track at which passenger trains do not stop.

Bronco,—273 miles from San Francisco, is a meeting place for trains with a store and a summer station-agent. Soon after leaving the station, there will be noticed a post marked "State Line," standing on the 120th meridian west of Washington D. C., and this passed, the traveler is in the Golden State of California.

Between Bronco and Boca, at what was Camp 18, a flag station has just been located and named Dover.

Boca,—a telegraph station, is 267 miles from San Francisco, with a population of about 150. It is at the mouth of the Little Truckee River, and is the Spanish name for "mouth." The only business is that of the Boca Lumber Mill and Ice Company, and the Boca Brewery, the latter the largest on the Pacific Coast, and on account of the equable temperature, expected to produce the best lager-beer in the world. About 8,000 tons of ice are cut yearly from the pond. The cold is sometimes severely felt, the mercury standing at 22° below zero during the winter of 1875–6.

Prosser Creek—is 265 miles from San Francisco at the mouth of a creek of the same name, called from a hotel keeper in early days. It is a flag station, and the terminus of a flume for several milling stations, and the ice-field for two companies that supply San Francisco. Continuing west 3.3 miles, we reach

Proctor's,—262 miles from San Francisco, but trains do not stop. On the left will be noticed a large tract of flat land covered with timber, or stumps, and a ranche or two. Across this and over the range of hills beyond, lies Lake Tahoe, but keeping to the river, 3.2 miles from Proctor's, we reach

Truckee,—259 miles from San Francisco, the dividing line between the Truckee and Sacramento divisions of the railroad, with a roundhouse for 24 engines. It has a tri-weekly newspaper, the *Republican*, and is the most important town in the Sierras, on account of the business done, as a summer resort, and because of its convenience to other favorite resorts. It is the seat of a large lumber trade, and would be benefited by the establishment of an extensive fire insurance business. The town was burned in 1868, 1869, twice in 1870, in 1874, and "ChinaTown" in 1875.

GALLERY IN SNOW SHEDS, C. P. R. R.

The prevailing winds are west, and in summer one might think the great width of the street is designed to prevent fires from the locomotive sparks, but in winter the more probable suggestion is that it is for the convenience of piling up the snow when the people shovel out their houses. The population is about 1,500, nearly one-third of which are Chinamen. A large number of good stores are arranged on the north side of the street, and considerable trade carried on with Sierra and Pleasant Valleys on the north.

Its hotels are first-class—the "Truckee Hotel," where the train stops, and the Cardwell House across the wide street and a little removed from the noise of passing trains. Many desiring the benefit of mountain air, and the convenience of the railroad, spend their summer months in Truckee, from which Donner Lake is distant only two miles, and Tahoe 12.

Stages leave Truckee on Tuesdays, Thursdays and Saturdays for Randolph, 28 miles, time four hours, and fare $4; Sierraville, 29 miles, time four and one-fourth hours, fare $4; Sierra City, 60 miles, time ten hours, fare $8; Downieville, 72 miles, time twelve hours, fare $10; Jamison City, 55 miles, time ten hours, fare $8, and Eureka Mills, 58 miles, time ten and one-half hours, fare $8. On Mondays, Wednesdays, and Fridays for Loyalton, 30 miles, time five hours, fare $4; Beckwith, 45 miles, time seven and one-half hours, fare $5.

The stages leaving on Mondays, Wednesdays and Fridays, are also the stages for Webber Lake, 16 miles north of Truckee, and Independence Lake, about the same distance. At each of these is a good hotel.

Webber Lake is about the size of Donner, encircled by high, snow-capped mountains, but beautified by a rim of fertile meadow around its pebbly beach.

Cardwell's stages leave the summit daily, passing along Donner Lake to Truckee, thence to Tahoe City on Lake Tahoe. Fare from the summit to Tahoe, $2.50. Truckee to Tahoe, $2; John F. Moody, of the Truckee Hotel, also runs an elegant open coach, of the Kimball Manufacturing Company, between Truckee and Tahoe City, daily, fare $2; and Campbell's stages leave every morning for Campbell's Hot Springs on Lake Tahoe.

Truckee was named after General Fremont's old Indian, who was engaged to guide the unfortunate Donner party across the Sierras. It is full of business and beauty in summer and winter. Here, among good hotels, is the best place in the Sierras to be snowed in, although twice as much snow may be seen falling at the summit.

A Snow-Storm at Truckee.—At midnight, the mountain peaks stood clear and white, with deep shadows here and there, and above, a cloudless sky; but, at daylight, a foot of new snow lay upon many previous snows.

The one-story houses were hid from view. While the air was full of falling flakes, busy men were shoveling off the roofs of their dwellings—shoveling all the while, and half a hundred Chinamen were loading cars with snow from the railroad track to throw it down some steep mountain side. Men are coming in with their shoes in hand—not number thirteens, but—thirteen feet long, and stand them up against the wall.

These snow-shoes are about six inches wide, turned up in front like the runner of a skate, and waxed to make them slip easily over the snow. Near the middle is a leather that laces over the instep (a skeleton half-shoe), and out of which the foot will slip in case of a fall or accident.

A long pole is carried like a rope-dancer's to preserve a balance, and to straddle and sit upon for a brake, when descending a hill. They are essential to safety in these storms.

MARY'S LAKE, MIRROR VIEW.

As I watched the falling snow, nothing could exceed the beauty. As it curled and shot through the air, the mountains were shut out with a gauzy veil and darker mists. Now and then I caught a glimpse of a clump of pines on the mountain side, indistinct and gray in shadow, and as the fitful snow favored the straining eye, the long white boughs seemed bending as if conscious of the enormous weight that threatened every living thing.

When the clouds broke suddenly away, a flood of golden light leaped from hill to hill. The tall pines, partly green, but now like pyramids of snow, lift their heads above the mountain sides. But in less than fifteen minutes after the first sight of the sun, a long stratum of dark cloud came down the mountain, and the snow falls thicker and faster than ever. Its hard crystals were driven so furiously as to make one's cheeks burn, and give exquisite torture to the eyelids. I looked upon the rapid river, and around its snow-capped rocks the water played in foaming cascades.

The enormous snow-plows at length grappled with this monster of the elements.

From east and west came reports of avalanches, snow sheds down, trains wrecked and snow-bound, and soon the telegraph refused to do its bidding.

The ponderous engines were thrown from the rails in the streets, before our eyes, by the hard crystals which they crushed into glacier-like ice. With five of them behind the largest snow-plow on the road, we started toward the summit. The snow flew and even the ground trembled, and every piece of the short snow sheds was welcomed with joy and misgiving. The blinding snow, I thought, will cease to fly, but suppose that, when crushed into ice like granite, it lifts the ponderous plow of 30 tons, or that we go crashing into the shed prostrate beneath twenty or forty feet of snow; or that an avalanche has come down and our way lies through the tangled trunks of these huge Sierra pines; five boilers behind that may soon be on top of us.

Never before did I realize the need of the snow sheds, but I often rebelled against the shutting out of nature's mountain charms from the weary or unoccupied traveler.

Let the discontented not forget that five feet of snow may fall in one day; that twenty and thirty feet may lie all over the ground at one

TUNNEL NO. 12, STRONG'S CANON.

time; that forty and fifty feet are sometimes to be seen, where the road-bed is secure beneath it, and that the canons often contain a hundred feet.

These capacious reservoirs are the pledge of summer fruitfulness. A winter scene in these Sierras without even the sight of unfriendly *bruin*, will beget a fondness for the snow sheds that the summer tourist cannot imagine, and a better appreciation of the boldness and daring of the men who brave the hardships of these mountain storms, and peril their lives at every step for other's safety. Day and night I saw the servants of the public, from highest to lowest, haggard and worn, yet never ceasing in their battle against the tremendous storm, and was overwhelmed thinking of our indebtedness to their energy, skill and endurance, as well as by viewing the wonderful works of God. "The feeding of the rivers and the purifying of the winds are the least of the services appointed to the hills. To fill the thirst of the human heart with the beauty of God's working, to startle its lethargy with the deep and pure agitation of astonishment are their higher missions."

Snow Sheds.—The snow sheds, so important to winter travel, are found east of Strong's Canon Station, and west of Emigrant Gap, wherever there is no side hill, and the removal of the snow would be difficult for the plow. Between these two stations, they are without break, except for tunnels and bridges. In all, there are about 40 miles of the sheds.

They are of two kinds, the flat roof, built to hold the weight of 25 or 30 feet of snow, or slide it down the mountain side, and those with the pitched or steep roof, and "batter brace." The massiveness of the huge pine trunks, or sawed timbers, twelve or sixteen inches on a side, may be easily seen from the cars. The cost per mile varied from $8,000 to $10,000, and where it was necessary to build heavy retaining walls of masonry, some dry and some cement walls, the cost was at the rate of $30,000 per mile. Sometimes the heavy square timbers are bolted to the solid ledge, that avalanches may be carried by, and the sheds remain.

At a distance the sheds look small, but they are high enough to insure the safety of breakmen who pass over the tops of the freight cars.

During the summer months when everything is sun-scorched, the destruction of the sheds by fire is often imminent, and great loss has been suffered in this way. To prevent fires, the greatest precaution is used, and the most effective measures adopted to extinguish a conflagration. At short intervals, both sides and roof are of corrugated iron to stop the progress of a fire, and the whole line from Strong's Canon to Emigrant Gap, provided with automatic fire-alarms, telegraphing the place of danger, and at the summit is a train with tanks, and the engine ready to become instantly a well-equipped fire-brigade.

Near Truckee the railroad leaves the river which turns to the south, and it follows Donner Creek, the outlet of Donner Lake, for a short distance and then turns up the great and magnificent canon of Cold Stream Creek, in a direction nearly south-west. Before leaving Donner Creek, we are hard by

"Starvation Camp," where in the winter of 1846-7 a company of eighty-two persons, coming to California, were overtaken by snow, lost their cattle, and were reduced to such straits that many survivors fed on the remains of their starved companions. The company comprised eighty-two persons, of whom thirty-two were females, a large proportion of the whole being children. Thirty-six perished, of whom twenty-six were males. Of a party of thirteen, who went out for help, ten perished. Relief was sent to the company, but it was impossible to save all. Mrs. Donner, when the alternative was presented her, early in March, of leaving her husband, and going away with her children, or remaining with him and soon perishing, refused to abandon him, and when, in April, the spot was visited again, his body was found carefully dressed and laid out by her. How long she survived him is not known. The sufferings of this party were insignificant in amount when compared with the whole aggregate of misery endured in the early peopling of California by the Overland, the Cape Horn, and the Panama Route, but no other tale connected with these early days is so harrowing in its details as this, and no one thinking of Donner Lake, turns from its quiet and beauty, to think of this tragedy that gave it its name, without a shudder.

The old road across the mountains to Sutter's Fort, followed up the Cold Stream, where snows no longer forbid a passage across the dangerous summits.

Along and rounding this Cold Stream Canon are the finest views on the eastern side of the Sierras, not shut out by snow sheds from the traveler by rail. The canon is wide and long, and far above and across, the road-bed is cut on the steep mountain side, and then protected by long snow sheds till at last it enters tunnel No. 13. Looking up the canon, on the right, soon after entering, or back, after the Horse-Shoe Curve has been made, a long line of purple pyramids and jagged precipices surround the valley, and if the road is not at the bottom of everything, the enormous face of the mountain seems to forbid the most daring attempt to ascend. But upward —still looking back to the valley of the Truckee far below, and the train reaches

Strong's Canon,—252 miles from San Francisco, which is a side track, telegraph office and turn-table, for snow-plows, principally. Cold Stream must not be confounded with Strong's Canon, for the latter will not be reached till the train has passed half-way along the lofty wall of Donner Lake. The station was originally at Strong's Canon, but was afterward moved to tunnel No. 13, the point where the road leaves Cold Stream Canon.

Donner Lake—the gem of the Sierras, is just below, and the vigilant eye will be rewarded by a sight of it through the observation holes in the snow sheds, and when the train crosses a bridge in doubling Strong's Canon. After leaving this Canon, the road-bed is cut out of rough, rugged, granite rocks; and before the summit is reached, it has passed through the seventh tunnel from Cold Stream. These are almost indistinguishable from the sombre snow sheds, and Nos. 11 and 12 and likewise 7 and 8, are almost continuous. The longest are Nos. 13 and 6, the former 870 feet, and the latter, 1,659 feet, and the longest on the line of the road. Emerging from tunnel No. 6, the

Summit,—244 miles from San Francisco, is announced, and the train is ready to descend rapidly to the valley of the Sacramento. It is a day and night telegraph station, and has an altitude of 7,017 feet—119.8 feet above Truckee—and is the highest point on the line of the road. Many of the surrounding peaks are two and three thousand feet higher.

The Summit House is the largest hotel along the line of the road, accommodates 150 guests, and is one of the most popular in the Sierras.

One who lets the train go by, to climb to the top of the ridge through which the tunnel leads, or some higher peak, will never be sorry, for an enchanting panorama will be unrolled.

Summit Valley, with its bright pastures, and warm with life, while it touches bleak rocks, and receives the shade of the inhospitable pine or the drip of the snow—one of the loveliest valleys at such an altitude—lies toward the setting sun. In the rim that shuts out the south-west wind, towers the Devil's Peak, a bold cliff rising from out of wild surroundings; and following the ridge eastward with the eye, and around toward the point of vision, there are prominent, Old Man's Peak, just across the valley, sharpened by the wintry storms of his long life, and on the main ridge, Mount Lincoln, 9,200 feet high, and Donner Peak, 2,000 feet above the railroad, and 3,200 above the lake that sleeps in quiet beauty at its base; and across the railroad

DONNER LAKE, FROM NEAR SUMMIT, NEVADA.

BY THOMAS MORAN.

the peak from which Bierstadt sketched the "Gem" beneath. Then there are a thousand other charms in the vast heights above, and vast depths below; in contrasts of light and shade, form and color; in mists hanging over the lake, and clouds clinging to the peaks; in the twilight deepening into darkness, or colossal pyres, kindled by the coming sun, and going out in the clear light of the day; or, in the gloom of the forest mingled with the living silver of the moonlit lake.

The peaks may be ascended — some with difficulty, and some with moderate exertion— but persons of feeble constitution may enjoy all the varied charms.

The lake is of easy access, and has on its banks a hotel for tourists. The distance to the lake by the carriage road is 2 1-2 miles, and Truckee 9 miles. The summit divides the waters that flow east and sink amid desert sands, from those that flow west into the Sacramento river.

Summit Valley,—2 1-2 miles long and one mile wide, heads in the high peaks, south of the hotel. It has pasturage during the summer for many cattle, and its springs and abundance of products, fresh from the dairy, make it a delightful place for camping out.

LAKE ANGELINE.

Its waters are the source of the South Fork of the South Yuba River.

The railroad descends to the foot of this valley, keeping the divide on the north to the right, then, about three miles from the summit, crosses the most southerly branch of the Yuba. A few yards before the crossing, is a summer flag station, or

Soda Springs Station.—These springs are situated on the south side of the high ridge that forms the southern wall of Summit Valley, and are in the headwaters of the American River. They are numerous, flow abundantly, and are highly medicinal. Stages run to them both from the summit, and from Soda Station, and the ride is not surpassed, if equaled, by any in the Sierras north of Yosemite, in the number and beauty of the fine views it affords.

The hotel at the Springs is not an imposing structure, but it is kept in first-class style and is a favorite resort.

The dividing ridge, which the railroad now follows, is on the left, and on the right are great ridges and canons, which gather more water for the Yuba. Their extent alone impresses the beholder with awe, but the snow sheds allow no satisfactory view.

The first regular station after leaving the summit is 5.8 miles west, called

Cascade,—239 miles from San Francisco. The vertical descent from the summit to this point is 498 feet, and nothing here will check one's readiness to descend farther, for it is only a signal station, and there are none to signal, except such as are employed on the road.

South of the station are Kidd's Lakes, emptying into the South Branch of the South Yuba through the Upper and Lower Cascade Ravines. The bridges over the ravines will be a grateful but short-lived relief from the restraint of the snow sheds. The time in passing is too short to take in the charms of the water-falls in summer, or the ice-clad rocks in winter, and the extended view on the right.

Kidd's Lakes are dammed so as to impound the water during the winter and spring, and when the dry season approaches, it is let out over the Cascades into the river and carried, eventually, to Dutch Flat.

SCENERY OF THE SIERRAS, NEAR SUMMIT.

There is a great spur, called "Crockers" thrown out in this ridge, through which the road passes in tunnel No. 5, and thence along Stanford Bluffs to

Tamarack,—235 miles from San Francisco, another signal station. A stop will not be likely, unless to meet or pass a freight train. A small saw-mill is in operation during part of the year. Just below Tamarack, the Yuba has worn a large gorge, and the bold bluffs, which unfortunately are below the road-bed, have been called "New Hampshire Rocks," and the name may well suggest that the Granite State will soon cease to be regarded as the "Switzerland of America."

The road continues on the north or Yuba side of the divide, between the waters of the Yuba and American Rivers; and between Tamarack and Cisco, Red Spur and Trap Spur are passed by tunnels No. 4 and No. 3. Three and a half miles from Tamarack is

Cisco,—231 miles from San Francisco, a day and night telegraph station, with an elevation of 5,939 feet. It was named after John J. Cisco, the sterling, assistant treasurer of the United States, at New York City, during the late civil war. Cisco was for a year and a half the terminus of the road, and lively with business for the construction of the road, and for Nevada. It had a population of 7,000, and some dwellings erected at a cost of $5,000; large warehouses, and all the intensity of frontier life. After the removal of the terminus to Truckee, the deserted buildings were either taken down and removed or went fast to decay, until their destruction was hastened by a fire that left nothing for the morning sun to rise upon, but the freight house with a platform 1,000 feet long, standing alone amid the ashes and surrounding forests.

From Cisco there is a beautiful view on the north, with Red Mountain in the distance. Just back of Red Mountain is the Old Man Mountain, but hid from view until the train descends a few miles farther.

To detect in this any sharp or remote outline of the human profile, wrought in colossal proportion by the hand that moulded and chiseled the infinite shapes of nature, is probably beyond the keenness of any Yankee.

Leaving Cisco, the railroad continues on the

SCENES ACROSS THE SIERRAS.

1.—China Ranche. 2.—Looking across Blue Canon.

north side of the divide, with the canons of the many streams that form the Yuba on the right, and a deep valley near by through hard porphyry, passing Black Butte on the left, crossing Butte Canon, around Hopkins' Bluffs and Miller's Bluffs, eight and a half miles to

Emigrant Gap,—223 miles from San Francisco, another day and night telegraph station, is almost one vertical mile above San Francisco, the altitude being 5,221 feet. Just before reaching this station, the Yuba turns abruptly to the north, and just west of the turning place, with an elevation barely perceptible to one rushing by, Bear River heads in a valley of the same name, clothed in summer with a delightful green. At Emigrant Gap the divide is crossed by means of a tunnel, and the old Emigrant Road crossed the Gap here, and is crossed by the railroad, just a few rods west of the tunnel. Here the old emigrants let their wagons down the steep mountain side by ropes, with which a turn or two were taken around the trees at the Gap. How much better are iron rails than rugged rocks, and atmospheric brakes than treacherous cords!

On the right we have now the headwaters of the Bear River, but of the valley one can have only a glimpse except by ascending the rocks above the railroad.

Once over the divide, there are on the left, the headwaters of a branch of the North Fork of the American River, and the road follows Wilson's Ravine, and the valley of the same name is in sight for some distance. A number of little ravines may be noticed emptying in Wilson's, the largest of which, called "Sailor's," is crossed where the road doubles Lost Camp Spur, from which one may look across the ravine and see tunnel No. 1 on Grizzly Hill, and continuing he will pass along and around Blue Canon.

Blue Canon,—217 miles from San Francisco, at the crossing of which, 5.2 miles from Emigrant Gap, is the hotel, a store, a shipping point for six saw-mills, and a day and night telegraph station. The elevation is now 4,693 feet. The snow sheds are unfrequent and shorter, and the traveler will become more interested in the scenery now growing most wonderfully, until it becomes the grandest on the line of the road across the Continent.

A little mining is carried on in Blue Canon, but on too small a scale to interest a stranger.

Blue Canon is the limit of the snow which remains during the winter. It is noted for the best water on the mountains — water so esteemed by the railroad men that it is carried to supply their shops at Rocklin and Sacramento.

Flumes and ditches are almost constantly in sight. The canon grows deep rapidly and seems to fall away from the railroad, so that one instinctively wonders how he is to get down so far. This portion of the railroad has the steepest grade on the whole line—116 feet to the mile.

China Ranche.—About two miles west of Blue Canon, a side track is passed where the close-tilling Celestial gardened prior to and at the location of the road—and the fact lingers in the name, *China Ranche.* Mountains may be seen as far as the eye can reach. After passing the ranche, there is a very deep cut through Prospect Hill, the name suggesting the loss of the passenger in the cut. On the west side of Prospect Hill is Little Blue Canon, where Shady Run, a pretty little creek, is seen on the left. It was so named by engineer Guppy at the time the road was located, in honor of the good camping ground it afforded.

Shady Run,—212 miles from San Francisco, is a side track, but not even a flag-station, 4.7 miles from Blue Canon. Near it the railroad passes around Trail Spur, and, on the left is one of the finest views on the line of the road, the junction of Blue Canon Creek and the North Fork of the American River; there the great chasm, worn by glaciers to a depth of about 2,000 feet, extending a mile to the junction of the South Branch, the precipitous sides narrowing to the water's edge and forbidding ascent even on foot, through the narrow gorge—and mountain upon mountain, back toward the snow peaks left an hour and a half ago—and eastward for fifty or more miles, till they are mingled in the eye as the stars of the milky way, add to the impressiveness of the view which is enchanced by its suddenness.

Just west of Trail Spur, and after passing Serpentine Ravine, one may look down the Great American Canon into Green Valley and Giant's Gap, beyond. The view is sublime, with the bright emerald green of the pastures; the terraced and rounded, black, gloomy forests, overhead, and the frowning approach of the majestic mountains, stopped where the icy torrent slowly rent the very frame-work of the Continent.

For a time the tourist will be compelled to leave the main slope of the American River and be carried across the ridge or divide at Hog's Back, across Canon Creek, to

Alta,—208 miles from San Francisco; 3,607 feet elevation. Here are several stores and the center of considerable lumber trade. Its population does not exceed a hundred. It is a day telegraph station, 4.8 miles from Shady Run. At one time soap-root, a bulb, growing like the stub of a coarse, brown mohair switch, just emerging from the ground, was gathered by the Chinamen. It has strong alkaline properties, and is used for washing and for *genuine* hair mattresses. It has become too scarce to be gathered here with profit by even the keen, moon-eyed Celestial.

Below Alta we strike the slope of Bear River, and on this water-shed we travel, winding among

SCENES ACROSS THE SIERRAS.

1.—Cold Stream. 2.—Shady Run. 3.—Anderson Valley. 4.—Castle Peak. 5.—Lake Donner. 6.—Green Bluffs. 7.—Little Blue Canon. 8.—Prospect Hill.

hills, until we near Cape Horn. But only 1.9 miles from Alta, we arrive at

Dutch Flat,—206 miles from San Francisco, our approach to which is heralded by the unmistakable evidences of mining, seen in the upturned face of the country.

The water that came down in advance of the cars from Summit Valley and Kidd's Lakes is now utilized. It was gathered from the East Fork of the American River, from Monumental Canon and Wilson's Ravine, and carried in Bradley's ditch around Lost Camp Spur and emptied into Blue Canon, near Blue Canon Station, and taken up again at the station and carried by ditches and flumes to Fort Point, where the railroad crosses it, and soon after one of the spurs is tunneled in two places to find an easy grade, but it cannot descend safely as fast as the cars, and at Prospect Hill passes through a tunnel 100 feet above the railroad, and is then emptied into Canon Creek, from which it is again taken up and distributed by flumes or great iron pipes to the mines we overlook at Dutch Flat and Gold Run. There are three separate ditches, the "Cedar Creek," an English company, bringing water from the American River; the "Miner's Mining and Ditch Company," with water from Bear River, and the "Yuba Ditch Company." The first two companies own and work mines, and the latter derives all its revenue from the sale of water. For hydraulic mining, this is one of the most important regions in the State.

Dutch Flat, or German Level, has an altitude of 3,395 feet. It is an old town, the mining having begun in 1851. It was once more largely populated than now, yet it boasts 1,500 inhabitants. It has a Methodist and a Congregational Church, and the finest school-house in the interior of the State. It has a tri-weekly stage to Nevada City, 16 miles, leaving every Monday, Wednesday and Friday morning. The time is three hours and the fare $3.00. The route passes through the towns of Little York, 2 1-2 miles, You Bet, 6 miles, and Red Dog, 8 miles from Dutch Flat. The town is built at the head of Dutch Flat Canon, and is very irregular and hilly. It has good stores, hotels and restaurants, and an enterprising semi-weekly newspaper.

Placer Mining.—Where the earth-carrying gold could be easily dug, and water was of ready access, and the diggings *were rich enough*, the washing out was done by hand, and this form of gold hunting was called placer mining. It required no capital except the simple tools and implements used in digging and washing, with food enough to keep one till some return from labor could be obtained. Several hundred million dollars value of gold were thus washed out of the surface soil of California in early years. Little ground remains that can be made to pay by this process, and it is almost a thing of the past. It naturally led, however, to hydraulic mining which is as flourishing as ever, and promises to continue so for many years. Placer miners came occasionally upon ground which, though carrying gold, was not rich enough to pay if worked by hand, but would pay handsomely when handled on a large scale. The device was soon adopted of providing flumes in place of cradles and rockers. Into these flumes a stream was turned and the earth shoveled in. Large quantities could thus be washed as easily as small amounts had been before.

The gold in each case, except that portion which was impalpably fine, and would even float on water, was detained by riffles on the bottom of the rocker, or the flume, and gathered up from time to time. It was found eventually that large banks sometimes hundreds of feet high, were rich enough in gold to pay for working, and the device was next adopted of directing a stream against them to wash them down. Stiff beds of cement have been found rich in gold, but too stiff to yield to any except a mighty force. Higher heads of water have been sought, until even 500 feet of head have been employed, the usual range being from 50 feet to 300, and a force obtained which nothing can resist. Such a stream issuing from a six-inch nozzle, comes out as *solid to the touch as ice*, the toughest bed of cement crumbles before it, and boulders weighing tons are tossed about as lightly as pebbles. A man struck by such a stream would never know what hurt him. The strongest iron pipe is required to carry the water to the nozzle, through which it is played. No hose can be made strong enough to bear the pressure, and the directing of the stream to the point desired is effected by two iron jointed pipes, moving in planes at right angles to each other, and thus securing a sweep in every direction. The amount of the force exerted by such a stream as has been described, it is impossible to estimate except approximately, but 1,300 pounds to the inch is not too high. To provide the water required where "hydraulicking" is done on a large scale, streams are brought long distances.

The price for selling water is graduated by the size of the opening through which it is delivered, usually under six inches pressure. Practically it is found that there is in California, more gold than water, for there are many places rich in gold, which cannot be worked for lack of water.

The season varies in length, according to the situation and the rain-fall, but nowhere is it possible to work the whole year, and probably on an average the active season does not exceed seven or eight months. There is one feature connected with hydraulic mining which no one can contemplate without regret. It leaves desolation behind it in the form of heaps of shapeless gravel and boulders, which must lie for ages before blossoming again with verdure. One of the difficult

GIANT'S GAP, AMERICAN RIVER CANON.

BY THOMAS MORAN.

problems in hydraulicking is to find room for the debris which the streams, used in washing down banks of earth, are constantly carrying along with them. The beds of streams have been filled up in some parts of the State so as to increase greatly the exposure of the cultivated regions below the mining districts to inundation and ruin. Legislation has been sought by the farmers to protect their interests, but the effort was opposed by the miners and a dead-lock followed. The muddiness which will strike the tourist as affecting all the mountain streams on the west slope of the Sierra Nevadas, is the result of this mining. Once the Sacramento River, the Feather and the American Rivers were clear as crystal, but the hunt for gold has made them like the Missouri River in high flood and even muddier, and they are not likely, while this generation and the next are on the stage of life, to resume their former clearness and purity.

Gold Run,—204 miles from San Francisco, another mining town in the famous Blue Lode. It is a day telegraph station, with an altitude of 3,220 feet. It has a population of 700, with a large number of stores, and several hotels. A mile west of Gold Run and to the right, across Bear River, may be seen You Bet, Red Dog, Little York, and other mining towns can be pointed out from the cars by those familiar with the country; but Ophir will be seen by every one, looking out on the right-hand side.

A farmer from Lancaster or Chester County, Pa., would not be impressed with the worth of the country; but the lover of nature, who does not tire of the variety in the mountain scenery, will yet feel new interest in the signs of speedily emerging into an open and cultivated country. Over the Bear River Canon, on the right, may be traced the thin outline of the basin of the Sacramento River, and, in a favorable atmosphere, the Coast Range beyond is clearly visible.

Once, all the ravines in this vicinity around it, swarmed with miners. "They went to the land of Ophir for gold." The placer mines were very rich, and covered with only from one to three feet of surface. The days are long past, but every pioneer has fresh recollections of them.

"Off to the Mines."—"Hallo, Bill! where are you off to, on that mule?" [The boys all call him Bill, and so do I, but his name is William Graves.] "Wa'al, I guess I'll go'n prospect a little," says Bill, as he and his mule lazily trudge down the canon. I have known Bill these nine years, and he is a genuine prospector. I once paid him and a "pard" $5,000 in twenty-dollar gold pieces for a claim they had worked on a while. [The "pard" is not an "honest miner" any longer, but edits a one-horse paper in a little place out in the desert.] How much Bill got of the $5,000 I never knew, except that it did not long keep him from hard fare, camping out, cooking and washing for himself, and every once in a while finding a claim to work on, locate, praise up and try to sell, and then get sick of and abandon. I would like to know how many fortunes in which his fancy and confident belief have reveled, have vanished and been forgotten, like dreams. He has never struck it rich since he made his sale to me, and I fear he never will again, but no use to tell him so. There is the "Belle Boyden," on which he is keeping up assessment work, hiring out for a while to earn something ahead, so as to buy grub and keep himself going for a few weeks.

It would be cruel to call him back now and ask him about it, but he would like nothing better, and would talk about its dip, and the rock it lies in, and how much it looks like some vein or other that has turned out well,—it is astonishing how many veins run in his head—and how many feet there are in the claim, and what he values his feet at, and how much *he wouldn't take* for it, if he only had money to open it, till he and I were both tired. Bill has gone through too many tight squeezes, and seen too much of tough life to be very emotional, but get him going on about the claim that he now holds and believes in, and his eyes brighten, and he talks with unction. He is tall and loosely hung together, and to hear him drawl out his slow speech and move draggingly around, one would not think he could do much, but give him a pick, a drill, and a sledge-hammer, and set him to running a drift, or sinking a shaft, and not many will beat him. He is cute, too. When I bought his claim he went off to Frisco and New York, and it was rich to hear him tell how the sharpers of all hues and colors were after him, thinking they never had a better chance at a greenhorn, when they were never worse mistaken. What he does not know about holding one's own in a game with the boys, whether it be at cards or banter and jokes, is not worth knowing. He is honest and kind—a whole-souled fellow, true as steel, and would doubtless take a fine polish, but his prospect is small of ever getting it. He will go on walking the mountains, camping here and there, hunting for ledges while he has grub, and working when he has not, till his hard life tells on him, and he breaks down, and it is sad to know that then he will go quick. Such as he are the men that prospect the country, penetrating its canons, exploring its gulches, climbing over and over its mountain sides, and finding the outcroppings of its mineral treasures, but hardly ever are they any the richer for it themselves.

Secret Town,—and Secret Town Ravine. There is a side track but it is not now a station, and the high, curved trestle-work, at first 1,100 feet long will soon be entirely replaced by the more durable embankment. The ravine was named from its early history, to mark the efforts of a party, to conceal their discoveries of rich claims.

About a mile and half below Secret Town, there is a pretty view, where the railroad is near the edge of the side hill, and the deep ravine falls rapidly away to the American River.

A Chinese Idea of Poker.—"What's usee play poker?" remarked an almond-eyed denizen of Tucson, Nevada, the other day. "Me hold four klings and a lace; Melican man hold all same time four laces and a kling; whole week washee gone likee woodbine."

Cape Horn Mills—is a side track, at which the overland trains stop on signal, but the Virginia City passenger train will not stop. It is 5.9 miles from Gold Run, and not far from Cape Horn. Before the train "doubles" the point or Cape, Robber's Ravine will be seen on the left, deepening into the great canon of the American River.

Cape Horn.—Around the Cape, the railroad clings to the precipitous bluff at a point nearly 2,000 feet above the river and far below the summit, and where the first foot-hold for the daring workman on the narrow ledge was gained by men who were let down with ropes from the summit.

SECRET TOWN, TRESTLE-WORK.

When the Cape is rounded, Rice's Ravine will be on the left, and Colfax seen on the opposite side. At the head of Rice's Ravine the railroad crosses by trestle-work 113 feet high and 878 feet long, on the summit of the divide between Long's Ravine and Rice's Ravine—the waters from Long's going first northward to the Bear River, and those in Rice's Ravine southward into the American. At the foot of the trestle-work, and climbing up both ravines to Colfax, its terminus, on a grade of 113 feet to the mile, may be seen the narrow gauge railroad just opened to Grass Valley and Nevada City--the former 16.74 and the latter 22 1-2 miles from Colfax.

At the bottom of the deep gorge around Cape Horn, and on the mountain side across the stupendous chasm, may be seen the stage road to Iowa Hill, a mining town across the river. The railroad here is an achievement of engineering skill, genius and daring on the part of its bold projectors, triumphing over natural wonders and obstacles of which ever to be proud. The view is magnificent. No one passing can afford to miss it, or he will die poorer and worse for the loss. Unless it be the view at Giant's Gap, there is no railroad view to surpass it. The wonderful chasm is almost frightful to behold. The houses and even fields in the valley beneath are little things, and the buttresses to the deep water-gate are so enormous that large canons are as indistinct as the lines of masonry, and as the defying mountains open wild galleries back among the higher peaks, the mountain sculpture grows grander and grander until the rugged, but dimly outlined forms stretch away in a vast sea of pine, peak and snow,

"Though inland far we be."

The road-bed, to one looking down is apparently scooped out of perpendicular rock and overhanging the great abyss; and, to one looking up, is like a long skein of gray thread wound around the cliff.

Colfax and the descending railroad, and the less pretentious narrow gauge toiling up to meet each other, are clearly seen across Rice's Ravine.

Skillful Cookery.—Americans who dine with the Chinese, are surprised at the perfection to which they carry their cooking. During a recent Chinese banquet in San Francisco, an orange was laid at the plate of each guest. The orange itself seemed like any other orange, but on being cut open, was found to contain within the rind five kinds of delicate jellies. One was at first puzzled to explain how the jellies got in, and giving up that train of reflection, was in a worse quandary to know how the pulpy part of the orange got out. Colored eggs were also served, in the inside of which were found nuts, jellies, meats and confectionery. When one of the Americans present, asked the interpreter to explain this legerdemain of cookery, he expanded his mouth in a hearty laugh, and shook his head and said, "*Melican man heap smart; why he not find him out?*"

Moonlight Scenery of the Sierras.—Travelers going westward have often the pleasure of a delightful ride by moonlight across the famous scenes of the Sierras. Just at evening, when the sun casts its last glorious rays across the mountains, and lights up the peaks and snowy summits with splendor—the train arrives at Cape Horn, and the thrill of interest of the excited tourist, will never be forgotten. Take a good look from the point, westward down the grand canon of the American River. Step toward the edge of the cut, and look down the fearful precipice, which is often broken ere it reaches the lowest descent of 2,000 feet. It is a scene more famous in railroad pleasure travel, than any yet known. A few miles beyond, near Shady Run, there suddenly opens on the gaze of the expectant traveler, just before the sunlight has quite disappeared, and the evening shades come on, the vision of

The Great American Canon,—by far the finest canon of the entire Pacific Railroad. The suddenness of approach, and the grandeur of scene are so overpowering, that no pen, picture or language can give to it adequate description. Two thousand feet below, flow the quiet waters of the American River. Westward is seen the chasm, where height and peak and summit hang loftily over the little vale. Southward is a sea, yea an ocean of mountains—and the observer, seemingly upon the same level, is bewildered at the immensity of Nature's lavish display of mountain wonders; night comes on, and the heights catch the soft light of the moon, as it shines and twinkles across and among the tops of the pines, lighting up the open canons, and rendering still more deep the contrast with the shady glens—the snow fields, cold, white and chilling, with ever changing turns of the railroad, make the evening ride, beyond a doubt, the most pleasurable that ever falls to the lot of the sight-seer. The tourist must stay up long—see for yourself all the beauties of the Sierras, while there is the least possible light—Emigrant Gap, Summit, Donner Lake, Blue Canon—all are delightful, and the lover of scene pleasures must not forsake his window or the platform, till the midnight hour finds him at Truckee. Travelers eastward will bear in mind that from Cape Horn to Summit, the best scenes are on south side of the train, the American River Canon on the right hand, or south side, and the Bear and the Yuba River Valleys on the north side; but from the Summit the scene changes, and the observer must find his pleasures on the north, until he reaches Truckee.

East of Truckee, the scene is again renewed, and the river and best views are mainly on the south.

Colfax,—193 miles from San Francisco. It was named in honor of the late Vice-President, has an altitude of 2,422 feet, is a day telegraph station, and the breakfast and supper station for the overland trains. Seventy-five cents, coin, are charged for meals, and 25 minutes allowed for eating them.

The old settlement was Illinoistown, but with the opening of the station, the old town was "finished." Colfax has a population of 700, two churches, Methodist Episcopal, and Congregational, three hotels and stores to indicate that it is the center of trade for a population of several thousand.

Stages run daily to Iowa Hill, eight miles, time one and one-half hours, fare $2.50, leaving on arrival of the trains from the East.

In the fall of 1876, a new road will be completed, and stages be run to *Forest Hill*, 14 miles, in two and one-half hours. The fare will be $2.50.

Grass Valley—is 16.74 miles distant, has a population of 7,000. It is the center of the best gold quartz mining region of the State, and has the largest Protestant Church (Methodist Episcopal) in the Sierra Mountains. It has also a Congregational Church, Roman Catholic, Episcopal and Christian or Campbellite. Until recently, it had two banks, but at present has none. It is the center of large lumber, fruit and mining interests, has a daily paper, the "*Union*," and one weekly, the "*Foothill Tidings*."

This city as well as Nevada, is reached from Colfax by the narrow gauge railroad, on which two trains connect daily with the trains of the Central Pacific. The fare to Grass Valley is $7.07, and to Nevada City $2.25, the maximum allowed by the law of the State.

Nevada—has a population of 5,000, and is the county-seat of Nevada County. The people

CAPE HORN.

1.—View looking down the American River. 2.—View of Cape Horn and American River Canon, looking East. 3.—Point of Cape Horn.

of Truckee are compelled to attend court in this city. It is in the same mining region as Grass Valley, and was for many years the largest town in the mining regions. From an area of six miles, not less than $75,000,000 have been taken, and $2,000,000 are now produced annually. Slight snows fall in the winter. The route of the narrow gauge railroad lies through the valley of the Bear River, over which one looks in descending the Sierras. At the crossing of Bear River, where it joins the Elkhorn, there is some fine scenery, and although in the distance of 22 1-2 miles there are 16 stopping places, there are no towns or villages except at the termini and at Grass Valley. San Juan North, Comptonville, and Downieville, Sierraville, Lake City, Bloomfield, Moore's Flat and Eureka South, and Marysville are all connected with Grass Valley or Nevada by stage.

In passing along near Colfax, and in all the foot hills, the manzanita is seen, but the bushes are smaller here than in many other parts of California. It is a queer shrub, and like the madrona tree does not shed its leaf, but sheds its bark. Its small, red berry ripens in the fall and is gathered and eaten by the Indians. Crooked canes made from its wood are much esteemed. The bark is very delicate until varnished and dried, and great care should be taken in transporting them when first cut.

The foot hills are partly covered with chaparral, a low evergreen oak, which, in early days, afforded hiding places for Mexican robbers, and now accommodates, with cheap lodgings, many a "road agent" when supplied by a raid on Wells, Fargo & Co's treasure boxes or the coin and watches of stage-passengers. White blossoms load the air with fragrance in April and May.

On the right, the valley of the Sacramento is coming faster into sight, and the Coast Range growing more distinct. The next station, 5.1 miles west of Colfax, is

New England Mills,—at the west end of a plateau where there is no grade for three miles. Lumbering in the vicinity has declined, and the trains do not stop. The roadway continues on the south side of the divide between the Bear and American rivers, but this has so widened that the cars seem to be winding around among small hills far away from either river.

Water taken from Bear River, near Colfax, is quite near the railroad, on the right, for a number of miles, and will be seen crossing over at Clipper Gap.

Below New England Mills there is an opening called George's Gap, named from an early resident, George Giesendorfer, and farther west is Star House Gap, called from an old hotel; then signs of farming are again seen in Bahney's Ranche, at the foot of Bahney's Hill, and Wild-Cat Ranche farther west, where Wild-Cat Summit is crossed by a tunnel 693 feet long, and Clipper Ravine is then found on the left-hand side.

This tunnel was made in 1873, to straighten the road, and the ends are built of solid masonry.

Across Clipper Gap Ravine, the stage road from Auburn to Georgetown may be seen winding up the mountain side.

About half-way between New England Mills and Clipper Gap, there is a side track and day telegraph station, called *Applegates*, for the running of trains and a point for shipping lime; but passenger trains run, without stopping, from Colfax 11 1-3 miles, to

Clipper Gap,—182 miles from San Francisco. The few buildings have a store and a hotel among them. It was the terminus of the road for three or four months, and then a lively place.

Hare and mountain quail abound in these foot hills. The latter roost, not on the ground, but in trees, never utter the "Bob White," so familiar to sportsmen, and fly swifter than the eastern quail.

Auburn,—175 miles from San Francisco, is a day telegraph station, 6.6 miles from Clipper Gap, with an elevation of 1,360 feet.

From Auburn Station a daily stage runs 22 miles to Forest Hill on arrival of the train from the east, fare $4.00, and to Michigan Bluffs, 30 miles, fare $6.00, and another runs daily, except Sunday, to Greenwood, 16 miles, fare $2.50, and Georgetown, 21 miles, fare $3.00, Pilot Hill, 11 miles, fare $1.50, Colma, 21 miles, fare $2.50, and Placerville, 32 miles, fare $4.00. Alabaster Cave on the route of the latter, six miles from Auburn, is an opening in a limestone formation, and the seat of the kilns in which the best lime of California is made. What little beauty the cave once possessed has been invaded and it has now no attraction for the tourist.

The town of Auburn proper is situated below the station. It has a population of 1,000, two churches, good schools, fine orchards, and is the county-seat of Placer County. It is one of the oldest towns in the State. It has three hotels, one of which is the Railroad House. Many of its buildings are constructed of brick or stone, and grapes are extensively grown in the vicinity, and with great success. The *Placer Herald* is a weekly Democratic paper, and the *Argus*, a weekly Republican paper.

From the point where the locomotive stands, the Sacramento River can be seen on the left, as also from other points as the train continues westward. Soon after leaving the station, the railroad crosses Dutch Ravine, at the head of which is Bloomer Cut, where the train passes through an interesting conglomerate, showing a well-exposed strata of boulders, sand and coarse gravel. The trestle work at Newcastle Gap Bridge is 528 feet long and 60 feet high.

A VISION OF THE GOLDEN COUNTRY.

BY THOMAS MORAN.

As the train nears Newcastle, the Marysville Buttes, rough, ragged peaks, are easily discerned. They are about 12 miles above the city of Marysville, and the town near the railroad, but clinging to a side hill opposite, is the decayed town of Ophir.

From the trestle work, just before reaching and also after passing Newcastle, there are fine panoramas of the Sacramento Valley, on both the right hand and the left. Mount Diablo may be seen on the left.

Newcastle,—170 miles from San Francisco, is a day telegraph station, five miles from Auburn, 956 feet above the sea. It has a hotel and several stores, every man in the place a Good Templar, and some promising quartz mines in the vicinity. It was named after an old resident and hotel-keeper called Castle. An earnest of what may be seen in the lovely valley, that has such unlimited extent before the traveler, may be seen in a flourishing orange tree, growing in the open air, in a garden only a few yards from the railroad track.

BLOOMER CUT.

Almost every one will have noticed an evergreen of attractive hue, a shrub and a vine, always trifoliated. It is the poison oak or poison ivy, and unless one knows that he cannot be affected by it, he should avoid an intimate acquaintance.

Below Newcastle about a mile, the railroad leaves Dutch Ravine, along which it has kept its way from Auburn, and enters Antelope Ravine, by which it descends the plain.

Penryn—is a side track near a valuable granite quarry. The rock is susceptible of a high polish—probably unsurpassed in the State, and was used for building the dry dock of the U. S. Navy Yard, at Mare Island, and other public buildings. In summer, 200 men are employed in the quarries.

Pino,—164 miles from San Francisco, is about where the limit of the pines is found, in a country full of huge boulders, with quarries of granite, slightly softer than that of Penryn.

Rocklin—is 162 miles from San Francisco, a day and night telegraph station, with 249 feet of elevation, and is the point at which east-bound trains take an extra locomotive to ascend the mountain. The roundhouse of the railroad company, with 28 stalls, situated here is a most substantial structure, made from the granite quarries near the station. From these quarries, many of the streets of San Francisco are paved, public and private buildings erected, and here were cut the immense blocks used for the pavements of the Palace Hotel.

Junction—is 157 miles from San Francisco. It is a day telegraph station, and 163 feet above the sea. The town is called Roseville, in honor of the belle of the country who joined an excursion here during the early history of the road, and will probably be known as Roseville Junction.

Here the Oregon division of the Central Pacific leaves the main line. On the left may be seen the abandoned grade of a road that was built to this point from Folsom on the American

River. By this road, Lincoln, Wheatland, Marysville, Chico, Tehama, Red Bluff, Redding, and intermediate points are reached. One hundred fifty-one and a half miles have been built from the junction northward. Passengers going north may use their tickets to San Francisco for passage over this division, and at Redding take stage for Portland, Or. Four miles from the Junction is

Antelope,—a side track at which passenger trains do not stop, and 6.6 miles farther on, a place of about equal importance called

Arcade.—The soil is light, much of it gravelly, but it produces considerable grass, and an abundance of wild flowers. Prominent among the latter are the Lupin and the Eschscholtzia, or California Poppy. The long fence will interest the Eastern farmer, for here is a specimen of a Mexican grant. It is the Norris Ranche, now owned by Messrs. Haggin, Tevis and others, and nearly ten miles long. When California was first settled, these plains were covered with tall, wild oats, sometimes concealing the horseback rider, and wild oats are now seen along the side of the track. No stop is made, except for passing trains, until the American River bridge is reached.

About four miles from Sacramento we reach the American River. It has none of the loveliness that charmed us when we saw it winding along the mountains. The whole river-bed has filled up, and in summer, when the water is almost wholly diverted to mining camps or for irrigation, it seems to be rather a swamp. It is approached by a long and high trestle work. After crossing the bridge, on the right, you will notice some thrifty vineyards and productive Chinese gardens in the rich deposits of the river. On the left you will obtain a fine view of the State Capitol; also you get a fine view of the grounds of the State Agricultural Society. Its speed-track, a mile in length, is unexcelled. Its advantages, including the climate of the State, make it the best training track in the United States. It was here that Occident trotted in 2.16 3-4, and is said to have made a record of 2.15 1-4 in a private trial. The grand stand was erected at a cost of $15,000.

Should you pass through the city in September or October, do not fail to see for yourself the Agricultural Park and the Pavilion, and test the marvellous stories about the beets and the pumpkins, and secure some of the beautiful and delicious fruit that is grown in the foot hills.

On the left you will also see the hospital of the Central Pacific Railroad. It contains all modern improvements for lighting, heating, ventilation and drainage, and a library of 1,200 volumes. It can accommodate 200 patients, and cost the company $65,000. Fifty cents a month is deducted from the pay of all employes for maintaining the institution. No other railroad has made such generous provision for its faithful employes.

Railroad Works.—North of the city there was a sheet of water known as "Sutter's Lake" and "The Slough," and a succession of high knolls. The lake was granted to the city by the State, and to the railroad company by the city. Its stagnant waters have given place, at great cost, to most important industries. The high knolls have been levelled, and are also owned, in part, by the railroad company. Not less than fifty acres of land are thus made useful for side tracks and fruitful in manufactures. Six and a half acres of it are covered by the railroad shops. *Twelve hundred men* are constantly employed.

These are the chief shops of the railroad. Some you saw at Ogden, Terrace, Carlin, Wadsworth, Truckee and Rocklin, and you will find others at Lathrop and Oakland Point, and at Tulare and Caliente on the Visalia Division. At Oakland Point, 150 men are employed, but all these shops and even those of the California Pacific Road at Vallejo center here. These are the largest and best shops west of the Mississippi River, and form the most extensive manufacturing industry of the city.

The best locomotives, and the most elegant and comfortable passenger cars on the coast are built, and a large portion of the repairs for the whole road is done here. All the castings of iron and brass, and every fitting of freight and passenger cars, except the goods used in upholstering, is here produced; boilers for steamers put up, the heaviest engine shafts forged, telegraph instruments made, silver plating done, and 12,000 car wheels made every month. All the latest and best labor-saving tools and machinery used in wood, iron and brass work can here be seen in operation.

The capacity of the shops is six box-freight, and six flat cars per day, and two passenger, and one sleeping car per month. Twelve years ago, the work of the company at this point, was all done in a little wooden building 24 by 100 feet, and with less men than there are now buildings or departments.

Last year a million and a half dollars was paid out for labor in these shops alone, and 4,000 tons of iron consumed. Some of the buildings, like the roundhouse, are of brick. This has 29 pits each 60 feet long, with a circumference of 600 feet. Some of the buildings have roofs or sides of corrugated iron. Seven large under-ground tanks, 1,600 gallons each, are used for oil and 2,000 gallons of coal oil, and 400 of sperm consumed every month.

In connection with the shops, is a regularly organized and well-equipped fire-brigade, and in two minutes the water of two steam fire-engines can be directed to any point in the buildings.

Soon a rolling mill will be erected, and upon the location but lately pestilential. The whole

GARDENS AND GROVES OF CALIFORNIA.

1.—An Avenue in Oakland, California. 2.—Fountain on Hillside Garden, near Napa. 3.—Flower Garden in Oakland.

coast will be laid under further tribute to these shops for the facilities of travel and commerce.

Just before entering the depot you will cross the track of the California Pacific Railroad, and see the Sacramento River on the right.

Sacramento.—Trains stop twenty minutes in the depot. This affords ample time to get a lunch at the Palace Saloon in the depot, or to visit the City and Capitol. Take one of the "free busses" for the Capitol, Golden Eagle, Grand or Orleans Hotel, all first-class, comfortable and well patronized; or the street-cars will convey you near any of these. They leave the depot and go up K street—one line to Third, along Third to O, along O to Twentieth, and along Twentieth to P, and the other line, out K to Tenth, thence to H, and thence to the Agricultural Park.

The population of the city is about 20,000. The streets are regularly laid out, and beginning at the river or depot, with Front or First, are numbered to Thirty-first, and the cross-streets are lettered, beginning with A on the north side of the city. The stores are chiefly of brick, and residences of wood. The broad streets are shaded by trees of heavy foliage, the elm, walnut, poplar and sycamore prevailing, and in summer are almost embowered by these walls of verdure, that are ready to combat the spread of fires. It is a city of beautiful homes. Lovely cottages are surrounded by flowers, fruits and vines, while some of the most elegant mansions in the State are in the midst of grassy lawns or gardens filled with the rarest flowers. The orange, fig, lime and palm flourish, and the air is often laden with nature's choice perfumes. It is lighted with gas, and has water from the Sacramento River, supplied by the Holly system. Two million gallons are pumped up daily.

The climate is warm in summer, but the heat is tempered by the sea breeze which ascends the river, and the nights are always pleasantly cool. Notwithstanding its swampy surroundings and the luxuriance of its semi-tropical vegetation, statistics establish the fact that it is one of the healthiest cities in the State.

Among the more prominent buildings are the Court-house, Odd Fellows', Masonic, Good Templars' and Pioneer Halls; the Christian Brothers' College, the Churches, Schools and the Capitol. The grammar school building is a credit to the educational structures of the State, and attracts attention from visitors second only to the Capitol.

The Pioneers are an association of Californians who arrived prior to January, 1850. Their hall has an antiquarian value—especially in a very accurate register of important events extending back to A. D. 1650. Another association, the Sons of the Pioneers, will become the heirs of these valuable archives, and perpetuate the association. Geographical convenience and natural advantages have given to the city

The State Capitol.—This is the most attractive object to visitors. It cost nearly $2,500,000. It stands at the west and thrice terraced end of a beautiful park of eight blocks, extending from L to N street, and from Tenth to Fourteenth street. Back of the Capitol, but within the limits of the park and its beautiful landscape gardening, are the State Printing Office and the State Armory.

The main entrance to the Capitol is opposite M street. The edifice was modeled after the old Capitol at Washington and has the same massiveness, combined with admirable proportions, and rare architectural perfection and beauty. Its front is 320 feet and height 80 feet, above which the lofty dome rises to 220 feet, and is then surmounted by the Temple of Liberty, and Powers' bronze statue of California. The lower story is of granite, the other two of brick.

Ascending by granite steps, which extend 80 feet across the front, we reach the portico with ten massive columns. Passing through this, we stand in the lofty rotunda, 72 feet in diameter. The chambers and galleries are finished and furnished in richness and elegance befitting the Golden State. The doors are of walnut and California laurel, massive and elegant. The State library has 35,000 volumes. The great dome is of iron, supported by 24 fluted Corinthian columns and 24 pilasters. Rising above this is a smaller dome supported by 12 fluted Corinthian pillars.

The beauty of the whole is equaled in but few of the public buildings in the country, and the California laurel with its high polish adds no little to the charm. The steps leading to the top of the outer dome are easy, except for persons of delicate health, and the view to be gained on a clear day, will amply repay any exertion. The extended landscape is incomparably lovely. You are in the center of the great Sacramento Valley, nearly 450 miles long by 40 wide, where fertile soil and pleasant clime have contributed to make one of the loveliest pictures to be seen from any capitol in the world.

Just beneath lies a city with many beautiful residences, half concealed in the luxuriant verdure of semi-tropical trees. Lovely gardens enlarged into highly cultivated farms—then, wide extended plains, on which feed thousands of cattle and sheep, groves of evergreen oak, long, winding rivers, and landlocked bays, white with the sails of commerce, and along the eastern horizon stretch the rugged Sierras, with their lines of arid foot hills, perpetual verdure, and snowy summits, shining like white summer clouds in a clear blue sky.

On the west the Coast Range limits the vision with its indistinct and hazy lines, out of which the round top of Mount Diablo is quite distinct. Southward, the eye takes in the valley of the San Joaquin, (pronounced, Wah-keen), with its rapidly populating plains.

In 1850, a fire left only one house standing, where are now 21 of the principal business blocks, and in 1854, a second fire nearly destroyed the city, after which lumber was scarce at $500 a thousand.

In the winter of 1851-2, a flood covered the whole city, and led to the construction of levees, which were afterward enlarged. Part of the city, too, was raised above high-water mark. Ten years later a flood occurred, with from eight to ten feet of water in all the parts of the city not raised, and flooding the first stories of all houses and stores. In the winter of 1875-6, the river was three inches higher than ever before known, yet the city was perfectly safe.

As a distributing point, the commercial advantages of the city are second only to San Francisco. Freight by the Overland route is here started north or south. Merchants of Nevada, Northern California and Utah secure their freight from this point with less charges and greater despatch than from San Francisco, and all shipments to the mountains or beyond, must go through this gate. Fruit from the foot hills, of choicer flavor than that grown in the warmer valleys, and vegetables, enormous and abundant, from the rich alluvial soil of the rivers, concentrate here to supply the dwellers from the Sierras eastward. During the summer of 1875 the average weekly shipment, of fruit alone, to the East, was 400 tons.

The industries that already give the city prominence, and not directly connected with the railroad, are more than can be mentioned. Among them are the Capital Woolen Mills, several carriage, wagon and furniture factories, several flouring-mills, one of which, the Pioneer, is the largest in the State, with capacity for producing 600 barrels of flour and 950 tons of barley per day, boiler, general iron and brass works. Wineries are permanently established and productive.

Beet Sugar—is manufactured about three miles from the city. The works were erected at a cost of $275,000, and 1,450 acres of land are in use for the factory. Ninety tons of beets can be used, per day, yielding about 13 1-2 per cent. of saccharine matter, while the refuse is mixed with other feed and used to fatten cattle.

This promises to become one of the chief industries of California, and the only occasion where the descriptive powers of Mr. Nordhoff seem to have failed him, was in the presence of the machinery of the Johnson process used in this manufacture.

The sugar-beet does not grow to enormous size, but the mangel-wurzel continues to grow, summer and winter, until it attains enormous size. Southern California is said to have produced one of 1,100 pounds, and a farmer of Sonoma County, had one (not considering the top), three feet above the ground. We believe he fenced around it, lest a cow should get inside of it and eat out the heart.

The city has a paid Fire Department, and five newspapers—the *Daily* and *Weekly Record-Union*, the *Daily* and *Weekly Bee, The Sacramento Valley Agriculturalist* (weekly), *Sacramento Journal* (German tri-weekly), and *The Weekly Rescue*, the organ of the I. O. G. T.

Sacramento is also an important railroad center, second only to San Francisco. Here is the practical terminus of the California and Oregon Railroad, which uses the main track of the Central Pacific Railroad to Roseville, and is completed 170 miles north, to Redding. At Redding, daily stage connection is made for Roseburg, Or., 275 miles, and thence, by the Oregon and California Railroad, 200 miles to Portland. Time, four days ; Fare, $55.00, gold.

The California Pacific runs to Vallejo, 60 miles, at the head of San Pablo Bay, immediately north of, and connected with San Francisco Bay. At Vallejo, steamers connect, twice a day, for San Francisco. The whole distance is 83 miles. Davisville, Woodland, Knight's Landing, Vacaville and the Napa Valley, are reached by this road.

Here, too, is the terminus of the Sacramento Valley Railroad, the oldest in the State. The river, also, affords a pleasant route, either to Northern California, or to San Francisco.

On the upper Sacramento, steamers of light draft ascend 240 miles to Red Bluff, or by the Feather River, from its junction with the Sacramento, 65 miles to Marysville, at the confluence of the Yuba and Feather Rivers.

Below the city an active trade is carried on with steamers and sloops. The California Steam Navigation Company have a daily line of steamers leaving Sacramento at ten o'clock A. M., and reaching San Francisco about six P. M. The distance is 108 miles. The river does not present the picturesque scenery of the Hudson, but the tourist will be interested at every point, whether as he looks out over the rich lands awaiting reclamation, or the thriving villages and fertile fields on either side, or the islands well protected by high and broad levees. The spacious bays — Suisun, San Pablo, and San Francisco — afford a series of views, in which the interest is like a good novel, increasing to the end. Mount Diablo is nearly always in view. You pass the United States Arsenal at Benicia, once the rival of San Francisco, and through the Straits of Carquinez. The United States Navy Yard, on Mare Island, overlooked by the town of Vallejo, and the beauty of the approach to San Francisco, noticed more at length in connection with the California Pacific Railroad, will amply compensate for the difference in time between the all-rail route *via* Stockton and

REPRESENTATIVE MEN OF CALIFORNIA.

1.—Senator Sargent. 2.—R. B. Woodward. 3.—Senator Sharon, (Nevada.) 4.—D. O. Mills.
5.—James C. Flood. 6.—W. C. Ralston. 7.—M. S. Latham. 8.—Gov. Irwin.

the river. The river-boats, however, are not run with the regularity of the trains, nor are they as large and comfortable as they were a few years ago.

Leaving Sacramento on the Central Pacific Railroad, formerly the Western Pacific, we reach

Brighton,—134 miles from San Francisco, where the Sacramento Valley Railroad leaves the main track. This road extends to Folsom, 22 miles, where it connects with the Sacramento Valley and Placerville Railroad, to Shingle Springs 26 miles, whence daily stages leave for Placerville, 58 miles from Sacramento. The old town of Brighton was on the Sacramento River opposite the present station, and on the old Placerville road.

At the farm-houses along the country roads, you notice numerous windmills, of various sizes and styles, whirling away to fill reservoirs for household wants, or irrigate the vineyards or orchards and gardens, if any there be. They are common in all the valleys and plains of California, and numerous in the cities. The sobriquet of Stockton is the "Windmill City."

About California farms there is usually no garden. Perhaps a few vegetables are raised during the winter. In some localities certain fruits or vegetables do not grow well, and the farmer who has twenty or a hundred head of horses, before his gang-plows, or harvesting his wheat or barley, has no time for gardening and prefers to depend upon the daily visits of the vegetable wagon as well as the butcher. And among our cosmopolitan people, the only class we lack is the farming women of the Mohawk Valley, or the Pennsylvania Dutch.

Florin—is 131 miles from San Francisco, a flag station—side track, store and post-office. The hard pan is near the surface, and therefore but little moisture retained from the most copious winter rains. Trees cannot send down their roots until this hard pan is broken through for them.

Elk Grove,—123 miles from San Francisco. In early days the hunter here could find large game without visiting Shasta, Tulare Lake or the mountains. At the old hotel the sign of the elk horns invited the traveler, suggesting him a dish that even then was seldom seen. Beyond, on the right hand, is some of the best soil in the State in the low lands, comprising the delta of the Sacramento, Mokelumne and San Joaquin Rivers. There are Presbyterian and Methodist Episcopal Churches in the village.

McConnell's,—119 miles from San Francisco, on the banks of the Cosumne River, a stream like all others in California, turbid in winter, and an empty channel in summer.

In California the name "ranche" (a contraction of the Spanish *rancho,* which is primarily the rude lodging-place of herdsmen, or an establishment for raising horses and cattle), has almost superseded the "*hacienda,*" or farm. McConnell's Ranche is, however, devoted largely to stock raising, and on it are kept the finest imported thorough-bred merino sheep. Sheep raising is among the most profitable pursuits in the State, and the woolen manufactures of California are unequaled in whatever line they have hitherto sought to excel.

Galt—is 112 miles from San Francisco. The Central Pacific Company are now building a branch road to the coal mines at Ione City. Daily stages connect Galt and Ione, Sutter Creek, Jackson and Mokelumne Hill, and during the summer proceed to the Calaveras Grove of Big Trees, 30 miles from Mokelumne Hill.

Ione City—is in a prosperous mining and farming region, and has recently received new life from the development of large coal fields.

Sutter Creek,—on this stage route, is 31 miles from Galt, and ranks next to Grass Valley in Nevada County, as a quartz mining locality. Here is the famous Amador or Hayward Mine, where the excavations are now made several hundred feet below the level of the sea. It has been one of the richest mines in the State, and produces about $700,000 annually. With irrigation, fruit growing and agriculture succeed well.

Jackson—was formerly rich in placer mines, but the prosperous mining interests of today are in quartz. The soil and climate combine to produce fruit unexcelled in the State, and large quantities of wine and brandy are made.

Mokelumne Hill—is 41 miles from Galt, and was the county-seat of Calaveras County until 1867. It was one of the earliest mining settlements. The Gwin and other quartz mines are now successfully worked. This route to the Big Trees is traveled but little, except by those who desire to visit the towns between them and Galt. The tourist will, undoubtedly, proceed to Stockton or Lathrop.

Acampo,—only a flag station.

Lodi,—formerly called Mokelumne. A daily stage leaves Lodi at 2.20 P. M., for Mokelumne Hill, 37 miles distant; fare $5.

Just before reaching the village, the Mokelumne River is crossed. Lodi is one of a flourishing trio of villages.

Woodbridge—is 2 miles north-west, and

Lockford,—4 miles north. This is one of the best portions of the great valley, across which one now passes. The soil is a rich sandy loam, producing abundantly, and the intelligent, energetic people are surrounded with all the necessary appendages of first-class farms. The evergreen trees have given their name "*Live Oaks,*" to a large region in this part of the valley.

Castle—is 97 miles from San Francisco—a flag station. The Calaveras River is crossed before reaching Stockton, but except in winter is only an empty channel. On either side of the road will be seen abundant crops, or unmistakable promise of them. Much of the land is so level that the large fields of 100 or more acres can be completely submerged from either of their sides.

On the right, entering the town of Stockton, stands one of the

Insane Asylums—of the State. The other, recently opened, is located at Napa. The grounds at this place comprise 130 acres, all under a high state of cultivation. There are about 1,300 inmates. The first building passed is the largest and most imposing, has every modern convenience, and is occupied by female inmates. The male inmates occupy the other buildings.

Stockton—is 91 miles from San Francisco, and has a population of 12,000. It is 23 feet above the sea, and the county-seat of San Joaquin County. It was laid out in 1848 by Captain Webber, who named it to commemorate Commodore Stockton's part in the conquest of California. It is two miles from the San Joaquin River, at the head of Stockton Slough, which is navigable at all seasons for vessels of 250 tons.

The heart of the town was destroyed by fire in 1849 and again in 1851. It is laid out with broad streets at right angles, and has street-cars from the depot to the principal hotels and the Insane Asylum. "Free busses" also convey passengers to the Yosemite, Mansion, Grand or Central, all first-class hotels. The city was once the exclusive base of supply for a large mining and agricultural trade which is now diverted, yet the development of the country has caused a steady increase of its volume of business. It is admirably situated to control the trade of the whole San Joaquin Valley, but needs a ship canal that will enable ocean vessels to load at its wharves.

The water supply is from an artesian well, 1,002 feet deep, flowing 300,000 gallons of pure water daily, the water rising 11 feet above the surface of the ground. The city is lighted with gas and has an efficient volunteer fire department. Two daily and weekly papers, the *Stockton Independent* and *Evening Herald*, four banks and large woolen, leather, wood, iron and paper factories, wholesale and retail stores, and an extensive grain business are the foundations and measures of the prosperity of the city. The leather tanned here is considered equal to the best French, and commands as high a price.

The proximity of iron and coal should make this city the Pittsburg of the Pacific. It has fourteen organized churches, some of which have built houses of worship—Roman Catholics, Methodists, North and South, German and Colored, Episcopalians, Congregationalists, Baptists, white and colored Christians (Disciples), and Jews. Passing in the cars, nothing is seen of the better residences, of which there are many, provided with every convenience and comfort. Excellent public and private schools are the boast of the people, for, if Californians ever boast (which they never do), they do not forget to speak of their schools. Masons, Odd Fellows, Red Men, Knights of Pythias, Hibernians, Pioneers and other societies represent social and benevolent progress. Near the depot, on the left, may be seen the grounds of the San Joaquin Valley Agricultural Society.

Heat.—The city has the best climate of the valley. The hot air of the interior is usually tempered by the sea breeze, and the nights are always cool. The hot and sickly places of California are never reached by the traveler. In Sacramento it is said to be hot in Marysville, and in Marysville, one is referred to Oroville for heat, and in Stockton, men say it is hot at Merced. The simple fact is that all parts of the Great Central Basin of California are subject to occasional north winds—the dread, at once, of man and beast. They usually lull at night, but continue, at least, three successive days. The wind having swept over hundreds of miles of dry and scorching plains, breathes as from a furnace, the mercury marking 110° to 120° in the shade. One may fancy himself in Egypt or Barbary, withered and fainting under blasts from the Sahara Desert.

The origin of the name, California, is said to be from two Spanish words, "*caliente fornalo*," meaning a "heated furnace." This seems plausible. The extreme dryness of the climate, however, enables men and animals to endure this heat surprisingly. Sunstrokes are unknown. Rapid evaporation keeps the pores open, no perspiration accumulates, the skin is dry and cool, and a heat 20 to 30 degrees above what would mark an intensely heated term, in the moister atmosphere of the Eastern States, produces little exhaustion in the dry atmosphere of this central basin. Horses travel frequently 50 to 60 miles a day without injury, the thermometer marking 100° or over. Stockton has not yet attained the importance as a railroad center, to which her position entitles her. A narrow gauge road to Ione City was commenced, but there is no prospect of its early completion. The Stockton and Copperopolis Railroad extends easterly into Calaveras and Stanislaus Counties, the main branch 30 miles to Milton, with a branch at Peters, 15 miles from Stockton, to Oakdale, 34 miles from Stockton.

To the Big Trees, Calaveras Group.—The best route to the Calaveras Grove of Big Trees is *via* Stockton and Milton. There is another grove of big trees at Mariposa, which is best reached from Lathrop and Merced. The comparative inducements to visit one or the other, will be stated hereafter, and here will be described only the route from Stockton to the Calaveras Grove. Cars leave Stockton at 12.35 P. M.,

1.—Grizzly Giant, Mariposa Grove. 2.—Three Graces, Calaveras Group. 3.—Scenes in Mariposa Grove.
4.—Trunk of Big Tree, Mariposa Grove. 5.—Natural Arch, Big Tree, Mariposa Grove. 6.—Calaveras Group, Big Trees.

for Milton; stages leave Milton at 2.45 P. M., and reach Murphy's at 7 P. M., where the first night is spent.

The Grove, 15 miles from Murphy's, is reached the next day at 11 A. M., and those who desire can leave at 3 P. M. the same day, and return to Murphy's for the second night. On the following day one may reach San Francisco, or go to Garrote, 45 miles from the Yosemite Valley. To visit the Calaveras Grove and Yosemite Valley by this route requires 145 miles of staging. This route to the Yosemite Valley *via* Milton, is called the Big Oak Flat, or Hutching's Route, the former name from a local point on the road, and the latter after the man who in past years did more than any other to make the Yosemite Valley known, and by whose untiring energy the stage road to it was opened. It is one of three routes by which the valley is reached without horseback riding. It is the shortest route from Stockton or San Francisco, but it requires more staging than the other two. To go directly to the valley by this route, one leaves Stockton for Milton at 12.35 P. M., and spends the night at Chinese Camp, 23 miles from Milton, reaching the valley the second day after, at 2 P.M. For the other three routes to the valley, see Lathrop, the next station. The decision whether to visit the Calaveras or the Mariposa Grove of Big Trees, substantially determines the route taken to and from the valley. The considerations that enter into this decision are as follows: There are seven known groves of big trees. Of these only the Calaveras and Mariposa have accommodations for tourists, are easily accessible and convenient to other points so as to be visited in comparatively little time and without large expense. It is true, that the Tuolumne and Merced Groves are directly on different routes to the valley, but the number of trees in these is small, and their size is not great. In the Tuolumne there are but ten, the largest only 24 feet in diameter. In both the Calaveras and Mariposa Groves are prostrate trunks one-sixth larger than the largest living trees, which enable one to realize, as cannot be done by looking at and walking round living trees, the enormous size of these forest giants. As the tourist will probably see one of these two groves it may be well to note for him that

	In the Calaveras Grove.	In the Mariposa Grove.
The No. of trees is	93	600
Diameter of largest,	33 feet.	33 feet.
Circumference of largest living tree, six feet above the ground,	61 feet.	90 feet.
No. of living trees between 80 and 90 feet in circumference,	0	1
No. between 70 and 80 feet,	0	6
No. between 60 and 70 feet,	1	2

The largest tree yet known in any of the groves is on King's River, 40 miles from Visalia, and is 44 feet in diameter.

The Calaveras Grove was the first discovered, the first opened to tourists, has been long and well known, has a first-class hotel directly at the edge of the grove, where a summer vacation may be pleasantly passed; the trees all the while growing on the visitor in size and beauty, as Niagara does on him who tarries there.

Private teams for either the big trees or the valley, or both, may be had at Stockton, Milton, or Merced, but unless one's time is absolutely unlimited, the public conveyance is to be chosen. By relays of horses these hurry one over the dry plains, and once in the midst of the charming scenery of the foot hills, one can tarry at pleasure.

The most notable trees in the Calaveras group are:

The Father of the Forest, which measures 435 feet in length, 110 feet in circumference.
Mother of the Forest,—321 feet high, 90 feet in circumference.

Hercules, ...	320 feet high,	95 feet circumference.
Hermit, ...	318 feet high,	60 feet circumference.
Pride of the Forest, .	276 feet high,	60 feet circumference.
Three Graces, . . .	295 feet high,	92 feet circumference.
Husband and Wife, .	252 feet high,	60 feet circumference.
Burnt Tree, . . .	330 feet long,	97 feet circumference.

"Old Maid," "Old Bachelor," "Siamese Twins," "Mother and Sons," "Two Guardians."

Lathrop,—82 miles from San Francisco. Lathrop has a fine hotel, erected by the railroad company, and is the junction of the Visalia Division of the Central Pacific Railroad, which runs southward to Goshen. There is a roundhouse for six engines—and a *California Grizzly,* caught when a cub, in 1870, in the Coast Range.

Southern Pacific Railroad.

This connects at Goshen with the Central Pacific Railroad, and forms a through route from San Francisco to Los Angeles, 444 miles in twenty-seven hours' time. A gap of 93 miles staging between Caliente and San Fernando, will soon be closed by the completion of the railroad, and by mid-summer over 600 miles of the Southern Pacific Railroad will be completed and in operation. (Fare, San Francisco to Los Angeles, $20.) This is also the quickest route to Arizona. Stages leave present terminus of Southern Pacific every other day, Sundays not excepted. This road penetrates the entire length of the

San Joaquin Valley,—and will cross the great plains of Southern California. This great valley has the Sierra Nevada on the east, and the Coast Range on the west, is about 250 miles long, and from 20 to 150 miles wide. The area is 25,000 square miles. The greater portion of the land is a sandy loam, easily tilled. There are but few trees, but the farmers have begun to plant extensively. Frequent patches of the black, tenacious, alluvial soil, called *adobe* are found, in which the sun cracks, visible during summer, faintly suggest earthquakes. A hundred miles of wheat fields may be seen in the valley, broken only by roads and fences.

This immense valley, with a surrounding belt of timber for lumber and fuel, coal, iron, and the precious metals bordering it, adapted for growing the grains and fruits of two zones, is destined to have a teeming population and fabulous wealth. Irrigation will supply the lack of summer rains when needed. The summer tourist will be struck with the absence of all sod, and long for the refreshing sight of it once more. As it exists in the Eastern States, it is unknown in California, except where carefully nurtured. The beautiful mantle of green that covers the earth, in winter and spring, is here turned to hay without any artificial process. The juices of the grass are stored, the seeds ripened, and the roots die, and seeds sprout again.

Alfalfa, a species of clover is, however, an exception. Its roots, sometimes an inch in diameter, penetrate to a depth of 12 or more feet, and draw moisture from unseen springs. Several crops of hay may be cut from it in one season, and the quantity produced from an acre is almost fabulous. Ten years ago not a head of wheat was produced in Stanislaus County, one of the counties of this valley, and now it is the chief wheat-producing county in the State.

To the Yosemite.

There are several small stations between Lathrop and Merced. Modesto, at the crossing of the Tuolumne River, is the only town of importance. It is surrounded by a rich agricultural region, is a county-seat, with about 2,500 inhabitants, and has a grain warehouse, owned by the railroad, a quarter of a mile in length.

Merced,—57.3 miles from Lathrop, illustrates Californian growth and progress. The first building was erected in 1872, and in two years there were not less than 1,500 residents. The railroad company have erected at this point, one of the finest and most commodious hotels in the State outside of San Francisco. There are several churches and a number of public buildings, but the chief importance of the place to the tourist, is as the point of departure of stages for the

Yosemite Valley.—There are two "all wagon" roads, the Mariposa and the Coulterville. Leaving San Francisco after business hours, at 4 P. M.; Lathrop at 8.15 P. M.; one reaches Merced at 10.35 P. M., and passes the night. The next morning there is a stage at 6 A. M., Coulterville Route, and at 7 A. M., by the Mariposa. There will be 12 hours staging on either route, and one will then be ready to enjoy the rest of the mountain stillness, and the refreshment of its pure cool air.

On the Mariposa Route, the night is spent at Clark's Ranche, only five miles from the Mariposa Grove of Big Trees, and 22 miles from the hotels in the valley. The grove may be visited in the morning, and the same day at 1 P. M. one may leave for the valley *via* Inspiration or Glacier Point, arriving at 6 P. M.; but this is too much to accomplish satisfactorily in one day, and the hour of arrival in the valley will be too late to enjoy the beauty of the Bridal Veil Fall when passing it. A day is none too long to wander and wonder amid the Big Trees. It is wiser, therefore, to leave Clark's in the morning, and reach the valley about 2 P. M.

By a new road from Clark's to Glacier Point, it is possible to see the most prominent points of interest and spend only one night in the valley. The other road, entering by Inspiration Point, passes the Bridal Veil, El Capitan, the Cathedral Rocks and Spires, the Three Brothers, and Sentinel Dome to one of the hotels, opposite the Yosemite Falls. Having taken all these points of interest on the way, one may make an early start in the morning to Mirror Lake, Vernal and Nevada Falls, Glacier Point, Sentinel Dome and back to Clark's, and next day return to Merced. Taking this route, in four days from the railroad without retracing one's steps, the entire length of the valley is visited, also Mariposa Grove. One has looked up to the summit of the high, towering cliffs, and from above gazed down into the deeply eroded ravine, or far away at the high Sierras, listened to the falling waters, rambled at will among the giants of the forest, and over and over again reveled in looking into the pure depths of the purest mountain atmosphere.

No improvement on this route is possible. Every minute of time is delightfully occupied to the best advantage. One may, and should, if possible, linger in the valley to visit the South Dome, the Cloud's Rest, the foot of the Upper Yosemite, and take in gradually the growing wonders of the place. It will pay well to go twice, or more, over the same ground; or at least from Sentinel Dome one may descend again to the hotels in the valley, and thence leave it by either of the three routes.

By the Coulterville Route, after leaving Merced in the morning and passing through the towns of Snelling and Coulterville, Dudley's Ranche is reached for the first night. The valley is reached next day at 5 P. M.; passing into it along the foaming river, as it rushes out the narrow canon below the valley proper, the Bridal Veil is on the opposite side of the river, but too distant to see its rainbow, or appreciate its peculiar charms.

El Capitan, and all other features of interest spoken of on the Mariposa Route, are also passed. By this Coulterville Route, Bower's Cave is passed, and a fine view is obtained from Pilot Peak. The cave is an immense and picturesque crack or sink in the solid limestone of the mountain top, into which one may descend to an irregular bottom about a hundred feet square, in one corner of which is a small and beautiful lake.

SCENES IN THE YOSEMITE VALLEY.
1.—Bridal Veil Fall. 2.—Mirror Lake.

By both routes Merced is reached at night on the fourth day after leaving for the valley, or later according to the time spent there. The cars leave at 6 A. M., for Lathrop.

We distinctly advise travelers not to return the same way as they entered the valley, but always choose a different route. Likewise in horseback rides, always return to the valley from Glacier Point, or other points, and from there take the stage. There are three good hotels in the Yosemite, Black's, Leidig's and Walsh & Coulter's, all which are comfortable. Board, $3.50 gold per day.

Expenses.—The expense of a trip to the Yosemite will be as follows: Railroad fare to Merced and return, $15; board one week, at $3.50 gold, $24.50; stage fare Merced to valley and returning by different routes, say $40; horses and guides, say 4 days, $3 per day, $12. Total, $91.50.

As to the merits of the different stage routes, we can only say that it is preferable to enter the Yosemite *via* Inspiration Point, Mariposa and Clark's; especially in hot days, this route has most shade. The stage route from Milton is the longest. Parties with ladies will find it desirable to enter *via* Mariposa and return *via* Coulterville. Of the Yosemite hotels, Leidig's is reputed to furnish the best table and eating, Black's best rooms, and Walsh & Coulter's the best location near Yosemite Falls. The best season for visiting Yosemite is from May 1st to July 15. Later than this the falls will be dry, or have but slight volume of water.

Tickets for the Yosemite, by any route, or to go by one and return by another, may be had at Lathrop, or at 4 New Montgomery street, San Francisco.

San Joaquin Bridge,—79 miles from San Francisco, is a station at the railroad crossing of the San Joaquin River. The channel is on the west side, and in high water the country is overflowed for miles up and down the river, reaching back from it almost to Bantas, the next station.

Bantas,—74 miles from San Francisco, and 30 feet above tide-water, is named for an old family resident here. Stages leave at 10.50 A. M., for San Joaquin City, 10 miles, Grayson, 20 miles, Mahoney's, 35 miles, and Hill's Ferry, 40 miles. Through fare, $3.50. About midway between this and the next station, a railroad has been commenced to run to Oakland *via* Antioch, Martinez, San Pablo and Berkley, thus avoiding the heavy grades of the Coast Range. To the right of Bantas, down the San Joaquin River, or the branch called "Old River" is a vast extent of lowland, overflowed in June, by the melting snows of the Sierra Nevadas, and during most of the rainy season.

After the water passes off, flowers spring up, and the button willow blooms, affording excellent bee-pasture. From the first of July to the first of November, a single swarm of bees will often gather 100 lbs. of honey. Those who take care of the bees also take quinine with the honey to cure the "chills." This is believed to be the extent of their acquaintance with "Bitter-sweet." Hundreds of acres of floating land here rise and fall with the water.

Ellis,—69 miles from San Francisco, and 76 feet elevation, another village which bustles in the midst of vast wheat fields, during seasons following a wet winter, and sleeps under vast disappointments during other years.

This "West Side" of the San Joaquin River, was supposed, for many years, to be worthless. The old Spaniards left it out of their ranches except when a few square miles or leagues were taken in for the sake of securing a convenient "*loma*" as a landmark. In 1849–50, as the gold-digger urged his mule, well laden with tent, bedding, pan and rocker, and three months' provisions, his heart full of expectation of a "pile" to be speedily dug from the placers of the "Southern Mines," his eyes were often gladdened by a lake of bright water near the "trail" only a mile ahead. He saw white sails, waves chasing each other, and trees on the shores reflected from their bosom. He expected soon to camp in the grateful shade, and slake his burning thirst with the cool water. The white sails bounded away, antelope-like, across the burning plains, for alas! it was only a *mirage*—an emblem of his expected wealth. Even now many are deluded in seeing the distant water and green trees beyond.

The soil of this once desert region, now produces the best of wheat, when the rains are abundant, but from its peculiar position on the north-east of the Coast Range, the necessary rain is often wanting. A local adage is "every seven years a crop"—worse than ancient Egypt's famine. But the land-owners are moving to construct a ditch 60 feet wide and 300 miles long, to irrigate the entire valley on the west side of the river, and serve for transporting the produce to the tide-water of Suisun Bay. Once accomplished this almost desert land, will easily support a population of 3,000,000.

Fourteen miles south-west from this station is Corral Hollow or Pass, in the mountain range, at the head of which are extensive coal mines, toward which a branch railroad extends five miles. Here an extra engine is taken to overcome the steep grade of the Livermore Pass, in the Mount Diablo Range.

Medway,—64 miles from San Francisco, and 356 feet above the sea-level, was formerly called "Zinc House," from the only building in this hilly region, made of zinc a material used frequently as a substitute for lumber, then scarce and difficult to transport. The rolling hills are extensively farmed with varied success. The place has but a small population. From this station the train coils rapidly around the points of hills, across

VERNAL FALLS, YOSEMITE.

BY THOMAS MORAN.

high embankments, and through deep cuts, the engine often seen from the car window like the fiery head of a huge serpent.

The soil is coarse sand and gravel, the finer particles of which, and vegetation, too, it seems, have been blown away by the trade-winds, which, pent up by the long range, rush with concentrated fury over the summit of the pass, and sweep down with devastating force into the vacuum on the heated plains.

Suddenly the train enters a tunnel, 1,116 feet long, the only one between Sacramento and San Francisco, and is in total darkness for two minutes. Emerging, it soon arrives at

Altamont,—west of the summit of the Mount Diablo Range, 56 miles from San Francisco, and 740 feet above the level of the sea. The traveler will see numerous gray squirrels standing erect at the entrance to their homes. They are about as large as the fox-squirrel of the Eastern States, live in villages of their own, are the pest of the farmer, have increased since the land has been cultivated, and lay the grain fields under a tribute far heavier than the rent. It is a remarkable fact that both birds and squirrels have increased in variety and numbers all over the cultivated regions of the State since 1850. As the train descends into Livermore Valley, a truly picturesque scene is presented. The level valley, in form a square 12 miles across, with many narrow extensions far into the mountains, is spread out before one in full view, with rolling hills on all sides, except the west, where rises an abrupt, tree-clad mountain.

On the right, across the low hills, green with live oaks, may now be seen Mt. Diablo, not as before, a blue dome, but a real mountain, with deep gorges in its sides, covered with chaparral, and capped usually with gray mists.

It is an Indian legend that this country, west of the Sierra Nevada Mountains, was once covered with water, and the top of this mountain then a little island. At that period, says the legend, the devil was there imprisoned by the waters for a long time, and, therefore, great prosperity and quiet resulted to mankind; hence his name was given to it. However the name may have been first given, it now clings to it in Spanish form.

The western portion of this valley contains hundreds of acres of the best land in the State, much of it moist, vegetable land, in the midst of which is a lake of fresh water, near which are natural flowing wells. From these the creek derives its name "*Las Posivas*"—*i. e.*, little wells.

Much of the eastern part of the valley is covered, to a great depth, with small, angular stones, mixed with clay, and the region was thought to be useless, but it now produces the finest of wheat.

From Altamont, it is 8.1 miles to

Livermore,—47 miles from San Francisco. This is a live town, 485 feet above tide-water, with 1,000 inhabitants, a seminary of learning, beautifully nestled amid sturdy oaks, a Presbyterian and a Catholic church, a steam mill, newspaper, saloons, stores, and several large warehouses. Nine miles south, and at the head of Corral Hollow, are five veins of good coal yielding 100 tons per day, and six miles from the town another vein has been opened. These are probably an extension of the Mount Diablo Coal fields which have been worked for many years. Six and one-tenth miles down the valley is

Pleasanton,—41 miles from San Francisco, 353 feet above the sea, a village of 300 inhabitants, with several stores, a large warehouse, an abundance of good water, and a rich, beautiful country on the north connecting with other valleys, and extending to Martinez at the head of the Straits of Carquinez. This region, now Livermore Valley, was formerly called Amador Valley, from its original owner, and was an inland sea. In 1836, Mr. Livermore found the bones of a whale on the surface of the ground, near the town which bears his name. The vertebræ lay in order with the ribs scattered about like the rails of a "worm" fence. Abalone shells are also found in quantities near the old ranche house. Beautiful variegated wild pansies, the lupin and California poppy have taken the place of sea weeds.

In June may be seen, near Pleasanton, high above the grain, the yellow blossoms of the black mustard. In former years it stood 12 feet high, and so thick that it was difficult to force one's way through it. To

Sunol,—(Sun-yole) 36 miles from San Francisco, the train dashes down the narrow valley of the Alasal Creek, 5.2 miles, amid pleasing scenery, and relics of the Mexican and Indian civilization of California. On the right is the Contra Costa Range of Coast Mountains, so called because opposite the Coast Range, near and north of San Francisco. It is only a few miles across to the San Jose (San Ho-zay) Valley, where the train will pass in an opposite direction. Sunol Valley, a mile wide and three miles long, is south of this station. Seven miles above this is the Calaveras Valley, containing 1,500 acres—the proposed site of a vast reservoir to supply San Francisco with water in future years. The mountains about these valleys are extensive sheep and cow pastures, covered with wild oats.

The road passes down the canon of the Alameda Creek and over three fine bridges, yet winding with the canon, steep mountains on both sides, dressed in green or parched with summer heat; the bracing sea breezes, and the knowledge that in an hour and a half the cars will reach the bay, revive the spirits of the traveler. Soon a scene of wide extended beauty is to burst on his vision—the San Jose Valley, the Bay of San Francisco, the Serrated

Mountains that turn back the ocean tides of 8,000 miles travel, and all around him, as he hurries on to the great city, a garden spot more and more variegated with the choicest fruits and flowers, and abundant in homes of luxury and ease. From Sunol it is 6.4 miles to

Niles,—30 miles from San Francisco, 88 feet above tide-water. Here are a store, hotel, warehouse and mill. A stage runs from all trains to Centreville, three miles distant. Here is the junction of the San Jose Branch of the Central Pacific Railroad. This branch passes through *Washington Corners*, the seat of a flourishing college, under Rev. S. S. Harmon, and a pleasant village overlooking the bay, and near the old *Mission de San Jose.*

Three miles farther are the Warm Springs, in the midst of oak and other trees near the Aqua Caliente (hot water) Creek. The minerals that increase the value of the heated water are lime, sulphur, magnesia and iron. They were formerly a popular resort, but are now the property of Governor Stanford. When his designs of building and beautifying are completed, it will be one of the most attractive of the summer resorts.

Near Niles the Alameda Creek is turned into a ditch 30 feet wide, and distributed over the valley for irrigation, for although both the land and climate are moist, irrigation promotes the growth of fruits and vegetables called for by the San Francisco market.

Adjoining the south-east end of this bay, are 20,000 acres of salt marsh, now in process of reclamation by dikes and ditches.

Through this a narrow gauge railroad has been built from deep water, at Dunbarton Point, *via* Newark to Alviso, and will run thence through Santa Clara to Santa Cruz.

Along the east side of the bay are numerous salt ponds, the sea water being let in at high tide upon a large tract of land, when the rainy season is over, and this repeated several times. The concentrated brine is then drawn off in a planked reservoir, where it slowly crystallizes.

As the train passes down 2.8 miles to Decoto, the eye is pleased, in April and May, by the mountain on the right—round, green, shaven, like a lawn, or its sides rich with fields of grain; or yellow with large patches of buttercups, blue with lupin, or deep orange with the Eschscholtzia, or California wild poppy, gathered, no doubt, far east of this point, for many a sentimental nosegay, in honor of the traveler's acquaintance. It is a flower peculiar to the north-west coast of America. Wild flowers are so numerous in California that often from twenty to a hundred varieties may be gathered from one spot.

On the left, the trees mark the Alameda Creek, flowing down to the salt land. Beyond this lies the Old San Jose Road, and the richest and best cultivated portion of the valley. At Centreville, half-hidden in the distance, is an Alden fruit factory, convenient to large orchards, and, near by, on the farm of Rev. W. W. Brier, stands the tree from which originated the thousands of acres of Brier's Languedoc Almond, the soft-shelled almond, that no traveler has ever seen excelled in flavor.

The hill-sides from one to 500 feet above the valleys, are best adapted to its culture, because the warm air from the lowlands prevents injury from frost. At

Decoto,—27 miles from San Francisco, may be seen the Blue Gum Tree. Under favorable circumstances it will grow, in five years from the seed, to a height of 70 feet, with a circumference of four feet. The green wood splits readily, but the dry is as hard as the lignum-vitæ. They are highly prized for a supposed tendency to counteract malaria, and their cultivation is rapidly extending.

Soon after leaving Decoto, Alvarado may be seen. It was once the county-seat of Alameda County. The valley land in this vicinity sells for $150 to $250 per acre, and the mountain land from $10 to $30. It is a peculiarity of California, that the value of land is always stated separately from improvements.

Haywards,—21 miles from San Francisco, is 6.3 miles from Decoto. The town is seen a mile to the right, on the hill, at the outlet of Castro Valley—rich, rolling and beautiful, and well watered, four miles long by two wide. Castro Valley is named in honor of the original owner of the ranche, and Hayward's Hotel is a well-known resort.

On the hill, to the right, is seen a forest—that may be mistaken for evidence that these hills have been recently denuded of their timber. It is a forest of the Blue Gum Tree—200 acres, planted by James T. Stratton.

The town has churches, public schools, and the hotel, still kept by Mr. Hayward, is a popular place of resort for those who seek a good and quiet home without removing from business in the city. Stages leave this station for Alvarado at 9.20 A. M., and 4.20 P. M.; for Danville and Walnut Creek at 4.20 P. M., and from all trains to Haywards. For many years a railroad ran from Alameda to Haywards, but the track has been taken up.

Lorenzo,—18 miles from San Francisco, is near San Lorenzo Creek, and surrounded by a well improved country. It is a pleasant village, and contains an extensive establishment for drying fruit on the Alden process, a store, a neat church edifice and the usual places to "take a drink." The land is worth $600 per acre. The large building to the right on the mountain side, is the Poorhouse of Alameda County, with which there is a farm connected. The golden sands of California and the absence of severe winters do not keep poverty and age from every door, nor does a generous hospitality make public charity unnecessary.

This section of country is noted for its cherries and currants, but nearly every variety of fruit is extensively cultivated. One of the fine orchards on the right before reaching the station, has 100 acres of Almonds, and 200 acres of other fruits. The owner, Mr. William Meek, has constructed private water-works at an expense of $15,000.

San Leandro,—15 miles from San Francisco, was formerly a county-seat. It has a population of 1,000, a large factory for wagons and gang-plows, a Presbyterian, a Catholic and a Methodist Church, stores and saloons. In the mountains opposite, and on a creek of the same name, is located the reservoir of the Oakland water-works. The water is collected from the winter floods and is 65 feet deep.

Melrose—is 11 miles from San Francisco. Before reaching the station and after crossing the San Leandro Creek, there may be seen on the right, nestled in a beautiful vale at the foot of the mountains, the largest and best apportioned Protestant Seminary for girls, to which the Pacific Coast lays claim. The buildings were erected at a cost of about $100,000, $30,000 of which was contributed by public-spirited individuals. The 65 surrounding acres, with their oaks, sycamores, alders, willows, and laurel or bay tree; the orchards, lawns and flower-beds, the inspiring views, combining the fruitful plain, the water and the mountains beyond; a climate, always stimulating to mental effort—in short, the correspondence of attractions and advantages, without and within, make this a point of interest to all who desire to see the progress of education in one of nature's most gifted spots.

Near the race-track on the left, are several buildings with large, square chimneys, used to smelt and refine gold and silver, while on the right is a fuse factory. The town of Alameda is seen on the left, almost hidden by live oaks. A branch railroad connects it with this station, and the "local" trains of Oakland.

Between Melrose and the next station, we pass Fruit Vale, a station on the Alameda Road, and a spot of surpassing loveliness. The elegant lawns, and beautiful mansions are almost wholly concealed by the luxuriant foliage, and amid the strapping of shawls and gathering of valises, there will be no time to waste, where only a glimpse of the beauty may be had, and

Brooklyn—will be announced 2.3 miles from Melrose, and 9 miles from San Francisco. Here is the point of departure for the "local" trains that will be seen again at the Oakland wharf. It is now East Oakland, a delightful suburb of San Francisco.

The land rises gently toward the foot hills, almost from the water's edge. Since it has become a corporate part of the City of Oakland, it has made rapid improvement in the opening of new and well macadamized streets and the erection of fine residences. At this point there is a "local" train that passes directly through Oakland to Oakland Point. Before reaching the next station the train will cross the track of the Alameda Branch. This track is for the accommodation of local travel, and connects Alameda and Fruit Vale with Oakland and San Francisco. From the abundance of the evergreen oaks, one may quickly conclude that pleasure parties will find there a balmy retreat whether beneath the clear sky, or sheltered from the afternoon winds, and it has always been a popular picnic resort. On Sunday, the boats and trains are crowded with thousands seeking recreation and enjoyment there. Brooklyn is a splendid home resort for travelers; the comforts of so nice a hotel as Tubb's are worthy of appreciation.

Oakland—is 2 miles from Brooklyn. The train halts at the foot of Market Street, where many through passengers leave it, Oakland being really a suburb of the larger city near at hand, and the chosen residence of hundreds who do all their business and spend most of their daytime over there. It is beautiful for situation, and boasts a climate much preferred to that of San Francisco; the trade-winds from the Pacific, which are fierce and cold, and often heavy with fog there, being much softened in crossing the bay. This has attracted many to make it their residence, though obliged to do business in San Francisco, and about 10,000 passengers daily cross on the half-hourly and splendid ferry-boats, and the number of trips will be increased before long. The population of the city increases rapidly, and, a year since, exceeded 20,000. As measures of its enterprise and prosperity it may be stated that 1,200 new buildings are to be erected in 1876, and a quarter of a million dollars expended in building a court-house and county jail. There are three savings banks, two national gold banks, four lines of horse-cars, three flouring and four planing mills, an iron and a brass foundry, two potteries, one patent marble works, a jute bag factory, three tanneries and other establishments employing many mechanics. On the public schools, of which Oakland is justly very proud, nearly $6,000 are monthly expended, and nearly a quarter of a million dollars value in property is owned by the department. The State University is within the city limits. Its site, which has been named Berkley, is on the northern border of the city and has a direct ferry to San Francisco, and many families are planting themselves there, attracted by its natural beauty and the educational and social advantages which cluster around it. The University is open to students of both sexes, and tuition is free. The number of students exceeds 200. By special law, the

BIRD'S-EYE VIEW OF SAN FRANCISCO.

sale of intoxicating liquors is forbidden, within two miles of this University.

There are 20 churches in Oakland, of which 16 own houses of worship. Some of them are elegant and costly; the First Presbyterian Church has recently dedicated a new church building which cost them over $60,000. Seven newspapers are published, three daily, the rest weekly.

The rides in and around Oakland, for variety of attractive features, are rarely equaled. Many come over from San Francisco, in the morning, expressly to enjoy this pleasure. Lake Merritt, a beautiful sheet of water, Tubb's Hotel and the Grand Central Hotel, both spacious and admirably kept, are among the attractions which none fail to visit, and with which thousands have bright and happy memories associated.

Though incorporated as a city, Oakland is thoroughly rural. A very small portion of the business part around the chief railroad station is built up solidly, but everywhere else the houses stand detached and usually surrounded by a liberal expanse of gardens, grass-plat, and shrubbery which remind one of an eastern village. Live oaks abound, and show by their leaning over toward the east, the constancy and strength of the summer tradewinds. Geraniums, roses, fuchsias, callas, verbenas, and many tropical plants and flowers grow luxuriantly, never suffering from outdoor winter exposure, and finding a soil of surpassing richness and fertility. Fruit trees develop into bearing in a third or half the time usually required on the Atlantic Coast. The city is favored with one rare advantage. The railroad company charge no fare on their local trains, between stations within the city limits.

These trains are half-hourly, most of the day, and there are nearly five miles of railroad, . and eight stations within the city limits. The convenience of thus riding freely at all hours, can hardly be understood by those who have not experienced it. The line of the local road is directly through the city, and only local trains run upon it, all other passenger trains, and all freight trains taking the main road close to the water's edge. Of all the suburbs of San Francisco, Oakland is the most popular. Its growth exceeds that of San Francisco. The time required to reach it from California Street, is less than is required to get up-town from Wall Street in New York, and once reached, the merchant, weary with the cares of the busy day, may find a home with a more tropical luxuriance of fruit and flowers, almost the same in summer and winter, and scenery scarcely less picturesque than the banks of the Hudson afford.

Oakland Point—is the last station before reaching the ferry. The stop is made to pass over the long trestle work with a light engine. Here the railroad company own about 125 acres of land, and have extensive buildings and repair shops. On their dock they remodel, or build their ferry-boats, the boats of the California Steam Navigation Company, and here the Western Development Company build all the bridges and frame all hotels, warehouses, and other buildings for the Central, California, and Southern Pacific Railroads. About 300 men are constantly employed. There is a roundhouse for 21 engines, and tracks for the extra passenger cars needed at this important terminus.

A channel has been dredged out from this yard to the bay, which shows plainly from the cars on the left hand. The train now runs out on the trestle work, which is built out into sea water farther than any other in the world, and is the largest in waters of this depth, and also the best built wooden pier in the world. It was built five years ago, and when examined a year since, a few *teredo* were found in piles without bark; but the strength of the pier was not appreciably impaired. It is 2.8 miles long.

To protect it from fire, all the engines employed on it are fitted with force pumps, and can be used as steam fire engines at a moment's notice. There are three slips and four piers, and the aggregate width of the latter is 396 feet, and over these an immense freight and passenger business is done.

Eight sea-going ships can be loaded with grain simultaneously. Nearly all the lumber for the whole treeless region in Southern California, now reached by the railroad, is loaded from vessels at this wharf. Wagons and carriages crossing between Oakland and San Francisco come over one of these piers to the ferry-boat at present; but it involves risk to horses, vehicles, and their passengers, and the company are building ferry-boats to run by San Antonio Creek directly to Oakland, by which all teams will be ferried between the two cities, and the increasing passenger traffic have the additional tracks now needed. Freight cars cross from this wharf to the immense freight depot at the foot of Fourth Street in San Francisco, and a boat is building to carry at once 20 loaded freight cars and 20 car loads of cattle.

There is fine angling, chiefly for smelt, from these wharves. Four or five of these fish may be caught at a single cast. Within two years, eastern salmon have been placed in these waters, and occasionally these are caught. California salmon do not take the hook, because people and fish are sharp on this side of the Continent.

At Oakland wharf, passengers and baggage are transferred to the spacious and elegant ferry-boats, on which hackmen and hotel-runners will be sure to speak for themselves.

The distance from the end of the wharf across the water to the ferry-house in San Francisco is 3.4 miles, and is ordinarily made in fifteen minutes. When the wind is blowing, none but the most rugged persons should venture to stand outside the cabin; but if it is practicable to gain the view, there are many points of great interest. At night, the city itself with long rows of lights extending over hills, more than "seven," or its wide extent by day, produces at once an impression of its greatness.

Bay of San Francisco.—The bay is large enough to float the navies of the world, and beautified by a rare combination of island, mountain, city and plain. On the right, passing to San Francisco, and near the wharf, is Goat Island, a military reservation, and the subject of considerable agitation in Congress. The quarters of the officers and men are seen on the east side, and on the south end is a fog-bell and whistle that are often called into requisition. The Golden Gate proper is north, or to the right of the city—five miles long and about a mile wide.

It is strongly fortified at various points. Alcatraz, a naval station, is an island at the end of the gate and entrance to the bay, and commands the whole passage from the ocean.

Angel Island, north of Alcatraz, is another military reservation, well fortified. North-west of this may be seen the towering peak of Mount Tamalpais, the highest near the city. On the right, one may look north to the San Pablo Bay, and behind him see classic Berkley, Oakland, and Alameda, with the Coast Hills in the background. South, the view extends over the bay toward San Jose, and everywhere, except where the city stands and through the Golden Gate, it is shut in by mountains.

The trade-winds and fogs are shut out from California by the Coast Range, the fogs not rising above 1,000 feet, and when they sweep down the coast, drive through the Golden Gate with pent-up fury. The heated interior makes a funnel of this passage and creates a demand for the lace shawl and seal-skin sacque on the same day.

The ferry-house where the trip across the Continent ends, is well arranged and provided with everything necessary for the accommodation of the throngs of passengers passing through it. The baggage department of the railroad is here, and is connected by telegraph with every station on the road, giving all possible facilities for tracing stray baggage. The loss of baggage by this railroad company is almost an unknown incident, and the Pacific Transfer Company is equally reliable.

San Francisco.—The ferry-boat lands at the foot of Market Street, which is fast becoming the leading business artery of the city. Every horse-car line, except one, either runs in or crosses it, and by direct communication or transfer, all connect with the ferry at its foot. By these cars, or by carriages in waiting, the hotels which are about a half mile away are easily reached. The Grand and the Palace Hotels are on Market, at the corner of New Montgomery Street, the Lick on Montgomery, a few steps from Market Street, the Occidental and the Russ near at hand on the same street, and the Cosmopolitan at the corner of Bush and Sansome Streets, close to Market. As to their respective merits, we must decline to make comparisons or give free advertisements. Hotel coaches charge uniformly $1.00 gold for transfer of each passenger and baggage from ferry to hotel. The Transfer Company will carry baggage alone for 50 cents. Whether the overland traveler resorts to a hotel or to the home of friends, the change from a week in the railroad cars to hospitable quarters and richly spread tables will be so grateful as at first to dispel all consciousness of fatigue; but tired nature will assert herself, and the first night especially, as the arrival is at evening, will be given to rest.

Perhaps the luxury of a Turkish bath should be had at the earliest moment. "The Hammam," erected by Senator Jones on Dupont Street, near Market, at a cost of nearly $200,000, is in truly Oriental style. The building is an ornament to the city, and in it dusty travelers will experience mingled wonder and delight at its Mohammedan architecture, perfect appointments, and complete adaptation to restore a sense of cleanliness and give solid refreshment to both body and spirit.

Thus refreshed and looking about next morning, there confronts the traveler a city, the growth of twenty-seven years, which counts 275,000 inhabitants, and covers a territory of 42 square miles. On its eastern front it extends along the bay, whose name it bears, is bounded on the north by the Golden Gate, and on the west washed by the Pacific Ocean along a beach extending five or six miles. From the Golden Gate on the north, to the city and county-line on the south, is a distance of about seven miles, and the same from the bay across to the ocean. The surface is varied by hills, several of which have been built upon, and from whose summit commanding views may be obtained. Telegraph Hill looks down on the point where the Golden Gate leads into the bay and harbor. Clay Street Hill is farther south and west, and may be ascended in cars drawn up its steep-graded sides by an endless rope running just below the surface. This hill extends some distance southward, and makes the streets crossing Montgomery to the west, steep, and some almost impracticable for wheeled vehicles. Along its heights some of the railroad directors and others have erected, or are erecting, princely dwellings. That of Governor Stanford is perhaps unsurpassed in almost every respect. Rincon Hill is in the southern part of the city, and slopes down to the water's edge. Until a recent period, it was noted for elegant private dwellings and grounds; but these are now found in all directions, more clustering, however, around Clay Street Hill, perhaps, than elsewhere. The growth of the city is rather toward the west than the south.

Russian Hill is west and north of Telegraph Hill, and looks down toward the Golden Gate and what is called the North Beach, a portion of the city less in favor of late years than formerly. Smelting works, woolen factories, potteries, artificial stone-works and establishments of this general character, have clustered here.

San Francisco is very regularly laid out. There are two systems of streets, between which Market Street is the dividing line. North of Market the streets are mostly 70 feet wide, cross at right angles and run almost north and south, east and west, and the blocks are 150 varas or 275 feet wide, and 150 varas or 412 1-2 feet long, the length being east and west. Market Street runs about north-east and southwest. South of it the streets for over a mile from the city front, run parallel with it or at right angles. At about a mile from the city front these parallel streets gradually curve toward the south till they run almost north and south. This change of course was caused by the low Mission Hills there lifting themselves, and by the tendency of travel along the narrow peninsula toward the country beyond it. The streets south of Market are some of them very broad, and some quite narrow. This portion of the city was laid out originally with very wide streets and in blocks 200 varas or 550 feet wide, and 300 varas or 825 feet long, but these proved too large and it became necessary to cut them up by intervening streets, which have no element of regularity except parallelism with the others. The streets are all numbered from the city front, or from Market Street, one hundred numbers being allowed to each block after the first, to which only 99 are assigned, the even numbers always on the right hand as the numbers run. It is thus easy to locate any street and number. There are a few avenues, but with the exception of Van Ness, which is 125 feet wide, and built up handsomely, and Montgomery Avenue, which is laid out to provide easy access to the North Beach portion of the city, they are usually short and narrow, or in the most newly laid out portion of the city, not yet built up.

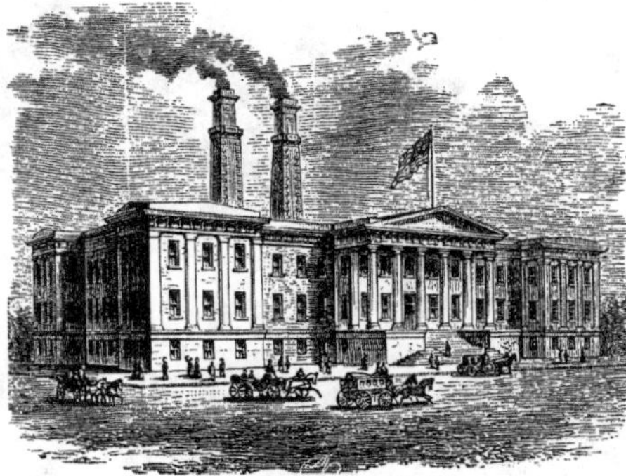

SAN FRANCISCO MINT.

The heavy wholesale business of the city is done along the water front and, mostly north of Market Street, extending back three or four streets from the front to where banks, brokers, insurance companies and office business generally have become established, the same territory south of this street being occupied by lumber merchants, planing mills, foundries, and machine shops. Retail business of all kinds is done along Kearney, the southern part of Montgomery, the upper part of Market, and along Third and Fourth Streets. Markets are scattered through the city. The Central is near Kearney to the west on Sutter Street, and the Californian between Kearney and Montgomery Streets extending through from Pine to California. Both are worth visiting, and display everything in the market line in rich profusion and perfect neatness and order. California Street and Montgomery at their junctions, are the great resort of the crowd dealing in stocks. All sorts of men may be seen there, between 9 A. M. and 6 P. M., hovering around quotations displayed on various brokers' bulletin-boards, and talking mines, for speculation centers in mining shares. Kearney Street and the southern part of Montgomery are the favorite promenade of ladies, and especially on Saturday afternoons, the Hebrew holiday, when a profusion of them, richly dressed and bejeweled, may be met there.

The theaters are all near this region. Two of them are quite new. Wade's Opera House boasts the finest chandelier on earth, and Baldwin's Academy of Music is claimed to be unsurpassed on this Continent, in beauty of interior decoration and finish.

Sidewalks throughout the city are wide and good. Most are of plank, many of asphaltum, which is well suited to the climate, the heat rarely being sufficient to soften it. A few are of cut stone or artificial stone. The last material is fast coming into favor for many uses. Streets are paved with cobbles, Russ pavement and plank, and off from lines of heavy business teaming, are macadamized. Wooden pavements are retained in many, but are not approved. The Nicholson pavement cannot be long kept down. It shrinks during the long dry summer, and with the first heavy rains swells and is thrown hopelessly out of place. Good paving material is not abundant, and the question is yet unanswered, what shall be the pavement of San Francisco in the future?

The water supply comes chiefly from reservoirs in the Coast Range Mountains south of the city, and is controlled by the Spring Valley Water Company. The rates are double and treble those charged in New York City, and are due monthly in advance. Many families pay more for their water than for their bread. It should be borne in mind, however, that some families use much more water for irrigating gardens and grass-plats, than for all household purposes.

The only government building in San Francisco that is finished and in use, and worth visiting, is the United States Mint, on Fifth Street, near Market. The machinery here is believed to be unapproached in perfection and efficiency. Visitors are admitted between 10 and 12 A. M.

BANK OF CALIFORNIA.

A Custom House is in process of erection, and a City Hall; but both are far from completion.

There are many fine buildings erected for business purposes. A number of new blocks of stores, on Kearney and Market Streets, combine spaciousness, solidity and elegance. The Ne-

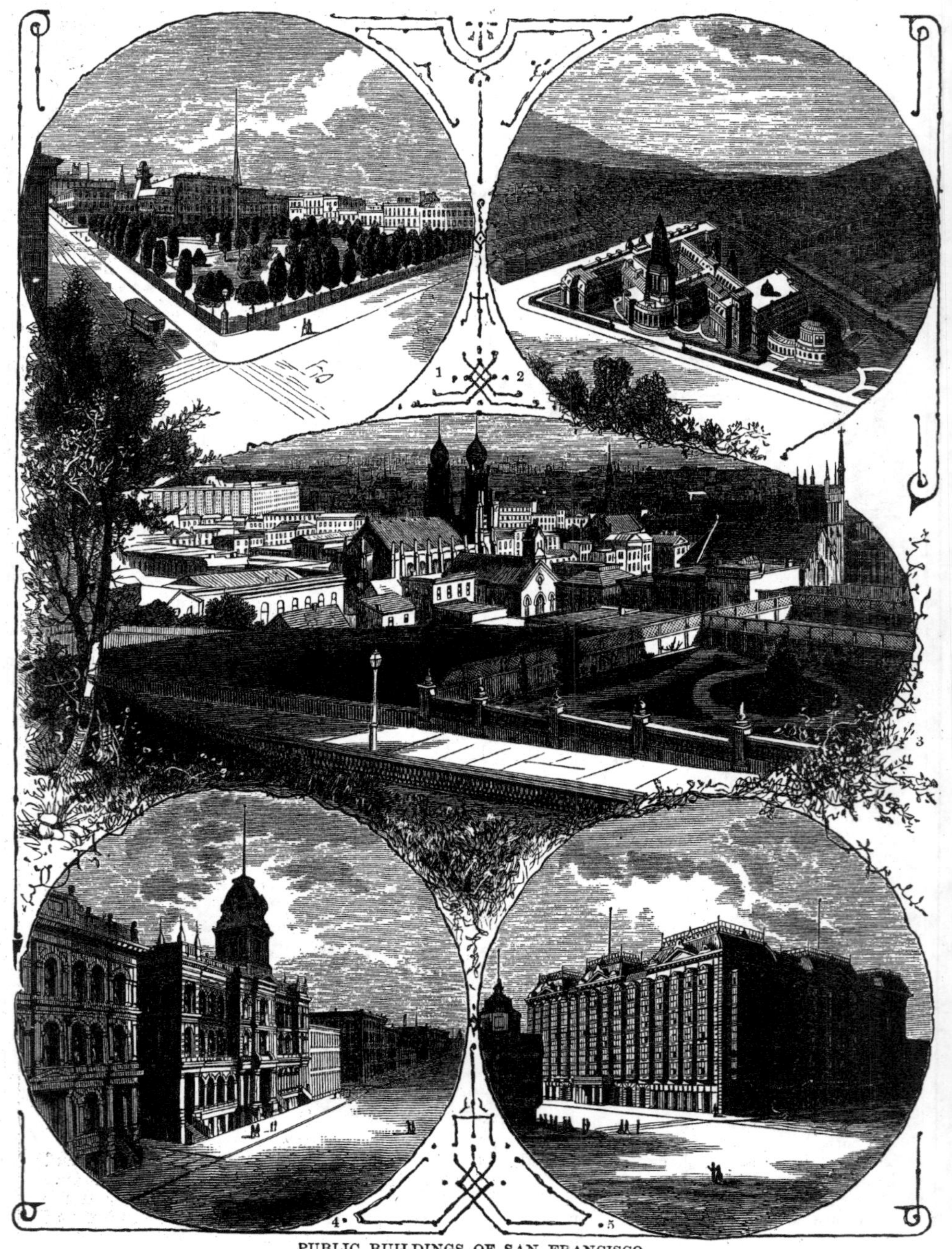

PUBLIC BUILDINGS OF SAN FRANCISCO.

1.—City Park. 2.—New City Hall. 3.—General View of City, looking towards the Bay.
4.—Merchants' Exchange. 5.—View on Market Street.

vada Block, the Safe Deposit Building, the Anglo Californian and the California Bank, the Mercantile Library and Merchants' Exchange, all combine pleasing and impressive features, and are thoroughly built and costly erections. The building, corner of California and Montgomery Streets, occupied by Wells, Fargo & Co's Express, was the first substantial erection in the city. It was imported from China, where the stone was all cut and fitted, ready for its place.

One feature of San Francisco architecture is bay-windows. Few private houses are without them, and the last built hotels, the Grand, the Palace, and Baldwin's, have their whole surface studded with them, to the great comfort of their guests, and equal defacement of their external appearance. San Francisco is called the Bay City. It might well be named the "bay-window city." The mildness of the climate and the instinctive craving for sunshine, are considerations which will always make bay-windows a desirable and a favorite feature here.

"HOODLUMS."

A stranger will observe here the great number of restaurants and furnished lodgings. A large proportion of the population live in lodgings and go out for their meals. The tendency to a more settled mode of life, however, increases, and a great number of private dwellings have been erected by individuals and building associations, of late years. The Real Estate Associates build and sell on an average a house a day, and have done so for three years past. They build by day's work, in thorough style, chiefly houses of six and eight rooms, and sell them for one-fifth cash, and the remainder in 72 monthly installments, based on 9 per cent. interest for the deferred payment. Most of the uniformly built blocks of detached houses in the city, were built by them. They always built detached houses, which are safer in case of fires.

A great conflagration may overtake any city, but this is more secure than its wooden appearance indicates. Owing to the dampness from summer fogs and winter rains, and the liability of injury by earthquakes, wood is the only desirable material for dwellings. Nearly all used is the *sequoia*, or redwood, so abundant in the Coast Range. It burns very slowly, compared

SCENES IN THE HARBOR OF SAN FRANCISCO.

with eastern woods, and the city has a very efficient steam fire department.

The city cemeteries are yet west of the best residences, but agitation has already commenced looking to an end of interments within city limits. Lone Mountain, an isolated mound within the Roman Catholic Cemetery and surmounted by a large cross, lately blown down, has long been a noted landmark and gives its name to the region adjoining, which is devoted to burying grounds.

South from Lone Mountain lies the Golden Gate Park, in which the city justly takes great pride, and which is destined to become one of the most beautiful of city pleasure grounds in the United States. It was a waste of sand only five or six years since, but, by careful planting of the yellow lupin, the sand is subdued, and by irrigation, grass-plats have been created, and a forest of trees brought rapidly forward. The drives are fine, and, on pleasant days, thousands of carriages resort here. Driving is a Californian's weak point, and more money is expended by him on livery and private stables in proportion to his means and other expenditures, than by his brother-citizens of the "States." It is a natural result of plentiful money, long distances and few railroads. Racing is also much in vogue, and a fine race-track is laid out, near Lone Mountain, in full view from the Park.

All the religious denominations are well represented, and there are some fine buildings for worship, among which the Synagogue, on Sutter, the First Congregational Church, on Post, and St. Patrick's Cathedral, on Mission Street, are most notable.

Benevolent mutual societies and secret orders are very numerous. Particulars concerning them and the churches, may be found in the city directory. The free schools of the city are a just source of pride. They are provided for with a liberality, and conducted with a skill which make them of incalculable value to the city in all its interests.

The Mercantile Library, the Mechanic's and the Odd Fellows,' are large and valuable, and the use of them may be obtained on easy terms. Roman's bookstore, on Montgomery, and Bancroft's, on Market Street, are prominent among many good ones. Books are generally sold at publisher's prices, in gold. Bancroft is a large publisher of law books, and has erected a building in which are carried on all departments of book-making.

Excursions.—For sight-seeing in San Francisco, no plan will suit the convenience of every one, but the best for a few days is the following:

Let the morning be spent in a ride to the Cliff House, where a good breakfast may be obtained, if not had sooner. The Cliff House toll-road has been the favorite route and is unsurpassed as a drive. The shell-road of New Orleans is no better. But the road through the Golden Gate Park, is splendidly macadamized, and should be traveled either going or returning. A drive should be taken along the beach to "Ocean House," and a return made to the city, through and over the hills. Coming into the city by this road, there bursts into view, one of the most magnificent sights on the coast. The city, the bay, Oakland and a vast extent of mountain, valley, loveliness of nature and art, are spread out below. If the Park can be reserved for a separate drive, go by the Cliff House Road, if not, go by the Park. The Cliff House may be reached also, by two lines of street-cars and omnibusses. The cost of a carriage for four persons will be $10.00 for the trip—by omnibus and cars, one dollar for each person. The trip should be made as early as possible to avoid the wind and fog.

The afternoon may be spent at Woodward's Gardens, making sure of the feeding of sea-lions at 1 or 3.30 o'clock. The aquarium is unique, suggested by one in Berlin, and has nothing like it in America. Birds, animals of various kinds, fruits, flowers, museum, art gallery and many other objects of attraction, make these gardens one of the chief attractions to tourists. They represent the Pacific Coast in its animals and curiosities, better than any other collection.

Another morning, go up Clay Street Hill in the cars, and ride to the end of the route. Fine views will be seen of the city and bay, from many points, and some handsome residences will be passed. On descending, climb Telegraph Hill on foot, the only way in which it can be done, and enjoy the view in all directions. After lunch take the Market Street cars, and ride to Twenty-first Street. At Sixteenth Street, one will be near the old Mission Church, an adobe building dedicated in 1776. Having reached Twenty-first Street, cross to Folsom, and return in the North Beach & Mission cars to the city, leaving them where they cross Market, or at the end of their route, corner of California and Montgomery. These rides will take one through the portion of the city rapidly growing and extending toward the south-west. There will be time after returning, to walk about Kearney and Montgomery Streets, near Market, also up and down Market, and see the finest retail stores, and look at new buildings, or even to climb up California Street to Highland Terrace, and see some of the finest private residences in the city, among which D. D. Colton's and Governor Stanford's are specially notable, the former on the north side of California Street, the latter fronting on Powell at the corner of California.

A pleasant place to visit is also the Mercantile Library on Bush Street, opposite the Cosmopolitan Hotel. Strangers, properly introduced, are granted the privilege of the library and reading-room free for a month, and odd hours can be put in there very pleasantly, especially in the read-

WOODWARD'S GARDENS, SAN FRANCISCO.

ing-room, which is light, cheerful, and supplied with the best papers, magazines and reviews of this and other lands.

Another day one can go to Oakland early, take a carriage at Broadway Station and ride to Berkley, Piedmont, and through Brooklyn, or East Oakland, along Lake Merritt, up and down streets and around the city at pleasure. Fine houses, beautiful grounds, good roads, flowers, shade trees and pleasant sights are everywhere. Returning to the city in season for the 4 P. M. boat up the Sacramento River, one can take it as far as Martinez, a 2 1-2 or 3 hours' ride, and see the northern part of San Francisco Bay, San Pablo Bay, Benicia and Suisun Bay, leaving the boat at Martinez and there spending the night. Early next morning a stage will take one to Mount Diablo, and three hours can be spent on its summit enjoying as fine a view as there is anywhere in California, after which the boat can be reached in season to be in San Francisco for the night, or one can stay for the night at a good hotel near the summit, see the sun rise, and return to San Francisco the next night. The fare for this round trip is ten dollars.

Most of San Francisco has now been seen. It would be well to ride through Van Ness Avenue and see the fine residences there; but one will begin to think of San Jose, Santa Cruz, the Geysers, &c. Another forenoon can be spent pleasantly in the city by taking the Central line of horse-cars (cars with white dashers) through the fast-growing western addition to the city, to the end of the route at Laurel Hill Cemetery, and walking about there for an hour. Returning by the same line in season to get off near the United States Mint, at corner of 5th and Market Streets, by 11 A. M., one can visit that institution, which is daily open for visitors until noon. In the afternoon, at 3.25, one may go to San Jose. The route leads through beautiful villages, some of which have been selected for the residence, most, if not all the year, of wealthy gentlemen of San Francisco. San Jose will be reached in season for a walk or ride about the city. The Auzerais House is a first-class hotel, and carriages can be obtained there at reasonable rates. The Court-House and State Normal School are the chief public buildings. General Naglee's grounds, which are open to visitors, except on Sunday, are well worth a visit.

If time allows, one may, by taking a private carriage, go to the New Almaden Quicksilver Mines, enjoy a fine ride, gaze upon a wide-spreading view upon the summit of the hill, in which the mines are situated, see the whole underground process of mining, provided the superintendent will grant a permit to enter them, which is not likely, and return to San Jose the same day, or if not able to afford time for this, can go over to Santa Clara by horse-car, through the shady Alameda, three miles long, laid out and planted, in 1799, by the Padres of the mission, visit the two colleges there, one Methodist, the other Roman Catholic, and return in season for the morning train to Gilroy, Watsonville, etc., and reach Santa Cruz the same night; or, if time will not allow of doing this, he may spend a little more time at San Jose and Santa Clara, ride out to Alum Rock Springs, through the Shaded Avenue, the prettiest drive in the State, and, taking the afternoon train, reach San Francisco at 5.35 P. M.

Whoever goes to Santa Cruz will want to stay there two nights and a day, at least, and there are so many charming rides and resorts near this watering-place of the Pacific Coast, that many days can be spent there very agreeably. The trip back to the city, unless made by steamboat at night, which can be done sometimes, and is a pleasant variety for those who are not afraid of a short exposure to ocean waves and tossing, will occupy an entire day, and the arrival is at about 5.30 P. M.

The next trip will naturally be to the Geysers and Calistoga, the Petrified Forest, White Sulphur Springs at St. Helena, etc., all of which are passed in the round trip. One may go by Calistoga, or return that way, as he prefers. Steamboats start at 7 A. M. for Vallejo, and at 8 for Donahue Landing. By the first route, one connects with cars for Calistoga, and by the second, for Cloverdale, and from each place stages take one to the Geysers the same day. After seeing the Geysers, travelers usually go on so as to return to San Francisco over the route they did not take coming to them, two days being required for the round trip, if one does not go to the White Sulphur Springs, which is a delightful place to spend a half-day, nor to the Petrified Forest, which is reached by a pleasant ride by private conveyance from Calistoga, and is a very interesting and romantic spot, and also requires a half day. To visit these one must take three days for the round trip. The fare for this trip, not including the carriage to the Petrified Forest, is sixteen dollars.

As the time of tourists is variously limited, it is well to say that the time required for all the trips above described, is twelve days, allowing one day at Santa Cruz, and one day for returning from there to the city. Not all persons have so much time to spend. By omitting the visit to Santa Cruz, the Petrified Forest and White Sulphur Springs, one may save four days, and by omitting, also, the trip to Mt. Diablo, the western addition to the city, and the United States Mint, one may save three days more, starting for the Geysers, after spending three days in the city and seeing the Cliff House, Golden Gate Park, Woodward's Gardens, climbing Telegraph Hill and Clay Street Hill, seeing the Mission and south-western part of the city, and passing most of a day in Oakland. Should one do this, it would be well to fill out the day begun in Oakland, by going through Van Ness Avenue, which is, and long will be, the finest street for private residences in the city. Two days more will enable one to visit the Geysers, and thus, in five days, all that is most notable in and about San Francisco, will have been seen.

Tourists who have time enough for it will find a trip to Pescadero, very pleasant. The route is by stage from San Mateo or Redwood City, on the Southern Pacific Railroad, across the Contra Costa Range, a ride very well paying of itself for the whole cost of the trip. Pescadero is in a narrow valley, about three miles from the famous Pebble Beach, about 100 yards long, which gives it its chief attraction. Most home-like quarters and delightful cooking are found at Swanton's, and one will be taken to the beach and brought back from it at hours of his own choosing. At this beach one will linger and linger, picking up finely-polished pebbles, many of which are fit to be set as jewels. Pescadero may be reached also by stage from Santa Cruz, and the ride along the coast is wild, interesting, unique and full of interest. The time required is a day, whether coming from San Francisco or Santa Cruz, and the same to return, and no one will spend less than a day there, so that to see Pescadero means three days, and there are few more enjoyable ways to spend so much time.

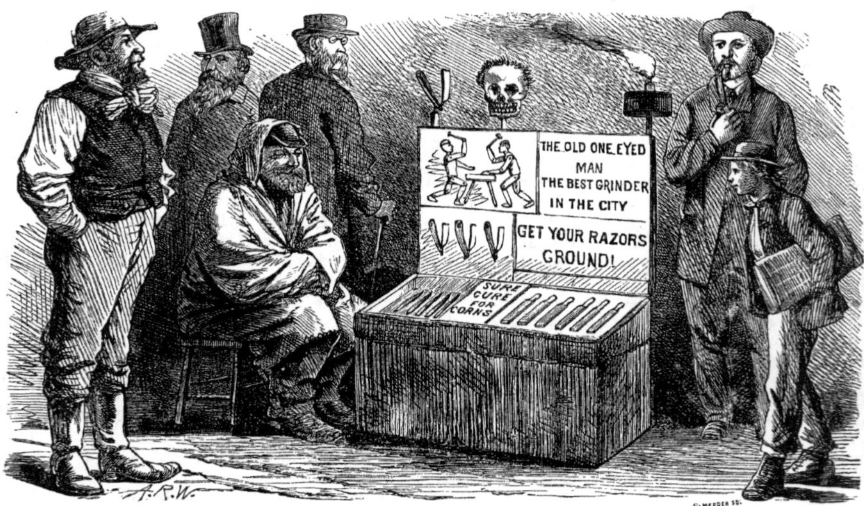

STREET SCENE IN SAN FRANCISCO.

Climate.—The climate of San Francisco is peculiar, and can not be described in a few words. It is equable on the whole, there being no great range of temperature, and the difference between that of winter and summer being small. Rain falls only in the winter half of the year, and does not much exceed one-half of the amount in the same latitude on the Atlantic shore, and the number of rainy days is very small, since it is apt to rain hard if it rains at all. The atmosphere in winter is quite moist, and though it is seemingly dry in summer, during the long absence of rain, pianos and furniture, and wood-work generally do not shrink as in many places, owing, doubtless, to the prevailing cool winds from the ocean. It is rarely cold enough for frost; plumber's work needs no protection, and hot days are equally rare, occurring only when the summer ocean winds yield for two, or at most three days, to winds from over parched and heated plains to the north. The air is rarely clear so as to reveal distinctly the outlines of hill and shore across the bay, a misty haze like that of eastern Indian summer, usually prevailing. After rains, and notably after frosts, and during the prevalence of winds from the north this sometimes vanishes, and a crystal clearness of atmosphere succeeds, in which Mount Diablo and the hills of Contra Costa and Alameda stand out mellow and clear as though just at hand. At such times, which are not frequent, and at others, more often, when it is sunshiny and the air is calm, and the haze thin, there is a spring and vitality and exhilaration in the air, and beauty in all out-door nature not often surpassed. Something of this is realized in the early part of most summer days, if fog does not hang over the city. As the day advances, the wind from the ocean rises and pours in mightily, cold and fierce—a bane and a blessing at once; a bane because it destroys all enjoyment of out-door existence, but a blessing because bearing away noxious exhalations, and securing health even to the most crowded and neglected quarters and thoroughfares.

There are few days in San Francisco when it is safe to dispense with outer wrappings, and when a fire is not needed morning and evening, both for health and comfort, and fewer yet when a room with the sun shining into it is not amply warm enough while it shines. Sunshine is therefore earnestly coveted, and many are the regrets of those who do not enjoy it. It is rare for persons to seek the shady side of the street, instinct suggests the contrary. Rooms are advertised as sunny, and many are so described which are sunny only a small part of the day. But whether the sun shines or not, it is never safe to sit by open windows or on door-steps without shawls, hats, or overcoats. Strangers do it sometimes, but never do it very long. San Francisco is not the place for out-door pleasuring. Bright and sunshiny and beautiful as it often is without doors, one prefers to look upon it from within, and if deciding to go out must wrap up almost as for a winter ride or walk in the older States.

San Francisco has few pleasure resorts. Seal Rocks, at the mouth of the Golden Gate, attract many to ride to the Cliff House, and gaze at sea-lions gamboling and snorting and basking on its sides. It is a beautiful ride thence south on the beach a couple of miles to the Ocean House, and thence back to the city by Lake Merced. Golden Gate Park is, however, the chief resort for pleasure. It is new, and its charms and beauty are still in the future, but much has been done already, and the promise for time to come is ample. The reclamation of sand wastes and dunes by planting yellow lupin and their conversion into beautiful grass-plots is a notable feature of the success already attained, which elicits the admiration of all who contrast what they see in the park with the proof of what it was once, shown in the still shifting sands around it. The park embraces about 1,100 acres, and when the thousands and ten thousands of trees planted in it have gained their growth, which they are doing almost too fast for belief, and other improvements in progress are carried out, it will rank among the most attractive and admired city parks on the Continent. It is reached by several streets leading west from Market, but most of the many drivers and riders who resort there find their way either by Turk, Tyler or McAllister Streets.

A favorite resort is also Woodward's Gardens. They are private property, and a quarter of a dollar is charged for entrance. It is a pleasant place to pass a half day visiting the collection of various living animals and birds, among which are camels born in the garden, and sea-lions caught in the Pacific, and paid for at the rate of seventy-five cents a pound. One big fellow, a captive for seven years, has grown to weigh over a ton. Sea-lions can be better studied at Woodward's than at Seal Rock, especially at the hour they are fed, when they do some fearful leaping and splashing. There are fine collections also of stuffed birds, and other curiosities, hot-houses with tropical plants, aquaria not surpassed on this Continent, a skating rink, and many other attractive features. The grounds are spacious and well sheltered, and a pleasanter spot cannot be found within the city limits for whiling away a few hours. The city line of horse-cars leads to the gardens from Market Street Ferry by two routes for part of the distance, both joining on Mission Street, on which the gardens front. They cover over six acres, and almost every taste can be suited somewhere in them. The active and jolly can resort to the play-ground and gymnasium, and those who like quiet, will find shady nooks and walks; those fond of sights and curiosities can spend hours in the various cabinets, and those who like to study mankind, can gaze on the groups standing around, and streaming passers-by. Through the whole season, from April to November, it is always genial and sunny, and enjoyable there.

Pleasure Resorts of California.

Mineral Springs.—California possesses an abundance of hot and mineral springs. Those most numerous are sulphur, both hot and cold. Of hot springs, the most frequented are Paso Robles in S. Luis Obispo Co., 143 miles by railroad and 99 by stage from San Francisco, Gilroy Hot Springs, 14 miles from the town of Gilroy, 81 miles south from San Francisco on the Southern Pacific Railroad, and Calistoga, at the terminus of the Napa Branch of the California Pacific Railroad, 66 miles north from San Francisco. Their waters are much used, both for drinking and bathing, with good repute for curative results. What are called mud baths are taken at Calistoga and Paso Robles, and many other places. There is nothing so muddy about them as one would fancy from the name, except at Paso Robles. They are simply baths taken in the spring itself just as it bubbles out of the ground, holding all its peculiar virtues unimpaired. At Paso Robles the mud baths are a literal plunging in thick mud. The waters of these springs, and of many others, must be used while retaining their original heat, and cannot be bottled to any purpose. The San Jose Warm Springs are only two hours from the city, but are not open to tourists.

There are three noted springs which are resorted to by health and pleasure seekers, whose waters are bottled in large quantities. These are the Napa Soda Springs, near Napa, and the Pacific Congress Springs, in the Coast Range, 10 miles from Santa Clara. They have been long

SCENE IN PARK AND PLEASURE GROUNDS AT OAK KNOLL, NAPA VALLEY, CALIFORNIA.—RESIDENCE OF R. B. WOODWARD.

known, and are very freely used on this coast, especially during the summer months. They are bottled by machinery, so as to carry their natural volume of gas, and are highly recommended by the medical faculty. The last named is on account of its natural attractions and its accessibility, being only 4 hours' ride from San Francisco, a very favorite summer retreat from the city. The water is said to resemble very closely that of the far-famed Saratoga Springs, after which it is named, and contains a larger proportion of mineral contents than either of the others. The last of these, not yet named, is that of the Litton Seltzer Springs, near Healdsburg, not long introduced to the public, but coming fast into favor, and claimed, not only to equal, but even excel the far-famed Congress water.

The analysis of these waters gives the following results :

NAPA SODA.	GRAINS IN A GALLON.
Bicarbonate Soda, .	13.12
Carbonate Magnesia,	26.12
Carbonate Lime, . .	10.88
Chloride Sodium, . .	5.20
Sub-Carbon Iron, . .	7.84
Sulphate Soda, . . .	1.84
Silicious Acid, . . .	0.68
Alumina, ...	0.60
Loss, ...	2.48
	68.76

PACIFIC CONGRESS.	
Chloride Sodium, . .	119.159
Sulphate Soda, . . .	12.140
Carbonate Soda, . .	123.351
" Iron, . .	14.030
" Lime, . .	17.295
Silica Alumina and trace Magnesia, .	49.882
	335.857

LITTON SELTZER.	GRAINS IN A GALLON.
Carbo'ic Acid (comb.),	42.76
Chlorine, ...	78.38
Sulphate Acid, . . .	2.36
Silicic Acid, ...	2.02
Oxide Iron, ...	2.85
Lime, ...	4.41
Magnesia, ...	5.24
Soda, ...	62.19
Alumina, Ammonia, Potash, Lithia, Boracic Acid, Organic matter,	27.38
	227.59

The quantity of *free* carbonic acid in the Litton Seltzer, *which escapes on standing*, is 383.75 grains per gallon. This large quantity of gas is very pleasant to the taste, and tests severely the strength of bottles, which sometimes explode even in a cool place.

The Paso Roble Springs (the name means Pass of Oaks) most used, have been analyzed with the following result :

	MAIN HOT SULPHUR SPRING.		MUD SPRING.	
Temperature 110,			122	degrees.
One imperial gallon contains, Sulphurated Hydrogen Gas, ...	4.55		3.28	inches.
Free Carbonic Acid, . .	10.50		47.84	"
Sulphate Lime, ...	3.21		17.90	grains.
Sulphate Potash, . . .	88		traces.	
Sulphate Soda, ...	7.85		41.11	
Perox Iron, ...	36			
Alumina, ...	22			
Silicia, ...	44		1.11	
Bicarbonate Magnesia, .	92	Carbon. Mag.,	3.10	
Bicarbonate Soda, . . .	50.74	Carbon. Soda,	5.21	
Chloride Sodium, . . .	27.18		96.48	
Iodi'e and Bromide trac's.				
Organic Matter, ...	64		3.47	
Total solid contents, .	93.44		168.38	

The Mud Spring contains also alumina and protoxide of iron. There are also three cold sulphur springs and three other hot springs, the hottest of the temperature of 140 degrees. There is, also, a chalybeate spring. Paso Robles is resorted to with good results by persons suffering from rheumatism, cutaneous diseases, and some constitutional disorders. They are no place for consumptives.

There are many other springs besides those named. Near Lake Tahoe, are Soda Springs. Near Vallejo and at St. Helena, are White Sulphur Springs. In Sonoma County, are Skaggs Hot Springs, and at Santa Barbara are springs much resembling those at Paso Robles. The Bartlett Springs are a delightful resort, and will amply pay for the time and cost going to them. They are reached by stage from Calistoga on the arrival of the morning train from San Francisco, going on 35 miles to Clear Lake, which is crossed by steamer, and a ride of six miles then brings one at evening to the springs. The ride is one of the most beautiful in California.

The Geysers.—Tourists will find the trip to the Geysers, the most interesting and easy of all the short excursions in the State. It is well to go by one route and return *via* another. The North Pacific Railroad *via* steamer by Donahue City, will give a delightful sail through the bay. Neat cars will convey the passengers to Cloverdale, where stages are taken for the Geysers. The ride to the Geysers is over a splendid road, amid beautiful mountain scenery, and occasionally there are examples of fine driving of the stage-teams. One day at the Geysers is usually enough, and the visitor will find it absolutely necessary to rise as early as 5 or 6 A. M., to see the finest display of steam from the Geysers.

The ground literally boils and bubbles under the feet. There are devil's inkstands, and caldrons, and tea-kettles, and whistles enough to overwhelm eyes, ears, smell, taste and touch with horrid reminiscences. Yet so great is the curiosity it should not be missed. Neither must the traveler omit the enjoyment of the natural steam bath, the sensation on emerging from which is most delicious. From the Geysers to Calistoga, the celebrated Foss drives a crack stage, and usually has his spanking team of six-in-hand. Reports are strong as to his fearless driving, but a glance at the way he beautifully manages his leaders and wheelers, gives no one any anxiety as to safety. The stage route is over very great heights, up the side of long mountains, from the summits of which the views are glorious, probably to many, more enjoyable than the Geysers.

The tourist must not fail, as he returns to San Francisco, to stop at Calistoga and visit the Petrified Forest—the best collection we know; and even a few days' tour to Lake County and the famous soda and borax deposits will be well spent. From Calistoga to Vallejo, stop at Napa and take stage to the famous vineyards of Sonoma, and see grape raising in perfection; also visit the Spout Farm and the Soda Springs. From Vallejo, go to Benicia, 8 miles and visit the fort, where often there are seen charming displays of flowers. Then cross to Martinez, by ferry, and visit the fruit orchards of Dr. Strentzel, where oranges and pears and peaches and apples grow side by side, and twine their branches together,—probably the choicest fruit orchard in the State. From here ascend Mount Diablo and remain over night, witnessing the sunrise scene on all the great valleys and the bay spread out so grandly before you. Descending, the traveler will return to Vallejo, and thence by steam through the bay to San Francisco. The cost of this trip will be, for round trip ticket, $16 to Geysers and return. Extra for trip to Mount Diablo, about $8. Board per day, in absence, $3 gold. Time for whole trip, about one week.

Hints to Invalids.—California has been the scene of many remarkable recoveries of health, and of many sore disappointments to invalids who thought that coming to this coast would insure them a new lease of life. There is no doubt that a judicious availing of its peculiar climatic features is highly useful in many cases, and it is equally certain that an arbitrary resort to them may even hasten the end which one seeks to avert.

A consumptive patient should never come to San Francisco expecting benefit from its climate. Cold winds from the Pacific, often loaded with fog, prevail eight or nine months in the year, for a good part of the day, and make warm wrappings necessary for well persons. When these trade-winds cease, the rainy season then commences, variable and uncertain, often very damp and chilly, the sky sometimes clouded for days in succession. In the interval between rains and summer winds, both spring and autumn, there is a period of variable duration, when the sky is often clear, the air balmy, the sun genial, and everything in the outer world is charming and exhilarating; but this period is not sufficiently fixed to be counted on, and is liable to be inhospitably broken upon by raw winds, and chilly, foggy days.

The cause which thus unfavorably affects the climate of San Francisco in so marked a degree, spread out as it is along the Golden Gate, the only interruption for hundreds of miles to the lofty Coast Range, erected as a barrier between the cold, foggy ocean on one hand, and the spreading central basin, gleaming bright and hot with sunshine on the other, affects in some degree many other places along the sea-coast. At a sufficient distance inland, the ocean breezes are tempered, and there are places near the sea-shore where the trend of the coast and outjutting headlands break the force of the trade-winds, and give delightful shelter from them. It is this circumstance which gives to Santa Barbara its celebrity. It lies on a bay facing to the south, the usual coast-line facing south-west, and is in the lee of Point Conception, a bold headland which turns away from it most of the cold ocean winds. San Rafael, near San Francisco, nestles under the lee of Tamalpais and adjacent hills, and is also sheltered. In a direct line, it is not over six or seven miles from San Francisco, and yet, when it is foggy or unutterably windy in the city, it is often warm, clear and still there.

The consumptive patient should carefully avoid exposure to the trade-winds by seeking some resort sheltered from them, or which they reach after being thoroughly tempered by inland travel. Neglect to heed this caution is the reason of many fatal disappointments experienced by California visitors seeking health.

In the summer season, beyond the range of the ocean trade-winds, the choice between locations for invalids in California will be governed as much by other, as their climatic advantages. Ease of access, hotel and boarding-house accommodations, social advantages, sources for amusement, comparative expense, are the considerations that will chiefly weigh in deciding the question. Sunshine will be found everywhere; the days, however hot, are always followed by cool nights; there are no storms, no sudden changes, the air is dry and clear and life-inspiring.

In winter it is desirable to go well south, where there is little rain and little cold weather, though even at San Diego, almost at the Mexican line, a fire is very comfortable sometimes, as the writer experienced one 10th of January, much to the surprise of some eastern invalids who arrived there with him. It will be wise for invalids to consult the physician best acquainted with the place they may choose, and carefully heed his advice about exposure, clothing, wrappings and the like. Every place has climatic features of its own, knowledge of which is gained only by experience and is of great value.

The following places are known as health resorts, and each has attractive and valuable features of its own: San Rafael near San Francisco, and Stockton in the San Joaquin Valley, Santa Barbara and San Diego on the southern coast, Paso Robles north from Santa Barbara, and back from the coast, a beautiful spot noted for sulphur baths; San Bernardino north-east from San Diego, and some distance from the coast, and fast coming into favor as it becomes more accessible and better known. Gilroy Hot Springs, 14 miles from Gilroy, on the Southern Pacific Railroad, 30 miles south of San Jose, is a favorite resort. It is in the hills of the Coast Range, and has good accommodations for visitors. Calistoga, at the terminus of the Napa Branch of the California Pacific Railroad, at the foot of Mount St. Helena, abounds in hot springs, and is resorted to for its baths of various kinds. On the railroad going to Calistoga the

White Sulphur Springs are passed at a distance of two miles. They are much frequented, but rather by visitors seeking summer recreation than by health seekers.

The best place for the consumptive patient is regarded by some good judges to be on an elevation among the hills of the Coast Range in summer, where the change of temperature will be only a few degrees, and in Southern California, a little back from the coast in winter. In such an equable climate, the patient can camp out, and keep in the open air, which is the best possible restorative.

The climate of San Francisco, which induces no perspiration, and by dampness aggravates rheumatic and neuralgic affections, is the most favorable in the world for mental invigoration and work.

Malaria is found in all the lowlands, and often among the foot hills, but elevated places are entirely free from it.

In short, there is such a variety of climate within a day's reach of San Francisco that the invalid may be sure of finding, somewhere on the Pacific Coast, whatever natural advantage will be most beneficial to his case.

California Pacific Railroad.

On the California Pacific Railroad two trains leave Sacramento daily for San Francisco, one at 6.30 A. M., and one 4 P. M. This is the shortest and favorite route between the capital and metropolis, and will no doubt ere long be the principal line over which the Overland Express Train will pass.

The train crosses the river by means of a "Y" and the Sacramento & Yolo bridge. Directly opposite Sacramento is the village of Washington, protected by a high levee, but retarded in growth by the toll for crossing the river. Along the river bank is a narrow strip of land sufficiently elevated for farming—but the train is soon beyond this on trestle-work, or a high embankment crossing the tules. On this narrow strip the ubiquitous pea-nut and chickory grow to perfection. No pea-nut surpasses these in size or flavor, and the chickory commands a price equal to the German. Coffee men consider it of superior quality, and the traveler will find it abundant in the *pure* coffee of all the hotels in the interior.

The tule land is the richest in the State—a fine vegetable mold and deposit from the winter floods. Many square miles of it up and down the river await reclamation, and much has been reclaimed. It will be difficult to reclaim the great extent of it now before the eye, because on the right of the railroad and several miles up the river, the waters of Cache Creek spread out and sink, and on the left the waters of Putah Creek are also emptied, and high levees would be required to carry off so much water. These tules are the temporary abode of some, and the permanent abode of other varieties of wild fowl, and the happy hunting grounds for many a Nimrod. After the first rains come, the geese arrive, the white brant coming first and in largest numbers. Three varieties are common, the white and speckled breasted brant, and the hawnker. Acres of the ground, where the dry tule has been burned off and the young grass has sprouted are covered with the geese, and sometimes they are like a great cloud in the air, and their noise heard for a mile or more.

The varieties of the duck are many, but the mallard, sprig tail, canvas-back, and teal are most esteemed. It is an easy and pleasant task for one acquainted with the flight of the ducks to bring down from twenty to a hundred in a single day, besides more geese than he is willing to "pack." About five miles from Sacramento is an island (of a hundred acres, dry and grassy) where two or three days camping may be enjoyed by a lover of the sport.

When the Sacramento overflows its banks and the creeks are high, the tules are hidden by the water, and if the wind blows, this region is like an open sea. Frequently the road-bed has been washed away, and now it is protected by an inclined breakwater and young willows. It has been generally but erroneously supposed that hogs and the Chinamen feed on the tule roots.

The bulbous root they eat is called by the Chinese "Foo tau," and is imported largely from China, where it grows to a greater size than in this country. Across the tules at Swingle's Ranche is a side track and flag station.

Davisville—is 13 miles nearly due west of Sacramento, has a population of 300, all gathered since the building of the railroad, and has two stores, a dozen saloons, four restaurants, and a Presbyterian, a Methodist Episcopal, and a Roman Catholic Church. About the same proportion of saloons to the population holds good over California, but that of churches does not. But "Davisville is not an immoral place, for the liquor is all sold to *non-residents*."

In 1862 land was worth from $6 to $10 per acre, and now sells at $75 to $100.

Near Davisville are large orchards, "Brigg's" covering 400 acres, and the "Silk Ranche" orchard 250 acres, but in dry seasons the quantity and quality of the fruit, is greatly impaired by the want of irrigation.

The failure of silk culture was largely owing to the hot winds from the north, killing the worms. Attention to fruit culture, has demonstrated the necessity of allowing nothing to grow between the trees. Nor are the trees trimmed so high up as in the Eastern States. Alfalfa has yielded in one season, $55 worth of hay to the acre.

At Davisville the railroad to San Francisco, turns directly to the south, and a branch runs north to Woodland and Knight's Landing.

Woodland is a town of 1,000 inhabitants, and 9 miles from Davisville. Near Woodland the road branches to the northern part of the valley of the Sacramento, but is not yet opened for business.

Knight's Landing is on the Sacramento River, and this railroad formerly continued on northward to Marysville, until the flood of 1872 destroyed the embankment for miles.

Continuing south from Davisville, Putah Creek is crossed near Davisville, a dry channel in summer, and a torrent in winter; and 4 miles south is

Foster,—a side track, and 4.17 miles farther,

Dixon—is reached. It has a large grain trade from the surrounding country, a Congregational, a Methodist and a Baptist Church; several hotels and a block or two of good stores. Since the completion of the railroad the town of Silveyville, about three miles distant, has been moved bodily to Dixon. Farther south 3.27 miles, is

Batavia,—a village in a promising region, with a large grain trade, a hotel and several stores, and next south 4.83 miles, is

Elmira,—formerly called Vaca Junction, the junction of the Elmira and Vacaville Railroad, extending to Vacaville five miles, and Winters 17 miles. Fare to Vacaville 50 cents, and Winters $1.70. South from Elmira 3.96 miles is

Cannon's,—a large ranche, and 6.55 miles farther is

Fairfield and Suisun City.—The former is on the right-hand side of the road, and the other on the left. Fairfield is the county-seat of Solano County, and Suisun the post-office and business center. Fairfield has a Methodist Episcopal Church, and Suisun a Protestant Episcopal, a Cumberland Presbyterian and a Methodist Episcopal. Suisun is at the head of Suisun Slough, navigable for small sloops and steamers, and on the edge of a large tract of tule land. Its streets are subject to a *slight overflow* during heavy rains, when its adobe soil is a very tenacious friend to one's feet. The hills which have been approaching closer and closer since we left Sacramento—one of the numerous ridges of the Coast Range are now not far off, and to avoid the grades in crossing them, a new road will soon be built along the edge of the "swamp and overflowed" land to Benicia, on the straits of Carquinez, and crossing these will continue along the east side of the San Pablo Bay and Bay of San Francisco, to Oakland Wharf and form part of the Overland Route.

Before reaching the next station, a small spur of the Suscol Hills is tunneled, and to the right from

Bridgeport,—5.45 miles from Suisun, and other points, may be seen fertile valleys in which the earliest fruits of the State are grown. In Green Valley — one of these, sheltered from wind and free from fog, fruits and vegetables ripen sooner than in the paradise of Los Angeles, about 400 miles south.

The tourist will be struck with the rolling character of the farming land, when he sees the highest hill-tops covered with golden grain or thick stubble. The soil is the rich adobe, the best adapted to dry seasons, and rarely found covering such hills. The crops are brought off on sleds.

Creston,—the summit, is 3.84 miles from Bridgeport, and simply a flag station. Soon after passing it, the Napa Valley lies below on the right, but almost before one is aware of it,

Napa Junction,—3.65 miles from Creston, is announced.

Napa Valley.

Here the road branches through Napa Valley, one of the loveliest and most fruitful of the State. It is enclosed between two ridges of the Coast Range, one of which separates it from the Sacramento and the other from the Sonoma Valley. Above Calistoga, Mount Saint Helena stands like a great sentinel across the head of the valley. The land is among the best in the State, and fruit growing extensively and successfully practiced.

The climate is well tempered and the season rare when crops fail. This branch is a part of one of the chief routes to the Geysers and other popular resorts.

The first station north from the Junction is called

Thompson,—from the owner of the ranche and orchard, which will strike the observer as closely related to the perfect arrangement and culture of the farms in Chester or Cumberland Valley of Pennsylvania, and a closer inspection would reveal one of the most convenient and complete farm-houses in the country. Suscol, a landing-place and ferry on the Napa River, is near by. The next station is 4.49 miles farther north, and called

Napa.—A town of great loveliness, with a population of 5,000, set in homes embosomed in fruits and flowers — a town not surpassed for beauty of situation in the State, and rivaled by San Jose only. It is at the head of navigation for steamers of light draft on the Napa River, and near it is located the new Branch Insane Asylum, erected at a cost of more than a million of dollars. The public schools rank high, and there are also four colleges and seminaries of high order. The *Register* is a daily and weekly newspaper, and the *Reporter*, a weekly. It has two good hotels, the "United States," and The Palace, many stores of high order, and good banking facilities. In no portion of the State is society more stable and cultivated. The churches are imposing and well attended. The Presbyterians have the largest, most convenient and tasteful house of worship outside of San Francisco and Oakland, and the Methodists, Baptists and Roman Catholics have good houses also. Daily stages connect with the morning train for Sonoma. Above Napa, 5.45 miles, is

Oak Knoll,—near which is hidden in a park of evergreen oaks, the pleasant residence of R. B. Woodward, Esq., one of the most enterprising and public-spirited men of California, near which may be seen his orchard, one of the largest and best in the county.

Yountville—is 3.45 miles farther north, a village with about 300 inhabitants, called after one of the early settlers. Near the depot is a large vinery. On the hill-sides are numerous vineyards, and in the village a Baptist and a Congregational Church.

St. Helena—is a village of about 500 inhabitants, surrounded with ranches where people of culture live in luxury, and two miles distant are the White Sulphur Springs. Stages for the Springs connect with every train, and for Knoxville in Lake County, with every morning train from San Francisco. Presbyterians, Baptists, and Methodists have churches here. The valley grows narrower until

Calistoga — is reached, with a population of about 500, and two hotels — one the "Hot Springs."

Here are hot and mud baths, and from Calistoga are numerous pleasant drives, especially to the Petrified Forest, five miles distant, on the top of the ridge lying toward the ocean, and in a sunken part of the high table-land where there was evidently a lake after trees had attained an enormous growth, and long after this the waters of the lake discharged by some sudden rupture of the surrounding wall. The mountain views, hunting, fishing and other attractions, make Calistoga a popular resort, and the recent discovery of many quicksilver and silver mines has given a fresh impetus to the business of the town.

The population is about 700, but varies with the summer freighting to Lake County. Foss's line of stages leaves every morning during the summer for the Geysers, and stages leave daily on arrival of morning train from San Francisco for Bartlett's and other resorts of Lake County, continuing toward San Francisco on the main line.

Vallejo.—The pronunciation of this Spanish word is Val-yay-ho, and the town was named in honor of an old family still residing there.

Just before approaching the town, the "Orphans' Home," set upon a hill, and under the auspices of the I. O. Good Templars, attracts attention. It is on the left-hand side, and the town on the right.

At the depot, street-cars connect with all the trains, and carriages to any part of the city may be had for "four bits;" the "bit" being equivalent to the old New York shilling.

The station for the town is called North Vallejo, to distinguish it from the new town that has grown around the railroad terminus, one mile south.

Vallejo was for a while the capital of the State. It has now a population of about 5,000, and derives much of its business from the United States Navy Yard on Mare Island.

It has a Methodist, a Presbyterian, a Baptist and a Roman Catholic Church, and South Vallejo has also a Congregational Church. Vallejo has a stage to Benicia, eight miles, and the steamer Parthenius runs daily to San Francisco, in addition to the steamers that connect twice a day with the trains on the California Pacific Railroad.

Its wharves are in deep water, and at them the immense quantities of grain brought from the valleys north, are loaded direct for Liverpool and other parts. A large elevator—the only one tried on the coast, was blown down during a south-east gale. The town has two newspapers, the *Chronicle*, a weekly, and the *Independent*, a daily. At

South Vallejo,—24 miles from San Francisco, passengers are transferred to a steamer, and by it transported to the foot of Market Street, in San Francisco.

On board the steamer a good meal may be secured, for one dollar coin; and a trip to San Francisco, for which an hour and a half, or two hours will be necessary, according to steam and tide, will be delightfully occupied with the attractions of the bay and the bordering hills. As the steamer leaves the wharf, the view of the Navy Yard is fine, and when it doubles the island, the straits of Carquinez, through which the Sacramento River empties, are immediately on the left, and when fairly out on the San Pablo Bay, by looking to the north, the town of Vallejo on the hill, and the Navy Yard on the island, appear to be one city. West of Vallejo may be traced the Napa Valley, and farther west, the Sonoma Valley, so famous for its wines, and far off to the north-west the Petaluma Creek, which forms an opening to the Russian River Valley, through which the North Pacific Railroad runs to Cloverdale, and forms a pleasant route to the Geysers.

These valleys are parallel to each other but separated by lofty ridges of the Coast Range.

After making this general survey of the northern end of the bay and then having breakfast or dinner, one will be in sight of the western metropolis. The city comes into view as the steamer turns to the south-east, around a point of land, off which are the "Two Brothers," corresponding to the "Two Sisters" on the west side, and enters the Bay of San Francisco. On one of the Brothers is a light-house of the fifth order, and just below is Red Rock, a bold and pretty landmark. Off to the right is Mt. Tamalpais, with a shoot for lumber, that looks like a swift road to travel, and at the foot of the mountain, nestled in a deep little cove, and overlooking the sheltered waters near by, is San Rafael, the home of some merchant princes of San Francisco, and the resort of many invalids, who are seeking a new lease of life in its genial clime. On the point of land just south of San Rafael, is San Quentin, where the State has a large boarding-house and workshop filled with unwilling inmates.

Farther south-east is Angel Island—separated from the promontory of the coast main-land by Raccoon Straits, through which one may look into the Golden Gate.

The island is a military reservation, fortified strongly on the south and south-west parts, with a road running around the entire island.

Passing the island, the Golden Gate is directly on the right, and Alcatraz, a naval station, mid-way across it, and directly in front, the hills of San Francisco, that ought to have been terraced.

On the east, beginning farther north are Berkley, with the buildings of the State University; and Oakland, the city of residences and gardens; Alameda, of like character, but of less extent, and more live oaks; and in the bay the Oakland Wharf and Goat Island.

Never, except during severe winter storms, or the prevalence of heavy fog, is the navigation of the bay unpleasant, and on a calm morning when the waters are placid, the skies Italian, and the mind free from anxious care, the bay from Vallejo to San Francisco will make some of the brightest and most lasting impressions of the Golden State.

INDEX.

INDEX.

INDEX.

HO! FOR CALIFORNIA!!!

THE LABORER'S PARADISE!

Salubrious Climate, Fertile Soil, Large Labor Returns.

NO SEVERE WINTERS,
NO LOST TIME, NO BLIGHT OR INSECT PESTS.

Daily Trains from Boston, New York, Philadelphia, Baltimore, Chicago, St. Louis, Omaha and Intermediate Points, for San Francisco.

EMIGRANT TICKETS AT LOW RATES.

Choice from Nearly Every Variety of Farming, Fruit, Grazing, and Timber Lands.

The Central Pacific Railroad Co.

Now offer, in sections, adjacent to their Railroad lines in CALIFORNIA, NEVADA and UTAH, a large body of Land, most of which is well adapted to cultivation, and offer unequaled advantages for settlement or investment.

IN CALIFORNIA the lands lying on each side of the main line of the Central Pacific Railroad extend from the navigable waters of the Sacramento, above the Bay of San Francisco, across the broadest and most populous portion of the Sacramento Valley and both slopes of the Sierra Nevada Mountains. They are diversified in soil, climate and conditions—embracing the semi-tropical productions in the lower valleys—corresponding with those of Spain, Italy, and the shores of the Mediterranean—the vine, orchard and grain lands of the foot hills—corresponding with those of France, Germany and Austria—and the timber lands of the mountain slopes—corresponding with those of Maine, Sweden, Norway, etc. This central portion of California is already noted for the excellence of its wheat, grapes, pears, cherries, strawberries, small fruits and garden vegetables generally, *and for the ease with which they can be grown to dimensions and perfection unattainable elsewhere.* The lands in this belt, purchased of the Company, have resulted in gratifying success to the settlers. Wheat can safely lie in the field till threshed and shipped, and the fruit trees and vines are not troubled by insects or blight.

Along the CALIFORNIA and OREGON BRANCH, in the renowned Valley of the Sacramento, extending from the center to the northern boundary of the State, the Company also offer a choice selection, with the same general characteristics. This valley is at present the seat of the most successful culture of small grains (wheat, barley, oats, etc.) in the country, and also offers unrivaled facilities for extensive and profitable sheep and stock grazing. The whole comprises *some of the Best Land in California.*

IN NEVADA the main line of the Central Pacific Railroad occupies the Truckee and Humboldt Valleys, the largest and best settled in the State, at a short distance from numerous and important mining regions, whose yield of the precious metals is estimated at from fifteen to twenty million dollars annually. The lands of the Company are so situated as to command these markets for their produce. Large herds of cattle are maintained with little or no trouble in the Humboldt Valley and the valleys which join it. Wherever the proper cultivation has been applied, these lands have yielded good crops of fruits, cereals and esculents.

IN UTAH, in the great Salt Lake and contiguous valleys, where the Mormons have so successfully demonstrated the fertility of the soil and the healthfulness of the climate, the Company have also good land.

Title, Patent direct from the United States Government.

These lands will be sold in quantities and on terms to suit. Immigrants, colonists and capitalists, who desire to acquire indestructible real property, certain to advance in value, will be benefited by an examination. Pamphlets, maps, etc., will be furnished by application to

B. B. REDDING.

Land Commissioner Central Pacific R. R. Co.

Railroad Buildings, Cor. Fourth & Townsend Sts., ***SAN FRANCISCO, CAL.***

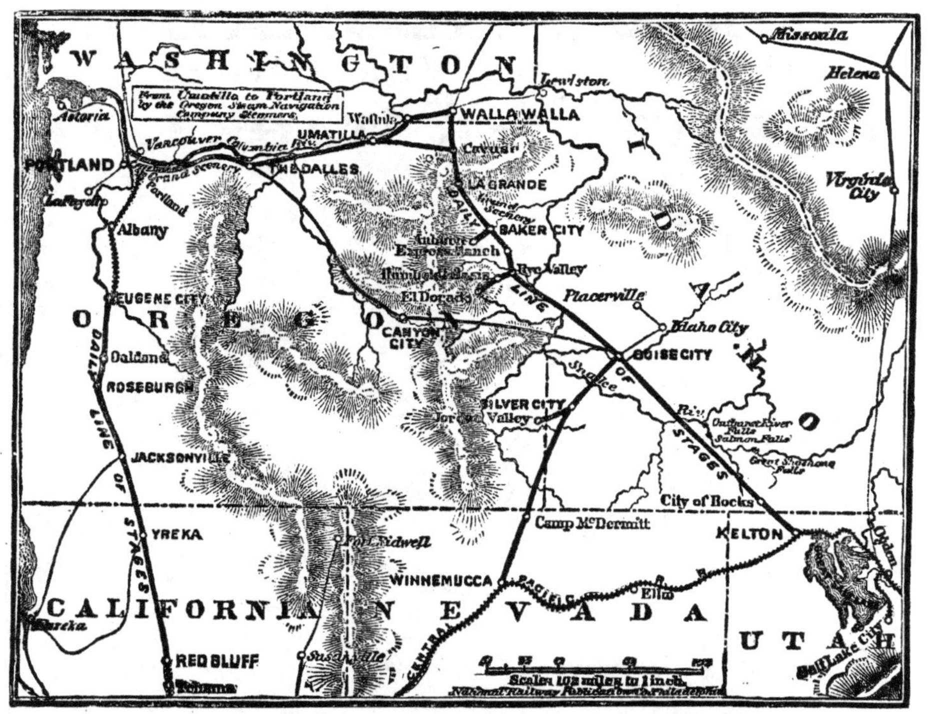

Idaho, Oregon, and Washington Territory,

—VIA—

The NORTH-WESTERN STAGE COMPANY,

IN CONNECTION WITH THE

Union and Central Pacific Railroads.

☞ Coaches leave KELTON, Utah, on the CENTRAL PACIFIC RAILROAD, **DAILY, at 6.00 A. M.**, for all points in Idaho Territory, Washington Territory, and Oregon,—among which are

SNAKE RIVER MINES,	IDAHO.	UNION,	OREGON.
BOISE CITY,	"	LA GRANGE,	"
SILVER CITY,	"	UMATILLA,	"
ELDORADO,	OREGON.	DALLES CITY,	"
CANYON CITY,	"	PORTLAND,	"
BAKER CITY,	"	WALLA WALLA,	"

New and elegant Concord Coaches, fine stock, and careful drivers. Time quick as is consistent with safety and comfort. This is the **SHORTEST, QUICKEST, CHEAPEST, and MOST DESIRABLE ROUTE**, affording the traveler views of some of the finest scenery on the Pacific slope. **THROUGH TICKETS** can be purchased at Omaha and Eastern Cities to all points on this Company's route.

WILLIAM B. MORRIS,
Gen'l Sup't, Boise City, Idaho.

S. S. HUNTLEY,
Gen'l Manager, Boise City, Idaho.

NEW ELDORADO!

The Big Horn and Wind River Country

IS REACHED BY THE

SWEETWATER STAGE LINE.

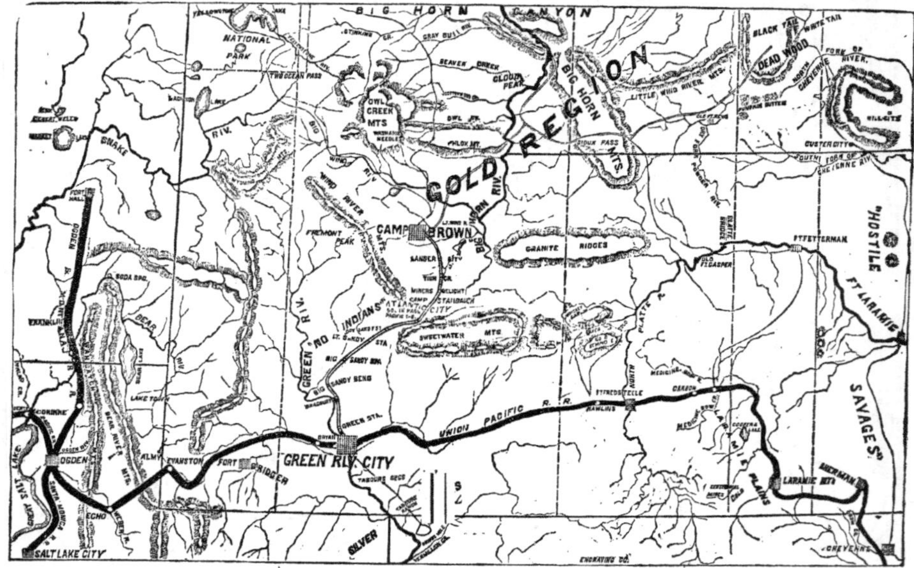

DAILY STAGES connect with the UNION PACIFIC RAILROAD at GREEN RIVER, thence via

Pacific Springs, South Pass City, Atlantic City, Camp Stambaugh,
Miners Delight, Sander City, Camp Brown.

A. E. BRADBURY, Supt., Green River, Wy. Ter.

S. S. HUNTLEY, General Manager.

TOWNSEND HOUSE,

SALT LAKE CITY, UTAH.

JAMES TOWNSEND, - - - Proprietor.

☞ Leading House in the City. One hundred and fifty Rooms, elegantly furnished, neat, clean and airy. The popular Resort for Tourists and the Traveling Public. The head-quarters of Excursions to the Lake, the Mountains and the Mines. Opportunities and facilities for becoming acquainted with representative men in the City, and the prominent business enterprises of the Territory. An old established House, only two stories high, with first-class accommodations in every respect. It is convenient to the Tabernacle, Churches, Theatre, and business portion of the City.

Omnibus and Street Car Lines to and from the House, with Livery accommodations near by.

☞ Every attention paid to the wants of Guests. Charges reasonable.

THE AMERICAN HOUSE

—AND—

THE INTER-OCEAN HOTEL,

DENVER, COLORADO.

Largest Hotel in the City—Two Hundred Rooms.

☞ *Overland Travelers from Pacific Railroad Trains may Telegraph in advance, at our expense, and have Rooms reserved for their arrival.* ☜

J. U. MARLOW, Proprietor,

Cor. 16th and Blake Streets, DENVER, COLORADO.